Realty Bluebook®

EDITION 31

Robert de Heer

Real Estate
Education Company
a division of Dearborn Financial Publishing, Inc.

This publication is designed to provide accurate and authoritative information in regard to the subject matter covered. It is sold with the understanding that the publisher is not engaged in rendering legal, accounting or other professional service. If legal advice or other expert assistance is required, the services of a competent professional person should be sought.

Publisher: Carol L. Luitjens
Acquisitions Editor: Diana Faulhaber
Project Editor: Debra M. Hall
Art Manager: Lucy Jenkins

CONTENTS

FINANCING

CHECK LISTS

ACKNOWLEDGMENTS

The author would like to acknowledge valuable assistance from the staff of Fannie Mae, FHA, the Department of Veterans Affairs, as well as from educators and authors John W. Reilly, John P. Wiedemer and Joan M. Harrison.

Thanks are extended to the following people who served as reviewers of the thirty-first edition: Rose S. Bock, Arvida Realty Sales, Ltd.; John A. Hamilton, Regional Director, Polley Associates; Vernon Hoven, CPA, Vern Hoven Tax Seminars; James M. Kinney, President, Rubloff Residential Properties; Judith Meadows; Jane Rosen, President, ACS, Assessment & Compliance Services; Barbara J. Stepp, Coldwell Banker School of Real Estate; and Michael L. White, President, Deed Transfer Report.

Special thanks are extended to the Hawaii Association of REALTORS® for permission to reproduce "Disclosure of Environmental Hazards," a section of its Risk Management Course.

Finally, comments and suggestions from many real estate professionals nationwide are sincerely appreciated.

PREFACE

The *Realty Bluebook*®, updated annually, has been a standard reference of the real estate profession since 1966.

The information in the *Realty Bluebook*® has been compiled from authoritative sources and reviewed by qualified legal and other specialists in the various fields to which the book has reference.

The *Realty Bluebook*® is not intended to provide legal, tax or other advice. Readers are encouraged to consult appropriate experts for specific advice.

HOW TO USE THIS BOOK

The ***Realty Bluebook***® is designed as a day-to-day reference tool. To become familiar with the wide variety of topics in the book read the tables of contents. Just open one of the six thumb indexes to locate the contents of a section. In addition, the alphabetical cross index at the end of the book provides instant access to any topic. The text is easy to understand and provides detailed essential information.

The convenient size and organization make the ***Realty Bluebook***® a walking memory! Let it be your constant companion in both field and office.

FINANCING

To receive advance notice of the
next *Realty Bluebook*® edition
(and information about
what's new), please call
1-800-322-8621
to register your name and address.

CONTENTS

FINANCING

Monthly Payment To Amortize a Loan of $1,000

The following table shows monthly payments for loans of $1,000. To find the payment for a loan of any amount, multiply the number found in the body of the table by the loan amount and divide by 1,000.

Example:

What is the monthly payment necessary to amortize a $90,000 loan at 8½% interest per year over a 30-year term?

Answer: Locate the point of intersection of the 30-year column and the line for 8½% interest. The number at that point of intersection is 7.6891, which is the monthly payment for a $1,000 loan at 8½% for 30 years. To find the monthly payment for a 30-year $90,000 loan at 8½%: 7.6891 × 90 = $692.02.

Amortization Table for $1000 Loans

	30 yr.	25 yr.	20 yr.	15 yr.	10 yr.	5 yr.
5	5.3682	5.8459	6.5996	7.9079	10.607	18.871
5⅛	5.4449	5.919	6.6688	7.9732	10.668	18.929
5¼	5.522	5.9925	6.7384	8.0388	10.729	18.986
5⅜	5.5997	6.0665	6.8085	8.1047	10.791	19.044
5½	5.6779	6.1409	6.8789	8.1708	10.853	19.101
5⅝	5.7566	6.2157	6.9497	8.2373	10.915	19.159
5¾	5.8357	6.2911	7.0208	8.3041	10.977	19.217
5⅞	5.9154	6.3668	7.0924	8.3712	11.039	19.275
6	5.9955	6.443	7.1643	8.4386	11.102	19.333
6⅛	6.0761	6.5196	7.2366	8.5062	11.165	19.391
6¼	6.1572	6.5967	7.3093	8.5742	11.228	19.449
6⅜	6.2387	6.6742	7.3823	8.6425	11.291	19.508
6½	6.3207	6.7521	7.4557	8.7111	11.355	19.566
6⅝	6.4031	6.8304	7.5295	8.7799	11.419	19.675
6¾	6.486	6.9091	7.6036	8.8491	11.482	19.683
6⅞	6.5693	6.9883	7.6781	8.9185	11.547	19.742
7	6.653	7.0678	7.753	8.9883	11.611	19.801
7⅛	6.7372	7.1477	7.8282	9.0583	11.675	19.86
7¼	6.8218	7.2281	7.9038	9.1286	11.74	19.919
7⅜	6.9068	7.3088	7.9797	9.1992	11.805	19.979
7½	6.9921	7.3899	8.0559	9.2701	11.87	20.038
7⅝	7.0779	7.4714	8.1325	9.3413	11.936	20.097
7¾	7.1641	7.5533	8.2095	9.4128	12.001	20.157
7⅞	7.2507	7.6355	8.2868	9.4845	12.067	20.217
8	7.3376	7.7182	8.3644	9.5565	12.133	20.276
8⅛	7.425	7.8012	8.4424	9.6288	12.199	20.336
8¼	7.5127	7.8845	8.5207	9.7014	12.265	20.396
8⅜	7.6007	7.9682	8.5993	9.7743	12.332	20.456
8½	7.6891	8.0523	8.6782	9.8474	12.399	20.517
8⅝	7.7779	8.1367	8.7575	9.9208	12.466	20.577
8¾	7.867	8.2214	8.8371	9.9945	12.533	20.637
8⅞	7.9564	8.3065	8.917	10.068	12.6	20.698
9	8.0462	8.392	8.9973	10.143	12.668	20.758
9⅛	8.1363	8.4777	9.0778	10.217	12.735	20.819
9¼	8.2268	8.5638	9.1587	10.292	12.803	20.88
9⅜	8.3175	8.6502	9.2398	10.367	12.871	20.941
9½	8.4085	8.737	9.3213	10.442	12.94	21.002
9⅝	8.4999	8.824	9.4031	10.518	13.008	21.063
9¾	8.5915	8.9114	9.4852	10.594	13.077	21.124

	30 yr.	**25 yr.**	**20 yr.**	**15 yr.**	**10 yr.**	**5 yr.**
9⅞	8.6835	8.999	9.5675	10.67	13.146	21.186
10	8.7757	9.087	9.6502	10.746	13.215	21.247
10⅛	8.8682	9.1753	9.7332	10.823	13.284	21.309
10¼	8.961	9.2638	9.8164	10.9	13.354	21.37
10⅜	9.0541	9.3527	9.9	10.977	13.424	21.432
10½	9.1474	9.4418	9.9838	11.054	13.493	21.494
10⅝	9.241	9.5312	10.068	11.132	13.564	21.556
10¾	9.3348	9.6209	10.152	11.209	13.634	21.618
10⅞	9.4289	9.7109	10.237	11.288	13.704	21.68
11	9.5232	9.8011	10.322	11.366	13.775	21.742
11⅛	9.6178	9.8916	10.407	11.445	13.846	21.805
11¼	9.7126	9.9824	10.493	11.523	13.917	21.867
11⅜	9.8077	10.073	10.578	11.603	13.988	21.93
11½	9.9029	10.165	10.664	11.682	14.06	21.993
11⅝	9.9984	10.256	10.751	11.761	14.131	22.055
11¾	10.094	10.348	10.837	11.841	14.203	22.118
11⅞	10.19	10.44	10.924	11.921	14.275	22.181
12	10.286	10.532	11.011	12.002	14.347	22.244
12⅛	10.382	10.675	11.098	12.082	14.419	22.308
12¼	10.479	10.717	11.186	12.163	14.492	22.371
12⅜	10.576	10.81	11.273	12.244	14.565	22.434
12½	10.673	10.904	11.361	12.325	14.638	22.498
12⅝	10.77	10.997	11.45	12.407	14.711	22.562
12¾	10.867	11.091	11.538	12.488	14.784	22.625
12⅞	10.964	11.184	11.627	12.57	14.857	22.689
13	11.062	11.278	11.716	12.652	14.931	22.753
13⅛	11.16	11.373	11.805	12.735	15.005	22.817
13¼	11.258	11.467	11.894	12.817	15.079	22.881
13⅜	11.356	11.562	11.984	12.9	15.153	22.945
13½	11.454	11.656	12.074	12.983	15.227	23.01
13⅝	11.553	11.751	12.164	13.066	15.302	23.074
13¾	11.651	11.847	12.254	13.15	15.377	23.139
13⅞	11.75	11.942	12.345	13.234	15.452	23.203
14	11.849	12.038	12.435	13.317	15.527	23.268
14⅛	11.948	12.133	12.526	13.402	15.602	23.333
14¼	12.047	12.229	12.617	13.486	15.677	23.398
14⅜	12.146	12.325	12.708	13.57	15.753	23.463
14½	12.246	12.422	12.8	13.655	15.829	23.528
14⅝	12.345	12.518	12.892	13.74	15.905	23.594
14¾	12.445	12.615	12.984	13.825	15.981	23.659
14⅞	12.545	12.711	13.076	13.91	16.057	23.724

FINANCE INSTRUMENTS

PROMISSORY NOTE

A *promissory note* is an unconditional written promise to pay a certain sum of money to another at a future specified time. In real estate financing, the note is evidence of the debt secured by a mortgage or deed of trust upon the property. The person signing the promissory note is called the maker, the person to whom the promise is made is the payee.

Most promissory notes in real estate financing are negotiable instruments. To be negotiable, the note must be made to a person or order or bearer, which enables the lender to endorse and transfer the note.

SECURITY INSTRUMENTS

A security instrument is a contract between lender and borrower by which property is given as security for repayment of a loan, evidenced by a note or bond.

In some states, the mortgage (in other states the deed of trust) is used as a real property security instrument. In a *mortgage*, the borrower is called the *mortgagor* and the lender, the *mortgagee*. In a *deed of trust*, the borrower is called the *trustor,* the lender is the *beneficiary;* the property is conveyed to the trustee (often a title company or bank) that holds title as security for repayment of the loan for the benefit of the beneficiary.

The *installment land contract,* also known as the *contract of sale,* is an installment-type contract between buyer and seller, whereby the buyer obtains the right to occupy but the seller retains legal title to the real property as security for payment of the purchase price. The seller agrees to convey title to the buyer upon fulfillment of certain conditions. During the term of the contract the buyer is said to have an *equitable ownership interest* in the property. A contract of sale is both a marketing instrument (like a sale/purchase agreement) and a security instrument (like a mortgage or deed of trust). Because a contract of sale is also a security instrument, brokers should not use such a form without having it reviewed by the buyer's legal counsel.

PRIORITY

An executed security instrument is a lien upon the property it secures, and the priority of a lien, in relationship to other liens, is determined by the date and time it is entered into the public records. A mortgage recorded before another mortgage is said to be prior or senior to a mortgage recorded later; a mortgage recorded after another mortgage is said to be junior or subordinate to one that is recorded earlier.

SUBORDINATION

A *subordination* clause in a mortgage or deed of trust is an agreement by the lender to subordinate its lien upon the property to a prior lien for the benefit of another creditor.

Subordination provisions are most commonly used when the holder of the mortgage agrees to subordinate its lien to a construction loan. A subordination clause may also be utilized when the holder of a second lien subordinates to a new, increased first lien used to improve the property and thus enhance the value of the lender's security.

To be enforceable, the courts ordinarily require that the lien to which subordination is granted be clearly and specifically described. An example of a subordination clause may be found in the "Contract Clause" section of the ***Realty Bluebook***®·

A partial release, partial satisfaction or reconveyance clause is used when the lender has agreed to reconvey a portion of the real property that secures its debt when a portion of that debt has been paid. Such clauses are common when the parties contemplate that the real property, which furnishes security for the mortgage or the deed of trust, will be subdivided and that portions will be sold to third parties. The creditor needs to be certain that the remaining property is sufficient to secure the remaining portion to the debt and that the reconveyance will not adversely affect the value of the remaining property. For example, when a large parcel of real property is being developed, it is common to include in the reconveyance provisions that the property reconveyed will be contiguous to other property that is reconveyed and that there be sufficient access to the property remaining subject to the encumbrance so that it will retain its value.

A real estate broker should not undertake to negotiate the provisions of either a subordination clause or a reconveyance clause. Such clauses are important contractual matters that should be drafted by legal counsel.

FORECLOSURE

Foreclosure is a procedure prescribed by law whereby real property, pledged as security for repayment of a debt, is sold to pay the debt in the event of default.

In the event the borrower defaults, the lender's remedy is foreclosure. The debtor, or any other person having an interest in the property (such as a junior lienholder), has the right to redeem the property any time after the obligation is due and before his or her right of redemption ends. The length of the redemption period varies from state to state.

Judicial foreclosure is a foreclosure ordered by a court following the filing of an action for that purpose by the holder of a mortgage or deed of trust. This procedure is used in states where there is no power of sale included in the mortgage or deed of trust or where there is a controversy about the terms of the mortgage or the deed of trust or the amount due. In some states, a deficiency judgment is allowed only in connection with a judicial foreclosure. In some states, the debtor has the right to redeem the property from sale within a specified period of time by paying the buyer the purchase price, interest and expense of maintaining the property.

Nonjudicial foreclosure proceedings are allowed in some states under a power of sale contained in a mortgage or deed of trust. The proceedings are conducted without the filing of any court proceeding. The lender, or the lender's trustee, has the right to sell the property upon default following the procedure set forth in state law and the terms of the mortgage or deed of trust. The procedure normally allows the debtor a period of time within which to cure the default under the secured obligation and requires that the sale be made at a public auction following proper notice. A period for redemption by the debtor is shortened or eliminated. In some states, the creditor cannot obtain a deficiency judgment if foreclosure proceedings take place without the aid of a court.

A *deficiency judgment* is a judgment against a debtor, endorser, guarantor or other party who may be liable for the debt when the security for the loan is insufficient to satisfy the debt because the sale proceeds are less than the amount due. A deficiency judgment may not be available in some states where the sale was made under a power of sale contained in the mortgage or deed of trust. Where available, a deficiency judgment can only be granted in a court proceeding. In some states, the court makes an independent determination with respect to whether or not the property was sold for less than its fair value at the foreclosure sale.

ACCELERATION—DUE ON SALE

The term *acceleration clause,* also called *alienation clause,* refers to a provision in a note and deed of trust or mortgage requiring immediate payment of the entire unpaid balance of principal and interest upon the occurrence of a specified event or events.

One of the two common types of acceleration clauses, contained in most notes, makes the entire amount of unpaid principal and interest become immediately due and payable upon default, at the option of the lender. Although this right of the lender is usually stated without qualification, in most states there are laws that permit the borrower to reinstate his or her right upon payment within a specified period of time and upon reimbursement to the lender of costs incurred.

The other type of acceleration clause, referred to as a *due-on-sale* or *alienation clause,* makes the entire amount of unpaid principal and interest become immediately due and payable upon the sale, transfer and sometimes further encumbrance of the property or any part thereof or interest therein, at the option of the lender.

Acceleration is a lender's optional privilege; but without an acceleration clause, the lender cannot accelerate the obligation upon default or transfer.

The due-on-sale clause enables the lender to exercise or waive his or her option to accelerate the payment date. The lender can, therefore, approve or disapprove of a buyer wishing to assume the loan; the lender can forbear his or her right to accelerate in return for an increased interest rate.

ASSUMING—TAKING SUBJECT TO A MORTGAGE

A mortgage loan is *assumed* when a written assumption agreement is executed between the lender and the purchaser of the property. Thus, the primary responsibility for repayment of the loan is placed upon the new owner.

In the event no due-on-sale clause is provided in the mortgage or trust deed, the lender cannot require a purchaser to sign an assumption agreement, nor can the lender raise the interest rate or make any other demands. In such event, the purchaser is said to buy the property subject to the mortgage loan, rather than to assume it.

In some states, either by statute or court decisions, due-on-sale clauses were made unenforceable.

The U.S. Supreme Court held in 1982 that a due-on-sale clause in a mortgage or deed of trust securing a note to a federal savings and loan association was enforceable notwithstanding state laws to the contrary.

Life insurance companies, due to the long-term nature of their investment objectives, rarely provide due-on-sale clauses in their mortgages. On the contrary, they charge high prepayment penalties and often lock in a mortgage during the initial portion of the term, which means that the loan may not be paid off under any circumstances.

From the seller's point of view, when a mortgage is assumed, the assumption agreement between the lender and the new owner places the primary responsibility for repayment of the mortgage upon the new owner. If, on the other hand, the property is sold subject to the mortgage, the person primarily responsible for repayment of the mortgage debt is the original maker of the note. The fact that the new owner makes the payments after the sale is consummated does not place the obligation to pay off the mortgage debt upon the new owner because he never agreed to do so in writing; the only party with whom the lender has a contractual relationship is the original borrower. However, for all practical purposes the seller has little reason for concern (except that the seller's credit may be adversely affected) unless the new owner has a very thin equity in the property. In the event of default, the lender would foreclose, and as long as the property can be sold for sufficient net proceeds to satisfy the balance of the mortgage, the lender is satisfied and the original borrower is released of all obligations with respect to the mortgage. Only if the property does not bring sufficient net proceeds to pay off the balance of the loan, will the lender have legal recourse to recover the deficiency. Some states do not permit deficiency judgments against the original borrower when the loan was made for the purpose of acquisition of the borrower's home or when the lender exercises his or her right to foreclose without a court proceeding.

PREPAYMENT

A *prepayment penalty* or *fee* in a loan document requires the borrower to pay a penalty for paying off the loan before maturity.

Where prepayment fees are not prohibited, the borrower cannot prepay a real estate loan before maturity unless the lender consents or unless expressly permitted by the terms of the note (stating periodic payments of a certain sum or more). Therefore, unless the mortgage note permits unlimited payments or provides for a specific prepayment fee, the lender is in a position to negotiate the charge he or she will accept in return for consent to an early payoff. This may be of particular concern in the case of private loans including those financed by the seller.

FHA, VA, Fannie Mae and Freddie Mac do not allow prepayment fees in their loan documents.

TYPES OF MORTGAGES

To increase available financing options to cover various financial situations, government agencies as well as the lending and real estate industries continue to create new alternative mortgage instruments and financing techniques. The term *creative financing* can best be defined as the ability to make effective use of all these instruments and techniques while at the same time exploring a buyer's chances to generate additional cash and/or improve his or her ability to handle mortgage payments.

ALTERNATIVE MORTGAGE INSTRUMENTS

Fixed Rate Mortgage (FRM)

A *fixed rate mortgage* provides for repayment of the principal amount (the unpaid balance of a loan) over a specified number of years in equal monthly payments, which include interest. Interest is computed on the remaining principal balance at the end of each month. As the principal of the loan is reduced, the interest portion of the monthly payment becomes less while the principal payment increases each month.

Biweekly Mortgage

A *biweekly mortgage* provides for payments amounting to one half the monthly payments and are due every two weeks. Because there are 52 weeks in a year, the program results in 26 biweekly payments or the equivalent of 13 monthly payments per year. The result is a considerable reduction in the term of the mortgage and a substantial savings in total interest paid. The comparison between a mortgage with monthly payments and one with biweekly payments in the following example shows a reduction in mortgage term from 30 years to about 21 years with an interest savings of $53,764.

	Monthly Payments	Biweekly Payments
Loan amount	$70,000	$70,000
Interest rate	10%	10%
Payments	$614.30	$307.15
No. of payments per yr.	12	26
Total No. of Payments per yr.	12 × $614.30 = $7,371.60	26 × $307.15 = $7,985.90
Terms in years	**30 years**	**20.96 years**
	$7,371.60 × 30 =	$7,985.90 × 20.96 =
Total payments	$221,148	$167,384
Minus principal	–$70,000	–$70,000
Total interest	$151,148	$97,384

Interest savings $151,148 – $97,384 = $53,764

Adjustable Rate Mortgage (ARM)

The concept of variable rate financing calls for the borrower to share with the lender the risks of a fluctuating economy.

An ARM, or *adjustable rate mortgage,* is a mortgage that provides for interest rate adjustments that are tied to an independent index.

Although the terms of one ARM may vary widely from another, there are several characteristics common to most adjustable rate financing plans:

1. **The index** is an indicator of current economic conditions and is used to calculate the new interest rate. Following are the only requirements a lender must meet in selecting an index.

    a. The index must be beyond the control of the lender.

    b. The index must be readily available to, and verifiable by, the public. Rate increases are at the option of the lender while rate decreases are mandatory.

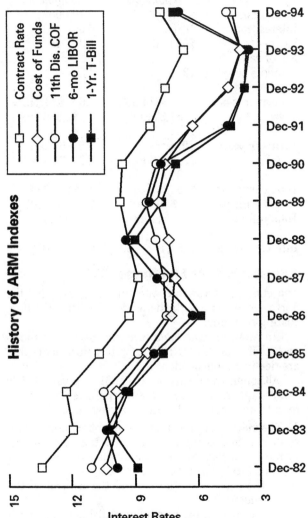

History of ARM Indexes

Legend:
- Contract Rate (□)
- Cost of Funds (◇)
- 11th Dis. COF (○)
- 6-mo LIBOR (●)
- 1-Yr. T-Bill (■)

Interest Rates axis: 15, 12, 9, 6, 3

Dates: Dec-82, Dec-83, Dec-84, Dec-85, Dec-86, Dec-87, Dec-88, Dec-89, Dec-90, Dec-91, Dec-92, Dec-93, Dec-94

A variety of indexes used by lenders are: One-Year Treasury Bill Rates, Three- and Five-Year Treasury Note Rates, Federal Reserve Discount Rates, Eleventh District Cost of Funds Index and LIBOR (London InterBank Offer Rate), the rate at which commercial banks lend money to one another in the international market.

Index Movements. The historical movements of ARM indexes are shown in the graph on the next page.

Cost of Funds. The national median cost of funds to SAIF-insured institutions as reported by the Office of Thrift Supervision, Washington, D.C., (202) 906-6000.

Contract Rate. The national average contract interest rate for major lenders as reported by the Federal Housing Finance Board, Washington, D.C., (202) 408-2500.

Eleventh District Cost of Funds. The cost of funds for the 11th District as released by the Federal Home Loan Bank of San Francisco. (California accounts for about 25% of all residential mortgage loans in this country.) (415) 616-2600.

One-Year Treasury Securities (T-Bills). The one-year constant maturity yield on U.S. Treasury securities as reported by the Federal Reserve Board, Washington, D.C., (202) 452-3400.

2. **The margin,** also referred to as the spread or differential, is the percentage added to the index rate in order to arrive at what is referred to as the *full indexed rate*. The margin should be clearly stated in the note and should remain constant throughout the term of the loan. At each adjustment interval, the interest rate is recalculated by adding the margin to the index rate. The margin varies with lender, type of index and market conditions.

CAUTION: When selecting an ARM, buyers should be cautioned about so-called incentive teaser rates offered by many lenders to help qualify the buyer. These are introductory below-market rates, referred to as *initial note rates,* in effect for a limited period of time (typically 6 or 12 months). At the end of that period, the interest rate is adjusted to the *full indexed rate.* In the event of a large difference between the teaser rate and the full indexed rate, the increase in monthly payments could be a shocking experience to a home owner.

3. **The adjustment interval** is the frequency with which the interest rate and/or the monthly payment amount can be reset. There is a wide variety of ARM loans in the market today with adjustment intervals ranging from several months to a number of years and almost everything in between. Actual adjustments to the consumer's mortgage interest rate can only occur on a predetermined time schedule—such as monthly, every six months or annually. The interest rate and payment adjustments may or may not be scheduled to change at the same time. For example, the interest rate on some plans changes more frequently than the monthly payment, which may result in negative amortization. This means that the additional interest will be added to the principal balance of the loan and may accrue additional interest itself.

4. **The cap** is a restriction on the periodic or lifetime change in interest rate or payment amount. A *periodic cap* limits the percentage of change at periodic or annual intervals. A *lifetime cap* sets a maximum on the percentage the interest rate can change from the initial note rate over the entire term of the loan.

Negative Amortization. Although interest caps offer protection to the borrower, payment caps without corresponding interest caps can result in considerable negative amortization in which the interest portion not covered by payments is added to the balance of the loan. This can result in the borrower owing more than the original loan amount.

Lenders may restrict the amount of negative amortization by recasting the loan every few years, or whenever the loan balance has increased a certain percentage over and above the original loan amount. When a loan is recast, the monthly payment—regardless of any payment cap—is refigured based on the then-remaining loan balance, the remaining term of the loan and the interest rate then in effect. This can result in very considerable payment increases, as much as 30%.

As a result, it may be difficult to obtain secondary financing from lenders and sellers carrying back seconds behind assumed first loans with negative amortization.

The following example of interest rate adjustments incorporates a 2% annual interest cap.

Year	Index	+	Margin	=	Adjustm	New Rate
1	10.0	+	2.00	=	12.0	12%
2	11.5	+	2.00	=	13.5	13.5%
3	15.5	+	2.00	=	17.5	15.5%
4	11.0	+	2.00	=	13.0	13.5%
5	11.0	+	2.00	=	13.0	13%

Yr 1: Lender and borrower agreed to a contract rate of 12% for the first year, with annual adjustments based on the index plus a margin of 2%.

Yr 2: The index increases 1.5% (from 10% to 11.5%). *Index + Margin* = 13.5%. Because the increase is less than the 2% annual cap, the new rate is 13.5%.

Yr 3: The index increases 4% (from 11.5 to 15.5). *Index + Margin* = 17.5%; however, because of the 2% annual interest cap, the new rate is only 15.5%.

Yr 4: The index decreases 4.5% (from 15.5 to 11). *Index + Margin* = 13%. The annual 2% interest cap, however, limits the interest decrease, and the rate is 13.5%.

Yr 5: The index remains the same as in previous year. *Index + Margin* = 13%. This is within the annual cap, so the new interest rate will decrease to 13%.

Advantages of ARMs

1. The initial interest rate is generally quite a bit below the going fixed rate, which means that the monthly payments are lower and more buyers can afford them.
2. It may be easier to qualify borrowers for an ARM because the initial rate is lower. Borrowers may have a much harder time qualifying for a fixed rate mortgage because their monthly payments are higher, which may put their income-to-debt ratio beyond the maximum.
3. Lenders usually permit assumptions, provided the new buyer meets credit standards. This is not nearly as common with a fixed rate mortgage.
4. Generally, there are no prepayment penalties.

Convertible ARMs

Convertible ARMs were introduced to the market by Fannie Mae in 1987. This type of ARM allows the borrower to convert to a fixed rate mortgage, usually any time from the 13th through the 60th month.

When a borrower converts, the new interest rate will usually be ⅝% over Fannie Mae's 60-day posted yield for fixed rate mortgages. The borrower is sometimes charged a conversion fee of about 1% of the original principal balance plus a processing fee that may not exceed $250.

A borrower's cost to convert may be substantially less than the cost of refinancing, but this is not always true.

Lenders must provide borrowers with an adjustable rate program disclosure upon discussing any adjustable program.

Potential borrowers should be cautioned to carefully analyze the wide differences between ARMs before committing themselves to this type of financing.

DATE:_____	LENDER 1	LENDER 2
Name of Lender	_____	_____
Loan amount	$_____	$_____
Points charged	_____%	_____%
Index used	_____	_____
Current index rate	_____%	_____%
Margin used	_____%	_____%
Contract rate	_____%	_____%
Contract rate guaranteed as of:		
☐ Submission date	_____	_____
☐ Loan approval date	_____	_____
☐ Closing date	_____	_____
Fee (if any) to lock in rte. earlier	_____%	_____%
Initial monthly payment	$_____	$_____
APR	_____%	_____%
APR of fixed rate loan	_____%	_____%
Initial discounted rate, if any	_____%	_____%
Term of discounted rate	_____mos.	_____mos.
Interest rate when disc. rte. ends:		
☐ Contract rate	_____	_____
☐ Adjusted rate	_____	_____
First interest rate adjustment date	_____	_____
First interest rate adjustment %, assuming no index change	_____%	_____%

First payment adjustment date   _____   _____

Regular rate adjustment period   ____mos.   ____mos.

Regular payment adjustment period   ____mos.   ____mos.

Lifetime interest cap, if any   _____%   _____%

Periodic interest cap, if any   _____%   _____%

Can int. rte. increase in excess of cap be carried over to next adjustment?   _____   _____

Does periodic int. cap apply to index decreases?   _____   _____

Does lifetime int. cap apply to index decreases?   _____   _____

Method of calculating int. rte. if index decreases:

☐ Int. rate bottoms at contract rate   _____   _____

☐ Int. rate declines same % as index   _____   _____

☐ Other   _____   _____

Lifetime payment cap, if any   _____   _____

Periodic payment cap, if any   _____   _____

Can negative amortization occur?   _____   _____

When is loan recast to pay off increase in principal balance due to negative amortization:

☐ Periodically   _____yrs   _____yrs

☐ When balance exceeds original by   _____%   _____%

Does payment cap apply to payment
  increases resulting from
  recasting of the loan due to
  negative amortization?   _____   _____

Can ARM be converted to fixed rte.?   _____   _____

Can loan term be extended?   _____   _____

Open end (add on) feature?   _____   _____

Is ARM assumable?   _____   _____

Assumable for one time only?   _____   _____

Assumption conditions:

☐ Customary credit standards   _____   _____

☐ Assumption fee   _____   _____

☐ Original periodic caps
  remaining?   _____   _____

☐ Original lifetime cap remaining?   _____   _____

Prepayment penalty, if any   _____   _____

Growing Equity Mortgage (GEM)

A *GEM* provides for a gradual increase in monthly payments with all of the increase being applied to the principal balance, resulting in a relatively rapid accumulation of equity and an accelerated maturity.

GEMs offer borrowers an affordable starting monthly payment based on 30-year amortization and predetermined increases, usually 3% to 5% annually, for a specified period.

Because the payment increases are applied to principal only, the mortgage balance is reduced more quickly than usual. Homebuyers who expect to earn rising incomes, or who are interested in paying off their loan in less time than with a traditional loan, find GEMs appealing.

See GEM tables under Growing Equity Mortgages in the VA Section.

Graduated Payment Mortgage (GPM)

The interest rate remains fixed throughout the term of the loan, but the monthly payments start out at a low level and gradually increase (for example, at 3% a year) until they rise above the level at which a standard fixed rate mortgage would have been written.

The amount of house a family can buy depends upon its current income, and so the GPM is particularly attractive to the young family buying its first home because the income requirements to qualify for a GPM are significantly less than those for a fixed rate mortgage. A GPM enables a family to raise its housing standard to a level that averages out more accurately with its expected lifetime income.

Chart 1 compares the annual payments for a $30,000 fixed payment loan at 9% interest and a graduated payment loan at 9.5% with payments increasing 7.5% a year. It should be noted that four years elapse before the payments on the GPM even equal those of a fixed rate conventional loan.

A major drawback of the GPM is that a family's income may not increase in line with the rate of increase in the payments.

Chart I
ANNUAL PAYMENTS: Conventional vs.
Graduated-Payment Mortgage.
$30,000 Loan for 30 Years.

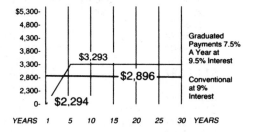

Chart 2
OUTSTANDING BALANCE: Conventional vs.
Graduated-Payment Mortgage.
$30,000 Loan for 30 Years.

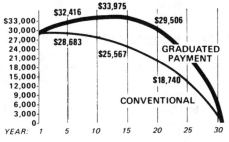

Note that GPMs involve negative amortization in the early years of the loan because the lower payments during that period frequently do not cover the full amount of interest. In that event, the loan balance would increase during the early years of the mortgage as illustrated in Chart 2, which shows the outstanding balance of a $30,000 GPM for 30 years compared to a conventional fixed payment loan.

GPM loans are available through FHA Sec. 245 and are also offered by the VA and the private sector in various forms.

15-Yr EQUAL™ Mortgage / 1-Yr Initial Payments

15-Year Term
Payment Increases in 2nd Year
Qualifying Rate: 6.125%

APR: 11.429%
Buydown Cost: $819.36
Level Payment in Year 7

Year	Mnthly Pmnt. Amnt.	Wthdrl. from Buydown Funds	Prin. Bal. at Yr End
1	$850.63	$66.04	$100,000.00
2	$914.43	$2.24	$100,000.00
3	$983.01		$99,162.49
4	$1,056.74		$97,297.30
5	$1,136.00		$94,215.72
6	$1,221.20		$89,701.97
7	**$1,311.97**		$83,520.03
8	**$1,311.97**		$76,622.73
9	**$1,311.97**		$68,927.29
10	**$1,311.97**	*Level*	$60,341.33
11	**$1,311.97**	*Payment*	$50,761.82
12	**$1,311.97**		$40,073.77
13	**$1,311.97**		$28,148.93
14	**$1,311.97**		$14,844.14
15	**$1,311.97**		$0.00
20	$0.00		$0.00
25	$0.00		$0.00
30	$0.00		$0.00

15-Yr EQUAL™ Mortgage / 2-Yrs Initial Payments

15-Year Term
Payment Increases in 3rd Year
Qualifying Rate: 6.250%

APR: 11.435%
Buydown Cost: $1,421.76
Level Payment in Year 9

Year	Mnthly Pmnt. Amnt.	Wthdrl. from Buydown Funds	Prin. Bal. at Yr End
1	**$857.43**	$59.24	$100,000.00
2	**$857.43**	$59.24	$100,000.00
3	$921.74		$999,935.95
4	$990.87		$98,991.80
5	$1,065.19		$97,000.20
6	$1,145.08		$93,769.63
7	$1,230.96		$89,081.06
8	$1,323.28		$82,684.48
9	**$1,415.76**		$74,380.25
10	**$1,415.76**		$65,115.09
11	**$1,415.76**	*Level*	$54,777.77
12	**$1,415.76**	*Payment*	$43,244.20
13	**$1,415.76**		$30,376.00
14	**$1,415.76**		$16,018.70
15	**$1,415.76**		$0.00
20	$0.00		$0.00
25	$0.00		$0.00
30	$0.00		$0.00

30-Yr EQUAL™ Mortgage / 1-Yr Initial Payments

30-Year Term   APR: 11.326%
Payment Increases in 2nd Year   Buydown Cost: $835.32
Qualifying Rate: 9.625%   Level Payment in Year 3

Year	Mnthly Pmnt. Amnt.	Wthdrl. from Buydown Funds	Prin. Bal. at Yr End
1	$849.99	$66.68	$100,000.00
2	$913.74	$2.93	$100,000.00
3	**$961.48**		$99,434.28
4	**$961.48**		$98,803.08
5	**$961.48**		$98,098.86
6	**$961.48**		$97,313.14
7	**$961.48**	*Level*	$96,436.52
8	**$961.48**	*Payment*	$95,458.42
9	**$961.48**		$94,367.16
10	**$961.48**		$93,149.63
15	**$961.48**		$84,592.85
20	**$961.48**		$69,798.85
25	**$961.48**		$44,221.27
30	**$961.48**		$0.00

30-Yr EQUAL™ Mortgage / 2-Yrs Initial Payments

30-Year Term   APR: 11.342%
Payment Increases in 3rd Year   Buydown Cost: $1,635.48
Qualifying Rate: 9.625%   Level Payment in Year 4

Year	Mnthly Pmnt. Amnt.	Wthdrl. from Buydown Funds	Prin. Bal. at Yr End
1	**$849.99**	$66.68	$100,000.00
2	**$849.99**	$66.68	$100,000.00
3	$913.74	$2.93	$100,000.00
4	**$966.96**		$99,365.12
5	**$966.96**		$98,656.76
6	**$966.96**		$97,866.42
7	**$966.96**		$96,984.63
8	**$966.96**	*Level*	$96,000.81
9	**$966.96**	*Payment*	$94,903.14
10	**$966.96**		$93,678.46
15	**$966.96**		$85,071.43
20	**$966.96**		$70,190.47
25	**$966.96**		$44,462.57
30	**$966.96**		$0.00

Graduated Payment Adjustable Rate Mortgage (GPARM)

The GPARM is a blend of the GPM and ARM. Buyers can take advantage of the initial low payments of a GPM while lenders get the flexible rate advantage of the ARM. The GPARM is not accepted by Fannie Mae.

EQUAL™ Mortgage

The EQUAL™ mortgage combines fixed rate interest, buydown, graduated payments without negative amortization and a known payment schedule.

- *Buydown:* By enabling the borrower to buy down the interest rate, the initial rate is substantially reduced from the note rate, thus producing lower monthly payments on which to qualify.
- *One- or Two-Year Initial Payments:* At the borrower's option, the initial payment is maintained for the first year or the first two years of the mortgage.
- *Yearly Increased Payments:* After one or two years the monthly payments are adjusted upward by 7.5% per year until level payments are reached to amortize the mortgage over the balance of its term.
- *EQUAL™ mortgages:* Available for 15- or 30-year terms.
- *Down Payment:* 20%
- *Other:* No prepayment penalty, limited documentation, no income verification.

Rate Improvement Mortgage (RIM)

A *RIM* is a 30-year fixed rate mortgage with a one-time interest rate improvement option. Lenders charge a conversion fee and a processing fee.

Pledged Account Mortgage (PAM) or Flexible Loan Insurance Program (FLIP)

The *pledged account mortgage* is a form of the GPM. In order to reduce the monthly payments during the first years of the loan, the buyer places part of the cash intended for the down payment into a pledged interest-bearing savings account. The lender makes a fixed rate mortgage. During the early years of the loan the borrower makes monthly payments considerably smaller than the payment that would amortize the fixed rate mortgage. The deficit is made up of monthly withdrawals from the pledged savings account. The borrower's portion of the payments increases and the withdrawals decline annually until the pledged account is exhausted at the end of the graduation period.

Example

Purchase price	$100,000
Available cash	20,000
Deposit in pledged account	15,000
Down payment	5,000
Fixed rate mortgage	
(with private mortgage insurance)	
@ 15% interest for 30 years,	
payable $1,200 per month	95,000
First year's monthly payments	800
First year's monthly pledged account withdrawal	400

Mortgage Guaranty Insurance Corporation (MGIC) of Milwaukee and FLIP Mortgage Corporation of Newton, Pennsylvania, have developed PAM loans that reduce the monthly payments by as much as 25% during the first year of a five-year graduation period.

Reverse Annuity Mortgage (RAM)

Senior citizen homeowners often face the reverse problem of young families in that their incomes are relatively low and that, although they may own their homes free and clear, they must move in order to utilize their equities.

Originally offered in only a few areas, *RAMs* provide senior citizen homeowners with money from the equity in their homes through government-backed or privately insured reverse mortgages.

Under the Home Equity Conversion Insurance Program, insured by the Federal Housing Administration (FHA), the lender pays the borrower a single lump sum, a credit line or monthly payments for as long as the person lives in his or her home. No repayment is required until the homeowner dies, sells his or her home or permanently moves. The program is open to homeowners at least 62 years old of all income levels who own their homes either free and clear or nearly so. (See also Home Equity Conversion Mortgage Insurance Program under the FHA section or call your local HUD field office.)

Cash Available from Federally Insured Reverse Mortgages*

Home Value	$50,000	$100,000	$150,000
Age 70	$19,700	$44,000	$68,300
Age 75	$23,100	$50,600	$78,100
Age 80	$26,800	$57,700	$88,600

*Based on national maximum at 7.25% interest; not available in all areas.
Source: National Center for Home Equity Conversion

Fannie Mae is also developing a privately insured reverse mortgage program. Privately insured reverse mortgages may offer higher cash advances than the FHA's program.

The nonprofit National Center of Home Equity Conversion has a list of participating lenders, the "Reverse Mortgage Locator," which includes information on FHA and privately insured reverse mortgage options by state, including company names and telephone numbers. Send $1 and a self-addressed, stamped business-size envelope to NCHEC, Suite 115, 7373 147th St. West, Apple Valley, MN 55124, (612) 953-4474.

The National Center of Home Equity Conversion also publishes an excellent book on the subject, *Retirement Income on the House* by Ken Scholen.

For a free booklet on reverse mortgages, write to the American Association of Retired Persons, 601 E Street N.W., Washington, DC 20049, (202) 434-2277.

Zero Percent Mortgage (ZPM)

With a typical *ZPM*, the buyer makes a large cash down payment, perhaps one-third of the purchase price, with the remaining balance payable in equal monthly installments over 5 years with no interest. The payments are comparable with those of a fixed rate 30-year mortgage at current interest rates.

Example

	ZPM	*Fixed Rate Mortgage*
Price	$100,000	$100,000
Down payment	33,000	20,000
Loan amount	67,000	80,000
Term of loan	5 years	30 years
Interest	0%	17%
Monthly payments	$1,100	$1,140

Taxation of ZPM Payments. For federal income tax purposes when there is a sale of property and a portion of the purchase price is deferred, interest is imputed when no interest is stated or when the interest is less than the minimum allowable. (See Imputed Interest in the Tax Information section.) Interest will be imputed at the lower of 9% or the applicable federal rate. Consequently, a portion of each payment will be interest income to the seller and will constitute deductible interest to the buyer subject to the limitations of the Internal Revenue Code.

Pros and Cons. To the buyer, the advantages of a ZPM are a home completely paid for in five years and avoidance of the high cost of interest. The problem, of course, is the requirement of a large down payment.

The seller has the advantage of facilitating the sale of his or her home, or in the case of a builder, moving his or her inventory. The disadvantage to the seller is the deferment of the receipt of the full purchase price without interest while incurring tax liability for imputed interest.

However, the interest-free benefit to the buyer may be illusory if the purchase price has been adjusted by adding a premium as an alternative to the stated interest. The buyer should compare the price of the property if purchased on an all cash basis against the price with the ZPM.

Variations of ZPMs. Any number of variations to ZPMs have been devised by homebuilders. In one variation, a buyer with a low down payment is offered a ZPM and a second mortgage at current interest rates accumulating for five years with no monthly payments. After five years when the ZPM is paid off, the buyer begins making payments on the second mortgage in the same amount as the payments on the ZPM. Example:

Purchase price: $100,000
Down payment: $15,000
ZPM: $65,000, payable @ $1,084 for five years
Second mortgage: $20,000, accumulating interest @ 17%

With a negative amortization of 17% per year for five years, the principal of the second mortgage has increased to $37,000. With monthly payments of $1,084 including interest at 17%, the second mortgage will be retired in less than four years.

Shared Equity Mortgage (SEM)

Through a sale-leaseback arrangement called a *shared equity mortgage,* parents sell their home to their children or to other investors, then lease it back for the remainder of their lives. Sales proceeds are invested in a life annuity on behalf of the parents. After deduction of rent, the annuity payments go to the parents.

Shared Appreciation Mortgage (SAM)

Under an *SAM,* the lender offers a below-market interest rate in return for a percentage in the appreciation of the property.

Unsecured Loan

A very well qualified borrower can obtain an *unsecured loan* or line of credit, which may be used for almost any purpose, from a lending institution. The individual must have outstanding income, savings and credit. Unsecured loans are not normally committed for more than a year at a time, and the interest rate is generally stated as the lender's prime rate plus an agreed upon percentage above that rate. Although this money could be used to purchase a home and would not appear as a lien against the property, an unsecured loan would not normally be suitable for financing real estate, other than perhaps as an interim loan or construction loan.

THE SECONDARY MORTGAGE MARKET

The *secondary mortgage market* is an investor market in which blocks of residential mortgage loans, originated by lending institutions, are purchased and assembled into mortgage pools for the issuance of mortgage-backed securities. The main players among these so-called poolers are Fannie Mae, Freddie Mac, investment bankers, a few large commercial banks and some state and local housing agencies.

Pool underwriting procedures began in the early 1970s on a small scale, reaching a peak level by 1982. There are now four agencies involved in this activity:

1. Fannie Mae,
2. Freddie Mac,
3. Ginnie Mae and
4. Farmer Mac.

Since 1992, these agencies have held in portfolio or issued underwriting guaranties on more than 45% of all residential mortgage debt in the United States. Because the ability to sell a mortgage loan into any of the agency pools represents good liquidity (the ability to convert any asset into immediate cash), many loan originators tend to follow agency requirements whether they expect to sell the loan immediately or not.

Investors of mortgage-backed securities look not only for yields in comparison with other investments but also for safety and salability. The safety factor is provided by government backing of FHA, VA and conventional loans. Salability and liquidity have been accomplished through standardization of mortgage instruments, terms and credit standards brought about by Fannie Mae and Freddie Mac, which contributed much toward the success of the secondary mortgage market. To make their loans salable in the secondary market, lending institutions incorporate these standards into their underwriting guidelines.

THE FOUR FEDERAL UNDERWRITING AGENCIES

Fannie Mae, Freddie Mac, Ginnie Mae and Farmer Mac differ somewhat in how they function and in how congressional authority within each of these agencies must work.

Fannie Mae, Freddie Mac and *Farmer Mac* are publicly owned by stockholders but maintain close ties to the federal government. *Ginnie Mae* is a government agency operating under the U.S. Department of Housing and Urban Development (HUD).

Fannie Mae and Freddie Mac are authorized either to purchase loans for their own portfolio or to underwrite loans, whereas Ginnie Mae and Farmer Mac are limited to approving loan pools and issuing guaranty certificates based upon approved pools. Neither makes outright purchases of mortgage loans.

Only one federal agency, Ginnie Mae, carries the authority to issue a government guaranty on its certificates, meaning the full faith and credit of the U.S. government. The other three issue "agency guaranties."

FEDERAL NATIONAL MORTGAGE ASSOCIATION (FANNIE MAE)

Fannie Mae was founded as a government agency in 1938 to purchase (not underwrite) FHA loans. In 1944, VA loans were added to its approved list of loans. All these loans were held in portfolio. In 1954, Fannie Mae was rechartered and granted authority to sell its mortgage loans with purchases made at discount prices rather than at par. In 1968, Fannie Mae became a private corporation through a partitioning that created the Government National Mortgage Association (Ginnie Mae). In 1972, Fannie Mae enlarged its mortgage operations by adding conventional loans.

To make the purchase of conventional loans practical, it was necessary to create a uniform pattern of documents, qualifying requirements and insurance against loan default, which was accomplished in cooperation with Freddie Mac. The result, called a conforming loan, is a standardized conventional loan written on uniform documents that meets the purchase requirements of both agencies.

Today, Fannie Mae is authorized to purchase FHA, VA and conventional loans that conform to its requirements. Loan purchases are made for two separate purposes

1. its own portfolio and
2. creation of mortgage pools.

The guaranty securities Fannie Mae issues, backed by its mortgage pools, are called MBSs (mortgage-backed securities) in financial markets.

FEDERAL HOME LOAN MORTGAGE CORPORATION (FREDDIE MAC)

Freddie Mac was created in 1970 and placed under the administration of the Federal Home Loan Bank Board. In 1989, the FHLBB was abolished and Freddie Mac was shifted to a new regulator and new management.

Almost from its inception, Freddie Mac purchased loans for the purpose of creating its own mortgage pools. A Freddie Mac pool generally is made up of a large, geographically diverse block of residential loans. Each designated pool collateralizes a series of mortgage participation certificates, called PCs in financial markets. In 1983, Freddie Mac issued the first collateralized mortgage (CMO).

GOVERNMENT NATIONAL MORTGAGE ASSOCIATION (GINNIE MAE)

Ginnie Mae was created when Fannie Mae was restructured in 1968. Ginnie Mae operates as a part of HUD. Of the four federal underwriting agencies, Ginnie Mae is the only true government entity, and it continues to serve as the government's agency whenever Congress authorizes housing assistance programs.

Ginnie Mae is limited to underwriting only FHA, VA and certain FHA loans.

Unlike Fannie Mae and Freddie Mac, Ginnie Mae does not purchase loans to create pools. It does set its own requirements for loans that can be accepted into a mortgage pool, then subsequently approves loan poolers who are committed to complying with those requirements. The loan poolers can be any Ginnie Mae–approved company, such as investment bankers, finance companies, mortgage companies, homebuilders, real estate brokers, insurance companies or others.

The poolers then either originate or buy qualified mortgage loans from other loan originators across the country. When a pool is designated, Ginnie Mae is asked to grant its underwriting certificate, called a Ginnie Mae. The servicing (collecting monthly payments and handling the escrow accounts) of individual loans remains with the loan originator or a specialized servicing company.

FEDERAL AGRICULTURAL MORTGAGE CORPORATION (FARMER MAC)

The Agricultural Credit Act of 1987 established Farmer Mac as a separate agency within the Farm Credit System to develop a secondary market in farm real estate loans.

To qualify for a pool, a loan must be collateralized by agricultural real estate in the United States that can include a home costing not more than $100,000 that is in a rural community with a population of 2,500 or less. The maximum loan is the larger of $2.5 million or that secured by no more than 1,000 acres.

LENDING SOURCES

INSTITUTIONAL LENDERS
Savings Associations (Formerly Savings and Loan Associations)

The deregulation of the savings and loan industry, brought about by the Depository Institutions' Deregulation and Monetary Control Act of 1980 and the Garn–St. Germain Depository Act of 1982, was intended to give relief from the adversities thrifts experienced in the 1970s. As a result, S&Ls were allowed to branch out from their traditional role as residential real estate lenders into nonresidential loans and consumer financing. A new downturn of the economy in the mid-1980s gradually led to riskier investments that resulted in growing numbers of thrift failures. It culminated in the dramatic S&L crisis, which cost taxpayers more than $100 billion.

In 1989, Congress passed the Financial Institutions Reform, Recovery and Enforcement Act (FIRREA), which eliminated the Federal Home Loan Bank Board and the Federal Savings and Loan Insurance Corporation. They were replaced by the Federal Housing Finance Board, the Office of Thrift Supervision and the Savings Association Insurance Fund. At the same time, FIRREA changed the name savings and loan association to *savings association*. The reorganized Federal Deposit Insurance Corporation (FDIC) now controls the Savings Association Insurance Fund (SAIF), which insures deposits in savings associations, and the Bank Insurance Fund (BIF), which insures deposits in commercial banks and savings banks.

FIRREA also imposed new restrictions on savings associations to reverse the practice of high-risk investments and to encourage more residential lending. The dominating market position savings associations once held in residential lending is now shared to a large extent by mortgage bankers and also by commercial banks.

Today, most savings associations invest the majority of their assets in residential mortgages and home

Lender Share of Single-Family Conventional Loan Originations*

Year	Mortgage Bankers	Thrifts	Commercial Banks	Others
1980	22%	46%	22%	11%
1981	24	43	22	11
1982	29	36	26	9
1983	30	40	22	8
1984	23	47	21	9
1985	38	38	20	5
1986	35	35	22	8
1987	33	34	25	8
1988	33	36	23	8
1989	37	30	27	6
1990	35	26	33	5
1991	47	22	27	4
1992	49	21	26	4
1993	52	18	26	4
1994	58	14	24	4

Source: Freddie Mac's *Secondary Mortgage Market,* 1994 Mortgage Market Review—HUD Survey.

equity loans and generally adhere to underwriting guidelines of the secondary market.

Savings Banks

Savings banks, traditionally located in the Northeast, generally provide the same services as savings associations.

Mortgage Companies (Mortgage Bankers)

Mortgage bankers or *mortgage companies,* now the largest force in residential lending, generally specialize in originating FHA, VA and conventional loans, using strict underwriting guidelines. They generally obtain financing from commercial banks via lines of credit and sell their portfolios in the secondary market. Mortgage companies also represent insurance companies and large pension funds as loan correspondents, originating and servicing loans for these investors.

Commercial Banks

Commercial banks remain major participants in the mortgage market by supplying lines of credit to mortgage companies. Commercial banks have surpassed savings associations in market share of residential lending. Most banks sell their residential loans on the secondary market. They tend to give preferential treatment to depositors because customers' deposits constitute most of their assets. Traditionally, banks are a good source for office and apartment building loans, also for commercial construction loans.

Mortgage Brokers

Mortgage brokers originate loans but send them to an institutional lender for underwriting and funding. A mortgage broker's profit is derived from wholesale fees that are built into the retail fees charged by the lender.

Often, mortgage brokers have the most competitive rates because they work with a pool of lenders and programs (some brokers have more than 500 programs to choose from), and they are aware of the lowest interest rates available. Also, they are capable of sending a borrower's loan package to two or three different lenders at the same time, locking in the best rates and securing quicker approval.

After the mortgage broker and the borrower select a program, the loan is processed and the completed package is sent to the lender for underwriting. Documents are drawn, and the lender funds the loan at closing.

Life Insurance Companies

Life insurance companies are regulated by the state in which they operate, as well as by the state in which the company is incorporated. They are usually represented by loan correspondents. Because they must carefully protect the safety of their funds, they tend to restrict their lending to large income-producing properties in prime areas. A borrower must have an excellent credit payment history to qualify, but insurance companies will sometimes allow higher income-to-debt ratios than other lenders.

Pension Funds

Pension funds generally have abundant funds available for investment. Comparatively high yields and their safety factor make mortgages ideal investments for their portfolios. Pension funds buy large blocks of mortgages on the secondary market, or they invest in large mortgages, usually through mortgage bankers.

Pension fund administrators include trust departments of commercial banks and life insurance companies, trustees of union pension funds and boards of trustees of government employee pension funds.

Endowment Funds

Many commercial banks and mortgage bankers handle investments for *endowment funds*. Endowment funds of hospitals, universities, colleges, charitable foundations and other endowed institutions offer a good source of financing for commercial and industrial properties.

Credit Unions

In the past, *credit unions* have specialized in short-term consumer loans for their members, but today they are playing an ever increasing role in the residential mortgage market by financing homes for their members.

"Wall Street" and Other Private Investors

"Wall Street" and other private investors often form pools for themselves or for public or private partnerships for the purpose of buying and selling mortgages both directly and in the secondary mortgage market, thus creating another source of mortgage funds.

Private individuals are also a source for second mortgage money. Much higher interest rates coupled with discounts render excellent yields to an investor.

LOAN UNDERWRITING

Underwriting a real estate loan is the process of evaluating an applicant as a credit risk and ascertaining that the property, pledged as collateral, is sufficient security for the mortgage.

The underwriting procedure includes the following seven steps:

1. Evaluation of the applicant's stable monthly income;
2. Verification of liquid assets available for down payment, closing costs and reserves;
3. Determination of the applicant's monthly financial obligations;
4. Use of income ratios to compare proposed housing expense with applicant's income;
5. Evaluation of the applicant's credit history (credit report);
6. Valuation of the property pledged as collateral (appraisal); and
7. Establishment of the loan-to-value ratio (LTV) from the maximum loan for which the applicant qualifies (step 4) and the valuation of the property (step 6).

INCOME

In evaluating the borrower's income, the underwriter looks at three aspects:

1. amount of monthly income,
2. dependability of the income source and
3. continuity of stable monthly income.

Acceptable Types of Income

Income from Regular Employment

The borrower should have a history of receiving stable income from employment, have been employed full-time for two full years preceding the loan application and have a reasonable expectation for employment income to continue in the foreseeable future. (To the

FHA this means through the first three years of the loan.)

A borrower who changes jobs frequently to advance within the same line of work should receive favorable consideration. On the other hand, job-hopping without advancement, or from one line of work to another, may indicate an inability to master a job and could lead to unstable income.

Borrowers who have recently entered the job market may be considered favorably if adequate future income can be anticipated due to their education and training.

Allowances for seasonal employment, typical in the building and other trades, may be made.

Commission Income

As a general rule, the lender develops an average of two years' commission income. The annual earnings trend is an important consideration.

Overtime and Bonus Income

As a general rule, the lender develops an average of two years' income and requires verification from the employer that such income will in all probability continue.

Part-Time Income or Second Job

Income should be uninterrupted for two years and have a strong likelihood of continuing.

Verification of Employment Income

There are two alternatives

1. the lender mails a *Verification of Employment* form directly to the employer; or
2. the borrower furnishes W-2 forms for the preceding two years, plus payroll stubs for the previous 30-day period, which the lender confirms with the employer by telephone.

If commission, bonus or overtime income exceeds 25% of the borrower's total income from the employer, the lender requires copies of signed income tax returns for the preceding two years.

Retirement Income

Retirement income may be verified by letters from the organization providing the income, copies of the retirement award letters, tax returns or W-2 forms. (If benefits expire within about five years, the FHA considers income only a compensating factor.)

Alimony, Child Support, Spousal Maintenance

These types of income must continue for at least three years (five years for the FHA). Acceptable verification is a copy of the divorce decree or separation agreement, which must specify the amount of the award and the period of time over which it will be received. The borrower must provide evidence that the funds have been received for the last 12 months in the form of deposit slips, canceled checks, court records or tax returns.

Public Assistance Payments

Unemployment and welfare benefits may be considered acceptable income if they are properly documented by the paying agency showing the amount, frequency and duration of the payments. (For the FHA the provided income is expected to continue for approximately five years.)

Notes Receivable

Payments must continue for at least three years. Evidence required is a copy of the note showing amount and length of payment, plus deposit slips, canceled checks or tax returns showing funds have been received during the last 12 months.

Interest and Dividends

Such investment income is counted, provided the investment is not cashed in to provide funds for closing. Photocopies of tax returns must show funds have been received for the past two years.

Rental Income

A stable pattern of rental income must be verified by submitting authenticated copies of the property's books showing gross rental income and operating expenses for the previous two years as well as two years' income tax returns. Lenders generally add only 75% of the verified income to the borrower's stable income.

For qualifying purposes, depreciation may be added. Positive rental income is considered gross income; negative rental income must be treated as a recurring liability.

Self-Employment Income

Any individual who has at least a 25% ownership interest in a business is considered to be self-employed and requires the following documentation:

- signed individual federal income tax returns, including Schedule C for sole ownership or partnership business, and other applicable schedules for the most current two years;
- signed corporate federal income tax returns for the most current two years with all applicable schedules, if the business is an S corporation;
- a business credit report, in addition to the individual credit report, if the business is a corporation, an S corporation or a partnership;
- a year-to-date profit and loss statement regardless of the type of entity; and
- a balance sheet for the previous two years if the business is a sole proprietorship.

Knowledge of the structure of the business and the length of time the self-employed borrower has successfully operated the business are important considerations. (The FHA requires the borrower to be self-employed for two or more years, unless the borrower has past employment experience, formal education or training in his or her occupation.)

VA Benefits

Direct compensation, such as for a service-related disability, is acceptable if documented by the VA and if it will continue for at least three years.

Mortgage Credit Certificates and Differential Payments

If the employer or a government entity subsidizes the mortgage payments, either through direct payments or through tax rebates, these payments can be considered acceptable income if verified in writing. Either type of subsidy may be added to gross income before calculating gross ratios.

Trust Income

Income from trusts may be used if guaranteed, constant payment will continue for at least three years (for the FHA, five years). The documentation includes a copy of the trust agreement or trustee's statement confirming amount, frequency and duration of payments.

Unacceptable Types of Income

- Expense account payments, except for any excess of receipts over expenditures
- Retained earnings in a company
- Rent from boarders in a single-family property that is also the borrower's primary residence or second home
- Temporary employment
- Unemployment compensation

ASSETS AVAILABLE FOR DOWN PAYMENT AND CLOSING

The underwriter verifies that the borrower has sufficient funds or liquid assets for closing and adequate reserves to handle financial emergencies, such as unexpected bills or interruption of income. Cash equal to at least two mortgage payments is considered an adequate reserve.

Typical Sources of Liquid Assets

Earnest Money Deposit on Purchase Contract

The required documentation is a canceled check and/or verification of deposit.

Bank Accounts

The request for verification of deposit is used to verify each checking and savings account. The underwriter checks the verifications for

- any information that does not conform to the statements in the loan application,
- recently opened accounts and
- any large increases in existing accounts.

Stocks and Bonds

Stocks and bonds must be properly verified.

IRA/Keogh Accounts

Only the net withdrawal amount may be counted.

Trust Account

Trust account funds can be used if the applicant has access to them and if they can be verified.

Gifts or Grants

If the applicant is short of funds for closing, gifts may be used to supplement the funds needed for closing, provided the donor is a relative, church, municipality or nonprofit organization, and provided further that the applicant makes a down payment of at least 5% of the purchase price.

A gift from a relative, evidenced by a signed letter, must

- specify the amount of the gift and the date the funds were transferred;
- indicate the donor's name, address, telephone number and relationship to the borrower; and
- include the donor's statement that no repayment is expected.

A gift (or grant) from a church, municipality or nonprofit organization must be evidenced by either a copy of the letter awarding the gift or grant, or a copy of the legal agreement that specifies the terms and conditions of the gift or grant.

The donor of the gift may not be a person or entity with an interest in the sale of the property, such as the seller, real estate agent or broker, builder or any entity associated with them.

Sales Proceeds

Proceeds from the sale of a currently owned home are a common and acceptable source for the down payment and closing costs on a new house as well as for the required reserve. A photocopy of the fully executed settlement statement on the sale of the home, showing sufficient net cash proceeds to consummate the purchase of the new home, must be used to verify the source of these funds.

Anticipated Sales Proceeds

If the borrower's currently owned home is listed for sale but has not yet been sold, the lender may temporarily qualify the applicant on the basis of his or her anticipated equity.

Formula to determine the equity in a house sold but not yet closed:

Sales Price – Sales Costs – All Liens = Equity

Formula to determine the equity in a house listed for sale:

Listing Price – 10% of Listing Price – All Liens = Equity

Bridge Loans

Bridge, or *swing loans,* are secured by the borrower's present home, which is usually for sale. By using funds from a bridge loan, the borrower can close on a new house before selling his or her existing house. This type of financing is acceptable if

- the purchaser has the ability to carry the payment on the new home, the payment on other obligations, the payment on the current home and the payment on the bridge loan; and

- the bridge loan is not cross-collateralized against the new property.

Construction Loans

For the purpose of financing the construction of a home on a lot owned by the applicant, any equity in the lot may be applied toward the down payment.

Example

Estimated construction costs	$100,000
Lot value	+ 20,000
Total property value	$120,000
Maximum loan at 80% LTV	−96,000
Down payment	$24,000
Lot value	$20,000
Mortgage against lot	− 5,000
Equity in lot	$15,000
Down payment	$24,000
Equity in lot	−15,000
Remaining down payment in cash	$9,000

Trade Equity

Property equity as part of the down payment when the seller takes a borrower's existing property in trade is acceptable as long as the borrower has made a 5% cash down payment and the equity contribution is a true-value consideration. This is determined as follows:

The lesser of the trade property's appraised value or agreed trade-in-value *minus* outstanding loan balance *minus* transfer costs.

The appraisal must be a residential appraisal (conventional, FHA or VA) not more than six months old.

Lease with Option to Purchase

Fannie Mae accepts as part down payment rental payments that exceed the market rent if a valid lease/purchase agreement is in effect, a copy of which must be attached to the loan application. The original term of the lease must have been at least 12 months. The

appraiser must develop the market rent figure, and
the lender must obtain copies of canceled checks or
money order receipts to document the rental payments for the last 12 months.

Real Estate Sales Commission

If the borrower is entitled to a real estate commission
from the sale of the property being purchased, that
amount may be used as part of the down payment.

Sweat Equity

FHA and VA (not Fannie Mae) consider labor performed on the property being purchased or materials
furnished by the borrower before closing as the equivalent of a cash investment to the extent of the estimated cost of the work or materials. (Sweat equity
may be "gifted.")

LIABILITIES

Recurring Obligations

Recurring obligations include all installment loans,
revolving charge accounts, real estate loans, alimony,
child support, spousal maintenance and all other continuing obligations, extending beyond ten months for
conventional financing (beyond six months for FHA
financing).

Contingent Liabilities

A contingent liability exists if a borrower is a cosigner
on an obligation or a coborrower on a mortgage.

For each liability, the lender verifies the unpaid
balance, terms and the borrower's payment history.

NET WORTH

Net worth is the excess of assets over liabilities. Accumulation of net worth, particularly in the form of
liquid assets, is a strong indication of creditworthiness. A borrower who accumulates net worth solely
from earnings and savings demonstrates a strong ability to manage his or her financial affairs. If the net

worth is in a liquid form, it can be used to service the debt, to pay unexpected obligations that may occur or to protect against short-term interruptions of income. Therefore, large liabilities may be offset by liquid assets.

QUALIFYING RATIOS

Qualifying ratios are used to compare the borrower's anticipated monthly housing expense and the total monthly obligations to his or her monthly gross income to determine whether the borrower will be able to meet the expenses involved in home ownership.

These ratios vary between conventional, FHA and VA financing and are discussed in detail under these respective headings.

CREDIT HISTORY

Lenders generally require a residential mortgage credit report from an independent consumer reporting agency. For self-employed borrowers doing business as a corporation or partnership, a business credit report is required to supplement the individual credit report. The borrower's credit history should demonstrate past willingness and ability to meet credit obligations in a way that will enable the lender to draw a logical conclusion about the borrower's commitment to making payments on the new loan.

Fannie Mae is more concerned about a borrower's overall payment pattern than about a few individual occurrences. Unless the borrower's credit history over the last 24 months raises some serious concerns or there are major indications of derogatory credit (undisclosed debts, judgments, bankruptcies, etc.) at any time during the last seven years, the lender generally considers a borrower's credit history as acceptable if, over the last 12 months, the borrower has had

- no payments 60 days or more past due and no more than two payments 30 days past due—for all of his or her *revolving credit accounts* (credit cards, etc.);

- no payments 60 days or more past due and no more than one payment 30 days past due—for all of his or her *installment credit accounts* (car loans, etc.); and
- no payments past due—for all of his or her *housing debt* (first or second mortgage, rent, etc.).

Major Indications of Derogatory Credit

The following items remain on credit reports for seven years.

Undisclosed Debt

If the credit report reveals significant debt not disclosed on the application, the borrower may have attempted to conceal liabilities to qualify for the mortgage.

Judgments, Garnishments or Liens

Any judgments, garnishments or liens must be paid in full before closing. The borrower must have re-established good credit.

Bankruptcy

A bankruptcy must be fully discharged, and the borrower must have re-established good credit for a period of at least two years between the discharge of the bankruptcy and the mortgage application.

Foreclosure of Real Property

Generally, Fannie Mae will not purchase a mortgage if the borrower has been a defendant in mortgage foreclosure proceedings that were completed in the past three years.

However, if the foreclosure was the result of extenuating circumstances that were beyond the control of an owner-occupant borrower—such as a serious, long-term illness, death of the principal wage earner, loss of employment because of factory slowdowns or shutdowns, reductions-in-force, etc.—Fannie Mae will purchase the mortgage as long as the lender's underwriting confirms the borrower has re-established good credit and has demonstrated an ability to manage his or her financial affairs.

PROPERTY APPRAISAL

As a direct result of the 1989 bailout of insolvent thrifts, a federal appraiser law requires all states to license or certify any appraiser who works on loans of $250,000 or more; and are involved with federally regulated lending institutions.

Three different levels of appraisal reporting are now in effect.

1. The Self-Contained Appraisal Report. This is the most detailed and encompassing of the three report formats. The length and descriptive details in such a report should fully support (in a self-contained format) the reasoning and conclusions of the appraiser.
2. The Summary Report. This report is less detailed than a self-contained report. Rather than describing in detail the information considered and the appraisal procedures followed, such information may be summarized.
3. The Restricted Report. This is the least detailed of the reporting options, with minimal presentation of information. It is intended for use only by a client. A restricted report must contain a prominent use restriction that limits reliance on the report to the client and warns that the report cannot be properly comprehended without additional information from the work file of the appraiser.

The Federal Reserve Board issued a rule, which became mandatory June 6, 1994, that requires residential mortgage loan creditors to provide certain applicants with either of two alternatives: (1) provide all covered applicants with copies of the appraisal no later than when notice of action taken on the application is given or (2) advise the applicant of the right to an appraisal upon receipt by the creditor of a written request from the applicant.

Because the valuation of real property is an integral part of loan underwriting, a basic discussion of the three appraisal methods is in order. They are

1. sales comparison approach to value,
2. replacement cost approach to value, and
3. income approach to value.

Sales Comparison Approach to Value

The sales comparison approach to value, also referred to as the market data approach, is an analysis of recently sold properties that are comparable to the subject property. This is the method most relied upon for appraising single-family residences.

Factors Considered in Comparing Properties

- Date of sale—Should be within the preceding six months
- Location—Proximity to transportation, shopping, schools, churches, recreational facilities
- Physical characteristics—Size, construction, quality, design, floor plan, amenities, energy efficiency
- Site—Lot size, topography, view, landscaping
- Terms of sale—Cash, seller financing, buydowns, closing costs paid by seller
- Arm's-length transaction—Assumes that both buyer and seller are informed about the local real estate market and are under no unusual pressure to buy or sell, that no conflict of interest exists between agents and principals and that the property has been exposed to the market for a reasonable period of time.

Replacement Cost Approach to Value

Residential appraisers use the replacement cost approach as a check to verify the result obtained from the sales comparison method. This approach measures the value of a property in a three-step process.

1. Estimating the cost of reproducing the improvements. A valid estimate of production cost per

square foot is multiplied by the square footage of the improvements.

2. Subtracting accrued depreciation. There are three principal types of depreciation: (1) physical depreciation, or deterioration, in the physical condition of the property; (2) functional depreciation, or obsolescence, caused by poor design; and (3) external depreciation, or economic obsolescence, caused by negative influences outside the property, such as a deteriorating neighborhood, expressways or industrial developments in the proximity of the subject property.

3. Adding the value of the lot. Appraisers use the sales comparison approach to arrive at the lot value, assuming the lot is vacant and available to be developed to its highest and best use.

Replacement cost of the property is obtained by adding the lot value to the estimated reproduction cost of the improvements minus depreciation.

Income Approach to Value

The income approach to value is based on the assumption that market value is related to the market rent less operating expense, equaling net income the property can be expected to earn.

The appraiser adjusts actual rents to market rent, adjusts expenses to realistic operating expense and obtains a capitalization rate by dividing the sale price of comparable properties by net income. An average cap rate is then applied to the subject property.

Although the income approach is of dubious value for appraising small residential income properties, gross multipliers are in common use. The *gross rent multiplier* (GRM) is arrived at by dividing the sale price of a comparable property by its total monthly gross rent. Conversely, a property value may be established by multiplying the total monthly gross rent by an established GRM. In lieu of gross rental multipliers, the appraiser may use *gross income multipliers* (GIMs), which simply use annual gross rent, rather than monthly gross rent.

In an appraisal, a gross rent multiplier (or gross income multiplier) is determined for each of a number of comparable properties. Using these multipliers, the appraiser establishes a GRM (or GIM) for the subject property, making adjustments for differences between the properties. If necessary, the appraiser may adjust the actual rents of the subject property up or down to bring them into line with market rents. Finally, a property valuation is arrived at by multiplying the adjusted total gross rent for the subject property by its GRM (or GIM).

Example

Property	Sale Price	Annual Gross Rent	GIM
1	$100,000	$ 8,300	12.05
2	150,000	12,400	12.10
3	125,000	9,920	12.60
4	140,000	11,400	12.28
5	115,000	8,960	12.83

If in the appraiser's judgment a GIM of 12.15 were appropriate, and assuming an adjusted annual gross rental income of $10,000, the appraised value of the subject property would be $121,500.

Final Reconciliation

In the final analysis, the appraiser must reconcile the reasonability and reliability of each approach to value and the reasonability and validity of the indicated values and the available data, and then select and report the approach or approaches that were given the most weight. The final reconciliation must never be an averaging technique.

Low Appraisals

Low appraisals are a continuous problem for real estate agents, buyers and sellers alike. Sales often fall apart due to low appraisals when the buyer is not willing or able to complete the transaction and the seller is unwilling to reduce the price to the appraised value.

In many cases, the problem can be avoided by listing the property at a fair market price, preparing a competitive market analysis for the seller when listing the property and offering a copy of the analysis to the appraiser. The agent should make every effort to be present when the appraiser inspects the property to answer any questions and to make sure the appraiser knows what the sale price is. Agents should be aware that items of personal property, which may be part of the transaction, are not included in the appraisal.

In the event comparable sales indicate that an appraisal is low, a request for reconsideration should be submitted to the lender. The request should be accompanied by an analysis of three recent sales of comparable properties, providing information along the lines of Fannie Mae's Uniform Residential Appraisal Report, see Sales Comparison Analysis on the following page.

Uniform Residential Appraisal Report (URAR)

The following appraisal reports are mandatory for all loans involving Fannie Mae, Freddie Mac, FHA and VA loans:

- Uniform Residential Appraisal Report (Fannie Mae form 1004, Freddie Mac form 70) for residential income properties;
- Small Residential Income Property Appraisal Report (Fannie Mae form 1025, Freddie Mac form 72) for two- to four-family units; and
- Individual Condominium Unit Appraisal Report (Fannie Mae form 1073, Freddie Mac form 465).

Sales Comparison Analysis

Item	Subj. Prop.	Comp.1	Comp. 2	Comp.3
Address				
Sales price				
Terms of sale				
Data source				
Date of sale				
Location				
Site/view				
Design/appeal				
Quality of construction				
Age				
Condition				
Total no. of rooms				
No. of bedrooms				
No. of baths				
Family room				
Square feet, living area				
Heating/cooling				
Garage/carport				
Patio, pool, etc.				
Energy efficiency				
Fireplaces				
Built-in kitchen equipment				
Other				

CONVENTIONAL FINANCING

A conventional loan is any loan made by an institutional lender that is not insured or guaranteed by a governmental agency.

Most conventional loans on residential properties of one to four units conform to the underwriting criteria established by Fannie Mae and Freddie Mac, the secondary market agencies that purchase conventional loans and mortgage-backed securities.

Loans that deviate from the criteria, called nonconforming loans, are made by lenders that keep loans in their portfolio rather than sell them in the secondary market.

Unless otherwise noted, underwriting guidelines for conventional mortgages discussed under this heading are criteria set by Fannie Mae or Freddie Mac.

DOCUMENTATION

Credit documents must not be more than 120 days old (180 days for new construction) on the date the note is signed. Appraisals must not be more than 180 days old (360 days for new construction).

- *Uniform Underwriting and Transmittal Summary* (Fannie Mae form 1008/Freddie Mac form 1077). Effective December 1992, Fannie Mae and Freddie Mac combined their forms under this new title.
- *Residential Loan Application* (form 1003)
- *Residential Mortgage Credit Report* and a *Business Credit Report* for self-employed borrowers if their business is a corporation, S corporation or partnership
- *Verification of Deposit* (form 1006)
- *Verification of Employment* (form 1005)
- *Federal income tax returns* (both individual and business returns) for past two years, with all applicable schedules; plus for self-employed borrowers and all business entities a year-to-date profit and

loss statement and balance sheet for previous two fiscal years

- A year-to-date profit and loss statement for self-employed borrower's business, if the loan application is dated more than 120 days after the end of the business's tax year
- A balance sheet for the previous two fiscal years for a self-employed borrower's business that is held as a sole proprietorship
- *Self-Employed Income Analysis* (form 1084A or 1088B)
- *Comparative Income Analysis* (form 1088) for self-employed borrowers
- A self-employed borrower's written permission to request copies of his or her federal income tax returns for the past two years directly from the IRS if they are needed for quality control purposes
- Purchase agreement and amendments
- Escrow instructions
- Verification of payment history on previous mortgages
- Any other documentation needed to make a prudent underwriting decision
- *Nontraditional Mortgage Credit Report* (NMCR). To establish a credit history for borrowers who do not use credit or whose credit history on traditional reports is insufficient. NMCRs include history of verified payments for rental housing, utilities, insurance premiums, payments to local stores, medical bills, school tuition, child care and documented debt payments to individuals. NMCRs are to be available by credit reporting repositories effective January 1, 1996, as announced by Fannie Mae July 17, 1995.

Loan-to-Value Limits Effective March 1993

Raw land loans	65%
Land development loans	75
Nonresidential construction loans	80
1–4 family construction loans	85
Improved property loans	85

Under the FDIC Improvement Act of 1991, there will be no ceiling on the following loans: permanent residential and home equity loans on owner-occupied one- to four-family properties, except that loans over 90% must have private mortgage insurance; FHA and VA loans; problem loans that must be renewed, refinanced or restructured; and loans that facilitate the sale of foreclosed properties.

ELIGIBLE MORTGAGES

First mortgages can be fixed rate or adjustable rate, purchase money or refinance loans.

Second mortgages must be secured by properties that are owner-occupied principal residences. The second loan must be a fixed rate interest loan and have a minimum term of five years. The borrower must make a cash down payment of at least 10%. The underlying first mortgage must be an institutional loan with an LTV not to exceed 75% and cannot permit negative amortization. A second mortgage can be a purchase money, refinance or home improvement loan.

Fixed rate first mortgages can be secured by properties that are owner-occupied principal residences (including one- to four-family properties), second homes or investment properties.

Adjustable rate first mortgages must be secured by owner-occupied principal residences or second homes. The maximum LTV for ARMs is 90%. The lifetime interest cap is 5%; the annual interest cap, 1%. They may not permit negative amortization.

ELIGIBLE BORROWERS

U.S. citizens and aliens who are lawful residents of the United States and who have reached the age at which the mortgage note can be legally enforced in the jurisdiction in which the property is located qualify as eligible borrowers.

A *coborrower* may be any party who does not have an interest in the property sales transaction. A coborrower must occupy the property if the LTV is over 90%. An occupant coborrower must have ratios of 35%/43% after the income and expenses of a nonoccupying coborrower have been excluded. If the LTV is over 80%, the occupant coborrower must make the first 5% of the down payment from his or her own funds.

Nonpermanent resident aliens (not foreign nationals without lawful residency status) with a maximum LTV of 75% who have an established two-year credit history in the U.S., or shorter if it can be supplemented by credit histories established in the country from which the borrower immigrated.

ELIGIBLE PROPERTIES

Mixed-use property—eligible under the following criteria:

- It must be a one-family property the borrower occupies as his or her principal residence.
- The mixed use of the property must represent a legal, permissible use of the property under the local zoning requirements.
- The borrower must be both the owner and the operator of the business.
- The property must be primarily residential in nature.
- The market value of the property must be primarily a function of its residential characteristics, rather than the business use or any special business-use modifications that were made.

Principal residence—a one- to four-family property that is the borrower's primary residence.

Second home—a single-family property that the borrower occupies in addition to his or her principal residence. (Rental income may not be used to qualify the borrower.)

Investment property—a one- to four-family property that the borrower does not occupy.

Multiple mortgages—When a mortgage delivered to Fannie Mae is secured by a one- to four-family property that is the borrower's principal residence, Fannie Mae does not impose any limitations on the number of mortgages the borrower can currently be financing. But if the mortgage is secured by a second home or an investment property, the borrower may not own more than four properties that are currently being financed. In these cases, the borrower's principal residence must be counted toward the limitation. Properties that are not being financed are not included in this limitation.

MAXIMUM LOAN AMOUNTS

The following maximum amounts for Fannie Mae or Freddie Mac mortgages remain in effect for 1995.

No. of Units	Maximum Loan	Alaska and Hawaii
1	$203,150	$304,725
2	259,850	389,775
3	314,100	471,150
4	390,400	585,600

Loans exceeding these ceilings are *nonconforming jumbo loans*.

DOWN PAYMENT

A minimum down payment of 5% must come from the borrower's savings or liquid assets. The remainder of a larger down payment may come from other sources (e.g., gift, trade equity, rent credit). If the LTV is 80% or less, the entire down payment may come from a gift or grant from a relative, church, municipality or nonprofit organization.

With secondary financing, the minimum down payment is 10% of the lesser of appraised value or purchase price.

The property seller may take the borrower's existing property, or an asset other than real estate, in trade as part of the down payment as long as the borrower has made a 5% cash payment and his or her equity contribution for the traded property is a true value consideration supported by a current, full appraisal.

In the event of a lease-purchase option, the property seller may give the purchaser credit toward the down payment for a portion of previous rent payments he or she made under a documented lease purchase agreement that had a minimum original term of at least 12 months in an amount up to the difference between the market rent and the actual rent paid. (The appraiser must determine "market" rent.) The buyer, in such case, does not have to make a 5% minimum cash down payment in order for the rental payments to be credited toward the down payment.

CASH RESERVES

Borrowers are generally required to have at least two months of *liquid reserves* as a cushion for unforeseen financial problems after paying the down payment, closing costs and prepaid expenses related to the mortgage.

LOAN-TO-VALUE RATIOS (LTV)

Loan-to-value ratios are determined by dividing the loan amount by the property value.

Example

The LTV of a property appraised at $100,000, secured by a loan of $90,000, is 90%.

CLASSIFICATION OF CONVENTIONAL LOANS

80% loans—Loans with an LTV of 80% or less
90% loans—Loans with an LTV of over 80%, but not more than 90%
95% loans—Loans with an LTV of over 90%, but not more than 95%

High-ratio loans are loans with LTVs over 80%. Due to the risk involved, private mortgage insurance (PMI) is required for high-ratio loans.

Maximum LTVs

	Units	Max. LTV	With Secondary Fin.
Primary residences	1	95%	75%
	2	90	
	3	80	
	4	80	
Second homes		80	75%
ARMs		90	
Investor (fixed rate only)		70	

PRIVATE MORTGAGE INSURANCE (PMI)

There are risks of varying degrees associated with mortgages, depending upon the loan-to-value ratio and other factors. *Private mortgage insurance companies* insure lending institutions against loss due to borrower default. The insurance covers the lender for the upper portion of the loan, typically 25% of the outstanding balance. For example, with a sales price of $100,000, a down payment of $5,000 and PMI coverage of 25%, the lender's exposure is calculated as follows:

Sales price	$100,000
Down payment	−5,000
Loan amount	$95,000
Coverage	× 25%
Amount of coverage	$23,750

The lender's exposure is $100,000 − $23,750 = $76,250.

Fannie Mae requires PMI coverage for high-ratio conventional mortgages (LTVs higher than 80%). Taking into consideration a lower risk factor associated with fully amortizing, fixed rate mortgages with an original term of 20 years or less, the PMI coverage requirement has been sharply reduced for these mortgages, as shown in the following chart.

PMI Coverage Requirements
(Effective November 11, 1994)

Mortgage Terms	LTV 0–85%	LTV 85–90%	LTV 90–97%
20 yr., fixed rate	6%	12%	25%
30 yr., fixed rate	12	25	30
15 & 30 yr. ARM	12	25	30
7 yr. Balloon	12	25	30

Premiums usually increase at intervals of 5% of LTV; so 85%, 90% and 95% loans have progressively higher premiums due to increased risk.

Borrowers may include the one-time PMI in the amount financed for first purchase money mortgages secured by owner-occupied properties. The one-time PMI is added to the loan before the monthly payment is calculated.

PMI is eligible for cancellation after two years if (1) the LTV, based on a current appraisal, is 80% or less due to an addition or improvement of the property; (2) the LTV, based on a current appraisal is 75% or less due to appreciation of the property; or (3) the loan has amortized to 80% or less (no appraisal required).

In an effort to reduce cash requirements at closing, private mortgage insurance companies began offering monthly premium payment plans rather than annual or single payment plans. Insurers are now reporting nearly half their new insurance business is in monthly premium payments.

QUALIFYING RATIOS

Two ratios are used to determine whether the borrower can reasonably be expected to meet expenses involved in home ownership. Fannie Mae's current benchmark ratios are:

1. Housing expense = max. 28% of gross income
2. Total obligations = max. 36% of gross income*

*With temporary buydowns, Fannie Mae's requirement for total obligations is 33% of gross income.

Housing expense means the monthly payment for principal, interest, hazard insurance, real estate taxes, mortgage insurance premium and any owners' association dues.

Total obligations means the sum of (1) housing expenses and (2) monthly recurring obligations on installment loans and revolving charge accounts extending beyond ten months, nonincome producing real estate loans, alimony, child support, spousal maintenance and payments on all other debts of a continuing nature.

Gross income means stable monthly income, reasonably expected to continue for at least three years.

Example of Qualifying a Buyer for Conventional Financing

Jim Miller wants to buy a home. His gross income is $5,000. He has monthly recurring obligations of $800. Calculate the maximum monthly housing expense for which he can qualify.

Gross income	$5,000	
	× 0.28	
Max. housing expense	$1,400	(Ratio 1)
Gross income	$5,000	
	× 0.36	
Max. total obligations	$1,800	
Recurring obligations	− 800	
Max. housing expense	$1,000	(Ratio 2)

Because the result of Ratio 2 is lower, the maximum monthly housing expense Mr. Miller qualifies for is $1,000.

High-Ratio Mortgages

For high-ratio mortgages (above 80% LTV), lenders look beyond the total obligations-to-income ratio to determine the borrower's eligibility, particularly with respect to the

- adequacy of the borrower's reserves after closing—cash that equals at least two mortgage payments represents adequate reserves;

- borrower's demonstrated ability to make monthly housing payments equal to or greater than the proposed monthly housing expense;
- borrower's ability to accumulate savings and to demonstrate prompt payment of debts;
- borrower's demonstrated capability for increased earnings in future years, based on his or her employment history (this is especially true for ARM borrowers); and
- borrower's ability to maintain an acceptable credit history.

Compensating Factors

Fannie Mae's debt-to-income benchmark ratios may be exceeded when compensating factors are present. The strongest compensating factor is a borrower's demonstrated history (12 to 24 months) of paying previous housing expenses equal to or greater than the proposed monthly housing expense while successfully handling other debt obligations. In such cases, lenders may approve the application of an otherwise qualified borrower even if Fannie Mae's benchmark ratios are exceeded. Additional compensating factors are a borrower's

- making a large down payment toward the purchase of the property;
- purchasing a property that qualifies as an energy-efficient dwelling;
- demonstrating the ability to devote a greater portion of income to basic needs such as housing expenses;
- demonstrating the ability to accumulate savings and to maintain a good credit history or a debt-free position;
- having a potential for increased earnings and advancement because of education or job training, even though he or she has just entered the job market;
- having short-term income (such as social security income, alimony child support, notes receivable,

mortgage differential payments, trust income, VA benefits) that could not be counted as stable income because it would not continue to be received for at least three years beyond the date of the mortgage application;

- purchasing the home as a result of corporate relocation of the primary wage-earner, and the secondary wage earner, who has a history of employment in the previous location, is expected to return to work (even if he or she has not yet obtained employment in the new location); and

- having a net worth substantial enough to evidence the ability to repay the mortgage.

In order to qualify under the higher ratios for mortgages with loan-to-value ratios above 90%, not only must borrowers fall into one of the above categories, but one of the following conditions must also exist:

- The borrower must have financial reserves that can be used to carry the mortgage debt for two to three months.

- The borrower must have a demonstrated ability to devote a greater portion of his or her income to housing expenses, an excellent payment history on any prior mortgage obligation and an acceptable credit history.

- A total obligation-to-income ratio (at the time of the application) of 30% or less, an excellent payment history on any prior mortgage obligation and an acceptable credit history.

Secondary Financing

The source of *secondary financing* is generally the seller who accepts a note for part of the purchase price, secured by a mortgage on the property. This is referred to as a *purchase money mortgage*. Secondary financing may also be obtained from a private third party or from an institutional lender (that may or may not be the lender making the first loan).

Most lenders have the following seven requirements for second loans (regardless of the source) in conjunction with conventional financing:

1. 10% minimum cash down payment. The combined first and second loans may not exceed 90% of the lesser of the appraised value or purchase price.
2. 75% maximum LTV for first mortgage.
3. Minimum term 5 years, maximum 30 years.
4. No prepayment penalty.
5. Regular scheduled payments. May be amortized or interest only, may provide for balloon payment, may be monthly, quarterly, and so on, but must be regular payments.
6. No negative amortization.
7. Buyer must qualify for combined payments of first and second loans. For qualification purposes, lenders base monthly payments of the second mortgage on an interest rate not less than 2% below the market rate for second loans.

Refinancing

Lenders' guidelines for refinancing are somewhat similar to purchase guidelines. Some differences follow.

- Seasoning, or age of loan, is important, and many lenders ask for at least one year and sometimes two years' seasoning.
- An excellent payment history on the present mortgage is important, with no late mortgage payments reported.

Cash-Out Refinances

Cash-out refinance mortgages must be secured by properties that will be owner-occupied principal residences only. Mortgage proceeds may include the unpaid principal balance of the existing first mortgage, closing costs, points, the outstanding balance of existing liens and additional cash the borrower may use for any purpose.

Limited Cash-Out Rate/Term Refinances

Limited cash-out rate/term refinances may be secured by owner-occupied principal or second homes or investment properties. Mortgage proceeds may include the unpaid principal balance of the existing first mortgage, closing costs, points, the outstanding balance of existing liens and additional cash to the borrower not to exceed 1% of the principal amount of the new mortgage.

No Cash-Out Rate/Term Refinances

No cash-out rate/term refinances must be secured by owner-occupied principal residences only. The mortgage must be fully amortizing and fixed-rate. When deciding to refinance for the purpose of reducing the rate of interest, a general rule of thumb is that the new interest rate should be approximately two percentage points lower than the current rate, and the borrower should plan to own the home for at least three more years. Of course, this rule does not apply where the borrower is mainly interested in refinancing for purposes other than interest rate reduction, such as converting an ARM to a fixed rate loan, retiring existing liens, making repairs or improvements or obtaining cash for other purposes.

CATEGORY	LTV
A. Limited Cash-Out Rate/Term Transaction	
• *Owner-occupied principal residence*	
—One- to two-family first mortgage	90%
—Three- to four-family first mortgage	80
—One- to four-family second mortgage	80
• *Second home*	70
• *Investment property*	70
B. No Cash-Out Rate/Term Transaction	**95**
C. Cash-Out Transaction	
• One- to four-family first mortgage	75
• One- to four-family second mortgage	70

Community Lending Mortgages

Many lenders are now playing a positive role in the revitalization of neighborhoods to reverse historic patterns of neglect and decay. Fannie Mae supports development of other community lending programs that combine acceptable risk with the flexibility required to make home finance opportunities available to low- and moderate-income households. Two community lending models are currently in place: The *Community Home Buyer's Program* model, generally available only to borrowers with incomes of not more than 100% of the median income for their locality, and the *Enhanced Fannie Neighbors* model, which opens up the Community Home Buyer's Program model to a wider range of borrowers by using as its qualifying criterion the location of the security property. Additional models (or changes to these models) may be announced from time to time.

Community Home Buyer's Program (CHBP)

Eligible borrowers. Mortgages are made to natural persons (not entities). But for certain types of transactions, borrowers may be nonprofit organizations or public agencies. A borrower's income generally may not exceed 100% of the median area income published by HUD.

Mortgages. CHBP mortgages are conventional fully amortizing first mortgages obtainable with a minimum investment. The one exception is the *start-up mortgage,* a graduated payment mortgage with interest-only payments for the first year. Payments increase 2% annually until the mortgage becomes fully amortizing. There is no negative amortization. Mortgages may have 15-, 20-, 25- or 30-year terms with either monthly or biweekly payments. Qualifying guidelines for CHBP mortgages are 33% for the monthly housing expense-to-income ratio and 36% for the total obligations-to-income ratio.

Properties. CHBP mortgages generally must be secured by one-family properties, including units in eligible condominium, PUD and cooperative projects. The properties may be new, existing or rehabilitated. Borrowers must occupy the security property as a principal residence and cannot concurrently have any ownership interest in any other residential dwelling. In addition, all coborrowers whose names appear on the mortgage note must occupy the security property as their principal residence.

Down payment options. Three down payment options are available.

1. *Regular down payment option.* Minimum down payment required under this option is 5% of the sales price of the property. Generally, this entire 5% must come from the borrower's own funds.
2. *3/2 Option.* Minimum down payment required under this option is 5% of the sales price of the property. However, the borrower only needs to make a 3% down payment from his or her own funds. The remaining 2% down payment may be obtained through a gift from a relative; a gift, grant or unsecured loan from a nonprofit organization or a public agency; or a secured loan from a public agency.
3. *Fannie 97.* Minimum down payment required under this option is 3% of the sales price of the property. This entire 3% generally must come from the borrower's own funds. However, the borrower may pool funds with a relative who lives with the borrower.

Homebuyer Education Requirement

Fannie Mae requires that all borrowers who obtain a start-up mortgage or who use the 3/2 Option or the Fannie 97 Down Payment Option participate in pre-purchase homebuyer education sessions. These sessions provide information on selecting a home, obtaining a mortgage, budgeting to meet monthly costs and maintaining a home. This requirement may not be waived unless her or she

- has previously owned a home;
- makes at least a 5% cash down payment from his or her own funds (and does not rely on a gift, loan or grant to obtain any portion of the down payment); and
- has cash reserves after closing that are at least equal to two monthly mortgage payments.

Education sessions generally must take the form of face-to-face tutorial or classroom or workshop sessions and may be conducted by a member of the lender's staff, a representative of a mortgage insurance company or a counselor using an approach and curriculum acceptable to the lender. Lenders that originate either a Fannie 97 Mortgage or a start-up mortgage must offer early delinquency intervention counseling to the borrower.

COMMERCIAL AND INVESTMENT PROPERTIES

Financing Sources

Generally, the best sources for financing of commercial properties are commercial banks, insurance companies and pension funds. Private investors are a good source for smaller properties and short-term loans. Many commercial loans are placed through loan brokers who represent insurance companies, pension funds and other lenders.

Property Qualification

Lenders require a positive cash flow, expressed as a *net operating income to annual debt service ratio,* to qualify commercial properties. The ratio is typically stated as 1:1, 1:3, and so on. Thus, a 1:3 ratio means the property must have a net operating income of $1.30 for each $1 of debt service. Most projects are expected to have a ratio between 1:1 and 1:5.

The cash down payment required for commercial property can range from 20 to 25%; office buildings, warehouses and shopping centers generally require from 25 to 35%. For unimproved commercial land, lenders will often require 50% down payment.

Quality of tenants, terms and safety of leases are other important criteria. Many lenders require 65% or more preleasing prior to funding. Lenders often require estoppel certificates wherein tenants state the amount of their rent, any advance payments, security deposits and any defaults or modifications of their lease.

In contrast to financing of residential property, most commercial lenders retain loans in their own portfolio. For that reason, they are not only more selective in the projects they fund but also favor particular types of properties in accordance with the lender's past experience. The size of loan is another criterion some lenders take into account. A lender may fund a loan of $5 million but turn down one of $800,000.

The term of most commercial loans generally does not exceed 10 years, although payments may be amortized over 30 years with a due date of 10 years or less. On the other hand, some commercial loans, such as insurance company loans, may have a high prepayment penalty or even a lock-in clause stating that the loan cannot be prepaid under any circumstances.

Construction

Construction loans are interim or short-term loans, normally about 12 months, at interest only. Usually, a sum of money is set aside in a special account for the borrower, who may be a builder, developer or future homeowner. Money is drawn out in installments as needed and as construction progresses. The monthly interest payment is calculated on the amount of funds disbursed, not on the overall amount of the loan. With this type of financing the lender often lends up to 90% of construction cost, provided that figure does not exceed 75% to 80% of the appraised value. At the end of the construction period, the borrower must obtain permanent financing, also referred to as a take-out, permanent or construction-permanent loan.

FHA FINANCING

The Federal Housing Administration (FHA) was created by Congress in 1934 as part of the National Housing Act.

FHA, a division of HUD, insures mortgage loans, secured by residential property, against default and foreclosure and compensates approved lending institutions for losses resulting from borrower default.

LOAN UNDERWRITING

Effective March 1995, FHA underwriting guidelines were revised as follows to enhance homebuying opportunities for a substantial number of American families.

- *Elimination of five-year test for income stability.* The number of years for which income is reasonably expected to continue for qualifying purposes has been changed from five years to three years.
- *Recognition of overtime and bonus income.* Overtime and/or bonus income received for less than a full two years is now acceptable when the lender determines there are reasonable prospects of its continuance.
- *Recognition of part-time income.* Part-time income, defined as income from jobs taken in addition to the normal, regular employment to supplement a borrower's income, received for less than two years, may be included as effective income provided the lender determines there are strong indications of its continuance.
- *Definition of long-term obligations extended from six to ten months.* Only those debts extending ten or more months need to be included in the debt-to-income ratios.
- *Mortgage credit certificates (MCCs).* Lenders may now consider the tax credit resulting from MCCs as a direct reduction in housing expense (PITI), although the tax credit results in an increase in the borrower's net monthly income. This will

reduce the borrower's qualifying ratios and increase the size of the mortgage

- *Elimination of child care as recurring debt.* The cost of child care is no longer considered in the computation of debt-to-income ratios. (Court-ordered or voluntary child support payments must continue to be counted as recurring debts.)
- *Unnecessary repair requirements on FHA appraisals.* HUD acknowledges some repair requirements should be eliminated. Lenders should exercise their authority to delete conditions that have little or nothing to do with the safety or soundness of the property.

DOCUMENTATION

Credit documents must not be more than 120 days old (180 days for proposed construction) at the time the loan closes. Verification forms must pass directly between lender and creditor without being handled by any third party. Credit documents and verification forms include the following:

- Uniform Residential Loan Application (HUD-92900-A).
- Borrower's Notification and Interest Rate Disclosure Statement (HUD-92900-B).
- Mortgage Credit Analysis Worksheet (HUD-92900-WS) and Attachment A if seller financing concessions are involved.
- Picture identification and evidence of Social Security number for each borrower.
- Residential Mortgage Credit Report on all borrowers who will be obligated on the note.
- Verification of Employment (VOE) and most recent pay stub. (In lieu of VOE, lenders may choose alternative method.)
- Verification of Deposit (VOD) and most recent bank statement. (In lieu of VOD, lenders may use original bank statements covering most recent three months.)
- Federal income tax returns for the past two years for commissioned individuals. For self-employed

borrowers, both individual and business returns with all applicable schedules. All business entities must also provide profit and loss statements and evidence of quarterly tax payments.

- Purchase (sales) agreement and amendments or other agreements, plus certification unless the agreement contains a clause stating that the document contains the entire agreement of the parties and supersedes all prior agreements and representations with respect to the property not expressed in writing in the agreement.

- Verification of payment history of previous mortgages, used in the credit report.

- Uniform Residential Appraisal Report (URAR) and Conditional Commitment/DE Statement of Appraised Value (HUD-92800.5-B), or VA Certificate of Reasonable Value (CRV).

Alternative Documentation

As of January 2, 1992, FHA can accept alternative documents to verify employment and assets. To verify employment, the past two years of original IRS W-2 forms (meaning any copy of the form not attached to the borrower's income tax form) along with original paycheck stubs for the most recent 30-day period can be used. Income must be computed over the 24-month period represented by the W-2s.

To verify assets, original bank statements for the most recent three months may be used. These statements may not be averaged.

A signed copy of IRS Form 4506, Request for Copy of Tax Form, must be submitted on all loans. During loan processing, the tax return must be reviewed by the lender who must report any discrepancies between that and documents furnished by the borrower.

The new procedures are intended to make loan processing faster and less expensive. Employment verifications have sometimes been slow or difficult to obtain, and some banks are now charging fees to verify deposits.

MAXIMUM LOAN AMOUNTS

Under most FHA programs, the maximum insurable loan is the lesser of (1) the statutory loan limit for the geographical area; (2) the applicable loan-to-value ratio; and (3) the applicable loan-to-appraised value limit.

Statutory Loan Limits

In accordance with legislation effective October 1994, FHA mortgage limits are indexed to annual Fannie Mae/Freddie Mac limits. Base limits *(floors)* are indexed at 38% and limits for high cost areas *(ceilings)* at 75% of the Fannie Mae/Freddie Mac limits, adjusted January 1 of each year (usually announced by the end of November or beginning of December).

Fannie Mae/Freddie Mac Loan Limits
(Continued in effect for 1995)

1-unit properties	$203,150
2-unit properties	$259,850
3-unit properties	$314,100
4-unit properties	$390,400

FHA Base Limits (Floors—38% of Fannie Mae/Freddie Mac)

1-unit properties	$77,197
2-unit properties	$98,700
3-unit properties	$119,350
4-unit properties	$148,300
1-condominium unit	$77,150

FHA Limits for High-Cost Areas (Ceilings 75% of Fannie Mae/Freddie Mac)

1-unit properties	$152,362
2-unit properties	$194,850
3-unit properties	$235,550
4-unit properties	$292,800

FHA Ceilings for Alaska, Guam, Hawaii and the Virgin Islands

1-unit properties	$228,543
2-unit properties	$292,250
3-unit properties	$353,300
4-unit properties	$439,200

Contact your local FHA office for limits applicable to your county. The mortgage amount must be a multiple of $50 for a mortgage that does not include financing of a mortgage insurance premium. For condominium mortgages and other mortgages affected by this requirement, the maximum mortgage amount is $77,150.

Maximum Loan-to-Value Ratios (LTVs)

The following *LTVs* establish an additional limit for individual loans effective in 1994. The new limits are 98.75% for loans of up to $50,000; 97.65% for loans between $50,000 and $125,000; and 97.15% for loans of more than $125,000 of appraised value or sale price, whichever is lower.

Closing costs may not be financed, but mortgage insurance premium may be added to the loan after the down payment calculation is made.

Example

The maximum mortgage amount for a property eligible for maximum financing with a value of $150,000 (including closing costs) is:

$$\$150,000 - 125,000 = \$25,000 \rightarrow \$25,000 \times 97.15\% = \$24,287.50$$
$$\$125,000 - 50,000 = \$75,000 \rightarrow \$75,000 \times 97.65\% = \$73,237.50$$
$$\$50,000 \qquad\qquad \rightarrow \$50,000 \times 98.75\% = \$49,375.00$$

Maximum Loan $146,900.00

For properties under construction and properties less than one year old not approved by and built under FHA or VA inspection and without a ten-year homeowners warranty, the maximum LTV is 90% of appraised value (or sales price, whichever is less) including closing costs.

For eligible veterans, the maximum LTV is 100% of the first $25,000 plus 95% of the amount between $25,000 and $125,000, and 90% of the amount over $125,000 (or sales price, whichever is less) including closing costs.

Nonoccupying coborrowers: When there are two or more borrowers, but one or more will not occupy the property as a principal residence, the LTV is usually limited to 75%. However, maximum financing is available for blood-related borrowers, or for unrelated individuals who can document evidence of a family-type, long and substantial relationship *not arising out of the loan transaction.* The occupant borrower must sign the security instrument and mortgage note.

Loan-to-Appraised-Value Limit

The 1990 housing legislation requires that the amount of any insured mortgage not exceed 97.75% of the appraised value of the property excluding closing costs (or 98.75% if the value is $50,000 or less.)

If the amount determined by the applicable LTV limit is less than the amount determined by the LTV ratio, the amount of closing costs that can be financed must be reduced by the amount the LTV ratio exceeds the LTV limit.

Calculating the Maximum Loan

1. Start with the lesser of the sales price or appraised value.
2. Add 100% of the borrower's closing costs shown on the good faith estimate form.
3. Add any repairs and improvements required by the appraiser to be paid by the borrower.
4. Add energy-related weatherization items to be paid by the borrower.
5. Subtract any closing costs paid by the seller.
6. Subtract any seller-paid sales concessions.
7. If the total of seller-paid closing costs and other financing concessions exceeds 6% of the selling price, subtract the excess.
8. The result is the mortgage basis, which is multiplied by the appropriate loan-to-value ratio.
9. The lesser of the amount thus obtained or the statutory LTV limit (without closing costs) is the maximum obtainable loan.

Closing costs may not include discount points or prepaid items. In the event the lender pays the borrower's closing costs by charging a premium interest rate or additional discount points, these closing costs may not be added to the sales price.

Repairs and improvements if required by the appraiser as essential for property eligibility are to be paid by the borrower. The sales agreement must identify the borrower as responsible for performing these repairs or improvements. The appraised value will already reflect these repairs and improvements.

Energy-related weatherization items, if the borrower is responsible for the payment of these items, include thermostats, insulation, storm windows and doors, weather stripping, caulking, and so forth.

Seller-paid sales concessions include prepaid items (tax and insurance escrows, association dues, etc.), personal property items, buyer-broker fees, decorating allowances, moving costs, payment of buyer's sales commission on present residence, excess rent credits, and so forth. Sales concessions must be subtracted dollar-for-dollar from the sales price before computing the loan amount.

Seller-paid financing concessions include closing costs, discount points, interest rate buydowns and other payment supplements, and payment of the UFMIP (up-front mortgage insurance premium). Financing concessions are not subtracted dollar-for-dollar from the sales price, but any excess of financing concessions over 6% of the sales price must be deducted before computing the loan amount.

Calculating the Cash Requirement

1. Start with the mortgage basis.
2. Subtract the maximum loan.
3. Add back the seller-paid sales concessions.
4. Add back any excess of seller-paid financing concessions over 6% of sales price.
5. Add buyer-paid discount points, UFMIP, prepayable expenses.

6. Subtract items financed in the mortgage.
7. Subtract proceeds of a second mortgage, if any.
8. The result is the minimum cash requirement (including any earnest money deposit).

It is permissible to use gift funds for all or part of the cash investment provided the donor is the borrower's employer, a close relative or a close friend with a clearly defined interest in the borrower.

With a *lease option* (lease with option to purchase), any rent over and above the market rent for the area may be applied toward the cash investment.

Three- and four-unit properties must be self-sufficient, regardless of occupancy. The maximum mortgage is limited, so monthly mortgage payments (PITI and owners' association fees) do not exceed the net rental income based on the appraiser's estimate of fair market rent less HUD's allowance for vacancies and maintenance.

Items that May Be Added Directly to the Loan Amount

1. Solar energy systems may increase the maximum mortgage amount. In addition, the statutory loan limit may be exceeded by 20%.
2. Buyer-broker fees may be added directly to the loan amount if the broker has been the exclusive agent of the buyer and a written agreement is submitted with the loan application.

FHA Maximum Loan Worksheet for properties with sales prices and appraised value of more than $50,000 is shown on the next page with information from the following example:

John Smith bought a home for $60,000 with an appraised value of $62,000. The seller paid the buyer's closing costs amounting to $2,500, discount points amounting to $1,500 and $500 of the buyer's prepaid expenses.

	FHA MAXIMUM LOAN WORKSHEET		
	WITH APPR. VAL. OVER $50,000		
	TRANSACTION DATA		
1	Sales price		$60,000
2	Appraised value		62,000
3	Total closing costs		2,500
4	Seller-paid closing costs	−	2,500
5	Buyer-paid closing costs (Line 3 − 4)	=	$ 0
6	Other financing concessions		1,500
7	Total financing concessions (Line 4 + 6)		4,000
8	Financing concessions exceeding 6% of price		400
9	Seller-paid sales concessions		500
10			
11	**MAXIMUM LOAN CALCULATION**		
12	The lower of sales price or appraised value		$60,000
13	Buyer-paid closing costs (Line 5)	+	0
14	Seller-paid sales concessions (Line 9)	−	500
15	Financing concession > 6% of price (Line 8)	−	400
16	Mortgage basis (Lines 12 + 13 − 14 − 15)	=	$59,100
17	97% × 25,000		24,250
18	95% × (Line 16 betw. 25,000 × 125,000)	+	32,395
19	90% × (Line 16 in excess of 125,000)	+	0
20	Maximum LTV (Lines 17 + 18 + 19)	=	$56,645
21	Max. LTV for new constr.: 90% × Line 16		
22	Mortgage limit: (97.75% × Line 2)		60,605
23	Max. loan (the lesser of 20 [21] or 22)		56,645
24	**CASH REQUIREMENT**		
25	Required cash investment (Line 16 − 23)		$ 2,455
26	Sales concessions (Line 14)	+	500
27	Financing concessions > 6% of price (15)	+	400
28	Discount points paid by buyer	+	0
29	Prepayable expenses paid by buyer	+	800
30	UFMIP paid in cash	+	
31	Total invested (25 + 26 + 27 + 28 + 29 + 30)	=	$4,155
32	Items financed in mortgage	−	1,788
33	Amount paid in cash (Line 31 − 32)	=	$2,367
34	Second mortgage proceeds (if applicable)	−	
35	Assets available (Line 33 − 34)	=	$2,367

SECONDARY FINANCING

Borrowers age 60 or older may borrow the required cash investment for purchasing a principal residence provided

1. the donor or lender is a relative of the borrower, a close friend with clearly defined interest in the borrower, the borrower's employer or an institution established for humanitarian or welfare purposes;
2. the donor or lender is not one whose interest is solely in the sale of the property, such as a builder or seller, or any person or organization associated with them;
3. the principal amount of the insured mortgage loan (the note or other evidence of indebtedness in connection with the property) may not exceed 100% of the value plus prepaid expenses; or
4. the note or other evidence of indebtedness may not bear interest exceeding that of the insured mortgage.

Second Mortgage Rule

The borrower may never use secondary financing from the seller or an *institutional lender* to finance any portion of the minimum cash investment.

However, in certain circumstances secondary financing to pay the minimum cash investment is permissible for borrowers over 60 years of age, provided the loan is secured by collateral other than the property being purchased and provided further that the loan is made by an independent party, such as a government agency, relative, close friend or employer, but never the seller, lender or the real estate broker or agent in the transaction.

The following conditions must be met for secondary financing with FHA-insured mortgages.

1. The first and second mortgages together may not exceed HUD's applicable maximum loan-to-value ratio nor the maximum mortgage amount for the area.

2. The sum of required payments under the insured first mortgage and the second mortgage may not exceed the mortgagor's reasonable ability to pay, as determined by the Federal Housing Commissioner.
3. The second mortgage may not require a balloon payment before ten years.
4. Any periodic payments made on account of the second mortgage must be made on a monthly basis in substantially the same amount.
5. The borrower must be permitted to prepay the second mortgage without penalty.

CLOSING COSTS

Legislation, effective October 1992, rescinded the 57% limit on financeable closing costs.

Allowable Closing Costs

- Title examination and title insurance fee
- Escrow fee
- Document preparation fee (if performed by a third party not controlled by lender)
- Attorney fee
- Credit report (actual cost)
- Appraisal fee
- Loan origination fee
- Deposit verification fees
- Recording fees
- Home inspection fees (up to $200)
- Survey fee
- Test and verification fees

Costs that may not be financed include discount points, local transfer fees and prepaid expenses (impounds for property taxes, hazard insurance and prorated interest).

The seller is permitted to pay all or part of the buyer's closing costs or prepaid expenses to help the buyer qualify for the loan.

Lenders may pay the borrower's closing costs (and prepaid items) by charging a premium interest rate or additional discount points to the borrower.

QUALIFYING RATIOS

Two ratios are used to determine whether the borrower can reasonably be expected to meet the expenses involved in home ownership and otherwise provide for the family:

1. Mortgage payment expense = maximum 29% of effective gross income
2. Total fixed payments = maximum 41% of effective gross income

Mortgage payment expense means the monthly payment for principal, interest, hazard insurance, real estate taxes, one twelfth of the annual MIP, any owners' association fees and payments for any acceptable secondary financing.

Total fixed payments means the sum of (1) mortgage payment expense and (2) monthly recurring obligations on installment loans and revolving charge accounts extending beyond ten months, substantial monthly payments ($200 or more) extending for less than six months, real estate loans, alimony, child support, spousal maintenance and payments on all other debts of a continuing nature.

Effective gross income is the applicant's monthly gross income from all sources that can be expected to continue for the first five years of the loan term. Effective income includes salary, bonuses, commissions, overtime pay, interest, rent and other verified income. Any income, other than the principal salary must be supported with a two-year verified history. If the borrower has changed employment within the last two years, both present and previous jobs must be verified. For salaried borrowers, lenders must obtain two years' original W-2 forms and pay stubs (photocopies are not acceptable).

Energy efficient homes (EEH) when purchased or refinanced are allowed both ratios to be exceeded by up to 2%. The local HUD office determines if a property qualifies for the EEH designation.

Condominium fees with proper documentation, such as that available from the utility company, are allowed that portion of the condominium fee clearly attributable to utilities to be subtracted from the mortgage payment before computing ratios.

Compensating Factors

Ratios in excess of the above may be acceptable if significant compensating factors are presented. Typically, for borrowers with limited recurring expense, greater latitude is permissible on the mortgage payment ratio than on the total fixed payment ratio. The compensating factors include the following situations:

- The borrower makes a large down payment toward the purchase of the property (at least 10%).
- The borrower has demonstrated a conservative attitude toward the use of credit and an ability to accumulate savings.
- Previous credit history shows that the borrower has the ability to devote a greater portion of income to housing expenses.
- The borrower receives compensation of income not reflected in effective income, but directly affecting the ability to pay the mortgage.
- There is only a small increase (10% or less) in the borrower's housing expense.
- The borrower has substantial nontaxable income.
- The borrower has potential for increased earnings as indicated by job training or education in the borrower's profession.

Example of Qualifying a Buyer for FHA Financing

Alex Johnson wants to buy a home. His effective gross income is $5,000. He has monthly recurring obligations of $800. Calculate the maximum monthly mortgage payment expense for which he can qualify.

Effective gross income	$ 5,000	
	$\times 0.29$	
Max. mortgage payment expense	$1,450	(Ratio 1)

Effective gross income	$ 5,000
	× 0.41
Max. total fixed payments	$2,050
Recurring obligations	− 800
Max. mortgage payment expense	$1,250 (Ratio 2)

Because the result of Ratio 2 is lower, the maximum monthly mortgage payment expense Mr. Johnson qualifies for is $1,250.

MODEL ENERGY CODE

Under the Comprehensive National Energy Policy Act of 1992, the Counsel of American Building Officials developed the *Model Energy Code (CABO MEC)*. In addition to establishing performance standards for heating, cooling and ventilation components, CABO MEC defines performance standards for the building envelope—the barrier between the inside and the outside of the building.

If the home is not built to CABO MEC 1992 standards, neither FHA nor VA will insure mortgages on property where construction started on or after October 24, 1993.

Freddie Mac allows 2% to 4% higher qualification guidelines for such properties while Fannie Mae and FHA allow 2% stretches on their qualifying ratios for energy efficient homes under construction.

The act has the following four major provisions:

1. states must establish minimum commercial building codes and consider minimum residential codes based on current voluntary codes;
2. the legislation includes a tie with the availability of federal mortgage assistance for new residential buildings to compliance with model energy code requirements;
3. the legislation requires the development of voluntary home energy rating guidelines and the promotion of energy efficient mortgages; and
4. the legislation requires the secretary of energy to select five states to implement a pilot program

for energy efficient mortgages that include superinsulation.

MORTGAGE INSURANCE PREMIUMS (MIP)

For most FHA programs the borrower pays a onetime (up-front) premium plus annual premiums.

Up-Front MIP (UFMIP)

Effective April 17, 1994, the *up-front MIP* is 2.25% of the base loan amount.

The onetime MIP can be paid in cash at time of closing or it may be financed. If financed, the MIP is added to the base loan amount and becomes part of the total amount financed. Financing of the onetime MIP does not in any way affect the maximum loan amount for purposes of loan qualification.

A person, other than the borrower, may pay the onetime MIP, but only if the entire MIP is paid in cash at time of closing.

If the MIP is paid in cash at closing, the lender is required to round down the base loan amount to the nearest $50.

Upon payment in full of the principal obligation of the mortgage, HUD will refund all of the unearned onetime MIP paid.

There is an exception to the reduced UFMIP that applies to streamlined refinancing of loans originated before July 1, 1991. For these refinanced loans, the premium will remain at 3.8%.

Annual Premium

In addition to the onetime MIP, there is an annual premium of 0.5% of the outstanding loan balance, which is divided by 12 and added to the monthly payments.

The annual premium is charged for a period of years, depending on the down payment. Since October 1, 1994, the following terms apply:

INCOME CONVERSION

HOUR	WEEK	MONTH	YEAR	HOUR	WEEK	MONTH	YEAR
4.00	160.00	693.33	8320.00	17.00	680.00	2946.67	35360.00
4.25	170.00	736.67	8840.00	17.25	690.00	2990.00	35880.00
4.50	180.00	780.00	9360.00	17.50	700.00	3033.33	36400.00
4.75	190.00	823.33	9880.00	17.75	710.00	3076.67	36920.00
5.00	200.00	866.67	10400.00	18.00	720.00	3120.00	37440.00
5.25	210.00	910.00	10920.00	18.25	730.00	3163.33	37960.00
5.50	220.00	953.33	11440.00	18.50	740.00	3206.67	38480.00
5.75	230.00	996.67	11960.00	18.75	750.00	3250.00	39000.00
6.00	240.00	1040.00	12480.00	19.00	760.00	3293.33	39520.00
6.25	250.00	1083.33	13000.00	19.25	770.00	3336.67	40040.00
6.50	260.00	1126.67	13520.00	19.50	780.00	3380.00	40560.00
6.75	270.00	1170.00	14040.00	19.75	790.00	3423.33	41080.00
7.00	280.00	1213.33	14560.00	20.00	800.00	3466.67	41600.00
7.25	290.00	1256.67	15080.00	20.25	810.00	3510.00	42120.00
7.50	300.00	1300.00	15600.00	20.50	820.00	3553.33	42640.00
7.75	310.00	1343.33	16120.00	20.75	830.00	3596.67	43160.00
8.00	320.00	1386.67	16640.00	21.00	840.00	3640.00	43680.00
8.25	330.00	1430.00	17160.00	21.25	850.00	3683.33	44200.00
8.50	340.00	1473.33	17680.00	21.50	860.00	3726.67	44720.00
8.75	350.00	1516.67	18200.00	21.75	870.00	3770.00	45240.00
9.00	360.00	1560.00	18720.00	22.00	880.00	3813.33	45760.00
9.25	370.00	1603.33	19240.00	22.25	890.00	3856.67	46280.00
9.50	380.00	1646.67	19760.00	22.50	900.00	3900.00	46800.00
9.75	390.00	1690.00	20280.00	22.75	910.00	3943.33	47320.00
10.00	400.00	1733.33	20800.00	23.00	920.00	3986.67	47840.00
10.25	410.00	1776.67	21320.00	23.25	930.00	4030.00	48360.00
10.50	420.00	1820.00	21840.00	23.50	940.00	4073.33	48880.00
10.75	430.00	1863.33	22360.00	23.75	950.00	4116.67	49400.00
11.00	440.00	1906.67	22880.00	24.00	960.00	4160.00	49920.00
11.25	450.00	1950.00	23400.00	24.25	970.00	4203.33	50440.00
11.50	460.00	1993.33	23920.00	24.50	980.00	4246.67	50960.00
11.75	470.00	2036.67	24440.00	24.75	990.00	4290.00	51480.00
12.00	480.00	2080.00	24960.00	25.00	1000.00	4333.33	52000.00
12.25	490.00	2123.33	25480.00	25.25	1010.00	4376.67	52520.00
12.50	500.00	2166.67	26000.00	25.50	1020.00	4420.00	53040.00
12.75	510.00	2210.00	26520.00	25.75	1030.00	4463.33	53560.00
13.00	520.00	2253.33	27040.00	26.00	1040.00	4506.67	54080.00
13.25	530.00	2296.67	27560.00	26.25	1050.00	4550.00	54600.00
13.50	540.00	2340.00	28080.00	26.50	1060.00	4593.33	55120.00
13.75	550.00	2383.33	28600.00	26.75	1070.00	4636.67	55640.00
14.00	560.00	2426.67	29120.00	27.00	1080.00	4680.00	56160.00
14.25	570.00	2470.00	29640.00	27.25	1090.00	4723.33	56680.00
14.50	580.00	2513.33	30160.00	27.50	1100.00	4766.67	57200.00
14.75	590.00	2556.67	30680.00	27.75	1110.00	4810.00	57720.00
15.00	600.00	2600.00	31200.00	28.00	1120.00	4853.33	58240.00
15.25	610.00	2643.33	31720.00	28.25	1130.00	4896.67	58760.00
15.50	620.00	2686.67	32240.00	28.50	1140.00	4940.00	59280.00
15.75	630.00	2730.00	32760.00	28.75	1150.00	4983.33	59800.00
16.00	640.00	2773.33	33280.00	29.00	1160.00	5026.67	60320.00
16.25	650.00	2816.67	33800.00	29.25	1170.00	5070.00	60840.00
16.50	660.00	2860.00	34320.00	29.50	1180.00	5113.33	61360.00
16.75	670.00	2903.33	34840.00	29.75	1190.00	5156.67	61880.00

Down Payment	Term
More than 10%	11 years
10% or less	30 years

UFMIP and Annual MIP for Loans over 15 Years, as of October 12, 1994

UFMIP	LTV	Annual MIP	Years
2.25%	Up to 90%	0.5%	7
2.25	90–95	0.5	12
2.25	Over 95	0.5	30

UFMIP and Annual MIP for Loans 15 Years or less, as of October 12, 1994

UFMIP	LTV	Annual Premium	Years
2.00%	Up to 90%	None	n/a
2.00	90–95	.25%	4
2.00	Over 95	.25	8

DISCOUNT POINTS

Restrictions regarding *discount points* paid by the borrower were removed as of November 30, 1983. The 1% loan origination fee was not affected.

INTEREST RATES

Since November 30, 1983, FHA interest rates have been free from HUD control, except for Section 235 loans.

The interest rate on a fixed rate FHA loan is not raised after an assumption.

MAXIMUM LOAN TERM

Maximum term for most FHA-insured mortgages is 30 years.

MONTHLY PAYMENTS

Under FHA financing, it is the lender's responsibility to ascertain that property taxes and hazard insurance premiums are paid when due. Lenders, therefore, will insist that the monthly payments include proportionate amounts for taxes and insurance.

Trust Fund

The lender must deposit the property tax and hazard insurance portion of the monthly payments into a trust fund from which to pay taxes and insurance premiums when due. In order to ascertain that sufficient funds are in the trust fund to make the first tax payment after the loan has been funded, the lender will require that the buyer deposit a certain sum into the trust fund at closing.

PREPAYMENT

There is no penalty for full or partial prepayment of FHA loans insured on or after August 2, 1985. However, FHA loans provide for collection of interest to the first of the month following payment in full.

NOTE: If an FHA loan is paid off early, the borrower may be entitled to a refund of part of the up-front mortgage insurance premium (UFMIP).

REFINANCING

Refinancing is permitted for the purpose of retiring existing liens, making repairs and improvements to the property, obtaining a reduction in interest rate, paying off a mortgage subject to a balloon payment, paying a divorced spouse as a result of a court-ordered property settlement, paying heirs to settle an estate or obtaining cash to finance family related expenditures, such as college education.

Streamline refinances are designed to reduce interest on a current FHA mortgage and may not include cashback to the borrower. No appraisal or credit approval is necessary. The term of the mortgage is the lesser of 30 years or the unexpired term of the mortgage plus 12 years.

Cashback refinances are permitted for owner-occupied principal residences owned more than one year and are limited to 85% of appraised value plus closing costs.

NOTE: If an FHA loan is refinanced, the borrower may be entitled to a refund of part of the up-front mortgage insurance premium (UFMIP).

OPEN-END CLAUSE

An FHA home loan may contain an *open-end clause* by which the outstanding balance may be increased by amounts advanced to the borrower for improvements, alterations or repairs to the property. Such advances may not increase the outstanding balance to an amount greater than the original loan amount unless they are used to add rooms or other enclosed space to the dwelling. For the loan increase, monthly payments can be raised or the term can be extended.

ASSUMPTIONS

Loans Originated Prior to December 1, 1986

FHA loans originated prior to December 1, 1986, are freely assumable, which means a buyer can title subject to the mortgage without the lender's approval, in which case the seller remains liable for repayment of the mortgage debt.

Assumptions with release of liability are granted only if the assumptor is creditworthy and willing to execute an agreement to assume and pay the mortgage debt.

Loans Originated Between December 1, 1986, and December 15, 1989

Some FHA mortgages executed during this period contain language that is not enforced due to later congressional action, and such loans are now freely assumable despite any restrictions stated in the mortgage.

Restrictions of the HUD Reform Act of 1989

FHA loans originated after December 15, 1989, contain due-on-sale clauses, which means they can only be assumed by an owner-occupant buyer found creditworthy who executes an agreement to assume and pay the mortgage debt. Lenders cannot refuse release of liability if an acceptable borrower assumes the loan. The due-on-sale clause is triggered whenever an owner's name is deleted from title, except when that party's interest is transferred by devise, descent or in other circumstances when transfer cannot legally lead to acceleration of the mortgage debt.

Any Mortgage Originated Before January 27, 1991. If the original borrower is an owner-occupant and the assumptor is purchasing the property as a second home, the seller can obtain release of liability only if the remaining balance is paid down to 85% LTV.

Allowable Assumption Charges

- A maximum of $500, plus cost of credit report, based on the lender's actual costs. Half of the fee must be refunded if the borrower is found creditworthy, but settlement does not occur for reasons beyond the borrower's control.
- Nonrefundable fees or charges for credit reports and VOEs or VODs, which are collected by the lender.
- Closing fees, such as document preparation fees, attorney fees, recording fees, and so forth.

BUYER PROTECTION CLAUSES

Amendatory Clause

The following amendatory clause must be part of the purchase agreement unless the borrower has been informed of the appraised value prior to signing the agreement.

> *It is expressly agreed that notwithstanding any other provisions of this contract, the purchaser*

shall not be obligated to complete the purchase of the property described herein or to incur any penalty by forfeiture of earnest money deposits or otherwise unless the purchaser has been given, in accordance with HUD/FHA or VA requirements, a written statement by the Federal Housing Commissioner, VA or a direct endorsement lender, setting forth the appraised value of the property of not less than $[_____]. The purchaser shall have the privilege and option of proceeding with consummation of the contract without regard to the amount of the appraised valuation. The appraised valuation is arrived at to determine the maximum mortgage the Department of Housing and Urban Development will insure. HUD does not warrant the value nor the condition of the property. The purchaser should satisfy himself or herself that the price and condition of the property are acceptable.

Lead-Based Paint Disclosure Notice

HUD requires that FHA borrowers buying homes built before 1978 receive and read a lead-based paint notice before executing the purchase agreement. The borrower must sign and date the notice and provide a copy to the lender when applying for FHA financing. A reduced copy of the notice appears on the following pages. The full text of the notice is reproduced in the Risk Management section under Disclosure of Environmental Hazards.

HOME EQUITY CONVERSION MORTGAGE INSURANCE PROGRAM

Under the Home Equity Conversion Mortgage Insurance Program, HUD will insure reverse mortgages on the homes of elderly homeowners, enabling them to convert their equity into a single lump, monthly payments or line of credit draws.

Elderly homeowners who are 62 years of age or older and who live in a home that they own free and clear (or almost free and clear) are eligible to apply for a HUD-insured reverse mortgage from a participating lender.

All HUD-approved lenders are eligible to participate in this program. The department proposes to insure three types of home equity conversion mortgages: (1) tenure, (2) term and (3) line of credit. These mortgages may bear interest at either a fixed or an adjustable rate. HUD also proposes to insure fixed rate tenure mortgages that provide for shared appreciation between the borrower and the lender.

Tenure mortgages provide for monthly payments from the lender for as long as the borrower occupies the home as a principal residence.

Term mortgages provide for monthly payments for a fixed period agreed upon between the lender and borrower.

Line of credit mortgages permit the borrower to make draws up to a maximum amount at times and in amounts of the borrower's choosing.

Elderly homeowners retain ownership of their property and may sell at any time, retaining the sales proceeds in excess of the amount needed to pay off their mortgage. They cannot be forced to sell their home to pay off their mortgage even if the mortgage principal balance, including accrued interest and mortgage insurance premium (MIP), grows to exceed the value of the property. When the mortgage does come due, the lender's recovery from the borrower will be limited to the value of the home. There will be no deficiency judgment against the borrower or the estate.

Generally, monthly payments under tenure mortgages will be lower than those under term mortgages, and payments available under a term mortgage are comparable to the disbursements available under a line of credit mortgage. Monthly payments under a shared appreciation tenure mortgage are expected to be higher than under a tenure mortgage without shared appreciation. After consultation with a housing counselor and a lender, elderly homeowners can select the mortgage best suited to their needs.

A borrower is protected if the lender fails to make the required payments under the mortgage. HUD will make the payments to the borrower. A lender who defaults will lose all interest on payments made to or on behalf of the borrower. In addition, HUD may initiate administrative sanctions.

FHA LOAN PROGRAMS

Section 203(b) Fixed Rate One- to Four-Family Dwellings

The objective of Section 203(b) is to finance the acquisition or the refinance of one- to four-family units for owner-occupants. 203(b) loans are available for (1) new construction approved by and built under FHA or VA inspection, (2) new construction not built under FHA/VA inspection but with a ten-year homeowner's warranty and (3) existing construction more than one year old.

Section 203(b)(2) FHA Loans to Veterans

The objective of Section 203(b)(2) is to finance, at special low cash requirements, the acquisition or refinance of single family units for owner-occupant veterans.

Loan-to-Value Ratio (LTV)

The maximum LTV is 100% of the first $25,000 plus 95% of the amount between $25,000 and $125,000, and 90% of the amount over $125,000 of appraised value (or sales price, whichever is less) plus allowable closing costs.

The minimum cash investment is $750 less for veterans than for regular 203(b) borrowers of properties in excess of $50,000.

Eligibility Requirements

To be eligible for an FHA 203(b)(2) loan, the veteran must have served 90 days of continuous active duty (which includes active duty training) in any branch of the U.S. armed forces including the National Guard and U.S. Coast Guard. This service could have been at any time, not necessarily in time of war. If a veteran can establish that he or she served under hazardous duty conditions, he or she is eligible with service of less than 90 days.

Veterans who have used their eligibility to obtain a VA home loan are still eligible for this program. Veterans who were eligible for a VA home loan and did not use their eligibility are still eligible for the FHA program.

Use of the FHA program does not cause veterans to lose their VA eligibility for future use. Veterans who use the FHA program may use it again an unlimited number of times, provided certain other requirements are met.

Application

In addition to the normal application forms required for a regular Sec. 203(b) FHA loan, the veteran will have to furnish a *Certificate of Veterans Status* (VA Form 26-8261), which must be obtained from the Veterans Administration. *Requests for Certificate of Veterans Status* must be made by filling out VA Form 26-8261A and mailing it to the VA regional office together with separation and discharge papers. Real estate brokers can expedite the process by obtaining a supply of these 26-8261A forms from the nearest VA office and by assisting the veteran in filling out the form.

Section 203(k) Rehabilitation Home Mortgage Insurance

Section 203(k) provides mortgage insurance for a person to purchase or refinance a principal residence or investment property and to accomplish rehabilitation and/or improvement of an existing one- to four-family dwelling. It was originally offered as a pilot program. Section 203(k) has been available nationwide since October 1994.

Eligibility Requirements

- Borrower must meet standard FHA credit qualifications.
- Borrower may be an owner-occupant or an investor.
- MIP is paid monthly; there is no UFMIP.
- Borrower can purchase a one- to four-unit property completed for at least one year, subject to the number of units acceptable to local zoning requirements.
- Homes that have been demolished, or will be razed as part of the rehabilitation work, are eligible provided the existing foundation system is not affected and will still be used. The complete foundation system must remain in place.
- Mortgage limits are the same as for Section 203(b).

Permanent Construction Loans

Purpose—To assist approved FHA builders in obtaining construction financing by allowing borrowers to be approved prior to start of construction.

Closing—In name of borrower prior to start of construction.

Mortgage amount—Same as any other FHA loan. Appraisal from plans and specifications with requirement for completion inspection. Builder must supply HOW warranty policy to enable borrower to obtain an LTV in excess of 90%.

MIP—To be paid within 15 days of closing.

Documents—Construction documents must contain a provision that the construction terms cease to be effective and the FHA terms become effective at time of final inspection or certificate of occupancy.

Section 234(c) Condominiums

The objective of Section 234(c) is to finance the acquisition of individual units in approved condominium projects containing four or more units in conjunction with the following sections: 203(b), 203(b)(2) FHA Veterans, 245(a) GPM or GEM and 251 ARM.

Occupancy Requirements

At least 80% of the units on which there are HUD-insured mortgages in a project must be owner occupied before HUD can make insured financing available on additional units.

Guidelines

The project in which the unit is located must conform to the following guidelines:

1. The unit must be in a condominium project that provides for undivided ownership of common areas by the unit owners.
2. The project must be more than one year old. All units and all common elements and improvements must have been completed. (Exception: VA-approved complexes)
3. Satisfactory completion of all improvements must have been made, including the common areas and facilities. (Exception: VA-approved complexes)
4. Eighty percent of the total number of units must be occupied by unit purchasers. No more than 40% of the units shall be insured under Section 235. (If the VA has issued approval subject to a higher presale requirement, reconsideration must be sought through the VA.)
5. Parking and recreational facilities must be a legal part of the project and owned by unit owners. However, leasing of these facilities is permitted provided the lessors can terminate with no more than 90-days notice any contract entered into with the lessee.
6. The developer must have no special rights with respect to the project or common areas other than the marketing of unsold units. The project must not be subject to future expansion at the option of the developer.

   Any special rights of the developer (as developer and not as a unit owner) to do any and all of the following must have expired or have been waived in a recorded instrument:

a. add land or units to the condominium;
b. convert common elements into additional units or limited common elements;
c. withdraw land from the condominium;
d. use easements through the common elements for the purpose of making improvements within the condominium or within any adjacent land; or
e. convert a unit into two or more units, common elements, or into two or more units and common elements.

7. Each unit owner, his/her successors and assigns upon acceptance of the unit deed automatically must become members of the association. Each unit member must have a proportionate vote at association meetings and must be responsible to pay a proportionate share of the expenses of the association.

8. The project must demonstrate good management, maintenance and financial stability. There must be an adequate reserve fund for the periodic maintenance, repair and replacement of the common elements.

9. The master deed, bylaws and any other similar documents must be in accordance with current state law. The legal documents clearly must designate
   a. unit composition, description of common areas and the party responsible for repair and maintenance of the property;
   b. a mechanism for amendment of the documents;
   c. the allocation on an equitable basis of the unit owner's voting rights and responsibilities for assessments; and
   d. the methods to be used in operating and governing the condominium.

   Each condominium unit owner should have a clearly specified interest in the common area.

10. The association must have a master or blanket policy, protecting against loss or damage by fire

and other hazards, sufficient to cover the replacement cost of the common areas of the project, and a comprehensive public liability insurance policy covering the common areas. If the project is in a flood zone, flood insurance also is required.

11. The project will not qualify if circumstances or conditions concerning the project will have a substantially adverse effect upon the project or be a contributing cause for the unit mortgage to become delinquent.

Application Forms and Exhibits

Application for an appraisal must be submitted on Form HUD-92800, *Application for Property Appraisal and Commitment*.

The application on the first unit submitted for HUD insurance in an existing condominium project must be accompanied by the following exhibits:

1. Master deed or equivalent document (including amendments), with the recordation date of the project.
2. Bylaws for the association.
3. Recorded plat, plan, survey or map (including amendments) of projects.
4. Articles of incorporation, if any, executed in connection with the establishment of the association.
5. Mortgagee's certification that
   a. the deed of the family unit and the deed or other recorded instrument committing the project to a plan of condominium ownership comply with all legal requirements of the jurisdiction;
   b. the mortgagor has good marketable title to the family unit, subject only to the mortgage, which is a valid first lien on the same; and
   c. the family unit is assessed and subject to assessment for taxes pertaining only to that unit.
6. Statement of insurance and fidelity bond coverage for the common areas.
7. The project's annual income, expenses and budget. The reserve funds for commonly owned replacements must be sufficient to meet current costs.

Submission must include copies of the minutes of the last two meetings of the council of co-owners.

8. Certification from the association that 70% of the units are owner occupied.
9. Certification from the mortgagee's attorney that legal documents submitted for review meet HUD's objectives.

Condominium Conversions

Units in any project (including VA approved) converted from rental housing to condominiums less than one year prior to the application for insurance are not acceptable unless

1. the mortgagor or comortgagor was a tenant of that rental housing or
2. the conversion of the property is sponsored by a bona fide tenants' organization representing a majority of the households.

Condominium Projects Approved by the FNMA and VA

The approval of condominium projects by the FNMA and/or VA will waive the requirement for project approval procedures as a condition of accepting applications (i.e., appraisal requests will be taken, but evidence of approval must accompany the first application.) Form 1028* must be submitted by the lender demonstrating that the project was approved by FNMA and evidence that the project is more than one year old. The CRV will be accepted as evidence of approval by the VA. The VA project is not limited to the one-year age restriction. Specific requirements to meet eligibility criteria established in the regulations will be made conditions of the commitment.

Any other documentation is not acceptable. FNMA's streamlined procedure is not acceptable, and submission of the above documentation is required.

Section 245(a) Graduated Payment Mortgage (GPM)

The objective of Section 245(a) is to finance the acquisition of owner-occupied single-family dwellings in order to meet the needs of homebuyers priced out of the market because of the high cost of housing. There must be a strong possibility that the borrower's income will increase substantially in the future.

Plans

GPMs permit increasing monthly payments each year during the first five years under Plans I, II and III. After that, payments will remain level. Buyers are qualified based on first year's payments.

Plan	Percentage of Increase in Monthly Payments	During
I	2½% each year	
II	5% each year	first 5 years
III	7½% each year	

Refinancing

Refinancing an existing level payment mortgage to any GPM plan is not permitted. However, a GPM may be refinanced at any time to a level payment mortgage. The amount of the monthly payment due under the refinancing mortgage must be less than that due under the existing mortgage for the month in which the refinancing mortgage is executed.

Maximum Loan

Because payments in the early years frequently do not cover the full amount of interest, the outstanding loan balance will increase (negative amortization). Because the principal obligation may not exceed at any time the maximum insurable loan, minimum down payment requirements will, in most cases, be greater than under standard FHA loans.

GPM HIGHEST OUTSTANDING BALANCE OCCURS AT END OF:

INTEREST	PLAN 1	PLAN 2	PLAN 3
6.00	0 MONTHS	12 MONTHS	24 MONTHS
6.25	0 MONTHS	12 MONTHS	24 MONTHS
6.50	0 MONTHS	12 MONTHS	36 MONTHS
6.75	0 MONTHS	24 MONTHS	36 MONTHS
7.00	0 MONTHS	24 MONTHS	36 MONTHS
7.25	0 MONTHS	24 MONTHS	36 MONTHS
7.50	0 MONTHS	24 MONTHS	36 MONTHS
7.75	0 MONTHS	36 MONTHS	36 MONTHS
8.00	12 MONTHS	36 MONTHS	48 MONTHS
8.25	12 MONTHS	36 MONTHS	48 MONTHS
8.50	12 MONTHS	36 MONTHS	48 MONTHS
8.75	12 MONTHS	36 MONTHS	48 MONTHS
9.00	24 MONTHS	36 MONTHS	48 MONTHS
9.25	24 MONTHS	36 MONTHS	48 MONTHS
9.50	24 MONTHS	48 MONTHS	48 MONTHS
9.75	24 MONTHS	48 MONTHS	48 MONTHS
10.00	24 MONTHS	48 MONTHS	48 MONTHS
10.25	36 MONTHS	48 MONTHS	48 MONTHS
10.50	36 MONTHS	48 MONTHS	48 MONTHS
10.75	36 MONTHS	48 MONTHS	60 MONTHS
11.00	36 MONTHS	48 MONTHS	60 MONTHS
11.25	36 MONTHS	48 MONTHS	60 MONTHS
11.50	36 MONTHS	48 MONTHS	60 MONTHS
11.75	36 MONTHS	48 MONTHS	60 MONTHS
12.00	48 MONTHS	48 MONTHS	60 MONTHS
12.25	48 MONTHS	60 MONTHS	60 MONTHS
12.50	48 MONTHS	60 MONTHS	60 MONTHS
12.75	48 MONTHS	60 MONTHS	60 MONTHS
13.00	48 MONTHS	60 MONTHS	60 MONTHS
13.25	48 MONTHS	60 MONTHS	60 MONTHS
13.50	48 MONTHS	60 MONTHS	60 MONTHS
13.75	48 MONTHS	60 MONTHS	60 MONTHS
14.00	48 MONTHS	60 MONTHS	60 MONTHS
14.25	48 MONTHS	60 MONTHS	60 MONTHS
14.50	48 MONTHS	60 MONTHS	60 MONTHS
14.75	48 MONTHS	60 MONTHS	60 MONTHS
15.00	60 MONTHS	60 MONTHS	60 MONTHS
15.25	60 MONTHS	60 MONTHS	60 MONTHS
15.50	60 MONTHS	60 MONTHS	60 MONTHS
15.75	60 MONTHS	60 MONTHS	60 MONTHS
16.00	60 MONTHS	60 MONTHS	60 MONTHS
16.25	60 MONTHS	60 MONTHS	60 MONTHS
16.50	60 MONTHS	60 MONTHS	60 MONTHS
16.75	60 MONTHS	60 MONTHS	60 MONTHS

HIGHEST OUTSTANDING BALANCE
FACTORS FOR $1000 GPM

INTEREST	PLAN 1	PLAN 2	PLAN 3
6.00	1.0000000	1.0011164	1.0098941
6.25	1.0000000	1.0019924	1.0118886
6.50	1.0000000	1.0028495	1.0145304
6.75	1.0000000	1.0043290	1.0173401
7.00	1.0000000	1.0059388	1.0200991
7.25	1.0000000	1.0075117	1.0228056
7.50	1.0000000	1.0090487	1.0254642
7.75	1.0000000	1.0107019	1.0280728
8.00	1.0000195	1.0128612	1.0309550
8.25	1.0005895	1.0149700	1.0341945
8.50	1.0011422	1.0170321	1.0373748
8.75	1.0016774	1.0190464	1.0404961
9.00	1.0023085	1.0210154	1.0435617
9.25	1.0033130	1.0229397	1.0465678
9.50	1.0042870	1.0251491	1.0495186
9.75	1.0052329	1.0275358	1.0524197
10.00	1.0061505	1.0298668	1.0552637
10.25	1.0071479	1.0321469	1.0580559
10.50	1.0084361	1.0343732	1.0607998
10.75	1.0096866	1.0365482	1.0635966
11.00	1.0108994	1.0386770	1.0667347
11.25	1.0120765	1.0407556	1.0698110
11.50	1.0132190	1.0427859	1.0728295
11.75	1.0143280	1.0447740	1.0757962
12.00	1.0154746	1.0467166	1.0787075
12.25	1.0168544	1.0486287	1.0815692
12.50	1.0181935	1.0508556	1.0843740
12.75	1.0194922	1.0530313	1.0871336
13.00	1.0207547	1.0551590	1.0898424
13.25	1.0219801	1.0572369	1.0925044
13.50	1.0231699	1.0592689	1.0951202
13.75	1.0243257	1.0612612	1.0976904
14.00	1.0254476	1.0632080	1.1002174
14.25	1.0265382	1.0651109	1.1026993
14.50	1.0275961	1.0669754	1.1051467
14.75	1.0286283	1.0688029	1.1075476
15.00	1.0296759	1.0705897	1.1099107
15.25	1.0308638	1.0723406	1.1122353
15.50	1.0320183	1.0740560	1.1145245
15.75	1.0331387	1.0757364	1.1167789
16.00	1.0342318	1.0773807	1.1189949
16.25	1.0352944	1.0789991	1.1211798
16.50	1.0363243	1.0805804	1.1233313
16.75	1.0373310	1.0821356	1.1254505

FHA GPM PLAN I

RATE	YEAR 1	YEAR 2	YEAR 3	YEAR 4	YEAR 5	REMAIN.
6.000	5.4229	5.5585	5.6974	5.8399	5.9859	6.1355
6.250	5.5720	5.7113	5.8541	6.0005	6.1505	6.3042
6.500	5.7230	5.8661	6.0127	6.1630	6.3171	6.4751
6.750	5.8758	6.0227	6.1732	6.3276	6.4858	6.6479
7.000	6.0303	6.1811	6.3356	6.4940	6.6563	6.8227
7.250	6.1865	6.3412	6.4997	6.6622	6.8288	6.9995
7.500	6.3444	6.5030	6.6656	6.8323	7.0031	7.1781
7.750	6.5039	6.6665	6.8332	7.0040	7.1791	7.3586
8.000	6.6651	6.8317	7.0025	7.1775	7.3570	7.5409
8.250	6.8277	6.9984	7.1733	7.3527	7.5365	7.7249
8.500	6.9918	7.1666	7.3458	7.5294	7.7177	7.9106
8.750	7.1574	7.3364	7.5198	7.7078	7.9005	8.0980
9.000	7.3244	7.5075	7.6952	7.8876	8.0848	8.2869
9.250	7.4928	7.6801	7.8721	8.0689	8.2706	8.4774
9.500	7.6625	7.8541	8.0504	8.2517	8.4580	8.6694
9.750	7.8335	8.0293	8.2300	8.4358	8.6467	8.8629
10.000	8.0057	8.2058	8.4110	8.6213	8.8368	9.0577
10.250	8.1791	8.3836	8.5932	8.8080	9.0282	9.2539
10.500	8.3537	8.5626	8.7767	8.9961	9.2210	9.4515
10.750	8.5295	8.7427	8.9613	9.1853	9.4150	9.6503
11.000	8.7063	8.9240	9.1471	9.3757	9.6101	9.8504
11.250	8.8842	9.1063	9.3340	9.5673	9.8065	10.0516
11.500	9.0631	9.2897	9.5219	9.7600	10.0040	10.2541
11.750	9.2430	9.4740	9.7109	9.9537	10.2025	10.4576
12.000	9.4238	9.6594	9.9009	10.1484	10.4021	10.6622
12.250	9.6056	9.8457	10.0918	10.3441	10.6027	10.8678
12.500	9.7882	10.0329	10.2837	10.5408	10.8043	11.0744
12.750	9.9717	10.2210	10.4765	10.7384	11.0069	11.2820
13.000	10.1560	10.4099	10.6701	10.9369	11.2103	11.4906
13.250	10.3411	10.5996	10.8646	11.1362	11.4146	11.7000
13.500	10.5269	10.7901	11.0599	11.3364	11.6198	11.9103
13.750	10.7135	10.9814	11.2559	11.5373	11.8257	12.1214
14.000	10.9008	11.1734	11.4527	11.7390	12.0325	12.3333
14.250	11.0888	11.3660	11.6502	11.9415	12.2400	12.5460
14.500	11.2775	11.5594	11.8484	12.1446	12.4482	12.7594
14.750	11.4667	11.7534	12.0472	12.3484	12.6571	12.9736
15.000	11.6566	11.9480	12.2467	12.5529	12.8667	13.1884
15.250	11.8471	12.1432	12.4468	12.7580	13.0769	13.4039
15.500	12.0381	12.3390	12.6475	12.9637	13.2878	13.6200
15.750	12.2297	12.5354	12.8488	13.1700	13.4992	13.8367
16.000	12.4217	12.7323	13.0506	13.3768	13.7113	14.0541
16.250	12.6143	12.9297	13.2529	13.5842	13.9238	14.2719
16.500	12.8074	13.1276	13.4558	13.7921	14.1370	14.4904
16.750	13.0009	13.3259	13.6591	14.0006	14.3506	14.7093

FHA GPM PLAN II

RATE	YEAR 1	YEAR 2	YEAR 3	YEAR 4	YEAR 5	REMAIN.
6.000	4.9095	5.1550	5.4127	5.6833	5.9675	6.2659
6.250	5.0470	5.2993	5.5643	5.8425	6.1346	6.4413
6.500	5.1862	5.4455	5.7178	6.0037	6.3039	6.6191
6.750	5.3273	5.5937	5.8733	6.1670	6.4754	6.7991
7.000	5.4701	5.7436	6.0308	6.3323	6.6489	6.9814
7.250	5.6146	5.8953	6.1901	6.4996	6.8246	7.1658
7.500	5.7607	6.0488	6.3512	6.6688	7.0022	7.3523
7.750	5.9085	6.2040	6.5142	6.8399	7.1819	7.5410
8.000	6.0579	6.3608	6.6789	7.0128	7.3634	7.7316
8.250	6.2089	6.5193	6.8453	7.1875	7.5469	7.9243
8.500	6.3613	6.6794	7.0134	7.3640	7.7322	8.1188
8.750	6.5153	6.8410	7.1831	7.5422	7.9193	8.3153
9.000	6.6706	7.0042	7.3544	7.7221	8.1082	8.5136
9.250	6.8274	7.1688	7.5272	7.9036	8.2988	8.7137
9.500	6.9856	7.3349	7.7016	8.0867	8.4910	8.9156
9.750	7.1451	7.5023	7.8775	8.2713	8.6849	9.1191
10.000	7.3059	7.6712	8.0547	8.4575	8.8804	9.3244
10.250	7.4679	7.8413	8.2334	8.6451	9.0773	9.5312
10.500	7.6312	8.0128	8.4134	8.8341	9.2758	9.7396
10.750	7.7957	8.1855	8.5948	9.0245	9.4757	9.9495
11.000	7.9613	8.3594	8.7774	9.2162	9.6771	10.1609
11.250	8.1281	8.5345	8.9612	9.4093	9.8798	10.3737
11.500	8.2960	8.7108	9.1463	9.6036	10.0838	10.5880
11.750	8.4649	8.8881	9.3325	9.7992	10.2891	10.8036
12.000	8.6348	9.0666	9.5199	9.9959	10.4957	11.0205
12.250	8.8058	9.2461	9.7084	10.1938	10.7035	11.2386
12.500	8.9777	9.4266	9.8979	10.3928	10.9124	11.4581
12.750	9.1505	9.6081	10.0885	10.5929	11.1225	11.6787
13.000	9.3243	9.7905	10.2800	10.7940	11.3338	11.9004
13.250	9.4990	9.9739	10.4726	10.9962	11.5460	12.1233
13.500	9.6745	10.1582	10.6661	11.1994	11.7594	12.3473
13.750	9.8508	10.3433	10.8605	11.4035	11.9737	12.5724
14.000	10.0279	10.5293	11.0558	11.6086	12 1890	12.7985
14.250	10.2059	10.7161	11.2520	11.8145	12.4053	13.0255
14.500	10.3845	10.9038	11.4489	12.0214	12.6225	13.2536
14.750	10.5639	11.0921	11.6467	12.2291	12.8405	13.4825
15.000	10.7440	11.2812	11.8453	12.4376	13.0595	13.7124
15.250	10.9248	11.4711	12.0446	12.6469	13.2792	13.9432
15.500	11.1063	11.6616	12.2447	12.8569	13.4998	14.1748
15.750	11.2884	11.8528	12.4455	13.0678	13.7211	14.4072
16.000	11.4712	12.0447	12.6470	13.2793	13.9433	14.6404
16.250	11.6545	12.2372	12.8491	13.4915	14.1661	14.8744
16.500	11.8384	12.4304	13.0519	13.7045	14.3897	15.1092
16.750	12.0229	12.6241	13.2553	13.9180	14.6140	15.3446

FHA GPM PLAN III, VA GPM, 5-YEAR GPARM

RATE	YEAR 1	YEAR 2	YEAR 3	YEAR 4	YEAR 5	REMAIN.
6.000	4.4491	4.7828	5.1415	5.5271	5.9417	6.3873
6.125	4.5122	4.8506	5.2144	5.6055	6.0259	6.4779
6.250	4.5758	4.9189	5.2879	5.6845	6.1108	6.5691
6.375	4.6397	4.9877	5.3618	5.7639	6.1962	6.6610
6.500	4.7042	5.0570	5.4363	5.8440	6.2823	6.7534
6.625	4.7690	5.1267	5.5112	5.9245	6.3689	6.8466
6.750	4.8343	5.1969	5.5867	6.0057	6.4561	6.9403
6.875	4.9000	5.2675	5.6626	6.0873	6.5438	7.0346
7.000	4.9662	5.3386	5.7390	6.1695	6.6322	7.1296
7.125	5.0327	5.4102	5.8160	6.2521	6.7211	7.2251
7.250	5.0997	5.4822	5.8934	6.3354	6.8105	7.3213
7.375	5.1671	5.5546	5.9712	6.4191	6.9005	7.4180
7.500	5.2349	5.6275	6.0496	6.5033	6.9910	7.5154
7.625	5.3031	5.7008	6.1284	6.5880	7.0821	7.6133
7.750	5.3717	5.7746	6.2077	6.6732	7.1737	7.7118
7.875	5.4407	5.8487	6.2874	6.7590	7.2659	7.8108
8.000	5.5101	5.9233	6.3676	6.8452	7.3585	7.9104
8.125	5.5799	5.9983	6.4482	6.9318	7.4517	8.0106
8.250	5.6500	6.0738	6.5293	7.0190	7.5454	8.1113
8.375	5.7206	6.1496	6.6108	7.1066	7.6396	8.2126
8.500	5.7915	6.2258	6.6928	7.1947	7.7343	8.3144
8.625	5.8628	6.3025	6.7752	7.2833	7.8295	8.4168
8.750	5.9344	6.3795	6.8580	7.3723	7.9252	8.5196
8.875	6.0064	6.4569	6.9412	7.4618	8.0214	8.6230
9.000	6.0788	6.5347	7.0248	7.5517	8.1181	8.7269
9.125	6.1516	6.6129	7.1089	7.6421	8.2152	8.8314
9.250	6.2246	6.6915	7.1934	7.7329	8.3128	8.9363
9.375	6.2981	6.7704	7.2782	7.8241	8.4109	9.0417
9.500	6.3719	6.8498	7.3635	7.9158	8.5094	9.1476
9.625	6.4460	6.9294	7.4491	8.0078	8.6084	9.2541
9.750	6.5204	7.0095	7.5352	8.1003	8.7079	9.3609
9.875	6.5952	7.0899	7.6216	8.1932	8.8077	9.4683
10.000	6.6704	7.1706	7.7084	8.2866	8.9081	9.5762
10.125	6.7458	7.2517	7.7956	8.3803	9.0088	9.6845
10.250	6.8216	7.3332	7.8832	8.4744	9.1100	9.7932
10.375	6.8976	7.4150	7.9711	8.5689	9.2116	9.9024
10.500	6.9740	7.4971	8.0594	8.6638	9.3136	10.0121
10.625	7.0507	7.5795	8.1480	8.7591	9.4160	10.1222
10.750	7.1277	7.6623	8.2370	8.8548	9.5189	10.2328
10.875	7.2050	7.7454	8.3263	8.9508	9.6221	10.3438
11.000	7.2826	7.8288	8.4160	9.0472	9.7257	10.4552
11.125	7.3605	7.9126	8.5060	9.1440	9.8298	10.5670
11.250	7.4387	7.9966	8.5964	9.2411	9.9342	10.6793
11.375	7.5172	8.0810	8.6871	9.3386	10.0390	10.7919

FHA GPM PLAN III, VA GPM, 5-YEAR GPARM

RATE	YEAR 1	YEAR 2	YEAR 3	YEAR 4	YEAR 5	REMAIN.
11.500	7.5960	8.1657	8.7781	9.4364	10.1442	10.9050
11.625	7.6750	8.2506	8.8694	9.5346	10.2497	11.0185
11.750	7.7543	8.3359	8.9611	9.6332	10.3556	11.1323
11.875	7.8339	8.4214	9.0530	9.7320	10.4619	11.2466
12.000	7.9138	8.5073	9.1453	9.8312	10.5686	11.3612
12.125	7.9939	8.5934	9.2379	9.9308	10.6756	11.4762
12.250	8.0742	8.6798	9.3308	10.0306	10.7829	11.5916
12.375	8.1549	8.7665	9.4240	10.1308	10.8906	11.7074
12.500	8.2358	8.8535	9.5175	10.2313	10.9986	11.8235
12.625	8.3169	8.9407	9.6112	10.3321	11.1070	11.9400
12.750	8.3983	9.0282	9.7053	10.4332	11.2157	12.0569
12.875	8.4800	9.1160	9.7997	10.5346	11.3247	12.1741
13.000	8.5618	9.2040	9.8943	10.6363	11.4341	12.2916
13.125	8.6440	9.2923	9.9892	10.7384	11.5437	12.4095
13.250	8.7263	9.3808	10.0843	10.8407	11.6537	12.5277
13.375	8.8089	9.4696	10.1798	10.9433	11.7640	12.6463
13.500	8.8917	9.5586	10.2755	11.0461	11.8746	12.7652
13.625	8.9748	9.6479	10.3715	11.1493	11.9855	12.8844
13.750	9.0580	9.7374	10.4677	11.2527	12.0967	13.0040
13.875	9.1415	9.8271	10.5642	11.3565	12.2082	13.1238
14.000	9.2252	9.9171	10.6609	11.4604	12.3200	13.2440
14.125	9.3091	10.0073	10.7579	11.5647	12.4321	13.3645
14.250	9.3933	10.0978	10.8551	11.6692	12.5444	13.4852
14.375	9.4776	10.1884	10.9525	11.7740	12.6570	13.6063
14.500	9.5621	10.2793	11.0502	11.8790	12.7699	13.7277
14.625	9.6469	10.3704	11.1482	11.9843	12.8831	13.8494
14.750	9.7318	10.4617	11.2464	12.0898	12.9966	13.9713
14.875	9.8170	10.5533	11.3448	12.1956	13.1103	14.0936
15.000	9.9023	10.6450	11.4434	12.3016	13.2243	14.2161
15.125	9.9879	10.7370	11.5422	12.4079	13.3385	14.3389
15.250	10.0736	10.8291	11.6413	12.5144	13.4530	14.4619
15.375	10.1595	10.9215	11.7406	12.6211	13.5677	14.5853
15.500	10.2456	11.0140	11.8401	12.7281	13.6827	14.7089
15.625	10.3319	11.1068	11.9398	12.8353	13.7979	14.8328
15.750	10.4183	11.1997	12.0397	12.9427	13.9134	14.9569
15.875	10.5050	11.2929	12.1398	13.0503	14.0291	15.0813
16.000	10.5918	11.3862	12.2402	13.1582	14.1450	15.2059
16.125	10.6788	11.4797	12.3407	13.2662	14.2612	15.3308
16.250	10.7660	11.5734	12.4414	13.3745	14.3776	15.4559
16.375	10.8533	11.6673	12.5423	13.4830	14.4942	15.5813
16.500	10.9408	11.7613	12.6435	13.5917	14.6111	15.7069
16.625	11.0285	11.8556	12.7448	13.7006	14.7282	15.8328
16.750	11.1163	11.9500	12.8463	13.8097	14.8454	15.9589
16.875	11.2043	12.0446	12.9479	13.9190	14.9630	16.0852

Section 251 Adjustable Rate Mortgage (ARM)

The objective of Section 251 is to finance the acquisition of or to refinance one- to four-family units. At least one unit must be owner occupied.

The term of an FHA ARM must be 30 years. LTVs and base loan amount calculations are the same as for 203(b) loans.

Interest Rate Keyed to Index

Changes in interest rate must correspond to changes in the weekly average yield on U.S. Treasury securities adjusted to a constant maturity of one year. Weekly average yields are published in the Federal Reserve Bulletin, easily obtained from the Federal Reserve Board by requesting to be placed on a mailing list for receipt of the weekly H.15(519) publication. Write to Publication Services, Mail Stop 138, Board of Governors, Federal Reserve System, Washington, DC 20551.

Frequency of Interest Rate Change

Interest rate adjustments must occur on an annual basis, except that the first adjustment may occur no sooner than 12 months nor later than 18 months from the due date of the borrower's initial monthly payment. Subsequent interest rate adjustments will occur on each anniversary date of the first interest adjustment date.

Caps on Interest Rate Changes

Maximum interest rate adjustment (up or down) is one percentage point from the interest rate in effect for the period immediately preceding that adjustment. Maximum of total interest increases over the entire term of the loan is five percentage points above the initial interest rate. No negative amortization is permitted.

Method of Calculating Interest Rate Adjustments

1. Determine the latest available index rate 30 days before the interest adjustment date of the mortgage.
2. Add to this index value the margin for the mortgage (margin is a permanent percentage established by the lender that is added to the index in order to arrive at the interest rate), and round the sum to the nearest ⅛% of 1%, referred to as the calculated interest rate.
3. The calculated interest rate becomes the new interest rate to the extent that it does not exceed one percentage point above or below the existing rate in effect for the past 12 months, subject to the 5% cap for the term of the loan.

   Increases in excess of 1% will be applied at the next adjustment date (subject to both caps) if the calculated interest rate remains at or above the existing interest rate. This means that, under certain circumstances, the index may decrease while the new interest rate actually increases, as shown in year four of the following example. (Decreases in excess of 1% will also be applied at the next adjustment date if the calculated interest rate remains at or below the existing interest rate).

YEAR	INDEX +	MARGIN =	CALCULATED INT RTE.	NEW INT RATE
1	N/A	N/A	N/A	12%(initial int. rate)
2	10.5	2.00	(10.5 + 2.00 = 12.5)	12.5%
3	14.5	2.00	(14.5 + 2.00 = 16.5)	13.5
4	13.5	2.00	(13.5 + 2.00 = 15.5)	14.5
5	13.5	2.00	(13.5 + 2.00 = 15.5)	15.5

Yr 1: Lender and borrower agreed to an initial interest rate of 12% for the first year with annual adjustments based on the index plus a margin of 2%.

Yr 2: Calculated interest rate (*Index + Margin*) is

12.5%. Because this is less than 1% above the initial interest rate, the new rate is 12.5%.

Yr 3: The index increases 4% (from 10.5 to 14.5) bringing the calculated rate to 16.5%. However, because of the 1% annual interest cap, the new rate is only 13.5%.

Yr 4: The index decreases 1% (from 14.5 to 13.5). After adding the margin, the calculated rate becomes 15.5%, which is again more than the existing rate of 13.5%. Therefore, the new rate will increase up to the 1% ceiling or 14.5%.

Yr 5: Index and calculated rate remain the same as in previous year. However, because the calculated rate (15.5%) is still more than the existing rate (14.5%), the new rate will increase up to the 1% cap, or 15.5%.

4. The new interest rate is then used to adjust the monthly payment to fully amortize the remaining principal balance as of the adjustment date over the remaining term of the loan. The adjusted monthly payment becomes effective 30 days after the interest adjustment date. This eliminates negative amortization.

Loan Disclosure

The lender is required to give the borrower a complete written explanation of the loan terms, including a hypothetical monthly payment schedule that shows a worst case scenario of the first five years of the loan. Such scenario shows what the monthly payments would be if the interest rate rose by 1% each year for five years to the maximum allowed total increase of 5%.

Additionally, the lender is obligated to inform the borrower at least 30 days in advance of any adjustment to the monthly payment of (1) the new interest rate and the amount of the monthly payment, (2) the current index figure and how the payment adjustment was calculated and (3) the method any interest rate change in excess of the cap is carried over to the next adjustment interval.

Title I Mobile Homes

The objective is to finance the acquisition of a new or used mobile home, which the borrower must occupy as his or her primary residence.

Qualifications

The mobile home must be new (not previously occupied); or a used mobile home being sold by a person who financed it with an FHA mobile home loan; or be occupied by the purchaser under a government lease after having been displaced from previous housing by a disaster.

The mobile home must be constructed according to standards prescribed by the American National Standards Institute and placed on a lot owned by the borrower that complies with certain standards or be in an approved mobile home park.

The mobile home must have a minimum floor space of 400 square feet.

Maximum Loan and Term

Multisection	$40,500
Multisection with lot	54,000
Lot only	13,500
Maximum term of loan	20 years

Minimum Cash Down Payment

The minimum cash down payment is 5% of the first $3,000 of the purchase contract amount plus 10% of any excess. A used mobile home with a blue book value of at least the required minimum down payment may be acceptable in lieu of cash down payment.

Interest Rate

Interest on loans may vary depending on the amount and term of the loan.

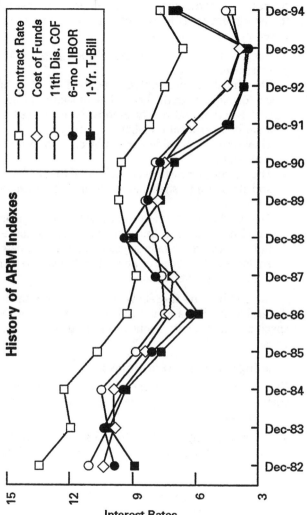

History of ARM Indexes

Legend:
- Contract Rate
- Cost of Funds
- 11th Dis. COF
- 6-mo LIBOR
- 1-Yr. T-Bill

Interest Rates

Dec-82, Dec-83, Dec-84, Dec-85, Dec-86, Dec-87, Dec-88, Dec-89, Dec-90, Dec-91, Dec-92, Dec-93, Dec-94

FHA Title I Manufactured Homes

Effective April 6, 1983, new or existing manufactured homes on a permanent site are eligible for insured financing under Title II, subject to the following criteria:

1. They must have a minimum floor area of 400 square feet.
2. They must be constructed after June 15, 1976, in conformance with the Federal Manufactured Home Construction and Safety Standards, evidenced by an affixed certification label.
3. They must be classified and subject to taxation as real estate.
4. The mortgage must cover the manufactured home and its site and shall have a term not to exceed 30 years.
5. The finished grade elevation beneath the manufactured home or, if a basement is used, the lowest finished exterior grade adjacent to the perimeter enclosure, shall be at or above the 100-year return frequency flood elevation.

In addition to the above general requirements applicable to all manufactured homes, the following specific requirements apply to existing or proposed construction.

Existing Manufactured Homes

Existing units permanently erected on a site more than one year prior to the date of application for mortgage insurance shall

1. be permanently anchored to and supported by permanent footings (anchoring straps or cables affixed to ground anchors other than footings will not meet this requirement);
2. have permanently installed utilities that are protected from freezing;
3. have the space beneath the dwelling properly enclosed as a crawlspace that provides for adequate crawlspace ventilation;

4. have been installed or occupied only at the location for which a mortgage is being requested; and

5. have a site, site improvements and all other features of the mortgaged property not addressed by the Federal Manufactured Home Construction and Safety Standards that meet or exceed applicable provisions of the requirements for existing housing one- to four-family living units.

Existing manufactured homes erected on a site less than one year prior to date of application for mortgage insurance that were not approved by HUD prior to their construction may not have been installed or occupied at any other site and shall comply with items 1 through 8 listed below for proposed construction. Such units are subject to a loan-to-appraised value ratio of 90% unless the unit is covered by a builder's warranty (as listed in item 10 below under proposed construction) and an insured ten-year protection plan accepted by HUD, in which case the unit could qualify for high ratio (97–95%) loans.

Proposed Construction

In addition to the general requirements listed above, manufactured homes shall meet the following requirements to qualify for proposed construction.

1. Be erected with or without a basement on a site-built permanent foundation that meets or exceeds applicable requirements of the Minimum Property Standards for One- and Two-Family Dwellings (MPS)

2. Be permanently attached to that foundation by anchoring devices adequate for all loads identified in the MPS, which includes resistance to ground movements, seismic shakings, potential shearing, overturning and uplift loads caused by wind, and so forth

3. Have the towing hitch or running gear, which includes tongues, axles, brakes, wheels, lights and other parts of the chassis that operate only during transportation, removed

4. Have any crawlspace beneath the manufactured home properly ventilated and enclosed by continuous permanent foundation-type construction designed to resist all forces to which it may be subject without transmitting to the building superstructure movements or any effects caused by frost heave, soil settlement or consolidation, or shrinking or swelling of expansive soils

5. Have the crawlspace perimeter enclosure, if separate from the supporting foundation, adequately secured to the perimeter of the manufactured home and constructed of materials that conform to MPS requirements for foundations

6. Be insulated so that envelope Uo values (the rate of heat loss through floors, walls, windows, doors and ceilings, measured in BTUs per hour per square foot of surface per degrees Fahrenheit difference between indoor and outdoor temperatures) do not exceed:

   a. 0.145 in Climactic Zone I, which includes the states of Alabama, Arkansas, Arizona, California, Florida, Georgia, Hawaii, Louisiana, Mississippi, New Mexico, North Carolina, Oklahoma, South Carolina, Tennessee and Texas.

   b. 0.087 in Climactic Zone III, which includes Alaska, Maine, Michigan, Minnesota, Montana, New Hampshire, North Dakota, South Dakota, Vermont, Wisconsin and Wyoming.

   c. 0.099 in Climactic Zone II, which includes the remainder of the states.

7. Have a site, site improvements and all other features of the mortgaged property not addressed by the Federal Manufactured Home Construction and Safety Standards that meet or exceed applicable requirements of the MPS except paragraph 311-2.2

8. Have had the manufactured home itself braced and stiffened before it leaves the factory to eliminate racking and potential damage during transportation

9. Be eligible for high-ratio (97–95%) financing, for which purpose the beginning of construction will be interpreted as the commencement of on-site work even though the manufactured home itself may have been produced and temporarily stored prior to the date of application for insured financing

10. Have submitted with the application for insured financing an agreement to execute a *Builder's Warranty,* Form HUD 92544, plus an addendum warranting that the manufactured home property substantially complies with the plans and specifications and that the manufactured home sustained no hidden damage during transportation and, if the manufactured home was manufactured in separate sections, the sections were properly joined and sealed. The agreement must provide that upon the sale or conveyance of the dwelling and delivery of the warranty, the seller/builder will promptly furnish the local HUD office with a copy of the warranty. This copy must be signed and dated by the purchaser to evidence that the original warranty was received.

VA FINANCING

VA loans are administered by the U.S. Department of Veterans Affairs (VA).

PURPOSE

VA is authorized to guarantee loans made to eligible veterans for the following purposes:

1. To purchase or construct a dwelling to be owned and occupied by a veteran
2. To purchase a farm on which there is a farm residence to be owned and occupied by a veteran
3. To purchase and occupy a one-family residential unit in a condominium housing development approved by the VA
4. To purchase a manufactured home, permanently affixed to its lot, provided that the laws of the state provide that the manufactured home is considered real property
5. To purchase a manufactured home
6. To repair, alter or improve a dwelling owned and occupied by a veteran and to install energy conservation improvements in a home, including solar heating or solar cooling.

    A veteran who purchases an existing home will be informed of the opportunity to include energy conservation improvements in the financing.
7. To refinance an existing mortgage secured by a lien of record on a dwelling owned and occupied by a veteran as a home
8. To refinance an existing VA loan for the purpose of interest rate reduction

TYPES OF LOANS

1. Fixed rate mortgage
2. Adjustable rate mortgage (ARM)
3. Graduated payment mortgage (GPM)
4. Growing equity mortgage (GEM)
5. Buydown

AUTOMATIC APPROVAL SYSTEM

Lenders are classified by the VA as supervised and nonsupervised. *Supervised lenders* are lending institutions that are subject to examination and supervision by an agency of the United States or of any state or territory, including the District of Columbia. *Nonsupervised lenders* are not supervised by any federal or state agency.

Loans that are automatically guaranteed without requiring specific prior VA approval may be made by supervised lenders and also by nonsupervised lenders that are specifically authorized by the VA to close loans on an automatic basis.

In the event the borrower defaults, the lender is compensated for the loss to the extent of the VA loan guaranty.

UNDERWRITING GUIDELINES

A VA loan may not be guaranteed unless the veteran is a satisfactory credit risk and the contemplated loan payments bear a proper relation to the veteran's present and anticipated income and expenses.

Please refer to the Underwriting Guidelines chapter for information on acceptable types of income and liquid assets available for down payment.

The VA has additional requirements with respect to active duty applicants and recently discharged veterans.

Active duty applicants. A Leave & Earnings Statement (LES) is required in addition to employment verification. Each active duty applicant must be counseled through the use of a Counseling Checklist for Military Home Buyers (VA Form 26-0592).

Recently discharged veterans. Special attention is given to veteran applicants recently discharged or retired who have little or no employment experience other than their military occupation.

DOCUMENTATION

Documents may be obtained before starting the loan application.

- The veteran needs to submit a Request for Determination of Eligibility and Available Loan Entitlement (Form 26-1880) together with discharge or separation papers in order to obtain
  - Certificate of Eligibility (Form 26-8320).
  - The veteran, seller or lender may also request an appraisal of the property to obtain a Certificate of Reasonable Value (Form 26-1843).

Important documents required for loan underwriting include a(n):

- Certificate of Reasonable Value (CRV) (Form 26-1843);
- Certificate of Eligibility (Form 26-8320);
- Uniform Residential Loan Application (URLA) with a revised HUD/VA addendum (Form 26-1802a);
- Loan Analysis (Form 26-6393);
- Original credit report and related documents;
- Request for Verification of Deposit (Form 26-8497a);
- Request for Verification of Employment (or equivalent) (Form 26-8497) and original pay stubs; verification of other income (e.g., tax returns, profit and loss statement and balance sheet);
- Purchase (sales) agreement (earnest money contract);
- Counseling Checklist for Military Home Buyers (if applicable) (Form 26-0592); and
- Interest Rate Reduction Refinancing Worksheet (if applicable) (Form 26-8923).

ELIGIBILITY REQUIREMENTS

Era	Dates	Length of Service
WWII	09/16/40–07/25/47	90 days
Peacetime	07/26/47–06/26/50	181 continuous days
Korean	06/27/50–01/31/55	90 days
Post-Korean	02/01/55–08/04/64	181 continuous days
Vietnam	08/05/64–05/07/75	90 days
Post-Vietnam	05/08/75–09/07/80	181 continuous days
Enlisted	09/08/80–08/01/90	2 years
Officers	10/17/81–08/01/90	2 years
Persian Gulf	08/02/90–undetermined	2 years or period called to active duty, not less than 90 days

Unremarried Surviving Spouse: Eligibility based on spouse's basic qualification.

Spouse of POW or MIA: Eligibility based on spouse's basic qualification.

ENTITLEMENT

In accordance with the VA Housing Act of 1970, all loan guaranty entitlement is available until used (it does not expire), whether derived from World War II, the Korean War or any other period. The act also revived unused, expired loan guaranty entitlement.

Restoration (Substitution) of Entitlement

The Veterans Housing Act of 1974 permits *restoration* (also called reinstatement) of a veteran's entitlement to the full extent of the current maximum guaranty if the property has been disposed of and the loan paid in full, or if the property is sold to another eligible, creditworthy veteran with entitlement equal to or greater than the loan's guaranty amount, and who assumes the VA loan and agrees to substitute his or her entitlement for the seller's.

Under the Veterans Benefits Improvement Act of 1994, a veteran's entitlement may be restored *one time only* if the veteran has repaid the prior VA loan in full, even if he or she is not disposing of the property securing the loan. Future restoration requires disposal of the property financed with that loan.

Remaining (Available or Partial) Entitlement

A veteran who has used up his or her entitlement and wishes to keep and rent the VA-financed home or who sold it without substitution of entitlement by another creditworthy veteran, or to a nonveteran, can still obtain a VA loan to finance the purchase of a new home by using any remaining entitlement. A veteran who used his or her entitlement several years ago is likely to have remaining entitlement now because VA guaranties have increased as property values have increased. (See the table below.) Remaining entitlement can be determined by subtracting the amount of entitlement used for prior guaranteed loans from the current maximum guaranty.

Maximum Guaranty

The VA sets no maximum loan ceilings but issues maximum loan guaranties. A veteran is entitled to the current maximum guaranty minus any entitlement used for prior guaranteed loans that have not been restored. As property values have increased over the years, so have VA guaranties, as shown in the following table.

History of Maximum Guaranties

Beginning of program	$ 2,000
12/28/45	4,000
4/20/50	7,500
5/07/68	12,500
12/31/74	17,500
10/01/78	25,000
10/01/80	27,500
2/01/88	46,000
10/13/94	50,750

Current Maximum Guaranty, as of December 1994

Loan Amount	Maximum Guaranty
Up to $45,000	50% of loan amount
$45,000 to $56,250	$22,500
$56,251 to $144,000	40% of loan amount
$144,001 to $184,000	25% of loan amount
$184,001 to $203,000*	25% of loan amount

Loans made for the purchase or construction of a home, to purchase a residential unit in a condominium or to refinance an existing VA-guaranteed loan for interest rate reduction. Cash-out refinances are limited to a maximum $36,000 guaranty.

Maximum Obtainable VA Loans

The VA does not set maximum loan amounts, except for the requirement that loans cannot exceed the CRV or the purchase price, whichever is less.

The veteran can obtain a larger loan by making a down payment. The loan amount is arrived at by multiplying the sum of down payment and guaranty by four (see item 2 of the following example).

Examples

1. Veteran Louise Brading bought a home in 1982 and used her maximum entitlement of $27,500. She sold her home in 1987 to a buyer who took title to the property subject to the existing VA loan. In May 1988, the veteran wanted to purchase a new home with a CRV of $80,000. What was the maximum obtainable VA loan?

   Answer: The veteran was entitled to the maximum guaranty of $46,000 (as of May 1988) minus used entitlement of $27,500 = $18,500. The maximum obtainable VA loan, therefore, was 4 × $18,500 = $74,000.

2. Veteran Brading (from the previous example) has saved $10,000, which she wants to use as down payment on her new house. How does this affect her maximum obtainable VA loan?

Answer: Her available entitlement of $18,500 plus her $10,000 down payment = $28,500, multiplied by 4 = $114,000, the maximum obtainable loan.

3. A veteran wants to purchase a house for $210,000. What is the maximum obtainable VA loan, and how much would he or she need for down payment?

   Answer: The maximum loan is four times the maximum guaranty of $50,750 = $203,000. Her or his down payment would be $210,000 − $203,000 = $7,000.

4. Veteran Larry Lombard bought a home in 1979 and used his entitlement of $25,000. In 1995, he sold his home to veteran Miller, who agreed to substitute his available entitlement for that of Lombard's. Lombard wants to buy a house with a CRV of $190,000. What is the maximum obtainable VA loan?

   Answer: Because Lombard's entitlement is reinstated, his available entitlement is the applicable guaranty of $50,750. The maximum loan obtainable would be $4 × $50,570 = $203,000 if it were not limited by the CRV of $190,000.

5. Had veteran Lombard (from the previous example) sold his home with release of liability, but to a nonveteran, what would his available entitlement be? What would the maximum obtainable VA loan be for the purchase of a home with a CRV of $190,000?

   Answer: Lombard's available entitlement would be the applicable guaranty of $50,750 minus the used entitlement of $25,000 = $25,750. The maximum obtainable VA loan would be $4 × 25,750 = $103,000.

ENERGY EFFICIENT MORTGAGES

The VA authorizes an addition to the purchase loan for the cost of energy efficient improvements up to $3,000, or $6,000 if the increase in the monthly payments for principal and interest does not exceed the likely reduction on monthly utility costs resulting from the energy efficiency improvements.

For a refinancing loan, the loan may not exceed 90% of the CRV plus the cost of the energy efficient improvements (CRV × .90 + cost of improvements).

Example

If a veteran has $20,000 remaining entitlement and applies for a loan of $80,000, plus $6,000 in energy efficient improvements, the VA will guarantee 25% of the full loan amount of $86,000. Thus, the dollar amount of the guaranty will be $21,500 even though the veteran's entitlement is only $20,000. (See Model Energy Code.)

QUALIFYING GUIDELINES

Lenders must follow two separate qualification guidelines based on (1) ratio of total obligations to income and (2) residual income (cash flow) for family support.

Ratio of Total Obligations to Income

The ratio is determined by dividing the total monthly obligations by gross income. Total monthly obligations include housing expenses (principal, interest, taxes, insurance, maintenance, utilities, homeowners' fees and special assessments) and recurring obligations (payments on debts with more than six months to go and other monthly obligations, such as alimony and child support.) Generally, the ratio should not exceed 41%.

Twenty Percent Rule

If the residual income (cash flow) exceeds the guidelines by at least 20%, lenders may approve loans with ratios in excess of 41%.

Example

Veteran Larry Halladay and his wife, Joan, are interested in buying a home and want to know the VA loan amount Larry can qualify for. Larry's monthly gross income is $3,500. They are making $200 monthly payments on a car with ten months to go and have other monthly obligations of $250.

Monthly gross income	$3,500
Multiply by ratio	× .41
Remaining for total obligations	$1,435
Recurring obligations	− 450
Remaining for housing expense	$985
Assume that taxes, insurance, utilities and maintenance amount to	− 125
Remaining for principal & interest	$860
At a VA rate of 7%, the veteran qualifies for a loan of about $141,000	

Residual Income (Cash Flow) for Family Support

Residual income is determined by subtracting from the monthly gross income not only the total monthly obligations (including housing expenses and recurring obligations), but also all federal, state and local taxes. A family's residual income should be at least the applicable amount in the following table.

The table shows minimum residual income for family expenditures of such standard items as food, health care, apparel and gasoline. The amounts are based on the loan amount, the region of the country where the veteran lives and family size.

Example

The Halladays from the previous example live in Phoenix, Arizona, and have three children. They saw a house they like with a CRV of $150,000. The payments, including principal and interest at 7% for a $150,000 loan, would be about $917. At the 41% total obligations-to-income ratio, they would not be able to qualify (the maximum for principal and interest in the previous example was only $860). However, they may have a chance to qualify for a higher loan if their

Residual Family Incomes by Region

Loan Amounts Below $70,000

Family size	North-east	Mid-west	South	West
1	$375	$367	$367	$409
2	629	616	616	686
3	758	742	742	826
4	854	835	835	930
5	886	867	867	965
6	961	942	942	1,040
7	1,031	1,017	1,017	1,115

Loan Amounts of $70,000 up

Family size	North-east	Mid-west	South	West
1	$433	$424	$424	$472
2	726	710	710	791
3	874	855	855	952
4	986	964	964	1,074
5	1,021	999	999	1,113
6	1,101	1,079	1,079	1,193
7	1,181	1,159	1,159	1,273

Northeast: Connecticut, Maine, Massachusetts, New Hampshire, New Jersey, New York, Pennsylvania, Rhode Island, Vermont

Midwest: Illinois, Indiana, Iowa, Kansas, Michigan, Minnesota, Missouri, Nebraska, North Dakota, Ohio, South Dakota, Wisconsin

South: Alabama, Arkansas, Delaware, District of Columbia, Florida, Georgia, Kentucky, Louisiana, Maryland, Mississippi, North Carolina, Oklahoma, Puerto Rico, South Carolina, Tennessee, Texas, Virginia, West Virginia

West: Alaska, Arizona, California, Colorado, Hawaii, Idaho, Montana, Nevada, New Mexico, Oregon, Utah, Washington, Wyoming residual income exceeds the guidelines by at least 20%.

Here is how to calculate their residual income:

Monthly gross income	$3,500
Principal and interest for a $150,000 loan at 7%	– 917
Property taxes, insurance, utilities, maintenance	– 140
Recurring obligations	– 450
Federal, state and local taxes	– 600
Residual income	$1,393

The minimum residual income for a loan in excess of $70,000 for a family of five living in Arizona is $1,113. Because the Halladays' residual income exceeds that amount by $280, in fact by more than 20%, they should have a good chance to qualify, providing, of course, that their credit history is satisfactory.

Compensating Factors

No single factor is a final determinant in an applicant's qualification for a VA-guaranteed loan. The residual income and ratio guidelines are never intended to be absolute determinants in deciding whether a VA loan should be approved but must be used only with discretion in conjunction with other factors. These factors become especially important when reviewing marginal loans with respect to residual income or the debt-to-income ratio. The following are examples of compensating factors.

- Excellent long-term credit
- Conservative use of consumer credit
- Minimal consumer debt
- Long-term employment
- Significant liquid assets
- Down payment or the existence of equity in refinancing loans
- Little or no increase in shelter expense
- Military benefits
- Satisfactory home ownership experience

- High residual income
- Low debt-to-income ratio

The VA's intention to advance the veterans' best interests is perhaps best expressed in this advice to lenders: "When making a credit determination for a VA-guaranteed loan, keep in mind that a veteran's benefit is involved. However, it serves no purpose to approve or make a loan to a veteran who would be unable to meet the repayment terms or is not a satisfactory credit risk. Such an approval would be, in fact, a disservice since it could well result in the veteran losing the home, a debt being owed to the U.S. government, and an adverse effect on the veteran's credit standing."

LOCK-IN AGREEMENTS

The VA will accept agreements between lender and borrower to lock in an interest rate when the VA maximum interest rate is expected to change prior to settlement.

Lock-in agreements must be in writing and unconditional, except for contingencies for approval of the property and of the borrower's income and credit. The agreement must be signed by both the veteran and the lender. The agreement must be for a specific rate of interest and must not exceed the effective rate on the date of the agreement.

The agreement may specify either the interest rate only or the interest rate and the number of discount points payable by the seller (or by the veteran in case of refinancing loans).

Lock-in agreements are typically valid for 45, 60 or 90 days. Prior to the expiration of a lock-in agreement, a lender and borrower may agree to extend the duration of the agreement.

No fee or charge may be imposed against the veteran for an interest rate lock-in agreement.

FEATURES AND REQUIREMENTS OF VA LOANS

Occupancy

Veterans are required to certify that they intend to occupy the home as their principal place of residence. Occupancy by the spouse of a veteran on active duty as a member of the armed forces meets the requirement.

In the event the veteran moves to another home at a later date, he or she may rent the old home financed by the VA-guaranteed loan.

Down Payment

No down payment is required by the VA except on GPMs. However, in the event the veteran agrees to a purchase price in excess of the CRV, the veteran is required to pay cash for such excess. The lender may require that the sum of the available entitlement and the down payment be at least 25% of the CRV.

Secondary Financing

The VA does not preclude second mortgages in conjunction with the VA first loan to obtain funds for closing costs, provided the following conditions are met.

1. The sum of the VA and the second loans may not exceed the amount of the CRV.
2. The veteran meets the qualification requirements based on payments of both loans.
3. The interest rate on the second loan does not impose an undue burden on the veteran.
4. The conditions of the second loan do not impose an undue burden on the veteran.

Interest Rate

Effective October 28, 1992, for the duration of a three-year test, VA home loan interest rates were freed from VA control and replaced by floating interest rates negotiated between veteran and lender.

Discount Points

Effective October 28, 1992, for the duration of a three-year test, discount points may be paid by the veteran for all types of VA loans and are negotiable between veteran, seller and lender. Discount points may not be included in the loan.

Closing Costs

Lenders may not charge a veteran-borrower any fees not included in the following schedule. Closing costs and prepaid items may not be included in the loan, except for refinancing loans.

Schedule of Allowable Fees for Loans under U.S.C. 1810

1. Appraisal and compliance inspection fees, and special inspections at request of veteran to satisfy concerns about condition of the property
2. Recording fees
3. Credit report
4. That portion of taxes, assessments and similar items for the current year chargeable to the borrower and the initial lump-sum payment for the tax and insurance account
5. Hazard insurance
6. Survey, if required by lender or veteran
7. Title examination and title insurance
8. VA funding fee

Permissible Charges and Fees for Refinancing Loans

1. Reasonable discount points
2. Title insurance (no escrow fees)
3. Recording fees for release of prior loans
4. Cost of repair and inspections
5. Cost of termite inspections and clearances

VA Funding Fee Table

Loan Type	Active Duty or Veteran	National Guard/ Reservists
Purchase/ construction 0% down	2.00%	2.75%
Purchase/ construction 5% down	1.50	2.25
Purchase/ construction 10% down	1.25	2.00
Cash-out refinance	2.00	2.75
Rate reduction refinance	0.50	0.50
Native American direct loan	1.25	1.25
Manufactured homes	1.00	1.00
Assumption	0.50	0.50
Vendee loans	1.00	1.00
Second or subsequent use—Does not apply on IRRRs or on purchase or construction loans with 5% or more down payment	3.00	3.00

Maximum Term of Loan

The maximum term of VA loans is the economic life of the property not to exceed 30 years and 32 days. In most cases, this allows for the first payment not later than 60 days after closing and an even 360 payments.

Monthly Payments

All VA loans, with the exception of term loans, GPMs and GEMs, must be amortized with approximately equal monthly payments. Under VA financing, it is the lender's responsibility to ascertain that property taxes and hazard insurance premiums are paid when due. Lenders, therefore, will insist that the monthly payments include proportionate amounts for taxes and insurance.

Trust Fund

Lenders deposit the property tax and hazard insurance portion of the monthly payments into a trust fund from which to pay taxes and insurance premiums when due. In order to ascertain that sufficient funds are in the trust fund to make the first tax payment after the loan has been funded, the lender requires that the buyer deposit a certain sum into the trust fund at closing. The VA has revised its procedures with respect to surpluses in escrow accounts so that they are in line with the Cranston-Gonzalez National Affordable Housing Act of 1990. The new policy allows a loanholder/servicer to release surplus escrow accounts offering borrowers a choice of options: (1) a lump-sum refund, (2) the surplus to be used to reduce or pay the next monthly payment(s) or (3) the surplus to be used to reduce principal or several other options.

Refinancing

The VA allows two types of refinancing: (1) refinancing of an existing mortgage secured by a lien on a dwelling owned and occupied by the veteran and (2) an interest rate reduction refinancing loan (IRRRL), which permits restoration of used entitlement.

With interest rate reduction refinancing loans, the lender may pay all closing costs and set an interest rate high enough to recover the advance of costs (but the rate must be lower than the loan being refinanced). A fixed rate loan may be refinanced with an ARM as long as the initial ARM rate is lower than the fixed rate.

Under the Veterans Benefits Improvement Act of 1994, veterans may obtain an IRRRL to convert their existing VA-guaranteed ARM to fixed rate loans even if the interest rate is higher than the rate of the ARM. The interest rate on the new fixed rate loan may be negotiated between the veteran and the lender.

Under the act, IRRRLs may include additional funds for energy efficiency improvements.

The table on page A-132 shows additional features of IRRRLs.

Comparison of VA Loan Refinancing

	Liens Other than VA	IRRRL*
Guaranty entitlement required	Yes	25% of loan, regardless of guaranty on the original VA loan, even if loan exceeds $184,000
Cash to veteran	Yes	No
Loan limit	90% of CRV plus funding fee	VA loan balance + closing costs + 0.5% funding fee, but no discount points
Must veteran own property?	Yes	Yes
Must veteran occupy property?	Yes	No (must have once occupied)
Maximum loan term	30 years + 32 days	Existing VA loan term + 10 yrs, not to exceed 30 yrs and 32 days
Lien of record required	Yes	Yes
OK to finance other liens	Yes	No
Appraisal required	Yes	No
Credit package required	Yes	No

The program permits restoration of used entitlement for the purpose of refinancing the same property with a new VA-guaranteed loan.

Veteran's Liability

Even though the lender is compensated by the VA for any loss up to the amount of the guaranty, the veteran remains liable for the full amount of his or her debt to the U.S. government in the event of default and foreclosure.

Assumption

Prior approval. The VA requires prior approval to any transfer of property securing VA loans committed or closed after March 1, 1988, unless the loan is paid in full at the time of transfer.

VA loans for which commitments were made before March 1, 1988, remain freely assumable, even by nonveteran buyers.

Release of liability. Upon approval of the prospective purchaser as an acceptable credit risk and upon full assumption of liability for repayment of the loan by the transferee and completion of the sale, the veteran is released from personal liability to the government.

Substitution of entitlement. Receiving an approved release of liability will not restore the veteran-seller's loan guaranty entitlement unless the purchaser is a veteran who has sufficient entitlement to substitute for that of the seller and consents to use his or her entitlement to the same extent the entitlement of the veteran-transferor had been used originally. In addition, the veteran-buyer must certify that he or she will occupy the property as his or her principal residence.

Prepayment. There is no prepayment penalty if a VA loan is partially or fully prepaid at any time.

Transfers Requiring No VA Approval

1. Creation of a lien subordinate to the lender's mortgage, which does not transfer right of occupancy
2. Creation of a purchase money security interest for household appliances
3. Transfer by devise, descent or operation of law on the death of a joint tenant or tenant by the entirety
4. Granting of a lease of three years or less not containing an option to purchase
5. Transfer to a relative resulting from the death of a borrower
6. Transfer when the spouse or children of the borrower become joint owner(s) of the property with the borrower
7. Transfer resulting from divorce, legal separation or property settlement
8. Transfer into an inter vivos trust, which does not relate to a transfer of occupancy rights, in which the borrower remains a beneficiary

9. Installment contracts of sale calling for transfer of title after a certain period of time, provided that VA approval is required at time of actual transfer

Joint Loans

To determine whether income and credit requirements are met for joint loans, the VA considers the income and credit of both the veteran and the other person joining in title. Income and assets of each party are combined to determine whether there is sufficient total income available to repay the loan (if the veteran alone cannot qualify) and adequate liquidity to cover any required down payment. This policy also applies to loans in which two or more veterans intend to use their entitlement and take title jointly. The only exception is a joint loan involving a veteran and a nonveteran who is not the veteran's spouse when the veteran's income must be sufficient to repay at least that portion of the loan allocable to the veteran's interest in the property and the nonveteran's income must be adequate to cover the balance of the payment obligation.

Option Agreement

The following agreement must be included in or presented as an amendment to purchase agreements providing for VA-guaranteed financing.

In the event of VA financing, it is expressly agreed that, notwithstanding any other provisions of this contract, the Buyer shall not incur any penalty by forfeiture of earnest money or otherwise be obligated to complete the purchase of the property, described herein, if the contract purchase price or cost exceeds the Reasonable Value of the property established by the VA. The Buyer shall, however, have the privilege and option of proceeding with the consummation of this contract without regards to the amount of the Reasonable Value established by the VA. Escrow fee to be paid by Seller.

MANUFACTURED-HOME FINANCING

A manufactured home that has been permanently affixed to the land on a permanent foundation is eligible for guaranty as is any other home. The unit must have been built in conformance with the Federal Manufactured Home Construction and Safety Standards or must comply with the VA's minimum property requirements as applicable. The home and land must be taxed as real property under each state's real property laws. The same interest rates, loan amounts, and so forth, are specified as on any other VA home loan.

The VA is authorized to guarantee loans for the following purposes:

1. the purchase of a manufactured home to be permanently affixed to a lot already owned by the veteran,
2. the purchase of a manufactured home and a lot to which the home will be permanently affixed,
3. the refinance of an existing VA-guaranteed loan which is secured by a manufactured home permanently affixed to a lot owned by the veteran, and
4. the refinance of an existing loan made for the purchase of, and secured by, a manufactured home permanently affixed to a lot and the purchase of the lot to which the home is affixed.

Manufactured homes are eligible for guaranty by the VA under a separate program that includes

- a loan of 95% of the purchase price,
- a maximum guaranty of $20,00,
- a maximum guarantee of 40% of the loan,
- a maximum interest rate permitted that is higher than that for normal VA loans and
- maximum loan terms of 15 to 25 years.

ADJUSTABLE RATE MORTGAGE (ARM)

Effective October 28, 1992, for the duration of a three-year test, VA's ARM is structured identical to the current FHA ARM, section 251.

VAARM loan applications are underwritten at one percentage point above the initial interest rate agreed upon by the lender and the veteran, as stated on the URLA. In cases with marginal income that are strong in other areas, the lower payment required by the initial rate may be considered as one compensating factor to support approval.

GRADUATED PAYMENT MORTGAGE (GPM)

Since November 1981, the VA has been authorized to guaranty graduated payment mortgages, allowing lower monthly payments than for a fixed payment mortgage during the first year and increasing annually by a fixed percentage for a stated graduation period. At the end of the graduation period, the payments remain level for the remainder of the loan. The reduction in the initial monthly payments is accomplished by deferring a portion of the interest due and adding that interest to the principal balance. This causes the outstanding balance to increase during the graduation period, an effect known as negative amortization.

Provisions Applying to VA GPMs

- The initial principal amount of the loan may not exceed the reasonable value of the property at the time the loan is made.
- The principal amount of the loan thereafter (including the amount of all interest deferred and added to principal) may not at any time be scheduled to exceed the projected value of the property.
- The projected value of the property may be calculated by increasing the reasonable value of the property from the time the loan is made at a rate not in excess of 2.5% per year, but not to exceed 115% of the reasonable value. This value projection is applicable only to new construction or existing homes not previously occupied.

- GPMs are limited to the acquisition of single-family units. This includes the purchase of new or existing homes, condominium units in VA-approved projects and existing homes for which the loan also includes funds for energy conservation improvements.

Amortization Plan

Plan III under FHA Section 245 is the only amortization plan authorized for VA GPMs. This plan provides for increasing loan payments at a rate of 7.5% per year for the first five years, increasing at annual intervals. At the beginning of the sixth year, the payments become level for the remaining term of the loan.

Down Payment

Because the outstanding loan balance increases during the graduation period, a down payment is required to prevent the loan balance from exceeding the CRV. The down payment must be paid in cash from the veteran's own resources. For existing homes, the amount of the down payment is equal to the highest amount of negative amortization that occurs during the graduation period. For new homes, the maximum VA GPM loan amount is 97.5% of the CRV or the purchase price, whichever is less, at the time the loan is made.

Computing the Amount of Down Payment

1. Find the GPM factor for the applicable interest rate on the following table.

Int. Rate	GPM Factor	Int. Rate	GPM Factor
7¾%	1.0280728		
8	1.0309550	12%	1.0787075
8¼	1.0341945	12¼	1.0815692
8½	1.0373748	12½	1.0843740
8¾	1.0404961	12¾	1.0871336
9	1.0435617	13	1.0898424
9¼	1.0465678	13¼	1.0925044
9½	1.0495186	13½	1.0951202
9¾	1.0524197	13¾	1.0976904
10	1.0552637	14	1.1002174
10¼	1.0580559	14¼	1.1026993
10½	1.0607998	14½	1.1051467
10¾	1.0635966	14¾	1.1075476
11	1.0667347	15	1.1099107
11¼	1.0698110	15¼	1.1122353
11½	1.0728295	15½	1.1145245
11¾	1.0757962	15¾	1.1167789

2. Find the maximum original loan amount by dividing the reasonable value of the property by the GPM factor, and round down to the nearest dollar.
3. The minimum down payment equals the reasonable value minus the maximum original loan amount found in Step 2.

Credit Underwriting

In determining whether a veteran-applicant meets statutory income requirements for a GPM, the loan analysis is based on the first year's payment only when there are strong indications that the income to support the application can be reasonably expected to keep pace with increases in monthly mortgage payments. In the absence of such strong indications, the

GPM will be underwritten based on the payment that would apply if the loan were a fixed rate loan at the current maximum VA interest rate.

BUYDOWN PROGRAM

Under the buydown program, sellers (usually builders) may temporarily reduce buyers' loan payments during the initial years of a mortgage by depositing buydown funds into a third party escrow without recourse. The buydown funds must be beyond the reach of prospective creditors of the builder-seller, lender or borrower. The funds must be used to reduce the buyer's loan payment and may not be used to pay past due monthly loan payments. The maximum loan may not exceed the CRV and funding fee.

Credit Underwriting

Underwriting based on full payment amount. Credit underwriting for loans with buydown plans is based on the full payment amount, except when there are strong indicators that the purchaser's income used to support the application can reasonably be expected to keep pace with the increases in the monthly mortgage payments.

Underwriting based on the first year's payment amount. For loans based on the first year's payment amount (the buydown rate), there must be strong indications that income used to support the application will increase to cover the yearly increases in loan payments and the following criteria must be met.

Assistance payments will run for a minimum of one year. Scheduled reductions in the assistance payments must occur annually on the anniversary of the first mortgage payment. The annual payment increases must be in equal, or approximately equal, amounts. Alternately, when the subsidy is calculated by setting the veteran's initial payments to a lower interest rate, the reduction in the assistance payments may be accomplished through equal annual increases in that interest rate.

SELLER CONCESSIONS

For VA purposes, a seller concession is defined as anything of value added to the transaction by the builder-seller for which the buyer pays nothing additional and that the builder-seller is not customarily expected or required to pay or provide.

Such concessions include payment by the seller of the buyer's VA funding fee, prepaid taxes and insurance, gifts such as a television set or microwave oven, extra discount points paid to provide temporary interest rate buydowns or the payoff of credit balances on behalf of the buyer.

Any concession or combination of concessions that exceed 4% of the established reasonable value of the property is considered excessive for VA loan purposes. Normal discount points and payment of the buyer's closing costs are not considered a concession for purposes of determining if total concessions are within the established limit.

SELLER FINANCING

Although seller financing may be in the best interest of a seller in certain circumstances, such as spreading tax on profit from the sale over a number of years or for investment reasons, it is usually done to induce a sale by assisting the buyer in some way.

Seller financing can take many different forms, including purchase money mortgage, buydown, wraparound mortgage, lease with option to purchase, installment sale or various degrees of seller-paid contributions.

PURCHASE MONEY MORTGAGE

When a seller accepts a note that is secured by a mortgage or deed of trust on the property for all or part of the purchase price, it is referred to as a purchase money mortgage.

Primary Seller Financing

A seller whose property is free and clear of any mortgages or other liens may consider carrying a first note secured by a mortgage or deed of trust on the property, or a contract of sale, either for tax reasons (as described in the tax section of the *Realty Bluebook®* under the heading Installment Sales) or as an investment.

Although the seller may benefit from financing the entire purchase, the buyer benefits in saving origination fees, discount points, flexibility in terms to suit the buyer's needs and more lenient qualification. Consequently, a seller who offers these benefits can usually command a higher price.

Secondary Seller Financing

Secondary seller financing is generally used as a marketing tool to supplement a buyer's required cash for down payment and closing costs but also to help a buyer qualify for a new first loan from an institutional lender.

In structuring the second purchase money mortgage, the broker needs to be aware of restrictions imposed by Fannie Mae, FHA and VA as shown in the following summary of requirements for second loans. (See Summary of Requirements for Second Loans.)

Examples

A particular buyer has 10% cash for down payment but cannot qualify for a new first loan. The seller offers to carry a second mortgage with the following types of financing:

- Conventional financing. The seller offers to carry a second for 15% of the appraised value, thus reducing the LTV of the first loan from 90% to 75% (the maximum LTV allowed with secondary financing). Additionally, the seller accepts interest payments only and a balloon payment in five years (permitted with conventional financing). The result is that the sum of monthly payments on both first and second is reduced to enable the buyer to qualify.
- FHA financing. A similar scenario could be structured with the combined amount of first and second limited to the maximum FHA loan amount (see chapter on FHA Financing under the heading Calculating Maximum FHA Loan) and the balloon payment not due before ten years.
- The VA may approve secondary seller financing provided that the sum of the VA loan and the second does not exceed the certificate of reasonable value and that the interest rate of the second does not exceed the rate of the VA loan.

  Note that in all three cases the buyer must qualify for the combined payments of first and second loans.

Seller's Risk and Broker's Liability

Needless to say, the seller's risk in carrying a mortgage increases proportionately with the amount of the note, the buyer's cash investment, the degree of the buyer's creditworthiness, the amount of periodic payments and the maturity of the loan. The broker structuring the transaction (down payment, the buyer's creditworthiness and qualification, interest rate, loan term, balloon payment, insurance coverage, etc.) accepts liability and should take the utmost care in the performance of his or her duties. A seller entering into such a sale should be aware of the effect the transaction may have on his or her tax liability, and the real estate broker or agent should advise the seller to consult his or her legal counsel before entering into such a transaction. Such disclaimer should also be included in the purchase agreement. (See Contract Clause section.)

Market for Purchase Money Mortgages

Notes secured by a first or second deed of trust (or mortgage) on real property are negotiable instruments and have a cash value that is normally lower than the face value of the note. The difference between the face value and cash value of the note is called the discount. Brokers can usually find private investors who buy such notes, provided the borrower's equity in the property and his or her creditworthiness meet the investor's standards, at a discount in order to realize a required return (yield) on their cash investment.

The discount needed to obtain the required yield depends upon the following terms included in the note

1. interest rate;
2. payoff rate (the amount of monthly payments expressed as a percentage of the face value of the note);
3. due date (the date the entire then remaining balance becomes due and payable in full, referred to as balloon payment); and
4. transferability (whether the note includes a due-on-sale clause).

Equity is the difference between the fair market value of the property and the total amount of outstanding loans against the property. Equity, therefore, represents the capital investment a borrower has in the property. Equity is an essential factor in determining the marketability of a note. The smaller the equity, the greater the risk for the holder of the note. When the equity is too small, foreclosure and resale costs could easily exceed the equity in the event the borrower were to default.

Example

1. Smith purchases a home from Brown for $100,000.
2. Smith obtains a new conventional loan of $70,000 for 30 years payable at $829.50 per month including interest at 14% per annum.
3. Smith executes a note secured by a second deed of trust in favor of Brown for $10,000, payable at $150 per month or more including interest at 13%, due and payable eight years from date of note or upon sale of the property.
4. Smith pays Brown the balance of $20,000 in cash.
5. Smith has a good credit rating, has no current debts, has a dependable monthly salary of $2,000 and has been employed for five years.
6. Three weeks after close of escrow, Brown decides to sell the note and asks his broker how much cash he can get for the note.
7. In view of the terms of the note, Smith's credit standing, his income and his equity in the property, the broker finds investor Green who offers to buy the note at a discount of 10%, giving him a yield of about 16% on his investment.

To protect the buyer in the above example, the broker structured the terms of the second loan so that the buyer would be able to make the balloon payment from the proceeds of refinancing the first loan at the time the balloon payment becomes due. This is demonstrated in the following scenario.

Eight years after purchasing the property, Smith faces a balloon payment of $3,025. The unpaid balance of the first loan at the end of eight years is $67,760. The combined total outstanding balance of first and second loans is, therefore, $70,785, which is the amount needed to refinance at the end of eight years to eliminate the second loan. Note that this is about the same amount as that of the original first loan.

As an alternative, Smith could have eliminated any balloon payment by increasing his monthly payments on the second mortgage from $150 to $168.

WRAPAROUND OR ALL-INCLUSIVE DEED OF TRUST

A *wraparound mortgage* includes the remaining balance of an existing first mortgage (to which it is subordinate) plus an additional amount carried by the seller. It is similar to a contract of sale, except that title to the property is actually transferred and may be insured by a policy of title insurance. When a deed of trust is used rather than a mortgage instrument, it is usually referred to as an all-inclusive deed of trust, but has also been known as a hold-harmless, overriding or overlapping deed of trust.

When Can a Wraparound Not Be Used?

A wraparound cannot be used unless there is no acceleration or any other alienation clause in any of the mortgages or deeds of trust that are to remain on the subject property. Sometimes these may be removed by agreement with the beneficiary.

When Is It Desirable To Use a Wraparound?

1. When there is a locked-in loan on the subject property
2. When the seller is anxious to sell but has a poor-risk buyer with a small down payment who is willing to purchase the property
3. When there is an overpriced property and the seller is firm as to the price, but not as to the terms of sale

4. When the seller does not want to lose the benefit of a present low-interest loan but is still anxious to sell, thereby retaining the use of funds already provided by the present financing
5. When there is little time to shop for loans and/or little likelihood of the new buyer qualifying for same
6. When there is insufficient cash down payment offered and the seller must carry back a large purchase-money trust deed

Advantages to Seller

1. Retains the good terms of the present financing should it become necessary to repossess the subject property at some future date
2. Probably is the only practical way of disposing of a property that has a locked-in loan against it without being forced to negotiate with the same lender for additional funds or for loan assumption
3. Can get a much higher *effective interest* on the true value of the all-inclusive trust deed
4. Can cash out the all-inclusive trust deed at a lower discount rate than a similar purchase money trust deed because of the higher effective rate of interest generated
5. Can get a higher price for the property because seller can afford to give better terms on the balance (apparent terms)
6. Better for the seller than a contract of sale because property may be repossessed by trustee sale, while a contract sometimes requires a court judgment in order to be canceled

Advantages to Buyer

1. Can acquire a much larger property for the same down payment
2. Can now purchase property for which he or she normally could not qualify were it necessary to apply for new financing

3. Can generate greater tax benefits through adjustment of price and terms
4. Saves cost of new loan appraisal fees, new loan points and loan escrow fees
5. Saves time required to make application, or shop, for new loans
6. Can tailor the cash spendable return to suit his or her needs more easily
7. Gets title to the subject property with an owner's policy of title insurance; while with a contract of sale, he or she would not
8. Can afford to overpay for the property by adjusting the terms of the all-inclusive trust deed to compensate for the overpayment
9. Is responsible for only one loan payment, rather than two or more

Precautions for Protection of Seller

1. Impound sufficient funds to cover cost of taxes and insurance.
2. Have the right to approve all leases that might have a detrimental effect on the value of the property (i.e., leases with prepaid rent provisions where the buyer may take the funds and then walk away from the property).
3. Provide for the availability of funds when required to meet due dates of the senior loans remaining on the property.
4. Limit or forbid the use of another all-inclusive trust deed on resale.
5. Have the right to refinance the property at any time, or at a specified time should certain events occur (i.e., expiration of lock-in clause on existing loan).
6. Assume the present loans at some time.
7. Spell out the exact circumstances that will bring about default, the exact amount that will be in default and the exact procedure to be followed upon foreclosure.

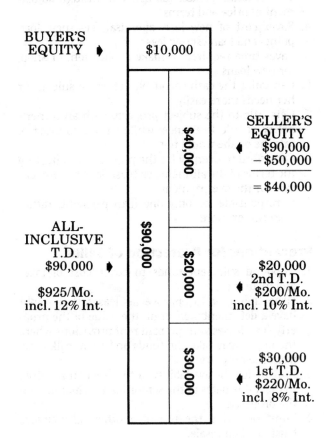

BUYER'S EQUITY → $10,000

SELLER'S EQUITY
$90,000
− $50,000
_____
= $40,000

$40,000

ALL-INCLUSIVE T.D. $90,000 →

$90,000

$925/Mo. incl. 12% Int.

$20,000

$20,000
2nd T.D.
$200/Mo.
incl. 10% Int.

$30,000

$30,000
1st T.D.
$220/Mo.
incl. 8% Int.

Seller gets $12\% \times \$90{,}000 = \$10{,}800$ Int.
and pays $10\% \times \$20{,}000$
        $8\% \times \$30{,}000 = \$\ 4{,}400$ Int.
Seller nets . . . . $\$\ 6{,}400$ Int.
on T.D. Equity of \$40,000 or

16% Effective Interest

Precautions for Protection of Buyer

1. Have some method of preventing the property from being lost through the failure of the seller to meet the payments or other terms of the senior loans of record.
2. Desirable to make the payments of the all-inclusive trust deed payable to a neutral collection agency such as a bank or to a trust specifically set up for that purpose. Cost of setting up these arrangements must be considered, as well as who shall be billed for same.
3. Should the payment on the all-inclusive trust deed not be sufficient to cover the payments needed to pay the senior remaining loans of record, some provision to provide them.
4. Desirable for the buyer to have the right to assume one or all of the senior loans of record upon a certain event, such as a lump-sum payment of X dollars.

Procedure to Set Up an All-Inclusive Trust Deed

1. Examine the existing trust deeds and notes, and ascertain the following:
   a. Is there any acceleration clause that becomes effective upon the change of ownership of the property? (Alienation clause).
      NOTE: If there is, then stop right here. The all-inclusive may not be used unless this clause is removed. You might be able to pay it off, or renegotiate it. (See also note at end of chapter.)
   b. Note the exact balance of each trust deed as of the projected transfer date.
   c. Note the monthly payments, interest rate and dates and amounts of any balloon payments due (both partial balloon payments or final).
   d. Determine the amount of monthly payments necessary to make the payments on all of the senior loans in addition to funds necessary to cover the taxes and insurances impounds (if required by seller).

2. Decide what the monthly payments on the all-inclusive trust deed shall be and draw up a schedule for same, including
   a. total value of all-inclusive (total price minus down payment);
   b. interest rate to be charged on the all-inclusive trust deed; and
   c. partial balloon payment or total balloon payments and due dates of remaining senior loans.
3. Decide who is to collect and disburse the payments on the all-inclusive trust deed: seller, bank, other collection agency, or a trust set up specifically for that purpose.
4. Decide who will pay for the cost of the collections or for the setting up and administration of the trust.
5. Decide on the exact procedure for handling the funds when received.
6. Spell out the exact circumstances that will bring about default on the all-inclusive trust deed and the exact amount that will be in default.
7. Spell out the exact procedure to be followed in case of default and subsequent foreclosure.

Preparation Is Essential

8. Provide your attorney with all of the above data as well as all of the documents involved. Your attorney will then be able to draw up the necessary phraseology that will be acceptable to the title company providing the policy of title insurance.
   NOTE: Title insurance companies in California have drafted and printed standard forms of all-inclusive notes secured by deed of trust. If these forms are used, the title company will provide title insurance.

As additional clarification it is pointed out here that the purchaser takes the property subject to the existing lien or liens, so that the seller remains the trustor. Obviously, this can only be done if the notes secured by such liens do not contain an enforceable due-on-sale clause. The all-inclusive deed of trust is recorded as a junior lien, subject to the existing liens.

The purchaser may later become the trustor of the deeds of trust that are prior to the all-inclusive deed of trust by assuming these liens in the form of assumption agreements; at such time, the seller must reconvey the all-inclusive deed of trust. It is strongly suggested that all-inclusive deeds of trust and contracts providing for their use be prepared by legal counsel.

NOTE: See Finance Instruments under the heading Assuming and Taking Subject to a Mortgage.

BUYDOWNS

Buydown is a form of seller contribution to help a buyer qualify for a new institutional loan by paying the lender a lump sum in return for reducing the buyer's interest rate, either for the life of the loan (permanent buydown) or for a period of years (temporary buydown). The lump-sum payment increases the lender's yield and has an effect similar to collecting discount points in lieu of a lower interest rate.

Permanent Buydown

The generally used rule of thumb is that it takes a lump-sum payment of 6% to reduce the interest rate of a 30-year loan by 1%. Thus, it would require $6,000 to reduce the rate of a $100,000, 30-year loan by 1%.

Temporary Buydown

Temporary buydowns reduce the interest rate, either by level payments or progressively increasing payments over the first few years of a loan. Buydown contributions may come from the seller, borrower, lender or other interested third party.

Borrowers will need to justify the increase in payments by the likelihood of increased income, and limitations are imposed for conventional, FHA and VA loans, shown in the chart on page A-152.

Fannie Mae Limitations of Buydown Contributions

Occupancy Type	LTV	Contr. Limited to
Investment Property	Fixed Rate- Regardless of LTV	2% of Sales Price or Appr. Value
Principal Residence	LTV over 90%	3% of Sales Price or Appr. Value
Principal Residence	LTV 90% or less	6% of Sales Price or Appr. Value
Second Home	LTV 80% or less	6% of Sales Price or Appr. Value

If seller contributions exceed the limits, the excess must be deducted from the sales price or appraised value before calculating the maximum loan amount.

FHA Limitations of Buydown Contributions

1. It must be a fixed rate loan on an owner-occupied principal residence.
2. The underwriting is based on a maximum interest rate reduction of 2% below note rate.
3. The increase in interest rate is limited to 1% once a year.
4. The lender must establish that the eventual increase in payments will not adversely affect the borrower and likely lead to default. One of the following criteria must be met.
   a. Potential for increased income to offset scheduled payment increases, as indicated by job training or education in the borrower's profession or by a history of advancement in the borrower's career with attendant increases in earnings
   b. A demonstrated ability to manage financial obligations in such a way that a greater portion of income may be devoted to housing expense
   c. Substantial asset to cushion the effect of increased payments

d. Borrower's cash investment that substantially exceeds the minimum required.

VA Buydown Requirements

Under the VA buydown program, sellers may temporarily reduce buyers' loan payments during the initial years of a mortgage by depositing buydown funds into a third party escrow without recourse. The buydown funds must be beyond the reach of prospective creditors of the builder-seller, lender or borrower. The funds must be used to reduce the buyer's loan payment and may not be used to pay past due monthly loan payments. The maximum loan may not exceed the CRV.

There must be strong indications that income used to support the application will increase to cover the yearly increases in loan payments and the following criteria must be met.

- Assistance payments will run for a minimum of one year.
- Scheduled reductions in the assistance payments must occur annually on the anniversary of the first mortgage payment.
- The annual payment increases must be in equal or approximately equal amounts.

OTHER SELLER CONTRIBUTIONS

The seller may pay a buyer's closing costs, discount points, mortgage insurance premium, moving costs and prepaid items; give a decorating allowance; give personal property; and so on. However, Fannie Mae and FHA limit the amount of contributions for the purpose of calculating the maximum loan amount.

LEASE WITH OPTION TO PURCHASE

A *lease with option to purchase* is another tool sellers can use to induce a sale when the buyer lacks sufficient funds for down payment and closing costs.

A lease with option to purchase, also referred to as lease-option, entitles the lessee to purchase the leased property for a price and upon terms provided in the agreement by exercising the option within a specified period of time (often a year). The lessee/buyer is referred to as the *optionee*, the lessor/seller as the *optionor*. The optionee pays the optionor upfront a nonrefundable *option consideration*, which is usually applied toward the purchase price in the event the option to purchase is exercised. Lease-options generally provide that a portion of the rent is applied toward the purchase if the option is exercised, referred to as *rent credit*.

Example

John Seller has a house on the market for $100,000. Jim Buyer wants to buy the house but does not have enough funds to qualify for a new loan. Instead of a purchase agreement, Seller and Buyer enter into a lease with option to purchase that includes the following terms: Buyer pays Seller a nonrefundable option consideration of $4,000, which is to be applied toward the purchase price if the option to purchase is exercised; Buyer agrees to lease the property for 12 months, at which time he may exercise the option to purchase the property for $100,000; Buyer agrees to pay rent of $800 per month, of which $400 is to be applied to the purchase price if the option is exercised.

If Buyer decides to exercise the option after 12 months, he or she will pay $100,000 minus the $4,000 option consideration, minus $4,800 (12 months rent credit at $400), amounting to $100,000 − $8,800 = $91,200.

Institutional lenders accept rent credits as part the down payment if rental payments exceed the market rent and if a valid lease/purchase agreement is in effect, a copy of which must be attached to the loan application.

Advantages of Lease-Option to the Optionee

- Low cash requirement
- Partial rent credit applied toward down payment
- Lock-in of purchase price at today's market value
- Time to plan and prepare for the finance of the purchase
- Possibility to sell the option (unless prohibited by the terms of the agreement)

Advantages of Lease-Option to the Optionor

- Monthly rent higher than market rent (reducing negative cash flow)
- Top market value for property
- Optionee is likely to treat the property as an owner would
- Tax-free use of option consideration until the option expires or is exercised
- Continued tax deductions for expenses and depreciation during the option period

TRUTH-IN-LENDING ACT

Truth in lending is a federal law enacted to promote the informed use of consumer credit by requiring creditors (lenders) to disclose various terms and conditions of credit. The law is enforced and administered by the Federal Trade Commission. Regulation Z, issued by the Board of Governors of the Federal Reserve System, implements this law that applies to individuals and businesses that regularly offer or extend credit to consumers for personal, family or household purposes.

Disclosures (12 Code of Fed. Regs. Sec. 226)—The Truth-in-Lending Act requires a creditor to furnish certain disclosures to the consumers before a permanent contract for loan is made. With respect to real estate loans, a creditor is a person who in any calendar year extends credit more than 25 times or more than 5 times for loans secured by a dwelling used as the borrower's residence, when the credit extended is subject to a finance charge or is payable by written agreement in more than four installments (excluding the down payment). A dwelling is defined as a residential structure including a mobile home or trailer that contains one- to four-family housing units.

REQUIRED ITEMS OF DISCLOSURE

Items of disclosure required of creditors by Regulation Z for real estate loans are summarized below. (The first four disclosures listed below must also have simple descriptive phrases of explanation similar to those shown.)

1. Amount financed—the amount of credit provided to you or on your behalf.
2. Finance charge—the dollar amount the credit will cost you.
3. Annual percentage rate—the cost of your credit as a yearly rate.

4. Total of payments—the amount you will have paid when you have made all the scheduled payments.
5. Identity of the creditor making the disclosure.
6. Written itemization of the amount financed or a statement that the consumer has a right to receive a written itemization and a space in the statement for the consumer to indicate whether or not the itemization is requested.
7. Payment schedule to include number, amount and timing of payments.
8. Demand feature of the loan excluding borrower default or due-on-sale clause.
9. Loan payment penalties—if not charged by the lender or if uncertainty exists, a statement to that effect. Rebate penalty disclosure.
10. Late payment charge stated either as a percentage or dollar amount.
11. Description of the security interest that will be retained by the lender as security for the loan.
12. Insurance and whether or not premiums are included in the finance charge.
13. Certain security interest charges or fees, such as taxes or other fees paid to public officials or the premium for insurance in lieu of perfecting the security interest, to be excluded from the finance charge.
14. Specific reference to terms of the contract related to nonpayment, default, acceleration or prepayment penalties.
15. A statement that a due-on-sale clause or other conditions about the loan assumption policy are contained in the loan documents. A statement as to whether the lender will allow subsequent purchasers to assume the remaining obligation.
16. Whether there is a required deposit by the borrower as a condition of the loan and a statement that the annual percentage rate does not reflect the effect of any such required deposit.

ARM Disclosure Rules

Effective October 1, 1988, the Federal Reserve Board implemented an amendment to Regulation Z. These rules apply to lenders that offer adjustable rate mortgages (ARMs) to borrowers. ARMs subject to the rules are for purchase money, refinance, house improvement, closed end equity second mortgages and any consumer purpose transaction secured by a principal dwelling.

At the time an application form is provided or before the consumer pays a nonrefundable fee, whichever comes first, certain information must be given to the consumer-borrower. The initial disclosures must be delivered or placed in the mail not later than three business days following receipt of the consumer's application.

At the time an ARM is initiated, lenders must make available the following information:

1. An educational brochure about ARMs, either the "Consumer Handbook on Adjustable Rate Mortgages," published jointly by the Federal Reserve Bank and the Federal Home Loan Bank, or a suitable substitute.

2. A loan program disclosure for each adjustable rate program in which a consumer expresses an interest. The disclosure information must reveal that the interest rate or term of the loan can change, identify the index applied and the source of information for that index plus provide an explanation of how the index is adjusted. A statement must be included advising the consumer to ask about the current margin value, the current interest rate and the amount of discount, if any.

3. An historic example must be given illustrating how payments on a $10,000 loan would have changed in response to actual historical data on the index to be applied. The consumer must be provided with an explanation of how to calculate payment amounts for the loan.

4. A statement reporting the initial and maximum interest rates and payments for a $10,000 loan

originated at the most recent rate in the historic example.

At time of settlement (close of escrow), the following disclosures must be made:

1. The transaction contains an adjustable rate feature.
2. A statement that the adjustable rate disclosures have been provided earlier.

Right of Rescission

The *right of rescission* with respect to real estate loans applies to consumer credit transactions in which the lender will retain or acquire a security interest in the consumer's principal dwelling including in many cases a mobile home (even if treated as personal property). The creditor must notify each consumer entitled to rescind under the provisions of this law with written notice to rescind. The consumer has the right to rescind under the provisions of this law with written notice of the right to rescind without penalty until midnight of the third business day following the later of these events

- consumption of the loan transaction;
- delivery of all material truth-in-lending disclosures; or
- delivery of two copies of the notice of the right to rescind.

Advertising

Regulation Z also requires that anyone who places an advertisement for consumer credit (including solicitation by mail or telephone) must comply with the advertising requirement of the Truth-in-Lending Act summarized as follows:

- The finance charge must be expressed as an annual percentage rate (APR), and if applicable, a statement that the APR is subject to increase after the loan is made.
- The variable rate mortgage ads should state the number and timing of payments, the amount of the largest and smallest of those payments and the fact that payments will vary between the two amounts after close of escrow.

- Buydowns or reduced interest rate advertisements must show the limited term to which the reduced interest rate applies, as well as the annual percentage rate determined in accordance with Section 226.17c of Regulation Z.

Failure to comply with the Truth-in-Lending Act may subject the creditor or advertiser to criminal and civil liability.

Exempt Transactions

- Credit for agricultural purposes
- Credit for business and/or commercial purposes
- Credit over $25,000 not secured by real property
- Credit to government agencies and other entities not considered "natural persons"
- Credit for nonoccupied rental housing if owner does not occupy for more than 14 days

IS THE REAL ESTATE BROKER SUBJECT TO THE TRUTH-IN-LENDING ACT?

Because a residential mortgage transaction is now exempt from the act, a broker involved in an ordinary sale will not be concerned with the purchaser's right to rescind.

Effective September 17, 1982, the following regulatory amendment was adopted in order to clarify the definition of *arrangement of credit*:

"Real estate brokers—The general definition does not include a person (such as a real estate broker or sales person) who, as part of the process of arranging the sale of real property or a dwelling, arranges for the seller to totally or partly finance the purchase, even if the obligation by its terms is simultaneously assigned by the seller to another person. However, a broker or sales person is not exempt from coverage in all transactions. For example, the real estate broker may be a creditor in the following situations:

"The broker acts as a loan broker to arrange for someone other than the seller to extend credit, provided that the extender of credit (the person to whom the obligation is initially payable) does not meet the 'creditor' definition.

"The broker extends credit itself, provided that the broker otherwise meets the 'creditor' definition.

"Under the revised regulation, a broker would not be required to make the disclosures required by the act, unless the broker is involved in more than five transactions in the current or preceding calendar year wherein he acts as a loan broker for a third party who is not a creditor or extends credit himself. Where loans are made by persons coming within the definition of creditor, the broker will not be responsible for the disclosures."

REAL ESTATE SETTLEMENT AND PROCEDURES ACT (RESPA)

The Real Estate Settlement and Procedures Act of 1974 is a federal law administered by the U.S. Department of Housing and Urban Development (HUD). RESPA is designed to protect homebuyers during the settlement phase of the purchase. Settlement (in many states referred to as close of escrow) is the process whereby the ownership of real property passes from the seller to the buyer. RESPA provides specific procedures, forms for settlement and detailed information that enable buyers to shop for settlement services and make informed decisions.

RESPA applies to all federally related purchase money and refinance mortgage loans, including home equity conversion mortgages (reverse mortgages) secured by a first or subordinate lien on residential real property of one- to four-family dwellings (including individual condominiums, cooperatives and manufactured homes). Subordinate lien loans include home-equity loans on one- to four-family dwellings, home-equity lines of credit and *dealer loans,* the latter being defined as residential mortgage loans secured by home improvement goods and services sold by a contractor.

Exemptions from RESPA include

- a loan secured by property of 25 acres or more;
- loans primarily for business, commercial or agricultural purposes;
- temporary financing, such as construction loans (not take-out loans);
- bridge loans or swing loans; and
- loans secured by unimproved property.

Disclosure requirements by providers of credit include the following:

- *HUD's special information booklet* describes and explains the settlement process. This booklet must be provided not later than three business days after the application is received or prepared. In case of a home equity line of credit, the brochure entitled "When Your Home Is on the Line: What You Should Know about Home Equity Lines of Credit" is provided.
- *A good faith estimate* listing the amount of, or range of, charges for the specific settlement services the borrower is likely to incur. The good faith estimate must be provided to loan applicants within three business days after the loan application is received or prepared. Terminology must conform to the HUD's Uniform Settlement Statement (HUD-1), and lenders are encouraged to use the same item numbers that appear on the HUD-1.

In the event the lender requires that a particular settlement provider (attorney or title company) be used, the lender is required to clearly identify such provider, stating whether or not each provider has a business relationship with the lender.

COMPUTERIZED LOAN ORIGINATION (CLO)

Under 1992 HUD regulations, real estate brokers are permitted to use CLO systems and charge customers a fee for loan services, provided the borrower is given a written disclosure specifying the fee to be charged and the CLO services to be provided. On July 21, 1994, HUD published proposed amendments that define the CLO system as a computerized system that provides prospective borrowers with information regarding rates and terms of mortgage loans; collects, assembles and transmits information about the prospective borrower, the property and other loan-related information to the lender; and based on the information transmitted, responds to the prospective borrower with detailed information on loan products available from the lender.

The proposed rules do not prohibit any payment made by a borrower to a CLO operator (whether mortgage or real estate broker*) for CLO services as long as the following CLO disclosure is provided:

YOU ARE ADVISED THAT YOU MAY AVOID THIS FEE IF YOU APPROACH A LENDER OR MORT-GAGE BROKER DIRECTLY. ADDITIONALLY, LOWER MORTGAGE RATES OR OTHER LOWER FEES MAY BE AVAILABLE FROM OTHER MORTGAGE LENDERS WHO ARE NOT LISTED ON THIS COMPUTER SYSTEM.

It appears that, under the proposed rules, CLO operators may charge customers whatever the market will bear.

NOTE: REALTORS® should be cautioned that the receipt of additional fees for CLO services must be for services that are actual, necessary and distinct from the primary services provided by many REALTORS® as ancillary to their principal real estate sales role.

NOTE: In some states, it is illegal for real estate licensees to use the CLO system.

CONTROLLED BUSINESS ARRANGEMENT

In the event a real estate broker or lender has a financial interest or an ongoing business relationship with a particular settlement provider, such as a title company or attorney, consumers must be informed of it in writing. Consumers must also be informed that under federal law they are free to choose whichever service provider they like.

REALTORS® are able to make referrals to affiliated lenders, CLOs, title companies, and so on, and employees of the realty company may be compensated by the realty company (but not by an affiliate) to provide incentive for such referrals. HUD's July 21, 1994, proposals would allow limited payments of bonuses and compensation to managerial employees provided that the compensation is not tied on a one-to-one basis or calculated as a multiple of the number or value of any referrals.

PROHIBITION AGAINST KICKBACKS

According to RESPA, no person may give and no person may accept any portion, split or percentage of any charge made or received for the rendering of a real estate settlement service in connection with a transaction involving a federally related mortgage loan other than for services actually performed.

TRANSFER OF SERVICING RIGHTS

At the time of application, lenders are required to disclose to the applicant whether the servicing rights may be assigned, sold or transferred to any other person or entity at any time during which the loan is outstanding.

DISCLOSURE REQUIREMENTS FOR ESCROW ACCOUNTS

Within 45 days of closing, borrowers are to be furnished an initial escrow statement clearly itemizing the estimated taxes, insurance premiums and charges that may be assessed, and the anticipated dates of such payments during the first 12 months of the escrow account. Annual escrow account statements must also be provided, and a final escrow statement must be furnished within 45 days of termination of the escrow account.

CONTRACT
CLAUSES

To receive advance notice of the
next *Realty Bluebook*® edition
(and information about
what's new), please call
1-800-322-8621
to register your name and address.

CONTENTS

CONTRACT CLAUSES

CLAUSES B

General Clauses B-19

Inspection Clauses B-34
Investment Property Clauses B-39

LEGAL ASPECTS OF CONTRACT PREPARATION

To practice law, one must be licensed as an attorney. The practice of law includes preparation of contracts and therefore requires a law degree. In most states, an exception is made for a licensed real estate broker or salesperson who, in the ordinary course of business, prepares a contract for the purchase or sale of real property. However, that right also includes a liability. Real estate licensees are charged with the responsibility of being experts in real property and experts in the preparation of real property contracts and thus may be liable in the same manner as lawyers are in the preparation of such agreements.

Historically, real estate contracts were prepared by lawyers without the benefit of printed forms. Gradually, printed forms gained popularity containing certain clauses that had become standard language. Over the years, modern forms were developed that include a maximum of printed standard and optional provisions. As a result, the work of the real estate licensee using these forms has been simplified. Ordinarily, the licensee need only fill in blank spaces and add a minimum of additional terms and conditions. The chance for errors and omissions is thus greatly reduced, and so is the broker's liability. While this makes for simplicity in the preparation of contracts, the real estate licensee has the obligation (1) to become thoroughly familiar with the printed clauses, (2) to accurately complete all of the blank spaces or mark them N/A (Not Applicable) and (3) to write into the contract additional items for the protection of their clients.

The mere fact that a provision is printed in a form does not mean it must remain in the contract. It can be deleted by striking it out or changing its terms. Any portion struck out or changed should be initialed by both parties. Ordinarily, anything written into the contract supersedes the printed words. However, writing provisions that are similar but not identical to printed clauses may create ambiguities in the agreement and may lead to disputes.

ENFORCEABLE CONTRACTS

To be enforceable, a *contract* (agreement) must meet the following conditions.

- Under the Statute of Frauds, an agreement for the sale of real property, or lease of more than one year, must be in writing to be enforceable. It is, therefore, essential that all terms and conditions of the agreement be included in the written agreement.
- The contract must have a lawful object. An example of an object not considered lawful would be an agreement to indemnify or hold one harmless for one's own negligence.
- There must be a promise of sufficient consideration by both parties, such as money by one party and transfer of property by the other. The terms of the agreement may not permit one party to choose unconditionally not to perform.
- Each party to the contract must be competent (i.e., of the age of majority and mentally capable of managing his/her own affairs).
- All conditions (contingencies) of the contract must have been satisfied or waived in writing within the time frame specified. It is essential to provide sufficient time for the obligated party to satisfy each condition. Conditions without time limits invite disputes and must be avoided.
- In the event the buyer is an entity (corporation, partnership, limited partnership or trust), the authority of the person(s) signing must be verified with an appropriate certificate of corporate resolution, statement of partnership, limited partnership certificate or trust agreement. Failure to do so may make the broker liable to the seller.

SATISFACTION OR WAIVER

The party responsible may either satisfy a condition in accordance with its terms or waive the condition in writing within the time frame provided. Failure to do so may permit the party benefiting from the condition to terminate the agreement or require performance by the other party. A condition should also make clear what the effect is if the time expires.

Examples

1. *Conditioned upon Buyer's ability to obtain, within [_____] days of acceptance, a commitment for new financing for the herein property from a lender of Buyer's choice, in the amount of not less than $[_____], for 30 years, payable at approximately $[_____] per month including interest at the rate of [_____]% per annum.*

2. *Buyer shall have the right, at his/her expense, to have the property inspected by licensed experts, for the following conditions. Within [_____] days of acceptance, Buyer shall approve or disapprove in writing all inspection reports obtained. In the event of disapproval, Buyer may terminate this agreement and all unused deposits shall be returned to Buyer.*

COMMISSIONS

Ordinarily, a commission is earned by a broker when he or she has procured a buyer, "ready, willing and able" to purchase the property, either upon the terms of the listing or upon terms satisfactory to the seller. Basically, a broker is entitled to a commission when there is a valid and enforceable contract (after all contingencies have been removed in writing). However, if the broker has no listing agreement and the parties to the purchase agreement rescind the contract, the broker will not be entitled to a commission unless the purchase agreement makes a specific provision to the contrary.

COUNTEROFFERS

An offer may be accepted by the offeree until it is revoked by the offeror or terminated by its own terms as long as acceptance is communicated by the offeree to the offeror.

The problem is that *communicated* can have different connotations, such as via telegraph, physical delivery, and so on. Therefore, it is important that the agreement provide for specific means of communicating acceptance.

Every offer and counteroffer should have a termination date. Without such termination or expiration date an offer or counteroffer remains open for a reasonable time and could conceivably be accepted by an offeree at some later time while the offeror had presumed all along that the offer had been rejected.

PURCHASE AGREEMENTS

The *purchase agreement* (otherwise known as sales agreement, deposit receipt or earnest money agreement) is a form used to incorporate the terms for the sale of real property. This type of form is designed to be used where title to the property is transferred at settlement (close of escrow or closing.)

The purchase agreement is in sharp contrast to the so-called installment contract of sale, (also known as land contract of sale or, simply, contract of sale), which is primarily a security device when title to the property is not transferred until a later date, subject to performance of certain conditions. While in most states licensed real estate brokers are authorized to use printed purchase agreement forms and to fill in simple terms and conditions, the preparation of security instruments should be left to legal counsel.

CLAUSES

The suggested clauses under the heading Terms and Conditions are in common use and cover most situations but will, of course, not necessarily all be needed in any one agreement. The clauses should not be used indiscriminately without consideration of their meaning relating to a particular transaction. Alterations of the suggested clauses may, therefore, be necessary to fit the particular situation. A blank line enclosed by brackets ([_____]) indicates there is information to be filled in; its length is not meant to indicate the amount of information.

SIGNATURES

Where more than one person is to acquire the property, the best procedure is to have all such persons sign as Buyer. Failure to have all of the owners of record sign as Seller may void the entire agreement and will limit the buyers' remedies in the event of default.

If the buyer or seller is an entity, such as a corporation, partnership, limited partnership or trust, the authority of the person(s) signing should be verified with an appropriate certificate of corporate resolution, statement of partnership, limited partnership certificate or trust agreement. Failure to do so may make the broker liable to the other party to the transaction.

FORMS OF OWNERSHIP

There are numerous ways in which persons may own real property. The broker should not attempt to advise buyers concerning corporations, partnerships, joint ventures or all of the legal relationships of cotenants. However, he or she should have a rudimentary knowledge of the problems and effects of the more common forms of property ownership, especially as related to ownership of real property by husband and wife. Cotenants (two persons owning property together but not necessarily husband and wife) may hold property as tenants in common or as joint tenants.

Tenants in common need not have equal interest; joint tenants must have equal interests.

Upon death of a tenant in common, the decedent's share passes to his or her heirs or devisees under his or her will; upon death of a joint tenant, the surviving joint tenant(s) succeed(s) to the decedent's interest in the property.

Most spouses acquire real property as joint tenants, but few are aware of the changes that they may be making in their property rights or of the effect on their tax basis at the date the first spouse dies. This may be an important consideration in some states with respect to property subject to depreciation or property that is likely to appreciate substantially in value. (See Tax Information section under the heading Basis.)

In community property states, the marital status of a grantee is often set forth in the deed. When a married person acquires property that is to be his or her separate property, it is important that this be noted in the deed. While it is not normally necessary to note that married persons acquire property as community property, this information is often noted in a deed.

The broker should not recommend any particular way of holding title but should alert the buyers to the above mentioned considerations, and if they have any questions, they should consult their lawyer.

DEPOSITS

It should be stated in what form the deposit is received: cash, personal check, certified check, cashier's check or note.

PERSONAL CHECKS

Checks should be made by buyer, but if made by a third party, then the check should be made payable to the buyer and endorsed by him or her to the office or escrow holder.

Do not accept checks if—to your knowledge—they are not covered by sufficient funds. Do not accept a postdated check without the seller's written approval; you might be held responsible if the check does not clear. Moreover, there is usually no recourse if you had knowledge that a check was not covered at the time you accepted it.

NOTES

If cash is not available, a *promissory note* can be taken as deposit.

Use a *straight note* or *flat note* form, make the note payable *On Demand to Broker at No Interest* and add:

This note is delivered in accordance with agreement of sale and deposit receipt dated [_____], covering the real property known as [_____].

PROPERTY DESCRIPTION

The Real Property commonly known as [Address]
If necessary, the broker may add:

also described as [Block #], [Lot #], [Unit #]
Or:

[District], [Section], [City], [State],
Or:

legally described as recorded in Book # [_____],
Page # [_____]
If desired, a brief mention of the type of property may
be made here, such as:

a single-family residence, a four-unit apartment
building, a vacant lot, etc.

BLANK SPACES

Unneeded blank spaces may be stricken or filled with
N/A (not applicable).

CORRECTIONS AND DELETIONS

Any corrections and deletions must be initialed by
both parties.

LEAVING COPIES

Buyer and seller must be given copies of all documents they sign at the time of signing.

DEFINITIONS OF TERMS

To avoid lengthy repetitions, the terms defined hereafter are used throughout the Contract Clause section.
Brokers may wish to insert these definitions into
their contracts.

Broker includes cooperating brokers and all salespersons.

Days means calendar days unless otherwise specified.

Acceptance the date the seller accepts the offer or
the buyer accepts the counteroffer.

Delivered personally delivered or transmitted by facsimile machine followed by a faxed acknowledgment of receipt or mailed by deposit in U.S. mail, postage prepaid. In the event of mailing, delivery shall be deemed to have been made on the fifth day following the date of mailing.

Date of closing the date title is transferred.

Terminate the agreement both parties are relieved of their obligations and all deposits shall be returned to buyer less expenses incurred by or on account of buyer to date of termination.

Property the real property and any personal property included in the sale.

FORMAT

Clauses in this edition are printed in italics. The user often needs to change the clause to fit a particular transaction. Such optional uses are shown **{italicized in braces}**.

Example:

Seller shall, within three days after acceptance, provide Buyer with copies of all notes and mortgages {deeds of trust} to be assumed {taken subject to}.

All clauses (except finance clauses) are arranged in alphabetical order in this edition.

FINANCE CLAUSES

All Cash

The clause *All Cash* or *All Cash to Seller* means that the buyer commits himself or herself to pay the entire purchase price in cash and should only be used if this actually conveys the buyer's intention.

In the event the buyer intends to but for some reason proves to be unable to obtain a certain loan, the buyer stands to lose his or her deposit and leaves himself or herself open to litigation unless the funds are available to fulfill the contract.

If, therefore, the buyer depends upon a loan to purchase the property, the agreement of sale should be made contingent upon his or her ability to obtain a loan of specific amount and terms.

Cash-Over New Conventional Fixed Rate Loan

Entire purchase price payable in cash. Conditioned upon Buyer's ability to obtain a fixed rate loan, to be secured by the property, in the amount of [_____]% of purchase price {in the amount of $[_____]}, with equal monthly payments to be amortized over a period of not less than [_____] years, with interest not to exceed [_____]% per annum. Buyer shall have [_____] days from date of acceptance within which to obtain such loan commitment or waive this condition in writing. Loan fee not to exceed [_____]%.

Cash-Over New ARM

Entire purchase price payable in cash. Conditioned upon Buyer obtaining an adjustable rate mortgage to be secured by the property in the amount of [_____]% of purchase price, for a term of [_____] years, at a contract interest rate of [_____]% and monthly payments including principal and interest of $[_____], tied to the index of [_____], with a margin of [_____]%, with an initial discounted interest rate of [_____]% and initial monthly payments of $[_____], in effect for a period of [_____] months. Interest rate to be adjusted every [_____] months. Payments to be adjusted every [_____] months. Periodic interest cap [_____]% per [_____]. Periodic payment cap [_____]. Lifetime interest cap [_____]%. Loan recasting every [_____] years (when negative amortization reaches [_____]% of contract rate). {Loan to be assumable for [_____] times.} Negative amortization allowed {not allowed}.

Seller To Carry First Mortgage

Cash down payment $[_____]. Buyer to execute a note secured by a first deed of trust {mortgage} on the property, in favor of Seller, for the balance of $[_____], payable at $[_____] per month, or more, including interest at [_____]% per annum {with the entire balance due [_____] years from date of note or upon sale or transfer of the property}.

Buyer shall furnish Seller, within three days after acceptance, a customary financial statement for the sole purpose of credit approval, which approval shall not be unreasonably withheld. Buyer authorizes Seller to engage the services of a reputable credit reporting agency for this purpose at Buyer's expense and Seller shall notify Buyer, within ten days after receipt of financial statement, of approval or disapproval of Buyer's credit.

New FHA Loan

Entire purchase price payable in cash. Conditioned upon Buyer obtaining an FHA loan to be secured by the property in the amount of $[_____] for [_____] years, payable at approximately $[_____] per month including interest at [_____]% per annum, plus taxes and hazard insurance.

Mortgage insurance premium to be financed {paid in cash}.

Loan fee not to exceed [_____]%. Discount points paid by seller (buyer) not to exceed [_____]%. Any work required by FHA to be paid for by Seller.

The following amendment must be signed by buyer and seller:

It is expressly agreed that notwithstanding any other provisions of this contract, the purchaser shall not be obligated to complete the purchase of the property described herein or to incur any penalty by forfeiture of earnest money deposits or otherwise unless the purchaser has been given, in accordance with HUD/FHA or VA requirements, a written statement by the Federal Housing Commissioner, VA or a direct endorsement lender, setting forth the appraised value of the property of not less than $[_____]. The purchaser shall have the privilege and option of proceeding with consummation of the contract without regard to the amount of the appraised valuation. The appraised valuation is arrived at to determine the maximum mortgage the Department of Housing and Urban Development will insure. HUD does not warrant the value nor the condition of the property. The purchaser should satisfy himself/herself that the price and condition of the property are acceptable.

New VA Loan

Entire purchase price payable in cash. Conditioned upon Buyer obtaining a VA loan to be secured by the property in the amount of $[_____] for [_____] years, payable at approximately $[_____] per month including interest at [_____]% per annum, plus taxes and hazard insurance.

The following amendment must be signed by the veteran buyer and the seller:

It is expressly agreed that, notwithstanding any other provisions of this Sales Agreement/Contract, the Veteran/Buyer shall not incur any penalty by forfeiture of earnest money or otherwise or be obligated to complete the purchase of the property described herein if the contract purchase price or cost exceeds the reasonable value of the property established by the VA. The Veteran/Buyer shall, however, have the privilege and option of proceeding with the consummation of this contract without regard to the amount of reasonable value established by the VA.

In the event the purchase price is in excess of the reasonable value determined by the VA and the veteran elects to proceed with the purchase, the veteran is required to pay cash for such excess.

Assumption of VA Loan with Release of Liability

Effective March 1, 1988, VA approval is required for transfer of property securing VA loans.

Loans originated prior to March 1, 1988, remain freely assumable by any buyer, including nonveterans.

Loans assumed after March 1, 1988, and any VA loans assumed with release of liability require the following clause:

Conditioned upon Buyer's ability to assume existing VA loan and to assume Seller's potential indemnity liability to the federal government for the repayment of the VA loan. The existing VA loan has an approximate balance of $[_____] and is payable at approximately $[_____] per month including interest at [_____]% per annum, taxes and insurance.

Balance of the purchase price in the approximate amount of $[_____] payable in cash.

Any net difference between the approximate balance of the existing loan and the actual balance of said loan at closing of escrow shall be adjusted in cash.

See Existing Loans under General Clauses.

If applicable, add the following to the assumption clause:

Buyer is a veteran and consents to substitute his or her remaining VA entitlement, in the amount of $[___] for that of the seller.

Subject to Existing First Loan

In the event the first loan does not contain a due-on-sale clause, the loan can be taken *subject to* without the need for obtaining the lender's approval. The lender, therefore, has no right to require approval of the buyer's credit, to charge an assumption fee nor to increase the interest rate. (See Introduction to Finance section.)

Subject to existing first loan in the approximate amount of $[_____], payable at approximately $[_____] per month including interest at [_____]% per annum {taxes and insurance}.

Balance of the purchase price in the approximate amount of $[_____] payable in cash.

Any net difference between the approximate balance of the existing loan and the actual balance of said loan at close of escrow shall be adjusted in cash.

See Existing Loans under General Clauses.

Assumption of Existing First Loan

Conditioned upon Buyer's ability to assume existing first loan in the approximate amount of $[_____] payable at approximately $[_____] per month including interest at [_____]% per annum (taxes and insurance).

Balance of purchase price in the approximate amount of $[_____] payable in cash. Buyer to obtain lender's approval within [_____] days after acceptance or waive this condition in writing.

Any net difference between the approximate balance of the existing loan and the actual balance of said loan at close of escrow shall be adjusted in cash.

See Existing Loans under General Clauses.

NOTE: In the event the loan to be assumed is a private loan, the due date, if any, should be stated. Also, if the note is due upon resale of the property it should be stated.

NOTE: Check with lender if the interest rate is to be adjusted and the amount of the assumption fee.

Assumption of ARM

Conditioned upon Buyer's ability to assume an adjustable rate mortgage secured by the property in the approximate amount of $[_____] with monthly payments including principal and interest of approximately $[_____], tied to the index of [_____], with a margin of [_____]%. Interest rate to be adjusted every [_____] months. Payments to be adjusted every [_____] months. Periodic interest cap [_____]% per [_____]. Lifetime interest cap [_____]%. Loan recasting every [_____] years (when negative amortization reaches [_____]% of contract rate). Loan to be assumable for [_____] times. Prepayment penalty [_____]. Balance of purchase price in the approximate amount of $[_____] payable in cash.

Any net difference between the approximate balance of the existing loan and the actual balance of said loan at close of escrow shall be adjusted in cash.

Wraparound or All-Inclusive Deed of Trust

Cash down payment $[_____]. Balance payable under an all-inclusive deed of trust that shall provide for monthly payments of $[_____] including interest at [_____]% per annum. Buyer to pay taxes and insurance. The lien of the all-inclusive deed of trust shall be subject to the following prior encumbrances: [_____], which are to be paid by Seller. Said all-inclusive deed of trust to be prepared by Buyer's attorney and approved by Seller's attorney.

Contract of Sale

Cash down payment $[_____]. Balance payable under a contract of sale that shall provide for monthly payments of $[_____] including interest at [_____]% per annum with entire balance due in [_____] years. Seller to pay existing loans on the property. Buyer to pay taxes and insurance. Said contract of sale to be prepared by Buyer's attorney and approved by Seller's attorney. Recordation of the contract of sale or memorandum *thereof shall be in lieu of recordation of deed or conveyance referred to in this sales agreement.*

New Conventional Loan—Second Loan to Seller

$[_____] (purchase price less second loan to seller) of the purchase price payable in cash.

Balance of purchase price in the amount of $[_____] in the form of a note secured by a second deed of trust (mortgage) on the property, to be executed by Buyer in favor of Seller, payable at $[_____] per month, or more, including interest at [_____]% per annum (with the entire balance due [_____] years from date of note or upon sale or transfer of the property).

Conditioned upon Buyer obtaining a first loan to be secured by the property in the amount of [_____]% of purchase price with equal monthly payments to be amortized over a period of not less than [_____] years, with interest not to exceed [_____]% per annum. Buyer shall have [_____] days after date of acceptance hereof within which to obtain such loan commitment or waive this condition. Loan fee not to exceed [_____]%.

Subject to Existing First Loan— Second Loan to Seller

Subject to existing first loan in the approximate amount of $[_____] payable at approximately $[_____] per month including interest at [_____]% per annum {taxes and insurance}.

Buyer to execute a note secured by a second deed of trust {mortgage} on the property, in favor of Seller, in the amount of $[_____], payable at $[_____] per month, or more, including interest at [_____]% per annum. {The entire balance shall be due [_____] years from date of note.} {The entire balance shall be due upon sale or transfer of the property or any interest therein.} Balance of purchase price in the approximate amount of $[_____] payable in cash.

Any net difference between the approximate balance of the existing loan and the actual balance of said loan at close of escrow shall be adjusted in [_____] (cash or note to seller).

Assumption of First Loan—Second Loan to Seller

Conditioned upon Buyer's ability to assume existing first loan in the approximate amount of $[_____] payable at approximately $[_____] per month including interest at [_____]% per annum (taxes and insurance).

Buyer to execute a note secured by a second deed of trust (mortgage) on the property, in favor of Seller, in the amount of $[_____] payable at $[_____] per month, or more, including interest at [_____]% per annum (with the entire balance due [_____] years from date of note or upon sale or transfer of the property).

Balance of purchase price in the approximate amount of $[_____] payable in cash.

Any net difference between the approximate balance of the existing loan and the actual balance of said loan at close of escrow shall be adjusted in [_____] {cash or note to Seller}.

Buyer shall furnish Seller within three days of acceptance a customary financial statement for the sole purpose of credit approval, which approval shall not be unreasonably withheld.

Buyer authorizes Seller to engage the services of a reputable credit reporting agency for this purpose at Buyer's expense, and Seller shall notify Buyer within ten days of receipt of financial statement of approval or disapproval of Buyer's credit.

NOTE: In the event the loan to be assumed is a private loan, the due date on the note should be stated; whether the note is due upon resale of the property should also be stated.

NOTE: Check with lender if interest rate is to be adjusted and about the amount of the assumption fee.

Second Loans on Income Property Containing Personal Property

In the event a buyer is to execute a note in favor of a seller secured by a second deed of trust {mortgage} on income property containing personal property, the following clause should be added:

All personal property conveyed will be pledged as additional security for the note in favor of Seller.

Buyer Assigning to Seller a Mortgage on Another Property

Buyer will transfer to Seller a note secured by a second (first or third) deed of trust (mortgage) on the real property described as [_____] with an unpaid balance of approximately $[_____] payable at $[_____] per month (or more) including interest at [_____]% per annum with the entire balance due [_____] [when paid in full] [or upon sale of the property]. Buyer shall furnish Seller a policy of title insurance.

If at close of escrow the unpaid balance of the above note is more or less than the amount shown herein, then such difference shall be adjusted in cash, but in no event shall such balance be more than $[_____] or less than $[_____].

Conditioned upon Seller's approval of (1) current title report, (2) offset statement executed by payor, (3) appraisal of property securing the note, (4) financial statement, (5) credit report and (6) hazard insurance declarations.

Buyer Trading in Another Real Property

This clause should not be used if a tax-deferred exchange is intended. In such case, see section on Exchange Agreements.

Buyer will convey to Seller the real property known as [_____] (subject to the following encumbrances): [list encumbrances].

A. A note secured by a first mortgage {deed of trust} having a balance of approximately $[_____]payable at $[_____] per month including interest at [_____]% per annum.

B. A note secured by a second mortgage (deed of trust) having a balance of approximately $[_____] payable at $[_____] per month (or more) and due and payable in full on [_____].

Buyer to be credited with the sum of $[_____] less the amount of the aforesaid encumbrances at the date of conveyance, upon the purchase price. Proration of insurance, taxes and other items to be made as provided hereinafter.

GENERAL CLAUSES

Addendum

If, due to lack of space, additional terms and conditions have to be attached on a separate addendum, the following clause may be inserted in the purchase agreement.

Additional terms and conditions in the attached addendum of same date, signed by both parties, have been made a part of this agreement prior to its execution.

Arbitration (Not for use in California, see next clause)

Buyer, Seller and Broker(s) agree that in the event any party defaults in the performance of the obligations of such party under the agreement, or in the event there is a dispute between any of them with respect to their obligations under the agreement, or their obligations arising out of the purchase and sale, exchange or lease of the property, that the matter shall be submitted to arbitration in accordance with the Commercial Rules of Arbitration of the American Arbitration Association.

The parties do further agree that the party or parties prevailing in such arbitration shall be entitled to receive from the other party or parties a reasonable attorney's fee and all costs incurred in connection with the arbitration in an amount to be determined by the arbitrator or arbitrators and in the event that any party shall fail to pay the amount due under the award of the arbitrator or arbitrators, and legal action is commenced for the enforcement of the award, the prevailing party or parties shall be entitled to receive a reasonable attorney's fee incurred in such action to be determined by the court in which such action is brought.

The parties further agree that they shall each have the rights of discovery set forth in provisions of local law, which is by this reference incorporated herein.

Arbitration (For Use in California)

Any dispute or claim in law or equity arising out of this contract or any resulting transaction shall be decided by neutral binding arbitration in accordance with the rules of the American Arbitration Association and not by court action except as provided by California law for judicial review of arbitration proceedings. Judgment upon the award rendered by the arbitrator(s) may be entered in any court having jurisdiction thereof. The parties shall have the right to discovery in accordance with Code of Civil Procedure Section 1283.05. The following matters are excluded from arbitration hereunder: (a) a judicial or nonjudicial foreclosure or other action or proceeding to enforce a deed of trust, mortgage or real property sales contract as defined in Civil Code Section 2985; (b) an unlawful detainer action; (c) the filing or enforcement of a mechanic's lien; (d) any matter that is within the jurisdiction of a probate or small claims court; or (e) an action for bodily injury or wrongful death, or for latent or patent defects to which that Code of Civil Procedure Section 337.1 or Section 337.15 applies. The filing of a judicial action to enable the recording of a notice of pending action, for order of attachment, receivership, injunction or other provisional remedies shall not constitute a waiver of the right to arbitrate under this provision.

Any dispute or claim by or against Broker(s) and/or associate licensee(s) participating in this transaction shall be submitted to arbitration consistent with the provision above only if the broker(s) and/or associate licensee(s) making the claim or against whom the claim is made shall have agreed to submit it to arbitration consistent with this provision.

NOTE: By initialing in the space below you are agreeing to have any dispute arising out of the matters included in the arbitration of disputes provision decided by neutral arbitration as provided by California law and you are giving up any rights you might possess to have the dispute litigated in court or jury trial. By initialing in the space below you are giving up your judicial rights to discovery and appeal, unless such rights are specifically included in the arbitration of disputes provision. If you refuse to submit to arbitration after agreeing to this provision, you may be compelled to arbitrate under the authority of the California Code of Civil Procedure. Your agreement to this arbitration provision is voluntary.

We have read and understand the foregoing and agree to submit disputes arising out of the matters included in the arbitration of disputes provision to neutral arbitration.

Attorney Fees

In any action or proceeding involving a dispute between Buyer and Seller arising out of the execution of this Agreement or the sale, the prevailing party shall be entitled to receive from the other party a reasonable attorney fee to be determined by the court or arbitrator(s).

Bonds and Assessments

In the event there is a bond or assessment that has an outstanding principal balance and is a lien upon the property, such principal shall be paid by Seller {or assumed by Buyer}. In the event of assumption, said obligation(s) shall [shall not] be credited to Buyer at closing. This Agreement is conditioned upon both parties verifying and approving in writing the amount of any bond or assessment within [_____] after receipt of the pre-liminary title report. In the event of disapproval, the disapproving party may terminate this Agreement.

Broker's Commission

In the event Buyer defaults in the performance of this Agreement, Buyer agrees to pay the Broker(s) any commission that would be payable by Seller in the absence of such default.

Building Code Violations

If a broker has knowledge of possible existing building code violations, he or she must state so in the contract. Examples:

Buyer understands that the social room was built without permit and may not meet building code requirements.

or

Contingent upon social room meeting local building code requirements.

Closing

Full purchase price to be paid and deed to be recorded on or before [_____], {within [_____] days after acceptance}. Both parties shall deposit with an authorized escrow holder, to be selected by Buyer, all funds and instruments necessary to complete the sale in accordance with the terms of this Agreement.

Closing Costs

Title Insurance to be paid by [_____]. Escrow fee {attorney fee} (if any) to be paid by [_____]. Seller to pay cost of clearing the title and any Transfer Tax; Buyer to pay all remaining costs.

Conditions Satisfied or Waived in Writing

Each condition or contingency, covenant, approval or disapproval shall be satisfied according to its terms or waived by written notice delivered to the other party or their Broker.

Consideration Clause

Regardless of an expression to the contrary in the offer (such as,

"[_____] days are hereby irrevocably allowed the agent for obtaining the seller's acceptance,"

any offer not given for consideration on the part of the broker may be revoked prior to acceptance. Occasionally, a broker may have to travel to present the offer to an out-of-town seller or he may have to wait an unusually long period of time for the seller to return from a trip. In such an event, it may be advisable to write a consideration clause into the agreement, such as the one suggested below. Whether such a provision is legally enforceable or not, there is no doubt that it will have a strong moral effect on the party signing such an agreement.

The undersigned Agent agrees to use diligence in effecting a sale of the property between Buyer and Seller, in consideration whereof Buyer agrees not to revoke this offer prior to midnight of [_____].

Contingent upon Closing of Buyer's Property

This Agreement is contingent upon closing of Buyer's real property at [_____] on or before

[____]. If Buyer's escrow is terminated, abandoned or does not close on time, this Agreement shall terminate without further notice unless the parties agree otherwise in writing.

Contingent upon Sale of Buyer's Property

This Agreement is contingent upon Buyer accepting an offer on his/her property at [____] within [____] days after acceptance of this Agreement, and that sale closing on or before [____]. Seller shall have the right to continue to offer the property for sale. When Buyer has accepted an offer on the sale of his/her property, Buyer shall promptly provide written notice of the sale and date of closing to Seller. If Seller accepts a bona fide written offer from a third party prior to Buyer accepting an offer on the sale of his/her property, Seller shall give Buyer written notice of that fact. Within 72 hours after receipt of the notice, Buyer shall waive the contingency on the sale and close of his/her property, or this Agreement shall terminate without further notice. Upon waiver of the contingency, Buyer warrants that funds needed to close will be available and Buyer's ability to obtain financing will not be contingent upon the sale and/or close of any property.

Counterparts

This Agreement may be executed in one or more counterparts, each of which is deemed to be an original.

Default

In the event Buyer shall default in the performance of this Agreement, Seller may, subject to any rights of Broker, retain Buyer's deposit to the extent of damages sustained and may take such actions as he/she deems appropriate to collect such additional damages as may have been actually sustained. Buyer shall have the right to take

*such action as he/she deems appropriate to
recover such portion of the deposit as may be
allowed by law. In the event that Buyer shall
default, unless Buyer and Seller have agreed to
liquidated damages, Buyer agrees to pay the Bro-
ker(s) any commission that would be payable by
Seller in the absence of such default.*

Deposit Increased by Secured Note

The following clause may be used if—at the time the
Agreement of Sale is made—the buyer does not have
sufficient liquid funds, but either has to refinance or
sell or has in escrow another property. It is necessary
for the broker to ascertain that the buyer's equity in
that property is amply sufficient for the cash down
payment; if it is marginal, it is suggested that the
broker guarantee the equity. (See Financing section
under Guaranteed Trade-In Plans.)

*Deposit to be increased to $[_____] in the form of
a note secured by a deed of trust {mortgage} to
be recorded against Buyer's real property
described as [_____] within [_____] days from
acceptance of this agreement.*

Destruction of Improvements

If the improvements of the property are destroyed,
materially damaged or found to be materially defective
prior to closing, Buyer may terminate the transaction
by written notice delivered to Seller's broker or agent,
and all unused deposits shall be returned to Buyer.
In the event Buyer does not elect to terminate the
agreement, Buyer shall be entitled to receive in addition to the property any insurance proceeds payable
on account of the damage or destruction.

Destruction of Premises

*If the improvements of the property are
destroyed, materially damaged or found to be
materially defective as a result of such damage
prior to closing, Buyer may terminate this*

Agreement. In the event Buyer does not elect to terminate this Agreement, Buyer shall be entitled to receive, in addition to the property, any insurance proceeds payable on account of the damage or destruction.

Entire Agreement

This document contains the entire Agreement of the parties and supersedes all prior agreements or representations with respect to the property that are not expressly set forth herein. This Agreement may be modified only in writing, signed and dated by both parties. Both parties acknowledge that they have not relied on any statements of the Real Estate Agent or Broker that are not expressed in this agreement.

Evidence of Title

Evidence of title to be in the form of a policy of title insurance {certificate of title} {abstract of title} {certificate of registration}, issued by [_____], paid by Buyer {paid by Seller}.

Examination of Title

In addition to any encumbrances assumed or taken subject to, Seller shall convey title to the property subject only to (1) real estate taxes not yet due, and (2) covenants, conditions, restrictions, rights of way and easements of record, if any, which do not materially affect the value or intended use of the property.

Within three (3) days after acceptance, Buyer shall order a preliminary title report and copies of CC&Rs and other documents of record if applicable. Within ten days after receipt, Buyer shall report to Seller in writing any valid objections to the title contained in such report other than monetary liens to be paid at closing. If Buyer objects to any exceptions to the title, Seller shall use due diligence to remove such exceptions at his/her own expense before closing. If such exceptions cannot be removed before closing, this Agreement shall terminate, unless Buyer elects to purchase the property subject to such exceptions. If Seller concludes he/she is unable in good faith to remove such objections, Seller shall so notify Buyer within ten days after receipt of said objections. In that event Buyer may terminate this Agreement.

Existing Loans

Seller shall, within three days after acceptance, provide Buyer with copies of all notes and mortgages (deeds of trust) to be assumed or taken subject to. Within five days after receipt, Buyer shall notify Seller in writing of his/her approval or disapproval of the terms of the documents. Approval shall not be unreasonably withheld. Within three days after acceptance, Seller shall submit a written request for a current statement of condition on the above loan(s). Seller warrants that all loans will be current at closing.

Expiration of Offer

This offer shall expire unless acceptance is delivered to Buyer or to Buyer's Broker on or before [_____] A.M./P.M., [_____], 19___ .

Fax Transmission

The facsimile transmission of a signed copy of this offer or any counteroffer to the other party or his/her Broker, followed by faxed acknowledgment of receipt, shall constitute delivery.

Fixtures

All items permanently attached to the property, including light fixtures and bulbs; attached floor coverings; all attached window coverings, including window hardware, window and door screens; storm sash; combination doors; awnings; TV antennas; burglar, fire, smoke and security alarms [unless leased]; pool and spa equipment;

solar systems; attached fireplace screens; electric garage door openers with controls; outdoor plants and trees [other than in movable containers] are included in the purchase price free of liens, excluding [_____].

Insurance

In the event of Seller financing, Buyer shall obtain hazard insurance prepaid for one year in an amount satisfactory to the loanholders and covering 100% replacement cost of improvements and shall name holders of the secured loans as additional loss payees. Buyer agrees further to annually increase said insurance, if necessary, to equal the then current replacement cost of the property during the term of the loanholder's mortgages. Buyer shall instruct the insurance carrier to deliver to Seller before closing a certificate of insurance providing for 30 days' written notice in the event of cancellation.

Loan Approval

Loan approval is conditioned upon Buyer's ability to obtain a commitment for new financing for the property from a lender or mortgage broker of Buyer's choice {and/or consent to assume existing financing} provided for in this Agreement, within _____ days after acceptance. Buyer shall in good faith use his/her best efforts to qualify for and obtain the financing and shall complete and submit a loan application within [_____] days after acceptance.

In the event a loan commitment [consent] is obtained but not honored without fault of Buyer, Buyer may terminate this Agreement.

Maintenance

Seller covenants that any existing heating, air-conditioning, electrical, solar, septic, gutters and downspouts, sprinkler and plumbing systems including well, sewer, water heater, pool and spa systems as well as built-in appliances and the mechanical apparatus shall be in working order on the date possession is delivered. Seller shall replace any cracked or broken glass including windows, mirrors, shower and tub enclosures. Double pane windows with damaged seals, and damaged door and window screens shall be replaced. Shower pans and enclosure shall be free of leaks. Until possession is delivered, Seller shall maintain all structures, landscaping, grounds and pool. Seller agrees to deliver the property in a neat and clean condition with all debris and personal belongings removed. The following items are specifically excluded from the above: _____.

Buyer and Seller understand and acknowledge that Broker shall not in any circumstances be liable for any breach in this clause. Seller's obligations under this provision are not intended to create a warranty with respect to the condition of the property to be maintained, or to create an obligation upon the Seller to repair any item that may fail after possession is delivered.

Mediation of Disputes

If a dispute arises out of or relates to this Agreement or its breach, the parties agree to first try in good faith to settle the dispute by voluntary nonbinding mediation before resorting to court action or arbitration.

No Tax Advice

Buyer and Seller acknowledge that they have not received or relied upon any statements or representations by the Agent regarding the effect of this transaction upon their tax liability.

Personal Property

The following personal property, on the premises when inspected by Buyer, is included in the purchase price and shall be transferred to Buyer free of liens and properly identified by a bill of sale at closing. No warranty is made as to the condition of the personal property. [_____]

Physical Possession after Recordation of the Deed

Physical possession of the property, with keys to all property locks, alarms, and garage door openers shall be delivered to Buyer on the [_____] day after recordation, not later than [_____]A.M./P.M. Seller agrees to pay Buyer in escrow [at closing], as a day-to-day tenant, for the period from recordation until the date specified above or any lesser sum in proportion to the actual date possession is delivered $[_____] per day {the sum of Buyer's principal, interest, taxes and insurance payments and homeowners' dues, if any, for said period.}

Seller understands that continued occupancy beyond the date specified above constitutes a breach of this Agreement in the absence of any written agreement between the parties to the contrary.

Physical Possession at Recordation

Physical possession of the property with keys to all property locks, alarms, and garage door openers shall be delivered to Buyer on the date of recordation of the deed, not later than [_____] A.M./P.M.

Prepayment

Seller shall pay any prepayment charge imposed on any existing loan paid off at closing. Buyer shall pay the prepayment charge on any loan that is to remain upon the property after closing. Seller is encouraged to consult his/her lender regarding prepayment provisions.

Property Tax

Within five days after acceptance, Seller shall deliver to Buyer for his/her approval a copy of the latest property tax bill. Buyer is advised that the property may be reassessed upon change of ownership, which may result in a tax increase. Buyer should make further inquiry at the assessor's office concerning any changes in the property tax. Within ten days after receipt of the tax bill, Buyer shall in writing approve or disapprove the tax bill. In the event of disapproval, Buyer may terminate this Agreement.

Prorations

Rents, real estate taxes, interest, payments on bonds and assessments assumed by Buyer and homeowners' association fees shall be prorated as of the date of recordation of the deed. Security deposits, advance rentals or considerations involving future lease credits shall be credited to Buyer.

Protection of Broker's Commission

In the event that Buyer fails to pay the balance of the purchase price, or to complete the purchase as herein provided, Buyer agrees to pay to Agent the commission that Agent is entitled to receive from Seller as hereinafter provided.

Rental Property

Buyer to take property subject to rights of parties in possession on leases or month-to-month tenancies. Within seven days after acceptance, Seller shall deliver to Buyer for his/her approval copies of the following documents: existing leases and rental agreements with tenants' estoppel certificates, any outstanding notices sent to tenants, a written statement of all oral agreements with tenants, existing defaults by Seller or tenants, claims made by or to tenants, a statement of all tenants' deposits held by Seller, a complete statement of rental income and expenses, any service and equipment rental contracts with respect to the property that run

*beyond the date of closing. Seller warrants all of
this documentation to be true an complete.*

*Within seven days after receipt of documents,
Buyer shall notify Seller in writing of approval or
disapproval of the documents. In case of disapproval, Buyer may terminate this Agreement. During the escrow (settlement) period of this
transaction, Seller agrees that no changes in the
existing leases or rental agreements shall be
made, nor new leases or rental agreements
longer than month-to-month entered into, nor
shall any substantial alterations or repairs be
made or undertaken without the written consent
of the Buyer.*

Right of First Refusal to Purchase Note

In the event of seller financing, it may be to the buyer's advantage to insert the following clause:

*If during the term of the note in favor of Seller, or
any extension thereof, Seller receives an acceptable offer to sell the note, or if Seller wishes to
offer the note for sale, Seller shall first deliver to
Buyer an option to purchase the note at the same
price and terms, to be exercised within 15 days
after receipt of Seller's option.*

Subject to Approval by Authorities

*Subject to Buyer obtaining final approval of his/
her intended use of the property as [_____] from
the appropriate government authorities within
[_____] days from acceptance of this agreement.*

Substitution of Collateral

*Buyer shall have the right, at any time,
upon reasonable prior notice to the holder
of said note, to substitute collateral, as
long as the fair market value of the
collateral, after deducting prior
encumbrances thereon, shall not be less*

*than 110% of the unpaid principal balance
of the note at the time of substitution.*

Survival

*The omission from escrow instructions of any
provision in this Agreement shall not waive the
right of any property. All representations or warranties shall survive the conveyance of the
property.*

Time

*Time is of the essence of this Agreement; pro-
vided, however, that if either party fails to comply
with any provision of this Agreement within the
time limit specified, or any extension thereof, this
Agreement shall not terminate until the other
party delivers written notice to the defaulting
party requiring compliance within 24 hours after
receipt of notice. If the party receiving the notice
fails to comply within said 24 hours, the nonde-
faulting party may terminate this Agreement
without further notice.*

Warranty Against Notice of Violations

*By acceptance hereof, Seller warrants that he/she
has no notice of violations relating to the property from city, county or state agencies.*

Zoning Violations

If a broker has knowledge of any existing zoning violations, he or she must state so in the contract:

*Buyer understands that property is zoned [_____]
and that the basement apartment may not meet
local zoning requirements.*

Or:

*Contingent upon local zoning restrictions
allowing the use of the basement apartment as a
rental unit.*

INSPECTION CLAUSES

Access to Property

Seller agrees to provide reasonable access to the property to Buyer, inspectors, appraisers and other professionals representing Buyer.

Building Code Violations

If a broker has knowledge of possible building code violations, he or she should state so in the contract. Examples:

Buyer understands that the social room was built without permit and may not meet building code requirements.

or

Contingent upon social room meeting local building code requirements.

City and County Inspections

Local ordinance requires that the property be inspected or a report issued for compliance with local building and permit regulations, standards and ordinances as a condition of sale or transfer, within [_____] days. Seller shall notify the appropriate local agency to cause the property to be inspected or to issue the required report at the earliest practicable date. If Seller is unable or unwilling to pay for correction of any violations shown in this report, this agreement shall terminate and all deposits be returned to Buyer unless Buyer agrees to pay the cost of corrections required.

Compliance with Local Laws

Seller shall comply with any local laws applicable to the sale or transfer of the property including but not limited to: (a) providing inspections and/or reports for compliance with local building and permit regulations including septic system inspection reports; (b) complying with minimum energy conservation standards; and (c) complying with water conservation measures. All such inspections and reports shall be at Buyer's expense, except where local law requires otherwise. If seller does not agree within [_____] days after receipt of the report to pay the cost of any repair or improvement required to comply with such laws, Buyer may elect to terminate this Agreement.

Home Protection Contract

A home protection contract [specify plan and company] paid for by [_____] shall become effective upon closing for not less than one year, unless both parties have waived such contract. The Brokers have informed both parties that such protection programs are available but do not approve or endorse any particular program.

Inspections of Physical Condition of Property

Buyer shall have the right to retain at Buyer's expense licensed experts including, but not limited to, engineers, geologists, architects, contractors, surveyors and structural pest control operators to inspect the property for any structural and nonstructural conditions including matters concerning roofing, electrical, plumbing, heating, cooling, electrical appliances, well, sewer, septic system, pool, boundaries, geological and environmental hazards, toxic substances including asbestos, formaldehyde, radon gas and lead-based paint. Buyer, if requested by Seller in writing, shall promptly furnish, at no cost to Seller, copies of all written reports obtained. Buyer shall approve or disapprove in writing all inspection reports obtained within [_____] days after acceptance. In the event of Buyer's disapproval, Buyer may elect to terminate this Agreement.

Maintenance Reserve

Seller agrees to leave in escrow a maintenance reserve in the amount of $[_____]. If in the reasonable opinion of a qualified technician any of the terms listed, under the heading Maintenance, are not in working order, Buyer shall furnish Seller a copy of said technician's inspection report and/or submit written notice to Seller of noncompliance of any of the conditions under Maintenance, within seven days from the date physical possession is delivered.

In the event Seller fails to make the repairs and/or corrections within five days from the receipt of said report or notice, Seller herewith authorizes the escrow holder to disburse to Buyer against bills for such repairs or corrections a total sum limited to the amount reserved. Said reserve shall be disbursed to Buyer or returned to Seller not later than fifteen days from date physical possession is delivered.

Pest Control Inspection

Within ten days after acceptance, Seller shall furnish Buyer, at Buyer's expense, a current written report of an inspection by a licensed structural pest control operator of the main building, all attached structures and the following other structures on the property:[_____].

Seller to pay for: (1) elimination of infestation and/or infection of wood destroying pests or organisms, (2) repair of damage caused by such infestation and/or infection, (3) correction of conditions that caused said damage and (4) repair of plumbing and other leaks affecting wood members, including repair of leaking shower stalls, in accordance with the structural pest control operator's report.

In the event the report recommends work to correct conditions deemed likely to lead to infestation or infection, but where no infestation or infection currently exists, the cost of such work shall be paid by [_____].

If the inspecting structural pest control operator recommends further inspection of inaccessible areas, Buyer may require that said areas by inspected. If any infestation of infection is discovered by such inspection, the additional cost of such inspection and additional work required to correct conditions shall be paid by Seller. If no such infestation or infection is discovered, the additional cost of inspecting such inaccessible areas and the work required to return the property to its original condition shall be paid by Buyer.

Funds for work specified in said report, to be done at Seller's expense, shall be held in escrow and disbursed by escrow holder upon receipt of a statement by said licensed structural pest control operator certifying that the property is free of evidence of active infestation or infection.

As soon as they are available, copies of inspection reports, certifications or other proof of completion of the work shall be delivered to Brokers of Buyer and Seller who are hereby authorized to receive the documents on behalf of their principals.

{Work to be performed at Seller's expense may be performed in whole or in part by the Seller; provided that, upon completion of Seller's work but before the area has been closed up, the property is reinspected by a licensed structural pest control operator at Seller's expense certifying that the inspected property is free of evidence of active infestation or infection.}

Roof Inspection

Buyer shall have the right to order, at Buyer's expense, a roof inspection report from a licensed general or roofing contractor. Copies of the report shall be delivered to the Broker(s) of Buyer and Seller who are authorized to receive them on behalf of their principals.

Within three days after receipt of the report, Seller may (1) elect to pay the cost of all work recommended by such report or (2) elect to pay none or only part of the cost of such work. Written notice of such election shall be delivered to Buyer or his/her Broker. In the event Seller does not agree to pay for any or all such work, Buyer may elect to pay the balance of the cost or terminate this Agreement.

In the event Seller shall have elected to pay the cost of any or all such work, Seller shall have the right to have the work performed by a licensed general or roofing contractor of Seller's choice.

Separate Pest Control Agreement

The Structural Pest Control Agreement of even date, attached hereto, has been made a part of this Agreement prior to its execution.

Stipulate Repairs To Be Made by Seller

If the buyer expects seller to repair broken windows, doors, locks or any other items, it should be clearly stated in the agreement.

Seller shall make the following repairs prior to close of escrow or allow the applicable credit against the cash portion of the purchase price. [List repairs].

Subject to Approval of Existing Pest Control Report

Within 24 hours after acceptance, Seller shall furnish Buyer a copy of the existing pest control report dated [_____], by [_____]. Seller agrees to pay for work, if any, recommended in said report. Within 15 days after acceptance, Buyer shall notify Seller in writing of approval or disapproval of the report. In case of disapproval, Buyer may terminate this Agreement.

{Work recommended in said report may be performed in whole or in part by the Seller, provided that, upon completion of Seller's work but before the area has been closed up, the property *is reinspected by a licensed structural pest control operator at Seller's expense certifying that the inspected property is free of evidence of active infestation or infection.}*

Waiver of Pest Control Inspection

Buyer has satisfied himself/herself about the condition of the property and agrees to purchase the property without the benefit of a structural pest control inspection. Buyer acknowledges that he/she or she has not relied upon any representations by either the Broker or the Seller with respect to matters that would normally be covered in a pest control inspection.

Walk-Through Inspection

Buyer shall have the right to conduct a walk-through inspection of the property within [_____] days prior to closing to verify Seller's compliance with the provisions of this Agreement. Utilities are to remain turned on until the walk-through is completed. This right is not a condition of this Agreement.

INVESTMENT PROPERTY CLAUSES

Changes During Transaction

During the escrow [settlement] period of this transaction, Seller agrees that no changes in the existing leases or rental agreements shall be made, nor new leases or rental agreements longer than month-to-month entered into, nor shall any substantial alterations or repairs be made or undertaken without the written consent of the Buyer.

Existing Leases

Subject to existing leases and rights of parties in possession under month-to-month tenancies. Within [_____] days of acceptance Seller shall

*deliver to Buyer for his/her approval copies of all
existing leases and rental agreements, as well as
copies of all outstanding notices sent to tenants,
and a written statement of all oral agreements
with tenants, uncured defaults by Seller or tenants, claims made by or to tenants, and a statement of all tenants' deposits held by Seller, all of
which Seller warrants to be true and complete.
Buyer's obligations are conditioned upon
approval of existing leases. Buyer shall be
deemed to have approved said documents
unless written notice to the contrary is delivered
to Seller or his agent within [_____] days of
receipt of said documents, in which case Buyer
may have his/her deposit returned and both parties shall be relieved of all obligations hereunder.*

Free Look Permit

*Buyer shall have the right to inspect the real and
personal property and materials described under
the headings Existing Leases and Income and
Expense Statement. Within ten (10) days following the furnishing of such materials, Buyer, in his/
her sole discretion, may by written notice to
Seller terminate all obligations of the parties
hereunder and any deposit shall be returned. If
such notice is not delivered within such time,
Buyer shall be deemed to have approved the condition of the property and the materials
submitted.*

Income and Expense Statement

*Seller shall deliver to Buyer a true and complete
statement of rental income and expenses within
five days of acceptance hereof. Buyer's obligations are conditioned upon approval of said statement. Buyer shall be deemed to have approved
said statement unless notice to the contrary is
delivered to Seller or Seller's agent within five
days of receipt by Buyer.*

Month-to-Month Tenancies

Buyer to take title subject to rights of parties in possession on a month-to-month basis.

Operating Permit

Seller warrants that an operating permit for the property is in effect.

Partial Reconveyances

Buyer intends to subdivide the property and improve the property in stages over a period of time. The mortgage securing Seller's note shall contain provisions for partial reconveyances and release of portions of the property. An agreement with respect to the amount of the note to be repaid for such partial reconveyances and the location of the portions of the property to be reconveyed shall be the subject of an agreement between Buyer and Seller to be prepared by their respective attorneys. In the event the parties are unable to reach an agreement with respect to such provisions within [_____] days from acceptance of this offer, this agreement, at the option of either party, shall be terminated and all deposits shall be refunded.

Permit of Occupancy

Seller warrants that a permit of occupancy for the property is in effect.

Personal Property in Furnished Income Units

The sale price includes all furniture and furnishings and any other personal property owned by Seller and used in the operation of said real property per attached signed inventory. Said personal property to be transferred by Bill of Sale in favor of Buyer at close of escrow.

Service Contracts

Seller shall furnish Buyer with copies of any service and/or equipment rental contracts with respect to the property, which run beyond close of escrow.

Soil Tests

Upon acceptance of this agreement, Buyer shall have the right to go upon the property to conduct soil tests, including percolation tests, to ascertain whether the property is suitable for the improvements that Buyer proposes to make. All expenses of such test shall be borne by Buyer, and Buyer shall be responsible for the repair and restoration of any damage to the property that may be caused by such tests. If in the reasonable opinion of the soil engineer, employed by Buyer, the property is not suitable for the proposed development, at the option of the Buyer, this agreement may be terminated and all deposits shall be refunded. Buyer shall have [_____] days from date of acceptance of this offer to complete said tests or waive this condition in writing.

Subordination Clause

It is recommended that agreements providing for subordination be drawn by legal counsel. The provision given herein is merely intended to acquaint the reader with considerations of a subordination.

The deed of trust {mortgage} securing Seller's note for the balance of the purchase price shall contain a provision permitting subordination of the lien within [_____] months from date of said note, to a prior deed of trust {mortgage} securing a note payable to a recognized financial institution, in an amount not to exceed $[_____], bearing interest at a rate not to exceed [_____]%, payable at a rate of not more than $[_____] per month, with principal not due prior to [_____]; provided that the proceeds of such a note to which Seller subordinates shall be used only for financing improvements on the securing property including a reasonable loan fee.

This right of subordination may be exercised once only {[_____] times only}.

Survey

Upon acceptance of this offer, the property shall be surveyed by a licensed surveyor at the expense of the Buyer, Seller. The purchase price is based upon the price of $_____ per acre square feet and shall be adjusted in accordance with the area set forth in such a survey.

Tax-Deferred Exchange

In the event that Seller wishes to enter into a tax-deferred exchange for the property or Buyer wishes to enter into a tax-deferred exchange with respect to property owned by him/her, in connection with this transaction, each of the parties agrees to cooperate with the other party in connection with such exchange, including the execution of such documents as may be reasonably necessary to complete the exchange provided that (1) the other party shall not be obligated to delay the closing; (2) all additional costs in connection with the exchange shall be borne by the party requesting the exchange; (3) the other party shall not be obligated to execute any note, contract, deed or other document providing for any personal liability that would survive the exchange; and (4) the other party shall not take title to any property other than the property described in this Agreement. It is understood that a party's rights and obligations under this Agreement may be assigned to a third party intermediary to faciliate the exchange. The other party shall be indemnified and held harmless against any liability that arises or is claimed to have arisen on account of the exchange.

DISCLOSURE CLAUSES
Agency Relationship Confirmation

The following agency relationship is hereby confirmed for this transaction: Selling Agent is the agent of the buyer exclusively, or the seller exclusively or both the buyer and seller.

NOTE: This confirmation *does not* take the place of any agency disclosure form that may be required by law.

The following agency relationship is hereby confirmed for this transaction: Listing Agent is the agent of the seller exclusively or both the buyer and seller.

NOTE: This confirmation *does not* take the place of any agency disclosure for that may be required by law.

Asbestos Disclosure

Reports recently documented by the U.S. Environmental Protection Agency (EPA) have indicated that there may be the presence of asbestos in certain types of sprayed ceiling and other building materials used in the construction of homes prior to the use of these materials being banned.

The various materials were banned between 1977 and 1979.

These documented reports and subsequent studies by other government and private agencies have shown that asbestos fibers may be airborne and may then present a health hazard.

PURCHASER MUST INITIAL ONE OF THE FOLLOWING TWO NUMBERED PARAGRAPHS:

[Buyer's initials] 1. Buyer acknowledges receipt of a copy of the booklet prepared by the U.S. Consumer Product Safety Commission and the EPA titled "Asbestos in the Home." Buyer shall have the option for [_____] days from acceptance of the purchase/exchange agreement to order, at Buyer's expense, an inspection and laboratory analysis on the property with regard to the

presence, or absence, of asbestos. In the event the written report of the analysis indicates the presence of asbestos, the Buyer, in Buyer's sole discretion, may elect to terminate the purchase/exchange agreement and have all deposits returned less any fees contractually expended for inspections.

[Buyer's initials] 2. Buyer acknowledges receipt of a copy of the booklet prepared by the U.S. Consumer Product Safety Commission and the EPA titled "Asbestos in the Home." The Buyer elects to waive the right to have the property inspected for the presence of asbestos building materials used in the construction materials of the home and accepts the property in its present unknown condition.

The booklet "Asbestos in the Home," prepared by the U.S. Consumer Product Safety Commission and the EPA, can be ordered by mail (not by phone) by enclosing payment of $1 (includes postage) from: Superintendent of Documents, U.S. Government Printing Office, Washington, DC 20402.

Balloon Payment

Both parties acknowledge that they have not received or relied upon any statements or representations made to them by the Broker regarding availability of funds or rate of interest at which funds might be available when Buyer becomes obligated to refinance or pay off the remaining balance of any loan pursuant to the terms of this Agreement.

Broker Buying as Principal

Seller understands that Buyer is a licensed real estate Broker [salesperson], acting as a principal, for his/her own account.

Broker's Disclaimer

Previously Owned Real/Personal Property: The real property, fixtures and personal property, referred to under Fixtures and Personal Property, may not be new and have been subject to normal wear and tear. The obligations of Seller under Maintenance are not intended to create a warranty with respect to the condition of the property to be maintained or to create an obligation upon the part of the Seller to repair any item that may fail after possession is delivered. Buyer understands that, except as may be provided to the contrary in Additional Terms and Conditions or in any addendum, Seller makes no express or implied warranty with respect to the condition of any of the real property or any personal property included in the sale.

Improvements, Size and Boundaries: Any oral or written representations by Seller or Broker regarding age of improvements, size and square footage of parcel or building, or location of property lines may not be accurate. Apparent boundary line indicators such as fences, hedges, walls or other barriers may not represent the true boundary lines. Only a surveyor can determine the actual boundary lines. If any of these issues are important to Buyer's decision to purchase, then Buyer should consider investigating the property independently.

Hazardous Materials: The real estate broker in this transaction has no expertise with respect to toxic wastes, hazardous materials or undesirable substances, including but not limited to asbestos, formaldehyde or lead or radon, and no representations, either expressed or implied, have been or will be made with respect to the existence or non-existence of such materials on the property. Buyers who are concerned about the presence of such materials are encouraged to have the property inspected by qualified experts.

Buyer acknowledges that he or she has not relied upon any representations that are not contained in this agreement or in the disclosure statements by either the Broker or the Seller with respect to the condition of the property. Both parties are advised that Broker does not investigate *the status of permits, zoning or code compliance; the parties are to satisfy themselves concerning these issues.*

Buyer acknowledges that he/she has not received or relied upon any statements or representations by Broker with respect to the effect of this transaction upon Buyer's tax liability.

Broker Representing Both Parties

By placing their initials here: Buyer: [_____] and Seller: [_____] acknowledge that [_____], the Broker in this transaction, represents both parties and Buyer and Seller consent thereto.

Building Code Violations

If you have knowledge of possible existing Building Code Violations, state so in the contract. Examples:

Buyer understands that the Social Room was built without permit and may not meet Building Code requirements.

Or:

Contingent upon Social Room meeting local Building Code requirements.

Buyer's Approval of Seller's Disclosure Statement

If such disclosure statement is delivered to Buyer after the execution of this offer, Buyer is allowed to terminate this agreement by written notice delivered to Seller or his/her Agent within three (3) days from receipt of said statement and have all deposits returned less expenses incurred to date of termination. Nothing disclosed by Seller shall require Seller to correct or improve the condition disclosed except as otherwise agreed in writing.

Buyer's Broker Disclosure

Seller understands that the Buyer's Broker named in this Agreement is the Agent of the

Buyer and is not the Agent of the Seller or a sub-agent of the Seller's Broker.

Common Interest Development Disclosure

Buyer shall take title of Unit # ___ of the common interest development known as [_____], subject to the governing documents of the development, including declaration of restrictions (master deed), CC&Rs, bylaws, articles of incorporation, rules and regulations currently in force, and financial statement of the homeowners' association, as applicable to the condominium [PUD, stock cooperative or time share], to be delivered to Buyer for his/her approval within 15 days after acceptance. Within 20 days after acceptance, Buyer shall notify Seller of Buyer's approval or disapproval of these documents. In case of disapproval Buyer may elect to terminate this Agreement.

In addition, Seller shall deliver to Buyer before closing a written statement from the homeowners' association documenting the amount of any delinquent assessments including penalties, attorney fees and other charges provided for in the management documents. Such charges (if any) shall be credited to Buyer at closing.

Dual Agency Disclosure

Seller and Buyer understand and acknowledge that Broker has been, and is now, representing both the Seller and the Buyer in this transaction as a dual agent.

The parties understand that this dual agency creates conflicts of interest and that the Broker cannot represent the interests of one party to the exclusion or detriment of the interests of the other party.

The parties understand, and Broker acknowledges, that Broker will act as facilitator or intermediary and will endeavor to be impartial between Seller and Buyer. Except as expressly provided below, Broker in his/her capacity as a dual agent shall disclose to both Seller and Buyer all known latent defects in the property, any matter that must be disclosed by law and information that Broker believes may be material or might affect Seller's or Buyer's decisions with respect to this transaction.

The parties acknowledge that Broker has not disclosed and Broker agrees not to disclose:

1. to Buyer information about what price or terms Seller will accept other than the listed price or terms without the express written permission of the Seller;

2. to Seller information about what price or terms Buyer will offer other than those offered in writing by Buyer without the express written permission of the Buyer; or

3. any information of a confidential nature that could harm one party's bargaining position or benefit the other's.

Both parties agree that Broker shall have the right to collect a commission or fee from both Buyer and Seller, and acknowledge that it has been disclosed that in connection with this transaction Broker will collect a fee of $[_____] or [_____]% of the purchase price, which shall be paid as a cost of said transaction and shall be charged 50% to the Seller and 50% to the Buyer.

In view of Broker's dual agency relationship, the parties understand they have the responsibility of making their own decisions with respect to the terms to be included in their agreement. The parties understand the implications of Broker's dual agency role as facilitator or intermediary rather than as advocate and exclusive representative and have determined that the benefits of entering into this transaction with Broker acting as dual agent outweigh said implications.

Therefore, Seller and Buyer both, and each of them individually, consent to Broker's dual agency and hereby waive any claims now or hereafter arising out of such conflicts of interest or for breach of fiduciary duty.

Both parties are advised to seek competent legal advice with regard to this transaction and with regard to all documents executed in connection therewith.

Seller and Buyer understand this document does not replace prior agreements entered into with Broker (i.e., the Exclusive Right to Represent Buyer agreement signed by Buyer on [_____], and the Exclusive Right to Sell agreement signed by Seller on [_____]).   However, in any areas where this document contradicts or conflicts with those documents, this Dual Agency Disclosure Amendment shall supersede.

Due-On-Sale Clause

If the note and deed of trust [mortgage] for any existing loan contains an acceleration or due-on-sale clause, the lender may demand full payment of the entire loan balance as a result of this transaction. Both parties acknowledge that they are not relying on any representation by the other party or the Broker with respect to the enforceability of such a provision in existing deeds of trust [mortgages], or deeds of trust [mortgages] to be executed in accordance with this Agreement. Both parties have been advised by Broker to seek independent legal advice with respect to these matters.

Earthquake Hazard Zone (For Use in California)

The property is situated in an earthquake fault zone or seismic hazard zone as designated under §2621-2625 and §2690-2699.6 of the California Public Resources Code. Construction or development of any structure for human occupancy may be restricted. No representations on the subject are made by Seller or Broker. Buyer may make further independent inquiries at appropriate governmental agencies concerning the use of the property under the terms of the above statutes. Within seven (7) days after acceptance, Buyer shall notify Seller in writing of satisfaction or dis-satisfaction of said inquiries. In case of dissatis-faction Buyer may terminate this Agreement.

Federal Fair Housing Law

The following clause may be inserted in contracts such as leases and purchase agreements:

Buyer and Seller understand that the federal Fair Housing Law prohibits discrimination in the sale, rental, appraisal, financing or advertising of housing on the basis of race, color, religion, sex, familial status, handicap or national origin.

The federal Fair Housing Act, as amended in 1988, provides that it is unlawful for any person or entity engaged in residential real estate–related transactions to discriminate against any person on the basis of race, color, religion, sex, familial status, handicap or national origin in the sale, rental, appraisal or financing of housing including

- refusing to sell or rent after a bona fide offer has been made, refusing to negotiate for the sale or rental of a dwelling;
- discriminating in the terms, conditions or privileges of a sale or rental or in providing services or facilities;
- making any statement or publishing any advertisement that indicates any preference, limitation or discrimination;
- making false representations with respect to the availability of a dwelling unit;
- attempting to induce owners to sell or rent dwellings by making representations about the entry of certain classes of people into the neighborhood (block busting); or
- discriminating in the making or purchasing of loans or in providing other financial assistance for purchasing, constructing, improving, repairing or maintaining a dwelling.

Protection against discrimination on the basis of familial status includes (1) individuals under the age of 18 living with a parent or other legal custodian and (2) any person who is pregnant or is in the process of securing legal custody (adopting) of any individual under the age of 18.

Housing providers are required to admit families with children unless the housing is categorized under the act as one of the following three categories of housing for older persons: (1) all housing specifically provided under state and federal programs for accommodating elderly persons; (2) housing intended for and solely occupied by persons 62 years of age or older; (3) housing commonly known as retirement communities, where at least 80% of the units must be occupied by one person in each unit who has attained the age of 55 with no restrictions on the remaining units.

Protection against discrimination on the basis of handicap includes persons with a physical or mental impairment that substantially limits such persons' major life activities. Such activities would include caring for one's self, performing manual tasks, walking, seeing, hearing, speaking, breathing, learning and working. Protection also includes persons with a record of such impairments or who are regarded as having such impairments.

Although landlords are not required to make modifications for handicapped persons, they must permit handicapped tenants to make reasonable modifications at the tenant's own expense if such modifications are necessary to provide the tenant with full enjoyment of the premises (e.g., installation of handbars in stall showers, lowering light switches and other environmental controls). The landlord may require the tenant to return the premises to its original state at tenant's expense. Landlords are also required to make reasonable exceptions in house rules and policies to accommodate handicapped tenants (e.g., allowing a guide dog or reserving a convenient parking place for a wheelchair tenant).

The foregoing discussion is a summary of the federal Fair Housing Act of 1968 and September 13,

1988, amendments. For additional information, contact HUD.

Please also refer to Fair Housing Laws in the Risk Management section.

Federal Safety Booklets

Buyer acknowledges receipt of the following safety booklet(s): ["Environmental Hazard Booklet," "Lead-Based Paint Disclosure," "Asbestos in the Home" and others.]

Flood Hazard Zone

Under the National Flood Insurance Reform Act of 1994, federally regulated financial institutions are required to escrow flood insurance premiums for covered loans along with taxes and other insurance premiums. The mandatory flood insurance escrow requirements apply to any covered loan that is made, increased, extended or renewed after September 23, 1995. Lenders and borrowers may now rely on a determination by the director of the Federal Emergency Management Agency (FEMA) stating whether the building is in a special flood hazard area.

Buyer has been advised that the property is located in a special flood hazard area designated by the Federal Emergency Management Agency (FEMA). It will be necessary to purchase flood insurance in order to obtain any loan secured by the property from any federally regulated financial institution or a loan insured or guaranteed by an agency of the U.S. government. The purpose of the program is to provide flood insurance at reasonable cost. For further information consult your lender or insurance broker.

Foreign Investment and Real Property Tax Act (FIRPTA)

Effective January 1, 1985, Sec. 1445 of the Internal Revenue Code requires a buyer of real property to withhold 10% of the sale price and deposit that amount with the IRS upon closing if the seller is a foreign corporation or partnership or a nonresident alien unless the seller or the property qualifies for an exemption under the act.

Exemptions to the withholding requirement include the following situations:

1. Buyer acquires the property for his or her personal residence, and the purchase price does not exceed $300,000.

2. Seller delivers a nonforeign affidavit stating under penalty of perjury that the seller is not a foreign person and stating the seller's U.S. taxpayer's identification number. (The brokers involved in the transaction may become liable for the tax if they have knowledge that an affidavit is false or that the seller is a foreign person and fail to disclose the facts to the buyer.)

3. Buyer receives from the IRS a Withholding Certificate stating that no withholding is required.

If the property is acquired for use as a residence and the price is $300,000 or less, the buyer, for his or her own and for the broker's protection, should sign a FIRPTA buyer certification in which he or she declares the intention to use the property as his or her residence.

Where the broker knows that withholding may be required, he or she should advise the buyer to consult with his or her attorney or accountant.

In some states, laws may require withholding of state income tax. For example, California requires withholding of 3⅓% of the gross sale price.

The following clause should be included in a FIRPTA buyer certification:

The Foreign Investment and Real Property Tax Act requires a Buyer of real property to withhold 10% of the sale price and to deposit that amount with the IRS upon closing if the Seller is a foreign person, foreign corporation or partnership, or nonresident alien unless the property qualifies for an exemption under the act.

Unless it is established that the transaction is exempt because the purchase price is $300,000 *or less and the Buyer intends to use the property as his or her primary residence, Seller agrees to:*

a. Provide Broker with a nonforeign seller affidavit (Professional Publishing Corporation Form 101-V) stating under penalty of perjury that Seller is not a foreign person;

or:

b. Provide Broker with a certificate from the Internal Revenue Service establishing that no federal income tax withholding is required;

or:

c. Subparagraphs (a) or (b) to be provided to Buyer within [_____] days of acceptance or Seller consents to withholding of 10% from the sale proceeds, to be deposited with the IRS.

Hazardous Materials Addendum

(This addendum may also be used with leases and other agreements.)

Various materials utilized in the construction of any improvements to property may contain materials that have been or may in the future be determined to be toxic, hazardous or undesirable and may need to be specially handled and/or removed from the property. For example, some electrical transformers and other electrical components can contain PCBs, and asbestos has been used in a wide variety of building components such as fireproofing, air duct insulation, acoustical tiles, spray-on acoustical materials, linoleum, floor tiles and plaster. Due to current or prior uses, the property or improvements may contain materials such as metals, minerals, chemicals, hydrocarbons, biological or radioactive materials and other substances that are considered, or in the future may be determined to be, toxic wastes, hazardous materials or undesirable substances. Such substances may be in above- and below-ground containers on the property or may be present on or in soils, water, building components or other portions of the property in areas that may not be accessible or noticeable.

Current and future federal, state and local laws and regulations may require the clean-up of such toxic, hazardous or undesirable materials at the expense of those persons who in the past, present or future have had any interest in the property including, but not limited to, current, past and future owners and users of the property. Sellers and Buyers are advised to consult with independent legal counsel of their choice to determine the potential liability with respect to toxic, hazardous or undesirable materials. Sellers and Buyers should also consult with such legal counsel to determine what provisions regarding toxic, hazardous or undesirable materials they may wish to include in purchase and sale agreements, leases, options and other legal documentation related to transactions they contemplate entering into with respect to the property.

The real estate salesperson and brokers in this transaction have no expertise with respect to toxic wastes, hazardous materials or undesirable substances in or on the property. The real estate salesperson and brokers in this transaction have not made, nor will make, any representations, either expressed or implied, regarding the existence or nonexistence of toxic wastes, hazardous materials or undesirable substances in or on the property. Problems involving toxic wastes, hazardous materials or undesirable substances can be extremely costly to correct. It is the responsibility of Sellers and Buyers to retain qualified experts to deal with the detection and correction of such matters.

Buyers and Sellers are directed to seek further information concerning any and all future correctional measures, if any, from municipal, county, state and/or federal agencies.

Receipt Acknowledged:

Seller/Owner [signature]
Buyer/Lessee [signature]
Dated: [_____]

Owners' Association Disclosure

Buyer shall take title subject to the governing documents of the development including declaration of restrictions or CC&Rs, bylaws, articles of incorporation, rules and regulations currently in force and financial statement of the owners' association, as applicable to common interests including condominiums, PUDs, stock cooperatives or time shares, to be delivered to Buyer for his/her approval within 15 days of acceptance. Buyer shall be deemed to have approved said documents unless written notice to the contrary is delivered to Seller or his/her agent within five (5) days of receipt by Buyer, in which case Buyer may have his/her deposit returned and both parties shall be relieved of all obligations hereunder.

In addition, Seller delivers to Buyer before close of escrow a written statement from the owners' association documenting the amount of any delinquent assessments including penalties, attorney's fees and other charges provided for in the management documents. Such charges shall be credited to Buyer at closing.

Property Tax

Within five (5) days after acceptance, Seller shall deliver to Buyer for his/her approval a copy of the latest property tax bill. Buyer is advised that the property may be reassessed upon change of ownership, which may result in a tax increase. Buyer should make further inquiry at the assessor's office concerning any changes in the property tax. Within ten (10) days after receipt of the tax bill, Buyer shall in writing approve or disapprove the tax bill. In the event of disapproval, Buyer may terminate this Agreement.

Rent Control Ordinance

Buyer is aware that a local ordinance is in effect that regulates the rights and obligations of property owners. It may also affect the manner in which future rents can be adjusted.

Seller's Disclosure Statement

On or before delivery of the accepted offer or counteroffer, Buyer shall receive a property disclosure statement prepared and signed by Seller. If Buyer is not satisfied with any condition of the property disclosed in the statement and that was not previously known to Buyer, he/she may terminate the transaction by written notice delivered to Seller's broker or agent within 72 hours of receipt of Seller's property disclosure statement or notify Seller's broker or agent in writing within said 72 hours of Buyer's election to order additional inspections of the property by appropriate professionals.

If Buyer is not satisfied with the result of any such inspections, he/she may terminate the transaction by written notice delivered to Seller's broker or agent, together with copies of all inspection reports, within 15 days of receipt of Seller's property disclosure statement.

Buyer understands that Seller's property disclosure statement is not a substitute for property inspections by professionals, including but not limited to engineers, architects, general contractors and structural pest control operators, and that Buyer has the opportunity to retain and pay for such professionals as he/she believes are appropriate. Buyer understands and acknowledges that the Brokers and Agents in the transaction cannot warrant the condition of the property or guarantee that all defects have been disclosed by Seller.

Seller agrees to hold all brokers and agents in the transaction harmless and to defend and indemnify them from any claim, demand, action or proceedings resulting from any omission or alleged omission by Seller in his/her property disclosure statement.

See also Buyer's Approval of Seller's Disclosure Statement.

Single Agency

Notwithstanding agreements with respect to payment of commissions or rights granted under multiple listing agreements, the parties agree that the Seller's Broker named herein is the agent of the Seller and is not the agent of the Buyer and that the Buyer's Broker named herein is the agent of the Buyer and is not the agent of the Seller or a subagent of Seller's Broker.

Special Studies Zone Act (California Only)

Buyer has been advised that the property is situated in a special studies zone designated under the act and that consequently construction or improvement of any structure for human occupancy may require the submission of a favorable geological report prepared by a registered geologist, unless such report is waived by the city or county under the terms of the act. Neither Seller nor Broker has made any representation with respect to either the cost of such report or the geological characteristics of the property.

Subject to Approval by Authorities

Subject to Buyer obtaining approval of his or her intended use of the property as [_____] from the appropriate governmental agency within [_____] days after acceptance.

Warranty Against Notice of Violations

By acceptance hereof, Seller warrants that he/she has no notice of violations relating to the property from city, county or state agencies.

Zoning Violations

If you have knowledge of any existing zoning violations, be sure to state so in the contract. For example:

*Buyer understands that the property is zoned
[＿＿＿] and that the basement apartment may
not meet local zoning requirements.*

or:

*Contingent upon local zoning requirements
allowing the use of the basement apartment as a
rental unit.*

DISCLAIMER CLAUSES

Boundaries

*Apparent boundary line indicators such as
fences, hedges, walls or other barriers may not
represent the true boundary lines of the property.
Any oral or written representations by Seller or
Broker regarding location of property lines may
not be accurate. If the exact location of boundary
lines is important to Buyer's decision to purchase, Buyer is encouraged to order a survey of
the property.*

Environmental Condition of the Property

*Buyer understands that the Broker has no exper-
tise with respect to toxic wastes, hazardous materials or undesirable substances including, but not
limited to, asbestos, formaldehyde, lead-based
paint, radon gas or underground storage tanks.
Buyer and Seller acknowledge that they have not
received or relied upon any statements, representations or characterizations by the Broker(s) with
respect to the environmental condition of the
property that are not expressed in writing.*

Previously Owned Real/Personal Property

*The real property, fixtures and personal property
included in the sale may not be new and may
have been subject to normal wear and tear.
Buyer understands that, except as provided to
the contrary in this Agreement, Seller makes no*

*express or implied warranty with respect to the
condition of such property included in the sale.*

Tax Liability

*Buyer and Seller acknowledge that they have not
received or relied upon any statements or representations by the Broker(s) regarding the effect of
this transaction upon their tax liabilities.*

COUNTEROFFER CLAUSES

Change in Price

Price to be increased to $[_____] in cash.
Or:

*{Price to be increased to $[_____] by increasing
the note to Seller to $[_____] payable at $[_____]
per month or more, including interest at [_____]%
per annum.}*

Contingency-Release Clause

*Subject to the sale and conveyance of Buyer's
Property, described as [address], within [_____]
days. Seller may continue to offer the herein
property for sale and accept written offers subject to the rights of Buyer. Should Seller accept
such an offer, then Buyer shall be delivered written notice of such acceptance. This agreement
shall terminate within [_____] days from receipt
of notice unless Buyer within said time (1) waives
this contingency in writing and (2) warrants and
demonstrates to Seller's satisfaction that adequate funds needed for closing will be available
and that Buyer's ability to obtain financing will
not be conditioned upon sale and/or closing of
any property.*

Contingent Upon Closing of Buyer's Property

*Contingent upon closing of Buyer's real property
at [_____] on or before [_____]. If Buyer's escrow
is terminated, abandoned or does not close on*

time, this Agreement shall terminate without further notice unless the parties agree otherwise in writing.

Contingent Upon Sale of Buyer's Property

Contingent upon Buyer accepting an offer on his/her property at [_____] within [_____] days after acceptance of this Agreement and on that sale closing on or before [_____]. Seller shall have the right to continue to offer the property for sale. When Buyer has accepted an offer on the sale of his/her property, buyer shall promptly provide written notice of the sale and date of closing to Seller. If Seller accepts a bona fide written offer from a third party prior to Buyer accepting an offer on the sale of his/her property, Seller shall give Buyer written notice of that fact. Within 72 hours after receipt of the notice, Buyer shall waive the contingency on the sale and close of his or her property or this Agreement shall terminate without further notice. Upon waiver of the contingency, Buyer warrants that funds needed to close will be available and Buyer's ability to obtain financing will not be contingent upon the sale and/or close of any property.

Counteroffer

In response to the offer to purchase the real property known as [_____], made by [_____], dated [_____], the following counteroffer is hereby submitted: 1. _____ 2. _____ 3. _____, etc.
Dated _____ Time _____ A.M./P.M.
Seller _____ Seller _____

Expiration

Each offer and counteroffer should provide for expiration after a certain period of time.

This counteroffer shall expire unless a copy with Buyer's written acceptance is delivered to Seller

or Seller's agent on or before [_____]
o'clock _____ A.M., _____ P.M., on [date].

Invitation to Submit New Offer

In lieu of delivering multiple counteroffers, the seller's agent should consider the possibility of advising each of the persons submitting offers that the seller has received more than one offer for the purchase of the property and has elected to reject all offers but will consider a new offer that the buyer may wish to submit at a designated time and place. Such a procedure will avoid controversy over acceptance of a counteroffer by more than one prospective buyer and may result in a higher price being offered by the prospective buyers.

The offeror is hereby alerted to the fact that several offers have been submitted, all of which are unacceptable. Therefore, the Owner elects to reject all offers and invites submission of new offers that will be reviewed for acceptance at [_____] o'clock _____ A.M., _____ P.M., on [date]. Such new offers may be submitted to Owner's agent, [Listing Agent's name], on or before said time.

Limitation of Pest Control Work

Pest control work chargeable to Seller not to exceed $[_____]. If work exceeds this amount, the herein Agreement shall be null and void unless Buyer relieves Seller in writing of responsibility for additional amount within [_____] days from acceptance of this agreement.

{Seller reserves the right to approve pest control report.}

{Seller will permit property to be inspected by a licensed pest control operator but will not pay for any work recommended. Buyer to relieve Seller

*in writing of any responsibility in connection
therewith within [____] days of acceptance.}*

Loan Approval

*Buyer shall use his or her best efforts to obtain a
commitment for new financing for the property
from a lender or mortgage broker of Buyer's
choice {and/or consent to assume existing financ-
ing} provided for in this Agreement, within
[____] days after acceptance. Buyer shall in
good faith use his or her best efforts to qualify for
and obtain the financing and shall complete and
submit a loan application within [____] days
after acceptance.*

Multiple Counteroffers

The problem with having the seller make simultaneous counteroffers is that the seller runs the risk of
having more than one of his simultaneous counteroffers accepted and, therefore, being in contract with
more than one Buyer. In an effort to avoid such risk
the following language may be inserted into multiple
counteroffers.

*Buyer understands and acknowledges that Seller
is making a counteroffer to more than one prospective Buyer and that the counteroffers may
not contain identical terms and conditions.*

*Until a copy with Buyer's signed acceptance
of this multiple counteroffer, or transmission by
facsimile thereof, is received by Seller's Agent
and confirmed in writing by Seller, Buyer's acceptance of this multiple counteroffer shall not be
binding, and Seller reserves the right to accept
any other offer or make counteroffers to any
other persons and shall have no obligation to sell
the property to Buyer.*

*In the event more than one accepted multiple
counteroffer shall be received by Seller simultaneously, Seller reserves the right to determine
which accepted multiple counteroffer to confirm.*

*This multiple counteroffer shall expire unless
a copy hereof with Buyer's signed acceptance is
received by Seller or his/her Agent not later than
[_____] o'clock _____ A.M., _____ P.M., on [date].*

Other Changes

Insert all other provisions deviating from the
terms and conditions on the face of the
agreement.

Other Terms

All other terms to remain the same.

Preventive Work

*Seller shall not be responsible for any work rec-
ommended to correct conditions usually deemed
likely to lead to infestation or infection of wood-
destroying pests or organisms but where no evidence of active infestation or infection is found
with respect to such conditions.*

Right To Accept Other Offers

*Owner reserves the right to accept any other
offer prior to Offeror's written acceptance of this
counteroffer. Acceptance shall not be effective
until a copy of this counteroffer, dated and
signed by Offeror, is personally received by [list-
ing agent's name], the agent of the Owner.*

SEPARATE AGREEMENTS

*In reference to Agreement of Sale between
[_____] the Buyer and [_____] the Seller, dated
[_____], covering the real property commonly
known as [_____], the undersigned Buyer and
Seller hereby agree to the following: [_____].*

*The herein Agreement, upon its execution by
both parties, is herewith made an integral part of
the aforementioned Agreement of Sale.*

BUYER [signature] [date]
SELLER [signature] [date]

BACKUP OFFERS

In the event the seller's broker receives an offer to purchase seller's property after seller has already entered into a legal contract with another buyer, it is the broker's obligation to inform the seller of such a secondary offer.

A seller may be tempted to accept such a secondary offer as a backup offer, to take effect in case the transaction under the existing contract cannot be completed. However, the seller should be made aware that, by accepting a secondary offer, he or she would have in effect two contracts, only one of which could be performed. The seller, therefore, would run the risk of being in breach under one contract and liable to that buyer for any damages occasioned by this breach.

If the seller instructs the broker not to present such a secondary offer, the broker should obtain such instruction in writing.

If the seller insists on accepting a secondary offer as a backup, the following form may be used as part of a secondary offer for approval and acceptance by seller and buyer. In such event the broker should advise the seller to obtain his or her own legal counsel's approval before signing such an agreement.

DISCLOSURE OF PRIMARY PURCHASE AGREEMENT

This disclosure is with reference to the offer to purchase the real property commonly known as made by [_____] dated [_____].

A. Seller acknowledges that this offer and the primary purchase agreement have been reviewed by Seller's legal counsel before entering into this contract.

B. Secondary Buyer acknowledges he/she is in a secondary position to a primary contract and further that the Seller reserves the right to make modifications to the terms and conditions of the primary contract without the modifications having the effect of placing the secondary offer in primary position.

C. *Secondary Buyer cannot see the primary purchase agreement unless granted written permission by the Seller.*

D. *The secondary offer deposit check shall be held uncashed by the Secondary Buyer's Broker, and escrow shall be opened only after the Secondary Buyer receives notice in writing from the Seller that the secondary contract is in a primary position.*

E. *All time periods for performance contained in the secondary offer shall begin on the date the secondary offer is placed in a primary position in writing.*

F. *Secondary Buyer reserves the right to terminate this contract without liability after [date] by giving written notice to that effect to the Seller or Seller's agent at any time prior to Buyer's receipt of notice from Seller advising that secondary contract is in first position.*

G. *In any event, this offer shall be null and void and all deposits shall be refunded to Buyer if this secondary offer is not placed in primary position before [date].*

Acknowledged:

SELLER [signature] [date]

SECONDARY BUYER [signature] [date]

OPTIONS

An *option* is an agreement to hold an offer open for a specified period of time, usually in consideration for the payment of a certain sum of money. The person granting the option is the optionor. The person receiving the option is the optionee. The optionor cannot withdraw the option before its expiration date. The consideration for an option is not returnable to the optionee if he or she fails to exercise the option; if the optionee does exercise the option, the consideration is usually applied to the purchase price.

OPTION AGREEMENT

In consideration of the payment by the undersigned optionee in the amount of $[_____], receipt of which is hereby acknowledged, optionor grants to optionee an option to purchase the real property described in the Agreement of Sale on the reverse side upon all the terms and conditions set forth therein. If not exercised, this option shall expire [_____] days from date. The option shall be exercised by mailing or delivering written notice to the optionor prior to the expiration of this option. Notice, if mailed, shall be by certified mail, postage prepaid, to the optionor at the address set forth below and shall be deemed to have been given upon the day following the day shown on the postmark of the envelope in which such notice is mailed.

In the event the option is exercised, the said sum of $[_____] shall [shall not] be credited upon the purchase price.

In the event the option is exercised, the Agreement of Sale on the reverse side shall be effective as if the offer and acceptance thereof had both been made upon the date the option is exercised.

LEASE WITH OPTION TO PURCHASE

A *lease with option to purchase*, also referred to as a *lease option,* entitles the lessee to purchase the demised property for a price and upon terms provided in the agreement by exercising the option within a specified period of time. Usually, the agreement provides for all or a portion of the rent to be credited toward the purchase price.

From the tenant-buyer's point of view, lease option advantages include (1) low cash requirement; (2) full or partial rent credit toward the down payment; (3) lock-in of the purchase price at today's market value; (4) lower rental payments than mortgage payments; (5) ability to sell the purchase option (unless prohibited by its terms) and (6) time to plan how to finance the purchase.

From the landlord-seller's point of view, lease-option advantages include (1) higher monthly rent than market rent, thus reducing negative cash flow; (2) an option price that can be set at top market value; (3) a tenant who usually will care for the home more like an owner; (4) tax-free use of the option money until the option expires or is exercised and (5) continued tax deductions for expenses and depreciation during the option period.

The terms and conditions of a lease option are as complex as the combined terms of a lease and purchase agreement.

LEASES

The real estate broker's concern in the lease transaction is its business aspect, which includes appraising the rental value of the premises, procuring a suitable tenant and negotiating the terms of the lease. With the possible exception of simple residential leases, brokers should not attempt to prepare leases without advice from qualified legal counsel. Printed form leases seldom meet all the parties' needs in a particular case, and substantial modifications in phraseology of the printed form or addition of complicated provisions are often necessary. A printed form lease should not be used or accepted without carefully reading and understanding all the terms and conditions.

Most printed forms are heavily weighted in favor of the owner and lessor and may provide little protection for the lessee. Generally, the importance of the individual provisions will vary directly with the term of the lease. Obviously, if the lease is to be of a very short duration, neither the lessee nor the lessor will be concerned with many of the terms because they will only be bound for a short time. However, even for a short period, a provision that could result in substantial expense to the lessee should not be utilized unless the lessee fully understands its import. For instance, in most form leases, the lessee is required to make all repairs with the usual exception of the roof and sidewalls. Where there are extensive electrical, plumbing, or other facilities on the premises that are likely to be troublesome, this provision should be carefully considered. Furthermore, most persons do not realize that the repairs may extend to concealed or buried pipes, electrical conduits or wiring.

In a long-term lease, the lessee may have a substantial investment in leasehold improvements or goodwill value created by advertising and promotion. A lease provision that would deprive the lessee of these benefits without compensation is unjust.

Provisions with respect to possible termination of the lease in the event of partial destruction should be examined and carefully considered by persons competent to do so. If the property is condemned, the law prevailing in most jurisdictions provides that, in the absence of an agreement to the contrary, the lessee is entitled to the bonus value of his or her leasehold interest. This bonus value may briefly be described as the value of the premises that is in excess of the balance of the rent that is required to be paid under the lease. Most form leases provide that in the event of condemnation the lease terminates and the landlord is entitled to all of the proceeds.

Other clauses that may be troublesome are provisions requiring the lessee to conform to local laws and ordinances when there is a possibility that the lessee will be required to make alterations in the premises to conform to revised building codes or other laws affecting the premises.

Another common provision is prohibition against assignment or subletting. This may be a severe financial burden on a lessee who can no longer use the premises, and it is common to add a provision that the consent will not be unreasonably withheld.

Not only is an attorney qualified by education and training to evaluate the importance of the various terms and conditions of a lease, but furthermore, when he or she is familiar with a client's business affairs, an attorney is better able to anticipate problems that may be caused by particular provisions in the lease as they relate to the business of the lessee.

ESSENTIAL PARTS OF THE LEASE

1. Names of lessor and lessee
2. Agreement to lease (demise)
3. Description of premises
4. Duration of lease
5. Rental amount and method of payment
6. Rights and obligations of lessor and lessee

Names of Lessor and Lessee

It is important that the lessor's name be exactly the same as it is in the instrument under which the lessor holds title or possession. The names of individuals should be accompanied by their marital status. A standard opening clause in a lease reciting the names of the parties, may read as follows:

THIS LEASE, made this [_____] day of [_____] , 19[_____], between [_____], Lessor, and [_____], Lessee;

Agreement to Lease (Demise)

The agreement to lease may read as follows:

Lessor does hereby lease to Lessee and Lessee does hereby lease from Lessor those certain premises with appurtenances, hereinafter called premises, situated in the city of [_____], county of [_____], state of [_____], and described as follows: [_____].

Description of Premises

The description of the property must be such that it can be readily identified. Depending upon the type of property, this may be the street address, the legal description, attachment of a blueprint of the space leased, and so forth.

Rights and privileges essential to the lessee's intended use of the premises are then stated (e.g., use of adjacent parking lot, railroad siding, and so forth). Restrictions and encumbrances that may limit the lessee's intended use of the premises are listed. Inventories of personal property included in the lease should be attached to the lease contract; the condition of the personal property should be stated and provisions made as to the lessee's obligation to maintain and replace such property.

Duration of Lease

The term of this lease shall be for [_____] and shall commence on the [_____], day of [_____], 19[_____], and end on the [_____] day of [_____], 19[_____], inclusive.

The day on which the lease is executed is not necessarily the day on which the lease goes into effect.

Rental Amount and Method of Payment

Rent in the total amount of $[_____] shall be paid to Lessor, without deduction or offset, at such place or places as may be designated from time to time by Lessor, in equal monthly installments of $[_____], in advance, on the [_____] day of each and every month during the term of the lease, commencing on the [_____] day of [_____], 19[_____], until the entire amount shall have been paid.

Rights and Obligations of Lessor and Lessee

The scope of this volume does not permit an extensive discussion of the covenants contained in most printed lease forms. Some simple clauses follow that may be inserted in a printed lease form and submitted to the client's attorney for approval. These clauses are primarily given for use in residential leases.

LEASE CLAUSES

Cost of Living Increase

The rent provided for herein shall be adjusted effective upon the first day of the month immediately following the expiration of [_____] months from date of commencement of the term and upon the expiration of each [_____] months thereafter in accordance with changes in the U.S. Consumer Price Index for All Urban Consumers (1982–84 = 100) hereinafter called the CPI. The monthly rent shall be increased to an amount equal to the monthly rent set forth herein multiplied by a fraction, the numerator of which is the CPI for the second calendar month immediately preceding the adjustment date and the denominator of which is the CPI for the second calendar month preceding the commencement of the lease term, provided, however, in no event shall the monthly rent be less than the amount set forth herein.

Estoppel Certificate

1. *Lessee shall at any time upon not less than ten (10) days' prior written notice from Lessor execute, acknowledge and deliver to Lessor a statement in writing (1) certifying that this Lease is unmodified and in full force and effect [or, if modified, stating the nature of such modification and certifying that this Lease, as so modified, is in full force and effect], the amount of any security deposit and the date to which the rent and other charges are paid in advance, if any, and (2) acknowledging that there are not, to Lessee's knowledge, any uncured defaults on the part of Lessor hereunder or specifying such defaults if any are claimed. Any such statement may be conclusively relied upon by any prospective buyer or encumbrancer to the premises.*
2. *At Lessor's option, Lessee's failure to deliver such statement within such time shall be a*

material breach of this Lease and shall be conclusive upon Lessee (1) that this lease is in full force and effect, without modification except as may be represented by Lessor, and (2) that there are no uncured defaults in Lessor's performance.

3. If Lessor desires to finance, refinance or sell the premises, or any part thereof, Lessee hereby agrees to deliver to any lender or buyer designated by Lessor such financial statements of Lessee as may be reasonably required by such lender or buyer. Such statements shall include the past three years' financial statements of Lessee. All such financial statements shall be received by Lessor and such lender or buyer in confidence and shall be used only for the purposes herein set forth.

Hazardous Materials

Lessee shall not store, use or dispose of any hazardous substance upon the premises, except that Lessee may use and store hazardous substances upon the premises if such substances are customarily used in the business of Lessee to be carried upon the premises and such use or storage is in compliance with all environmental laws. Hazardous substance means any hazardous waste, substance or toxic material that is regulated under any environmental laws or regulations applicable to the property.

Memorandum of Lease for Recordation

This contract, made this [_____] day of [_____], 19[_____], between [_____], hereinafter called Lessor, and [_____], hereinafter called Lessee, witnesseth:

Lessor has agreed to let and hereby does let and demise to Lessee and Lessee has agreed to take and hereby does take from Lessor the following described real property [_____], for a term of

> [_____] years, commencing [_____], 19[_____],
> subject to the terms and conditions more particu-
> larly set forth in a lease agreement between Les-
> sor and Lessee bearing even date herewith.
>
> IN WITNESS WHEREOF, the parties hereto
> have executed this instrument the day and year
> first herein above written.
>
> Lessor [signature] [date]
> Lessee [signature] [date]

Option to Purchase

In the event a lease is drawn with an option to purchase, the terms and conditions of such purchase are
as complex as in a regular sales agreement. It is,
therefore, suggested to simply insert a clause into the
lease referring to a sales agreement attached to the
lease, with a clause in the sales agreement referring
to the lease.

The following clause is to be written into the lease.

> The Lessee shall have the option to purchase the
> leased premises at any time prior to [_____]. The
> option shall be exercised by mailing a written
> notice to Lessor electing to purchase, prior to
> said date. The purchase shall be made in accor-
> dance with the terms and conditions set forth in
> the attached sales agreement of even date that
> shall be deemed to have been executed by both
> parties on the date of the exercise of the option.
>
> If the option is exercised, $[_____] of the rent
> paid hereunder shall be applied on the purchase
> price.
>
> In the event the Lessee purchases the herein
> described real property during the term of this
> lease or any renewal or extension thereof, the
> Lessor agrees to pay to [_____], the Broker in this
> transaction, a selling commission of [_____]% of
> the selling price.

The following clause is to be written into the sales
agreement attached to the lease.

> This agreement is effective only in the event the
> option to purchase provided for in the attached

lease of even date is exercised and shall be
deemed to have been executed by both parties
on the date of the exercise of the option.

Option to Renew

In the event that the Lessee shall not be in default
in the performance of any term or condition of
this lease, then upon the expiration of the lease
term, Lessee shall have the option to renew the
lease for an additional term of [_____] years. During such renewal period, all the terms and conditions of this lease shall remain in effect [including
the rent payable hereunder] [except that the rent
payable hereunder shall be $[_____] per month in
lieu of the rent provided for herein].

This option may be exercised by the Lessee at
any time prior to the date that shall be three (3)
months from the expiration of the original term
of the lease. The option shall be exercised by
delivering or mailing, postage prepaid, certified
mail, notice to Lessor stating that the Lessee is
exercising his/her option to renew. Such exercise
of the option shall automatically extend the term
of the lease upon the terms and conditions herein
set forth, and no further writing need be executed
by the Lessee or the Lessor. Once exercised, the
Lessee shall not have the right to revoke his/her
election to exercise the option. In the event that
the option is not exercised as provided for herein
within the time provided for, then the option shall
expire and the Lessee shall not have the right to
renew the lease.

Right of First Refusal

If, during the term of this lease or any extension
thereof, Lessor shall receive an acceptable offer
to purchase the premises [or the building in
which the premises are located] or if Lessor shall
wish to enter into an agreement for the sale of
said premises [said building], Lessor shall first
give Lessee written notice setting forth the name
of the proposed buyer, the purchase price, and all

the terms and conditions of the proposed sale. Within 15 days following the delivery, or mailing of said notice pursuant to the terms of this lease, tenant shall have the right to purchase the premises [the building] upon the same terms and conditions. Said right shall be exercised by delivering or mailing such election to owner prior to the expiration of said 15 days. If tenant shall not elect to make such purchase within said time and the sale is made in accordance with the terms set forth in the notice, tenant shall not have a right to purchase upon any resale.

Security Deposit

Lessor acknowledges receipt of $[_____] deposited by Lessee as security for the performance of his/her obligations hereunder. Lessor may, but shall not be obligated to, apply said sum, or a portion thereof, in payment of any obligation of Lessee or as reimbursement for any damage suffered on account of any breach by Lessee. Any balance remaining upon termination of the lease that is in excess of any claim by Lessor shall be paid over to Lessee.

Subrogation

When an insurance company pays a claim under its policy to the insured for damages sustained by the wrongful act or omission of a third person, the insurance company acquires the rights of its insured against the third person. This is known as subrogation. Insurance policies, in the policy or by endorsement, often grant the insured the right to waive subrogation for the benefit of such third person. This may be of great value to a lessee or lessor who might otherwise be responsible to pay for any damage, and consequently, a clause such as given below is often included in modern leases.

Lessor and Lessee, to the maximum extent permitted by insurance policies owned or that may be acquired by them, do waive for the benefit of each other all rights of subrogation that any insurer of either may otherwise have.

Tax Increase

In the event there is any increase during any year of the term of this lease in the city, county or state, real estate taxes over and above the amount of such taxes assessed for the year 19[_____]/19[_____], whether because of increased rate or valuation, Lessee shall pay to Lessor monthly* during the lease term an amount equal to ([_____]% of **) the increase in taxes upon the land and building in which the leased premises are situated. In the event that such taxes are assessed for a tax year extending beyond the term of the lease, the obligation of Lessee shall be proportionate to the portion of the lease term included in such year.

*Alternatives:
1. annually
2. upon presentation of paid tax bills
3. ten (10) days prior to the date upon which such taxes or any part thereof are due

**If the lessee occupies only a portion of the building, an equitable percentage of the tax increase should be paid by the tenant, determined by the proportion of rental value or square footage that the premises occupied bear to the total building.

TAX
INFORMATION

To receive advance notice of the
next *Realty Bluebook*® edition
(and information about
what's new), *please call*
1-800-322-8621
to register your name and address.

CONTENTS

TAX INFORMATION

TAX INFORMATION

The real estate broker is generally not trained or licensed to give tax advice and cannot take the resulting responsibility. This field belongs to the professional tax consultant—the attorney at law or the public accountant—who by virtue of his or her profession is trained and licensed to give tax advice and holds himself or herself responsible for the consequences of that advice.

The general public, however, often fails to avail itself of the services of professional tax consultants when real estate is concerned. It is then that the real estate broker is often the only one in a position to recognize certain opportunities or pitfalls with respect to the client's real estate holdings or transactions that could have serious consequences on the client's tax liability. If able to recognize such opportunities and pitfalls, the broker can perform an invaluable service for clients by pointing out tax effects resulting from certain situations and by urging clients to consult their tax advisers. While the broker has thus not given tax advice, he or she may well have saved clients from making a move that could otherwise have resulted in costly tax consequences; or the broker may have caused clients to make a profitable move taxwise that they otherwise might not have made.

The broker should protect himself or herself—and the client—by ascertaining that the client does not rely upon any statements or representations made by the broker with respect to the client's tax liability. It may be prudent to insert a clause to that effect into sales and exchange agreements.

BASIS

Basis (tax book value of property) has significant tax consequences to the owner.

1. It is the starting point for computing cost recovery deductions.
2. It determines the amount of gain or loss realized upon disposition of the property.
3. It controls the amount of any casualty losses.

During ownership of property, the basis is adjusted upward by adding any capital expenditures the owner may have made. Basis is adjusted downward by subtracting any cost recovery (depreciation) deductions.

The *Sale Price* less *Selling Expenses* is the *Amount Realized*.

The *Amount Realized* less *Adjusted Basis* is termed *Gain Realized*.

The taxable portion of the *realized gain* is called *recognized gain*.

I. Acquisition by Purchase

Basis is the cost of acquisition (purchase price plus purchase costs).

II. Acquisition by Gift

Basis is the donor's adjusted basis plus gift tax but does not exceed the fair market value at the time of the gift for the purpose of computing loss on sale.

III. Acquisition by Inheritance

When the property would be included in the transferor's gross estate for federal estate tax purposes and when basis is the fair market value at the date of death or at the alternate valuation date* if the alternate valuation date was elected for federal estate tax purposes acquisition is by inheritance or other transfer.

There is a limited exception to this rule for property acquired from a decedent who died between January 1, 1977, and November 7, 1978, when the executor of the estate elected to use the carryover basis provisions that were in effect at that time. The election would have been made only if the market value of the property passing from the decedent was less than the amount of the basis that could be established under the carryover basis provisions.

When property is held as community property and one spouse dies, both the descendant's and survivor's one-half interests receive a new basis (determined as previously stated) even though only one half of the commu-

Alternate valuation date is six months after death or the date of sale or distribution if prior to this date.

nity property is included in the gross estate for federal estate tax purposes. However, this advantage is not available when the property is held in joint tenancy. Only that portion of the property that is included in the decedent's estate receives a new basis, and the basis of the survivor's interest is equal to his or her adjusted cost.

IV. Acquisition in Tax-Deferred Transactions

These include exchanges, sale and purchase of personal residences and involuntary conversions (replacement of property condemned, requisitioned, destroyed or sold under threat of condemnation). In these transactions, the taxpayer is permitted to defer recognition of all or part of the gain realized on the old property. In general, the basis of the new property is equal to the basis of the old property plus any additional boot paid (such as cash, notes and other assets) plus any recognized (taxable) gain. Alternatively, the basis of the new property may be determined by subtracting that deferred gain from the cost of the acquired property. (See the sections on Tax-Deferred Exchanges and Personal Residences.)

V. Acquisition as Compensation for Services

Basis is the fair market value of the services at time of transfer.

VI. Acquisition Through Exercise of an Option

Basis is the cost of acquisition of the property plus the cost of the option.

VII. Basis Increase

Basis is increased by:

1. additions and improvements (as distinguished from repairs);
2. cost of insuring, perfecting and defending the title, and other purchase expenses; and
3. special assessments.

CAPITAL IMPROVEMENTS VERSUS REPAIRS

Capital improvements increase the basis and are subject to annual cost recovery deductions spread over the life of the asset whereas repairs are fully deductible expenses. The basic distinction between capital improvement and repair is that the former normally involves a relatively permanent increase in the value of the building or a lengthening of its useful life whereas the latter is usually a recurring type of expenditure to keep the property in operating condition and will not cause an increase in value or in useful life. Please refer to Deductible Expenses under Personal Residences.

Type of Expenditure	Capital	Expense
Foundation – new....................	X	
Foundation – repair..............		X
Pest control...........................		X
New front	X	
Painting – outside		X
Painting – inside...................		X
Papering................................		X
Plastering..............................		X
Floors – new	X	
Floors – resurfacing and patching...........................	X	
Floors – replacing with tile...	X	
Roof – replacement	X	
Roof – reshingling.................	X	
Roof – repair broken portions		X
Ratproofing...........................	X	
Fire escapes – new.................	X	
Fire escapes rails replaced.....		X
Stairway – new supports		X
Electric wiring – new	X	
Electric wiring – replaced (defective)		X
Iron water pipes replaced by copper	X	

Type of Expenditure	Capital	Expense
Plumbing – replaced (defective)		X
Stopping plumbing leaks		X
Heating – permanent conversion	X	
Furnace – relining	X	
Furnace – enameling		X
Insulating		X
Air-conditioning compressor replaced		X
Wells – cleaning and repairing.		X
Maintenance of property		X
Casualties – repairs resulting from		X
Damaged property restored to normal		X
Damaged property restored to something better and different	X	
Restoration of property purchased in rundown condition	X	
Alterations to suit taxpayer's use	X	
Repairs and improvements as part of a general plan of remodeling	X	
Alteration of building	X	
Architect's fee – addition	X	
Assessments for improvements	X	
Enlarging and adding bathrooms	X	
Office layout–nonpermanent change		X
Residence – converting upper floor for rental	X	
Keeping building in safe condition		X

Type of Expenditure	Capital	Expense
Shoring up building to prevent collapse....................		X
Installation of a swimming pool or landscaping.........	X	

Fees and Commissions*	Capital	Expense
For management and collecting rent......................		X
For negotiating lease deductible over original term of lease....................	X	
Points or discount in lieu of interest in whole or part deductible by cash basis taxpayer over the period of repayment of loan...............................	X	
Loan fee, if an expense for obtaining the loan and not interest, deductible as a business or investment expense...................	X	
For negotiating a sale or purchase	X	
Selling commission paid by dealers.............................		X
Legal and accounting for acquisition of property or protection of title........	X	
Legal and accounting, except as above		X
Tax advice, tax return, litigation..........................		X
Title search and title insurance......................	X	
Cost of removing clouds on title	X	
Cost of survey	X	

Fees and Commissions*	Capital	Expense
Appraisal fee............................	X	
Mortgage interest and pre-payment fees.....................		X

For investment properties.

CLASSIFICATION OF REAL ESTATE

For tax purposes, real estate can be classified into the following types of holdings:

1. R.E. Held for Investment or for Production of Income
   Gain is capital gain.
   Loss is capital loss.
   Expenses are deductible.
   Depreciation is allowed (if rented or available for rent).
2. R.E. Held for Use in Trade or Business
   Gain is capital gain.
   Loss is ordinary loss.
   Expenses are deductible.
   Depreciation is allowed.
3. R.E. Held as a Personal Residence
   Gain is capital gain.
   Loss is nondeductible.
   Expenses are nondeductible, except interest, property taxes and casualty losses.
   Depreciation is not allowed.
4. R.E. Held Primarily for Sale to Customers
   Gain is ordinary gain.
   Loss is ordinary loss.
   Expenses are deductible.
   Depreciation is not allowed unless property produces income or is held for the purpose of producing income.

R.E. Held for Investment or for Production of Income

These two categories include real property held as an investment, such as unimproved land or property that requires little or no supervision or maintenance.

Investment property is a capital asset. As such, profits are capital gains and losses are capital losses. Capital losses reduce the amount of capital gain if they occur in the same year. If the capital loss exceeds the capital gain, then the resulting deduction for net capital loss is limited to the lesser of $3,000 or taxable income per year; the remainder is carried forward to the next succeeding year until it is used up.

R.E. Held for Use in Trade or Business

This category includes real property used by the taxpayer in his or her trade or business. Generally, rental property falls into this category as the property is used in the trade or business of producing rental income.

Real estate in this category falls outside the definition of capital asset and qualifies for tax treatment that is especially advantageous.

1. If in any one year gains exceed losses on trade or business property, all gains or losses are treated as gain or loss from the sale of a capital asset, resulting in a net capital gain.
2. If in any one year losses exceed gains, all such gains and losses are treated as arising from the sale of noncapital assets, resulting in a fully deductible ordinary loss.

R.E. Held as a Personal Residence

When a personal residence is sold or exchanged, any resulting profit is treated as capital gain, but losses cannot be deducted against income.

If a personal residence has been converted to income-producing property, it may become trade or business real estate and, as such, qualifies for capital gain or ordinary loss treatment upon disposition. Special rules apply to calculation of losses in this situation.

Refer also to Personal Residences in this section.

R.E. Held Primarily for Sale to Customers

Real estate under this classification can be compared to merchandise on a dealer's shelf. Taxpayers who deal in real estate so classified are called *dealers*. Gains or losses resulting from the disposition of dealers' realty are ordinary gains or ordinary losses.

Rules as to whether a taxpayer is classified as a dealer have evolved from court decisions. Among the factors considered by the courts in the classification of taxpayers as dealers are the following:

1. The degree of activity in the purchase and sale of real estate. But merely reducing the frequency of real estate turnover is not sufficient to remove the dealer status once the taxpayer has been so classified.
2. The intent of purchasing and holding the property as an investment or as part of an inventory held for resale. It is important to make the intent a matter of record at the time of acquisition and to act consistently with such intent during the term the property is held.
3. The length of time the property is held.
4. The extent of involvement in real estate activity by the owner, such as promotion, advertising, listing the property with a real estate broker, and so forth.
5. The reason for purchasing or selling the property; whether the purchase or sale was voluntary or involuntary (because of a drop in rents, increase in maintenance costs, sudden rise in land values, etc.).
6. Undeveloped real estate is subdivided.
7. The extent income from real estate sales compares with income from another full-time occupation.
8. Real estate brokers, builders and subdividers will need additional evidence to establish that any of their real estate holdings are investments.

It should be noted that nonprofessional investors are not protected from being classified as dealers by the IRS even though they are in an entirely different business.

CAPITAL VERSUS ORDINARY GAIN OR LOSS

The nature of profit (capital and ordinary gain) derived from the sale or exchange of an asset depends upon whether or not the asset is a capital asset. Generally, real property will be either a capital asset or an asset held for sale in the ordinary course of business by a taxpayer commonly described as a dealer.

The importance of the distinction between capital and ordinary gain or loss was substantially diminished by the 1986 Tax Reform Act (TRA '86).

After December 31, 1986, no portion of the net long-term gain is excluded from the taxpayer's income. The provision that limits the deduction of net capital loss against other income up to $3,000 in each year was not eliminated. Long-term capital gain is now taxed at the same rates as other income, subject to a maximum effective rate of 28%.

ALTERNATIVE MINIMUM TAX

A taxpayer is subject to payment of the *alternative minimum tax* if such tax exceeds the taxpayer's regular income tax for the year.

The alternative minimum tax is 26% of alternative minimum taxable income up to $175,000 and 28% of alternative minimum taxable income in excess of $175,000.

Alternative minimum taxable income for most taxpayers will be the *adjusted gross income* plus *items of tax preference* minus *Alternative Tax Itemized Deductions.*

Alternative tax itemized deductions include (1) casualty and theft losses in excess of 10% of adjusted gross income; (2) charitable deductions; (3) medical deductions in excess of 10% of adjusted gross income; (4) interest paid on indebtedness for acquisition, construction or substantial improvement of taxpayer's principal residence or second home; and (5) investment interest to the extent of net investment income of the taxpayer. *Items of tax preference* include accelerated depreciation in excess of straight-line depreciation on real property and net loss from a passive activity. (As explained hereafter, net loss from the ownership of rental real property is a passive activity loss.)

The alternative minimum taxable income is reduced by an exemption of $45,000 for joint returns, $33,750 for single taxpayers and $22,500 for married taxpayers filing separately. However, the exemption amount is reduced by 25% of the amount by which the alternative minimum taxable income exceeds $150,000 for joint returns, $112,500 for single individuals and $75,000 for married taxpayers filing separately.

Example

Taxpayers file a joint return with an ordinary income of $100,000 and rental (passive activity) loss of $20,000. Their adjusted gross income is $80,000. Assume they have alternative minimum tax itemized deductions of $48,000 and nonalternative minimum itemized deductions of $2,000. Excess accelerated depreciation deducted is $23,333. Their regular income tax for the year is $4,504.

The alternative minimum tax would be computed as follows:

Adjusted gross income			$80,000
less			
alt. tax itemized deductions		$48,000	
plus			
Allowable rental loss	$20,000		
Excess depreciation	23,333		
		43,333	
			−4,667
Alternative minimum taxable income			$75,333
Exemption		45,000	
Less 25% AMTI excess over $150,000		None	
			−45,000
			30,333
Alternative Minimum Tax at 26%			$ 7,887

NOTE: *The alternative minimum tax is $3,383 greater than the regular tax.*

DEPRECIATION—COST RECOVERY

Historically, the law permitted taxpayers investing in depreciable property to take regular tax deductions for the amount of annual depreciation of an asset. Depreciation was computed on the basis of an asset and was spread systematically over its estimated useful life.

The Economic Recovery Tax Act of 1981 introduced the Accelerated Cost Recovery System (ACRS) for property placed in service after December 31, 1980. The new system substitutes the term *cost recovery* for *depreciation*. ACRS enables taxpayers to recover the cost of eligible (depreciable) property more rapidly than was formerly permitted. However, the TRA '86 substantially lengthened the period of time over which taxpayers can recover costs.

Cost recovery tax deductions do not result from current cash expenses; yet they reduce taxpayers' tax liability and thus increase the cash return on investments.

Eligible (depreciable) property. To be eligible for cost recovery, property must be held for production of income or for use in the taxpayer's trade or business.

Persons entitled to cost recovery (depreciation). To be entitled to cost recovery deductions, the taxpayer must have an economic interest in the property; just holding title to the property is not sufficient.

Elements of Cost Recovery (Depreciation)

To compute annual cost recovery tax deductions, one must determine the tax basis of the property and the recovery period.

Basis. In the case of real property, only the improvements are subject to cost recovery, not the land. Therefore, the basis of the improvements must be allocated. This is often done by using the assessment ratio of land to improvements or by using comparable sales or appraisals.

Adjusted basis. The original basis is adjusted by adding capital improvements and subtracting cost recovery deductions.

Recovery period and method. The recovery period for residential real property is 27½ years. The recovery period for nonresidential real property acquired after May 12, 1993, is 39 years. (Formerly, the recovery period for nonresidential real property was 31½ years.) Cost recovery must be taken on a straight-line basis for all property acquired after December 31, 1986.

Component Depreciation

Component depreciation is no longer available. When a taxpayer makes a substantial improvement to a building, the substantial improvement will be treated as a separate building rather than a component. An improvement is a substantial improvement if (1) the amounts added to the capital account of the building over a two-year period are at least 25% of the adjusted basis of the building (disregarding depreciation and amortization adjustments) as of the first day of that two-year period and (2) the improvement is made at least three years after the building was placed in service.

LIMITATION ON INTEREST AND OTHER DEDUCTIONS

Loss Limitation from Passive Activities

A passive activity is a trade or business in which the taxpayer does not materially participate. Section 469 of the Internal Revenue Code disallows the deduction of losses and tax credits of passive activities to individuals, estates, trusts, closely held Subchapter C corporations and personal service corporations. This is true subject to certain exceptions including closely held Subchapter C corporations, which may offset passive losses against net active business income, but not against portfolio income (dividends, interest and royalties.)

The following discussion is limited to the disallowance or allowance of losses attributable to real estate rental activities. With certain exceptions, the rental of real estate is considered a passive activity for many taxpayers even though they may actually participate materially in the activity.

There is an exception for losses not exceeding $25,000 in any tax year incurred by an individual who actively participates in the management of his or her property. The $25,000 amount is phased out between $100,000 and $150,000 of modified adjusted gross income (determined without regard to passive losses.)

Low-income housing credits may be taken (upon a deduction equivalent basis) under the $25,000 allowance against nonpassive income without regard to whether the individual actively participates.

The active participation with respect to the $25,000 allowance does not require regular, continuous and substantial involvement in operations. The requirement may be satisfied if the taxpayer participates in the making of management decisions, such as approval of new tenants or deciding on rental real estate activity if he or she owns less than 10% of the value of all interest in the activity.

There is a special exception for taxpayers in the real estate business. This exception applies to the taxpayer for a taxable year if more than one-half of the personal services performed in trades or business by the taxpayer during the year are performed in real property trades or business in which the taxpayer materially participates and if the taxpayer performs more than 750 hours of services during the taxable year in real property trades or business in which the taxpayer materially participates. The term *real property trade or business* means any real property development, redevelopment, construction, reconstruction, acquisition, conversion, rental, operation, management, leasing or brokerage trade or business. With respect to a closely held Subchapter c corporation, the requirements are satisfied if more than 50% of the gross receipts of such corporation for the taxable year are derived from real property trades or businesses in which the corporation materially participates. The personal services of an employee are not treated as performed in real property trades or businesses unless such employee is a 5% or greater owner of the employer.

Interest deductions attributable to passive activities are treated as passive activity deductions, not as investment interest (see explanation of investment interest under the subhead that follows). Thus, such interest deductions are subject to limitation under the passive activity loss rule, not under the investment interest limitation. Similarly, income and loss from passive activities generally are not treated as investment income or loss in calculating the amount of the investment interest limitation.

To the extent that passive activity losses are not deductible in any one year, they are carried forward from year to year. They may be deducted in subsequent years against passive activity income. When the passive activity is disposed of, the losses from prior years become deductible (offset by any gain).

Investment Interest

The allowable deduction for interest paid by a taxpayer was substantially changed by the TRA '86. (See also Residence Interest.)

Investment interest means interest paid or accrued on indebtedness on property held for investment. Interest on debt used to purchase or hold rental real property is *not* investment interest. If the taxpayer materially participates in the operation of the rental property, the interest would be incurred on a trade or business. If the taxpayer does not materially participate in the operation of the rental property, interest would be an expense in computing taxable income from a passive activity. Property subject to a net lease is not treated as investment property because it is treated as a passive activity under the passive loss rules.

The deduction for investment interest is limited to the amount of net investment income. In the event the net investment interest exceeds the net investment income in any one year, such excess is carried forward and treated as investment interest in the succeeding tax year.

Net investment income means the excess of investment income over investment expenses.

Investment income includes gross income from property held for investment, gains attributable to the disposition of property held for investment and gross portfolio income.

Portfolio income means dividends, interest and royalties.

Investment expenses are deductible expenses (other than interest) directly connected with the production of investment income.

INVESTMENT TAX CREDIT

Low-Income Housing

Commencing in 1987, a tax credit is allowed for investments in low-income housing. The credit may be claimed annually for a period of ten years. The credit rate is set so that the annualized credit amounts have a present value of 70% for qualified new construction and rehabilitation expenditures that are not federally subsidized and a 30% credit for other qualifying low-income housing expenditures. Expenditures qualifying for the 30% present value credit consist of the cost of acquisition, certain rehabilitation expenditures incurred in connection with the acquisition of an existing building and federally subsidized new construction or rehabilitation expenditures. The taxpayer's credit amount in any taxable year is computed by applying the appropriate credit percentage to the appropriate qualified basis amount in such year.

For buildings placed in service in 1987, the credit percentages are 9% annually over ten years for the

70% present value credit and 4% annually over ten years for the 30% present value credit. For buildings placed in service after 1987, these credit percentages are to be adjusted monthly by the Treasury to reflect the present values of 70% and 30% at the time the building is placed in service.

The qualified basis amounts with respect to which the credit amount is computed are determined as the proportion of the eligible basis in a qualified low-income building attributable to the low-income rental units. This proportion is the lesser of (1) the proportion of low-income units to all residential units or (2) the proportion of floor space of the low-income units to the floor space of all rental units. Generally, in these calculations, low-income units are those units presently occupied by qualifying tenants, whereas residential rental units are all units, whether presently occupied or not.

Eligible basis consists of (1) the cost of new construction, (2) the cost of rehabilitation or (3) the cost of acquisition of existing buildings acquired through purchase and the cost of rehabilitation, if any, to such buildings incurred before the close of the first taxable year of the credit. Only the adjusted basis of the building may be included in the eligible basis. The cost of land is not included.

The cost of residential units in buildings that are not low-income units may be included in the eligible basis only if such units are not above the average quality standard of the low-income units. Residential real property may qualify for credit even though a portion of the building in which the residential rental units are located is used for commercial purposes. No portion of the cost of such nonresidential rental property may be included in eligible basis. The qualified basis attributable to rehabilitation expenditures not claimed in connection with the acquisition of an existing building must equal at least $3,000 per low-income unit or 10% of the building's adjusted basis, whichever is greater, in order for rehabilitation expenditures to qualify for the credit.

Residential rental projects providing low-income housing qualify for the credit only if (1) 20% or more of the aggregate residential rental units in the project are occupied by individuals with incomes of 50% of the area median income as adjusted for family size, or (2) 40% or more of the aggregate residential rental units in the project are occupied by individuals with incomes of 60% or less of the area median income as adjusted for family size. The owner must irrevocably elect the minimum set aside requirement at the time the project is placed in service. The gross rent paid by families in units included in qualified basis may not exceed 30% of the applicable qualifying income for a family of its size. Gross rent is to include the cost of any utilities other than telephone.

Subject to provision for correction of inadvertent noncompliance, if a low-income housing project fails to continue to qualify during the 15-year compliance period, the credits allowed in the prior years are recaptured. Buildings will not receive credit allocations unless an extended low-income housing agreement is entered into between the allocating agency and the taxpayer. The extended agreement would be for an additional 15 years but may be terminated if the taxpayer requests the agency to find a buyer at a formula price contained in the agreement and the agency is unable to do so. Notwithstanding termination, the taxpayer may not increase the rent for 3 years after the agreement terminates. The effect of this is to extend the compliance period to 18 years if the allocating agency is unable to find a buyer pursuant to a request received 1 year before the end of the initial 15-year compliance period. If there is a change in ownership of the building, this is a recapture event unless the seller posts a bond to the Secretary of the Treasury in a satisfactory amount to assure compliance during the balance of the 15-year term. For partnerships consisting of more than 35 individual taxpayers and at the partnership's election, no change in ownership will be deemed to occur provided that within a 12-month period at least 50% in value of the original ownership is unchanged. A purchaser of a low-income housing project is eligible to continue to receive the credits based upon the original qualified basis.

Limitations are placed on the number of low-income housing projects qualifying for the credit in each state. In the case of projects financed with tax-exempt bonds, this limitation arises on account of the statewide limitation on the amount of bonds that are financed for the tax exemption. With respect to projects not financed by tax-exempt bonds, there is a procedure for the state to approve a limited number of units. The annual dollar limit for each state on the total amount of qualifying projects is $1.25 for each individual resident of the state.

Rehabilitation of Nonresidential Buildings

The tax credit for rehabilitation expenditures of older nonresidential buildings was modified by the TRA '86 with respect to property placed in service after December 31, 1986. The credit percentage is 20% for rehabilitations of certified historic structures and 10% for rehabilitation of buildings other than certified historic structures originally placed in service before 1936. Expenditures incurred by a lessee do not qualify for the credit unless the remaining lease term on the date the rehabilitation is completed is at least as long as the applicable cost recovery period under the general cost recovery rules.

There must be a substantial rehabilitation requiring that the rehabilitation expenditures during a 24-month period ending on the last day of the taxable year exceed the greater of the adjusted basis of the property or $5,000. At least 75% of existing external walls as well as 75% of the building's interior structural framework must remain in place. This limitation does not apply to historic structures.

EXCHANGE AGREEMENTS

BALANCING EQUITIES

Before an exchange agreement can be written, the equities of both parties must be balanced.

Case 1: Two-Way Exchange

Jones offers to exchange his property at 101 Atlantic for Brown's property at 505 Pacific.

Jones' property has an FMV (fair market value) of $100,000, and he has a first loan of $50,000, giving him an equity in Atlantic of $50,000.

Brown's property has an FMV of $200,000, and he owes $30,000 on it, which gives him an equity in Pacific of $170,000.

Jones proposes to obtain a new loan on 505 Pacific of $130,000; he has $15,000 cash to give to Brown and proposes to execute a second mortgage on Pacific in favor of Brown for the balance of $5,000.

Jones	Gives	Gets
Exchange value of Atlantic	$100,000	
Less loan on Atlantic	50,000	
Equity in Atlantic		$50,000
Cash to Brown		15,000
2nd loan on Pacific to Brown		5,000
Exchange value of Pacific	200,000	
Less new loan on Pacific	130,000	
Equity in Pacific		$70,000
	$70,000	$70,000

Brown	Gives	Gets
Exchange value of Pacific	200,000	
Less loan pay-off on Pacific	30,000	
Equity in Pacific	$170,000	
Exchange value of Atlantic	100,000	
Assume loan on Atlantic	50,000	
Equity in Atlantic	$50,000	
Jones' new loan		$130,000

Less loan pay-off on Pacific		30,000
Loan proceeds		$100,000
Cash from Jones		15,000
2nd loan on Pacific from Jones		5,000
	$170,000	$170,000

Case 2: Three-Way Exchange

Uses the same example as above but with this difference: Brown is not interested in Atlantic but wants to cash out. A buyer, Smith, offers to buy Atlantic for $100,000 on the following terms: $30,000 cash, conditioned upon Smith's ability to assume the $50,000 loan and with Brown to carryback a second loan on Atlantic for the balance of $20,000.

Brown	Gives	Gets
Equity in Pacific (see Case 1)		$170,000
Loan proceeds from Pacific (see Case 1)		$100,000
Cash from Jones (see Case 1)		15,000
2nd mortgage from Jones on Pacific (see Case 1)	5,000	
Cash from Smith	30,000	
2nd mortgage from Smith on Atlantic	20,000	
	$170,000	$170,000

Case 3: Four-Way Exchange

Uses the example of Case 1 but with the following complications: Brown wants to cash out. He is not interested in Atlantic. Builder Green offers a new apartment building at Sierra Avenue in exchange for the Atlantic property. Green's apartments have an FMV of $80,000 with an assumable first loan of $60,000. Green proposes to pay $30,000 cash in addition to his $20,000 equity in the Sierra apartments. Green would acquire Atlantic at the FMV of $100,000 and assume the $50,000 loan. Brown still is not interested in exchanging but says he would sign if a buyer is found for the Sierra apartments, provided he would not incur any extra expenses on account of the exchange. Before long, buyer Black makes an offer on the Sierra apartments for $80,000 with $20,000 cash, assuming the $60,000 loan.

Brown	Gives	Gets
Equity in Pacific	$170,000*	
Loan proceeds from Pacific		$100,000*
Cash from Jones		15,000*
2nd mortgage from Jones on Pacific		5,000*
Cash from Green		30,000
Cash from Black		20,000
	$170,000	$170,000

*See Case 1

The IRS approved the use of a clause in a sales agreement to the effect that the buyer would cooperate with the seller in effecting a tax-free exchange in the event the seller could find a suitable property. Such a clause may read as follows:

> *In the event the Seller elects to complete the transaction as a tax-deferred exchange under Internal Revenue Code Section 1031, Buyer agrees to cooperate with Seller in order to effect such an exchange provided, however, that Buyer shall not be required to incur any additional liability, nor shall the costs or expenses to be paid by Buyer be increased as a result of such a transaction.*

Directions for Using an Exchange Worksheet to Balance Equities

To use an *Exchange Worksheet To Balance Equities*, proceed as below. See sample worksheets on C-26, C-27, C-29, C-31 and C-32.

1. Inventory the real properties, cash, existing paper (not paper created in the exchange) and other boot going into the exchange by filling in the GIVE lines of A through F in columns 2, 3, 4, 6,

7, 9, 11, 12 and 14. (In the event the brokers have put any real property, cash, existing paper or other boot into the exchange, use the GIVE line in section F.)

2. Fill in the maximum potential financing in column 18.

3. Charge loan fee on each new loan to the party doing refinancing in column 13. Then fill in the totals on the GIVE lines in column 15.

4. Now fill in the Net Effective Equities in column 16.

5. Inventory the real properties coming out of the exchange by filling in the GET lines of A through F in columns 2, 3, 5 and 6. Inventory the boot (e.g., personal property) coming out of the exchange by filling in the GET lines of A through F in columns 2, 3, 5 and 6. Ascertain that all real properties and boot have been disposed of; if not, post to brokers in the GET line of G in columns 2, 3, 5 and 6.

6. Any differences between the Property Equities on the GET lines of column 6 and the Net Effective Equities (column 16) must now be made up in Escrow Accounts (columns 7, 8, 9 or 10). Balance the equities of the party cashing out last, giving him or her all the paper first (the grand total of column 9) and the balance in cash. Double check Net Effective Equities on the GET lines: Column $16 = 6 - 7 + 8 - 9 + 10$.

7. Total column 18 and transfer to column 7–I (see arrow).

8. Total column 15 and transfer to column 8–H (see arrow).

9. Total column 12 on line G.

10. Tentatively total columns 7, 8, 9 and 10 on line J and examine these totals. First ascertain that all the paper (the grand total of column 9) has been disposed of; if not, post the balance to Brokers in column 10–G. Then determine if any cash is available for commissions; if so, post available cash to 8–G. As a check: $12G = 6 - 7 + 8 - 9 + 10$.

11. Retotal columns 7, 8, 9 and 10, so that Cash In equals Cash Out and Paper In equals Paper Out.

The example filled in on page C-25 is based on the following data:

Jones offers to exchange his property at 101 Atlantic for Brown's property at 505 Pacific.

Jones's property has an FMV (fair market value) of $100,000, and he has a first loan of $50,000, giving him an equity in Atlantic of $50,000.

Brown's property has an FMV of $200,000, and he owes $30,000 on it, which gives him an equity in Pacific of $170,000.

Jones proposes to obtain a new loan on 505 Pacific of $130,000; he has $15,000 cash to give to Brown plus an existing mortgage valued at $4,000, secured by another property.

Brown wants to cash out; he is not interested in Atlantic.

Builder Green comes along and offers a new apartment building at Sierra Avenue in exchange for the Atlantic property. Green's apartments have an FMV of $80,000 with an assumable first loan of $60,000. Green proposes to pay $30,000 cash in addition to his $20,000 equity in the Sierra apartments. Green would acquire Atlantic at the FMV of $100,000 and assume the $50,000 loan.

Brown still is not interested in exchanging but says he would sign if a buyer were found for the Sierra apartments provided he would not incur any extra expenses on account of the exchange.

Before long, buyer Black offers to purchase the Sierra apartments for $80,000 with $20,000 cash, assuming the $60,000 loan.

Each party agrees to pay a commission of 6% on the property he conveys. For the sake of simplification, it is assumed that each party's closing costs amount to $1,000 and that loan fees are 1%.

EXCHANGE WORKSHEET TO BALANCE EQUITIES

1 PARTIES	2 PROPERTIES	3 MARKET VALUES	4 LOANS EXISTING LOANS	5 LOANS NEW OR ASSUMED LOANS*	6 PROPERTY EQUITIES GIVES 3-4 GETS* 3-5	7 ESCROW CASH IN (GIVES)	8 CASH OUT (GETS)	9 PAPER-OTHER BOOT IN (GIVES)	10 OUT (GETS)	11 GROSS EQUITIES 6+7+9	12 TRANSACTION COSTS COM'N/MISSION	13 LOAN FEES	14 OTHER COSTS	15 TOTAL OF 13+14	16 NET EFFECTIVE EQUITIES 11-12-15	17 NEW LOANS	18 GROSS LOAN PROCEEDS 17-4
A Jones	GIVES Atlantic	100,000	50,000		50,000	15,000		4,000		69,000	6,000	1,300	1,000	2,300	60,700		
	GETS Pacific	200,000		130,000	70,000			9,300								130,000	100,000
B Brown	GIVES Pacific	200,000	30,000		170,000					170,000	12,000		1,000	1,000	157,000		
	GETS Cash						136,900		20,100								100,000
C Green	GIVES Sierra	80,000	60,000		20,000	30,000		5,800		50,000	4,400		1,000	1,000	44,200		
	GETS Atlantic	100,000		50,000	50,000												
D Black	GIVES Cash					20,000		1,000		20,000			1,000	1,000	19,000		
	GETS Sierra	80,000		60,000	20,000												
E	GIVES																
	GETS																
F	GIVES																
	GETS																
G BROKERS GET							22,800				22,800						
H TRANSACTION COSTS DISBURSED THROUGH ESCROW							5,300							5,300			
I LOAN PROCEEDS DISBURSED THROUGH ESCROW (CASH IN must equal CASH OUT)						100,000											
J TOTAL ESCROW ACCOUNTS						165,000 = 165,000		20,100 = 20,100		(PAPER IN must equal PAPER OUT)							100,000

* Also includes loans taken "Subject To"
** Double check GETS line Column 18 = 6 - 7 + 8 - 9 + 10
‡ Equity in property acquired = Col 6 - Col 9 (But ONLY if a purchase-money note on property acquired)
Col 9 represents a purchase-money note on property acquired

Date: _____ Prepared by _____ Office: _____ (415) 472-1964 ___, CA 94903

FORM 123-A (8-88)   COPYRIGHT ___ PROFESSIONAL PUBLISHING CORPORATION '87   PROFESSIONAL PUBLISHING

The following case studies were developed by James F. Little, CCIM. They assume a 6% commission and a 2% loan fee.

Problem One

Bell owns a fourplex with an FMV (fair market value) of $200,000, subject to a $120,000 loan, which he would like to exchange for a 10-unit apartment complex. A new $160,000 loan is available. Bell's transaction costs, exclusive of the commission and loan fees, are estimated at $1,500.

Fry owns a 10-unit apartment complex with an FMV of $350,000 that is encumbered with $200,000 in loans, which he would like to exchange for an office building. A new $280,000 loan is available. Fry's transaction costs, exclusive of the commission and loan fees, are estimated at $2,500.

Katz owns an office building with an FMV of $500,000 subject to a $250,000 loan that he wants to exchange for a warehouse. A new $350,000 loan is available. Katz's transaction costs, exclusive of the commission and loan fees, are estimated at $3,500.

Sparks owns a warehouse with an FMV of $700,000 that is subject to a $380,000 loan. Sparks wants to get out of the warehouse business, take his money and move to Mazatlan. A new $455,000 loan is available. Sparks's transaction costs, exclusive of the commission, are estimated at $4,500.

Derr has $40,000 in cash with which he would like to purchase a fourplex. Derr's transaction costs, exclusive of loan fees, are estimated at $1,000.

NOTES: Sparks will go to Mazatlan with $192,100 in cash and four notes totaling $81,400 secured by a fourplex, a 10-unit apartment complex, an office building and a warehouse, for a total of $273,500 (his net effective equity). Notice that none of the parties exchanging properties put any cash into the exchange. The majority of transaction costs, commissions and cash paid to Sparks came from gross loan proceeds.

Problem One

EXCHANGE WORKSHEET TO BALANCE EQUITIES

	PARTIES	PROPERTIES	MARKET VALUES	EXISTING LOANS	NEW OR ASSUMED LOANS*	PROPERTY EQUITIES GIVES 3-4 GETS 3-5	ESCROW CASH IN (GIVES)	ESCROW CASH OUT (GETS)	PAPER-OTHER BOOT IN (GIVES)	PAPER-OTHER BOOT OUT (GETS)	GROSS EQUITIES 6+7+9	COMMISSION	LOAN FEES	OTHER COSTS	TOTAL OF 13+14	NET EFFECTIVE EQUITIES 11-12-15	NEW LOANS	GROSS LOAN PROCEEDS 17-4
			3	4 (LOANS)	5 (LOANS)	6	7	8	9	10	11	12	13	14	15	16	17	18
A Bell	GIVES	Fourplex	200,000	120,000		80,000					80,000	12,000	5,600	1,500	7,100	60,900		
	GETS	10 Units	350,000		290,000	70,000			9,100								160,000	40,000
B Fry	GIVES	10 Units	350,000	200,000		150,000					150,000	21,000	7,000	2,500	9,500	119,500		
	GETS	Office Bldg	500,000		350,000	150,000			30,500								280,000	80,000
C Katz	GIVES	Office Bldg	500,000	250,000		250,000					250,000	30,000	9,100	3,500	12,600	207,400		
	GETS	Warehouse	700,000		455,000	245,000			37,600								350,000	100,000
D Sparks	GIVES	Warehouse	700,000	380,000		320,000					320,000	42,000	none	4,500	4,500	273,500		
	GETS	Cash/Paper						192,100		81,400							455,000	75,000
E Derr	GIVES	Cash					40,000				40,000	none	3,200	1,000	4,200	35,800		
	GETS	Fourplex	200,000		160,000	40,000			4,200									
F	GIVES																	
	GETS																	
G BROKERS	GET											105,000						
H TRANSACTION COSTS DISBURSED THROUGH ESCROW								37,900							37,900			
I LOAN PROCEEDS DISBURSED THROUGH ESCROW							295,000											295,000
J TOTAL ESCROW ACCOUNTS							335,000	105,000	81,400	81,400		105,000						

(CASH IN must equal CASH OUT) 335,000 = 335,000   (PAPER IN must equal PAPER OUT) 81,400 = 81,400

* Also includes loans taken "Subject To"
.. Double check GETS line Column 16 = 6 - 7 + 8 - 9 = 10
... Equity in property acquired if Col 6 = Col 3 (But ONLY if Col 9 represents a purchase-money note on property acquired)

Date: _____ Prepared by: _____ Office: _____

FORM 122-A (6-88) COPYRIGHT PROFESSIONAL PUBLISHING CORPORATION SAN RAFAEL, CA 94903 (415) 472-1964   PROFESSIONAL PUBLISHING

Exchange Agreements   C-27

Problem Two

Assumes the same facts in Problem One with the following changes: There is no buyer (Derr) for the fourplex.

Sparks has refused to accept any paper on the 10-unit apartment complex.

The brokers will accept equity in the fourplex and the note on the 10-unit apartment complex for part of their commission (the $3,200 loan fee and $1,000 transaction costs will be paid from the brokers' commission).

NOTES: Sparks will go to Mazatlan with $205,400 in cash and two notes totaling $68,100 secured by an office building and a warehouse, for a total of $273,500 (his net effective equity).

In this exchange, all of the transaction costs, commissions and cash paid to Sparks came from gross loan proceeds.

The brokers have earned a $40,000 equity in a fourplex, a $9,100 note secured by a 10-unit apartment complex and $51,700 in cash for their efforts in this transaction.

Problem Three

Miller owns a $300,000, 8-unit apartment complex subject to a $150,000 loan, which he wants to exchange for a retail building. A new $240,000 loan is available. Miller's transaction costs, exclusive of commission and loan fees, are estimated at $2,000.

High owns a retail building with an FMV of $500,000 with a $250,000 loan, which he wants to exchange for an office building. A new $350,000 loan is available. High's transaction costs, exclusive of commission and loan fees, are estimated at $3,500.

Pope owns a $800,000 office building with a $450,000 loan and a free and clear fishing boat with an FMV of $50,000, which he wants to exchange for a medical building. A new $560,000 loan is available. Pope's transaction costs, exclusive of the commission and loan fees, are estimated at $5,000.

Lowe owns a $1,200,000 medical building with a $700,000 loan. He wants to sell his medical building,

Problem Two

EXCHANGE WORKSHEET TO BALANCE EQUITIES

					LOANS		PROPERTY	CASH		ESCROW ACCOUNTS				TRANSACTION COSTS				
												PAPER - OTHER BOOT						
PARTIES			MARKET VALUES	EXISTING LOANS	NEW OR ASSUMED LOANS*	PROPERTY EQUITIES GIVES 3-4 GETS 3-5		IN (GIVES)	OUT (GETS)	IN (GIVES)	OUT (GETS)	GROSS EQUITIES 6+7+9	COM-MISSION	LOAN FEES	OTHER COSTS	TOTAL OF 13+14	NET EFFECTIVE EQUITIES 11-12-15	NEW LOANS	GROSS LOAN PROCEEDS 17-4
1	2		3	4	5	6	7	8	9		10	11	12	13	14	15	16	17	18
A	Bell	GIVES	Fourplex	200,000	120,000		80,000					80,000	12,000	5,600	1,500	7,100	60,900	160,000	40,000
		GETS	10 Units	350,000		280,000	70,000			9,100									
B	Fry	GIVES	10 Units	350,000	200,000		150,000					150,000	21,000	7,000	2,500	9,500	119,500	280,000	80,000
		GETS	Office Bldg	500,000		350,000	150,000			30,500									
C	Katz	GIVES	Office Bldg	500,000	250,000		250,000					250,000	30,000	9,100	3,500	12,600	207,400	350,000	100,000
		GETS	Warehouse	700,000		455,000	245,000			37,600									
D	Sparks	GIVES	Warehouse	700,000	380,000		320,000					320,000	42,000	none	4,500	4,500	273,500	455,000	75,000
		GETS	Cash Paper						205,400		68,100									
E		GIVES																	
		GETS																	
F	Brokers	GIVES	Transaction Costs										(4,200)	3,200	1,000	4,200			
		GETS																	
G	BROKERS	GET	Fourplex	200,000		160,000	40,000		51,700		9,100		100,800			37,900			295,000
H	TRANSACTION COSTS DISBURSED THROUGH ESCROW								37,900										
I	LOAN PROCEEDS DISBURSED THROUGH ESCROW			(CASH IN must equal **CASH OUT**)		295,000		295,000											
J	TOTAL ESCROW ACCOUNTS							295,000 = 295,000		77,200 = 77,200			(**PAPER IN** must equal **PAPER OUT**)						

Date: _____ Prepared by: _____ Office: _____

FORM 122-A (8-86)   COPYRIGHT 1981 PROFESSIONAL PUBLISHING CORPORATION "J"   "ABEL, CA 94903   (415) 472-1964   **PP** **PROFESSIONAL PUBLISHING**

* Also includes loans taken "Subject To"
** Double check GETS line Column 16 = 6 - 7 + 8 - 9 + 10
** Equity in property acquired = Col 6 - Col 9 IN ONLY if Col 9 represents a purchase money note on property acquired)

Problem Three

EXCHANGE WORKSHEET TO BALANCE EQUITIES

1 PARTIES	2 PROPERTIES	3 MARKET VALUES	4 EXISTING LOANS	5 NEW OR ASSUMED LOANS*	6 PROPERTY EQUITIES GIVES 3-4 GETS 3-5	7 CASH IN (GIVES)	8 CASH OUT (GETS)	9 PAPER-OTHER BOOT IN (GIVES)	10 PAPER-OTHER BOOT OUT (GETS)	11 GROSS EQUITIES 6+7+9	12 COMMISSION	13 LOAN FEES	14 OTHER COSTS	15 TOTAL OF 13+14	16 NET EFFECTIVE EQUITIES 11-12-15	17 NEW LOANS	18 GROSS LOAN PROCEEDS 17-4
A Miller GIVES	8 Units	300,000	150,000		150,000					150,000	18,000	7,000	2,000	9,000	} 123,000	240,000	90,000
A Miller GETS	Retail Bldg	500,000		350,000	150,000			27,000 (PAPER CREATED)									
B High GIVES	Retail Bldg	500,000	250,000		250,000					250,000	30,000	11,200	3,500	14,700	} 205,300	350,000	100,000
B High GETS	Office Bldg	800,000		560,000	240,000			34,700 (PAPER CREATED)									
C Pope GIVES	Office Bldg/ Boat	800,000 / 50,000	450,000 / none		350,000 / 50,000			29,800 (BOOT GIVEN)		400,000	48,000	16,800	5,000	21,800	} 330,200	560,000	110,000
C Pope GETS	Medical Bldg	1,200,000		840,000	360,000												
D Lowe GIVES	Medical Bldg	1,200,000	700,000		500,000		307,500	(BOOT GIVEN)		500,000	72,000	none	6,000	6,000	} 422,000	840,000	140,000
D Lowe GETS	Boat/Cash/ Paper	50,000		none	50,000				64,500								
E GIVES															~		
E GETS																	
F Brokers GIVES	Transaction Costs				∴		74,700		27,000		(6,300)	4,800	1,500	6,300	~		
F Brokers GETS					∴						161,700						
G BROKERS GET	8 Units	300,000	240,000		60,000		57,800							57,800			
H TRANSACTION COSTS DISBURSED THROUGH ESCROW						440,000											
I LOAN PROCEEDS DISBURSED THROUGH ESCROW (CASH IN must equal CASH OUT)						440,000 = 440,000 (CASH OUT)											440,000
J TOTAL ESCROW ACCOUNTS								PAPER IN must equal PAPER OUT	91,500 = 91,500							

Notes (right margin):

* Also includes taxes taken "Subject To"

Double check GETS line Column 16 = 6 − 7 + 8 + 9 + 10

∴ Equity in property acquired = Col 6 − 7 + 8 − 9 + 10

∴ Col 9 represents a purchase-money note on property acquired)

Date: ____ Prepared by ____ Office: ____ (415) 472-1964

FORM 122-A (9-86) COPYRIGHT · 1987 PROFESSIONAL PUBLISHING CORPORATION. 122 PAUL DRIVE, SAN RAFAEL, CA 94903 PROFESSIONAL PUBLISHING

C-30 *Tax Information*

take his cash and spend the rest of his years on a fishing boat in the Bahamas. A new $840,000 loan is available. Lowe's transaction costs, exclusive of the commission, are estimated at $6,000. Lowe has indicated he will accept no more than $65,000 in paper.

The brokers will accept equity in the 8-unit apartment complex and paper for part of their commission. The transaction costs on the 8-unit apartment complex, exclusive of loan fees, are estimated at $1,500 (the $4,800 loan fee and $1,500 transaction costs will be paid from the brokers' commission).

NOTE: Lowe will go to the Bahamas in his "new" $50,000 fishing boat with $307,500 cash and two notes totaling $64,500 secured by an office building and a medical building, for a total of $422,000 (his net effective equity). In this exchange, all of the transaction costs, commissions and cash paid to Lowe came from gross loan proceeds. The brokers have earned a $60,000 equity in an 8-unit apartment complex, a $27,000 note secured by a retail building and $74,700 in cash for their efforts in this transaction.

Problem Four

Assumes the same facts as in Problem Three with the following changes: A new party, Wright, has offered to exchange four free and clear subdivision lots, valued at $15,000 each, which he has held for investment, for the 8-unit apartment complex. Wright will pay a 10% commission on the lots. Wright's transaction costs, exclusive of the commission and loan fees, are estimated at $2,000.

The brokers have a buyer, Marks, who will purchase two of the subdivision lots for cash. Marks has indicated that he has the cash to pay his transaction costs, which are estimated at $800. The brokers will accept the remaining two lots for part of their commission. The brokers' transaction costs, estimated at $800, will be paid from their commission.

NOTE: While the brokers have increased their commission by $11,500, the cash portion they will receive has increased from $74,700 to $103,400.

Problem Four

EXCHANGE WORKSHEET TO BALANCE EQUITIES

1 Parties	2 Properties	3 Market Values	4 Existing Loans	5 New or Assumed Loans*	6 Property Equities Gives 3-4 Gets 3-5	7 Cash In (Gives)	8 Cash Out (Gets)	9 Paper-Other Boot In (Gives)	10 Paper-Other Boot Out (Gets)	11 Gross Equities 6+7+9	12 Commission	13 Loan Fees	14 Other Costs	15 Total of 13+14	16 Net Effective Equities 11-12-15	17 New Loans	18 Gross Loan Proceeds 17-4
A Miller GIVES	8 Units	300,000	150,000		150,000					150,000	18,000	7,000	2,000	9,000	123,000	240,000	90,000
GETS	Retail Bldg	500,000		350,000	150,000			27,000 (participated)									
B High GIVES	Retail Bldg	500,000	250,000		250,000					250,000	30,000	11,200	3,500	14,700	205,300	350,000	100,000
GETS	Office Bldg	800,000		560,000	240,000			34,700									
C Pope GIVES	Office Bldg/Boat	800,000 / 50,000	450,000 / none		350,000 / 50,000					400,000	48,000	16,800	5,000	21,800	330,200	560,000	110,000
GETS	Medical Bldg	1,200,000		840,000	360,000			29,800									
D Lowe GIVES	Medical Bldg	1,200,000	700,000		500,000					500,000	72,000	none	6,000	6,000	422,000	840,000	140,000
GETS	Boat/Cash/Paper	50,000		none	50,000		307,500		64,500								
E Wright GIVES	Four Lots	60,000	none		60,000					60,000	6,000	4,800	2,000	6,800	47,200		
GETS	8 Units	300,000		240,000	60,000			12,800									
F Marks GIVES	Cash					30,800				30,800	none	none	800	800	30,000		
GETS	Two Lots	30,000		none	30,000												
G BROKERS GET	Two Lots	30,000		none	30,000		103,400		39,800		174,000 Total / (800) / 173,200 Net			59,100 Total / 800 / 59,900 Net	30,000		440,000
H TRANSACTION COSTS DISBURSED THROUGH ESCROW							59,900										
I LOAN PROCEEDS DISBURSED THROUGH ESCROW						440,000											
J TOTAL ESCROW ACCOUNTS (CASH IN must equal CASH OUT)						470,800 =	470,800	104,300 =	104,300 (PAPER IN must equal PAPER OUT)								

Col 12: Total 174,000 / (800) / Net 173,200 — Broker's Transaction Costs
Col 15: Total 59,100 / 800 / Net 59,900 — Broker's Transaction Costs

* Also includes loans taken "Subject To"
∴ Double check GETS line: Column 16 = 6 - 7 + 9 + 10
∴ Equity in property acquired = Col 6 - Col 9 (But ONLY if Col 9 represents a purchase-money note on property acquired)

Date: _____ Prepared by: _____ Office: _____

FORM 122-A (5-88) COPYRIGHT · 1987 PROFESSIONAL PUBLISHING CORPORATION 122 PAUL DRIVE, SAN RAFAEL, CA 94903 (415) 472-1964

PROFESSIONAL PUBLISHING

TAX-DEFERRED EXCHANGES

Tax-Deferred Exchange versus Sale and Purchase

The following illustration demonstrates the benefit of a tax-deferred exchange over sale and purchase of real estate held for investment or for productive use in trade or business.

Case 1: Sale and Purchase

Assume someone sells a property for $800,000, purchased a number of years earlier for $600,000, and that the tax basis is depreciated down to $500,000. The seller would have a federal tax liability of $84,000 (28% of $300,000), which would reduce the sale proceeds available for reinvestment.

Case 2: Tax-Deferred Exchange

In a tax-deferred exchange, the $84,000, which would otherwise go to Uncle Sam, can be fully used for reinvestment provided the taxpayer acquires like-kind real property of equal or greater value, held for investment or for productive use in trade or business, and provided further that the taxpayer owes at least as much on the property acquired as he or she owed on the property exchanged and that he or she did not receive any cash, notes, personal property or other assets referred to as boot.

Internal Revenue Code Section 1031

Under Internal Revenue Code Sec. 1031, gain or loss realized is not recognized (taxable) in an exchange if property held for productive use in trade or business or for investment is exchanged solely for property of like kind that is to be held for productive use in trade or business or for investment.

The taxpayer, however, has merely deferred (not avoided) tax on nonrecognized gain realized in a so-called tax-deferred exchange.

Real property of like kind includes improved and unimproved property, fixtures and leaseholds with a remaining term of at least 30 years. (If improved real property is exchanged for unimproved, gain is not recognized except for that portion of the gain treated as ordinary income under I.R.C. Recapture rules of Section 1250.)

The Revenue Reconciliation Act of 1989 provides that exchanges between U.S. and foreign property are no longer like kind.

Boot-Recognized Gain

Property not qualifying as like-kind property, if transferred partly in exchange for like-kind property, is termed *boot* and includes:

1. Mortgage boot (existing liens on the properties exchanged)
2. Other boot:
   a. Cash (including loan proceeds)
   b. Third-party notes
   c. Notes executed in escrow by one of the parties to the exchange
   d. Furniture, equipment and other personal property transferred in the exchange
   e. Real property held primarily for sale, usually referred to as *dealer property*
   f. Property used as taxpayer's residence

Gain may be recognized to the extent of the fair market value of such boot. (Rev. Rul. 72-456, 1972-2, C.B. 468 provides that in determining the amount of gain to be recognized by the taxpayer, the brokerage commission paid from the cash boot may be deducted.)

Because various kinds of boot may be given and/or received in such a partly tax-deferred exchange, the rule is that the taxable (recognized) portion of the gain realized is equal to the net boot received. However, part of the rule is that mortgage boot received (mortgage relief) can be offset by other boot given, but that mortgage boot given (new or assumed mortgages) cannot be offset by other boot received. Therefore, the mortgage boot must be netted first before the other boot is netted. From these principles, the following formula has evolved to determine the recognized portion of the gain realized:

Recognized Gain = (1) *Net Mortgage Relief** plus *Other Boot received* or less *Other Boot given* or (2) *Gain Realized,* whichever is lower.

**Net Mortgage Relief—Any excess of existing mortgages on the real property transferred over existing mortgages on the property acquired.*

The following examples illustrate the application of the above formula:

Example 1

Jones	Gives	Gets
Fair market values	$100,000	$200,000
Existing mortgages	25,000	150,000
Equities	$75,000	$50,000
Cash		25,000
	$75,000	$75,000
Net mortgage relief (25,000 – 150,000)		0
Plus other boot (cash) received		$25,000 (1)
Gain realized is assumed to be		$70,000 (2)
Recognized gain [the lower of (1) and (2)]		**$ 25,000**

Example 2

Brown	Gives	Gets
Fair market values	$150,000	$200,000
Existing mortgages	120,000	100,000
Equities	$30,000	$100,000
Third party note	70,000	
	$100,000	$100,000
Net mortgage relief (120,000 – 100,000)		$20,000
Less other boot given		($70,000)
		0 (1)
Realized gain is assumed to be		$60,000 (2)
Recognized gain [the lower of (1) and (2)]		**$0**

Example 3

Smith	Gives	Gets
Fair market value	$250,000	$225,000
Existing mortgages	130,000	100,000
Equities	$120,000	$125,000
Furniture		40,000
Cash	45,000	
	$165,000	$165,000

Smith buys the furniture for $40,000 in a separate transaction and gives $5,000 in the exchange, thus eliminating boot on one side.

Net mortgage relief ($130,000 − $100,000)	$30,000
Less other boot given	($5,000)
	$25,000 (1)
Realized gain is assumed to be	$70,000 (2)
Recognized Gain [the lower of (1) or (2)]	**$25,000**

Where properties of unequal equities are exchanged, recognition of gain can be reduced by avoiding payment of cash in escrow. This can be accomplished—as illustrated below—by reducing the loan on the property with the smaller equity before the exchange agreement is executed.

	Existing Position		Alternate Position	
	Jones	Smith	Jones	Smith
Fair market values	$100,000	$120,000	$100,000	$120,000
Loans	40,000	90,000	40,000	60,000
Equities	60,000	30,000	60,000	60,000
Cash transfer		30,000		0
Recognized gain	**30,000**	20,000	**0**	20,000

Regulation 1.1031 (b)-1(c) provides that mortgage boot given by the taxpayer cannot be offset by mortgage boot incurred by the taxpayer in anticipation of the exchange. There is some court authority that would permit such refinancing. However, refinancing

should not be undertaken without the advice of a qualified tax professional.

Transfer of Basis

Transferring the basis from the old to the new property becomes more complex as existing loans are involved and boot of various kinds is given.

Basis of New Property =
Fair Market Value of New Property
less *Realized Gain*
plus *Recognized Gain*

Basis of New Property =
Adjusted Basis of Old Property
plus *Boot given*
plus *Mortgages on New Property*
plus *Recognized Gain*
less *Boot received*
less *Mortgages on Old Property*

The following examples will demonstrate how—under increasingly complicated conditions—bases are transferred and to what extent gain is recognized by applying the above formula.

1. A taxpayer owns a real property free and clear with an adjusted basis of $20,000 and an FMV (fair market value) of $30,000. She exchanges her property plus $10,000 boot for another property of like kind worth $40,000.
   Realized gain = $10,000
   Recognized gain = None
   New basis = $20,000 + $10,000 = $30,000
2. The same taxpayer exchanges her property for another property of like kind worth $40,000. This time she gives no boot but assumes a loan of $10,000.
   Realized gain = $10,000
   Recognized gain = None
   New basis = $20,000 + $10,000 = $30,000
3. The same taxpayer exchanges her property for another property of like kind worth $22,000 and

receives $8,000 boot.

Realized gain = $10,000

Recognized gain = $8,000

New basis = $20,000 + $8,000 − $8,000 = $20,000

4. A taxpayer owns real property with a loan balance of $15,000, an adjusted basis of $20,000 and an FMV of $30,000. He exchanges his property for another property of like kind worth $50,000, assuming a $30,000 loan and giving the other party $5,000 boot.

Realized gain = $10,000

Recognized gain = None

New basis = $20,000 + $5,000 + $30,000 − $15,000 = $40,000

5. A taxpayer owns real property with a loan balance of $15,000, an adjusted basis of $20,000 and an FMV of $30,000. He exchanges his property for another property of like kind worth $19,000, assuming a loan of $10,000 and receiving $6,000 boot.

Realized gain = $10,000

Recognized gain = $10,000

New basis = $20,000 + $10,000 + $10,000 − $6,000 − $15,000 = $19,000

Because in this example all of the realized gain is recognized (taxable), there is no tax advantage of an exchange over a sale and a purchase.

6. A taxpayer owns real property with a loan of $10,000, an adjusted basis of $20,000 and an FMV of $30,000. He exchanges his property for another property of like kind worth $44,000, assuming a loan of $30,000 and receiving $6,000 boot.

Realized gain = $10,000

Recognized gain = $6,000

New basis = $20,000 + $30,000 + $6,000 − $6,000 − $10,000 = $40,000

Multiple Exchanges

It is highly unlikely that two property owners will wish to exchange their properties with each owner retaining the property received from the other.

The usual situation arises when a taxpayer, owning property A, wishes to make a tax-deferred exchange for Property B, owned by a seller who is not interested in Property A.

The taxpayer may enter into an exchange agreement with the owner of Property B, conditioned upon the sale at a specified price of Property A to a third party within a period of time acceptable to the owner of Property B.

Supposing the owner of Property B is unwilling to wait until the taxpayer has found a buyer for Property A, can the taxpayer still make a tax-deferred exchange of Property A for Property B?

The answer is yes, but it would probably be necessary to use a third party facilitator and additional financing will be required until Property A is sold. The taxpayer can enter into an exchange agreement with a facilitator for the exchange of Property A for Property B. The facilitator could purchase Property B and make a simultaneous exchange with the taxpayer for Property A. Alternatively, the facilitator could purchase Property B and exchange it for Property A when a buyer is found to purchase Property A. In either event, the facilitator will need funds with which to purchase Property B. The funds would ordinarily be borrowed and repaid from the sale proceeds of Property A.

In an alternative situation, the taxpayer receives an acceptable offer to purchase Property A before she has located a suitable Property B. Because buyers are often hard to come by, the taxpayer may enter into a *binder agreement,* whereby the party wishing to purchase Property A agrees to purchase Property B, to be selected by the taxpayer within a specified period of time, and then exchange it with the taxpayer for Property A.

Supposing the buyer is unwilling to wait until the taxpayer has found Property B, can the taxpayer still effect a tax-deferred exchange of Property A for Property B and allow the buyer to purchase Property A without delay? The answer is yes by effecting a delayed exchange.

Starker Delayed Exchanges

The term *Starker Exchange* stems from the famous 1979 Starker case, in which T.J. Starker survived an IRS attack. The case was legislatively sanctioned by the TRA '84 in amending Section 1031(a) (3). Final regulations of the IRS were published in May 1991.

The rules of a Starker exchange are outlined in three basis steps:

1. The exchanger finds a cash buyer for the smaller *like kind* property. When the sale closes, the cash must be held by a third-party *qualified intermediary.* (If the seller has access to that cash, called *constructive receipt,* the sale proceeds are taxable to the seller.)
2. Within 45 days of closing the sale, the exchanger must designate the property to be acquired, with the sales proceeds being held by the intermediary (plus any cash to be added).
3. The purchase of the designated property must be completed within 180 days after selling the old property.

A Starker delayed exchange agreement should be prepared by a tax or real estate attorney.

Definitions

A *deferred exchange* is an exchange in which, pursuant to an agreement, the taxpayer (*exchanger*) transfers property held for productive use in trade or business or for investment (*relinquished property*) and subsequently receives property to be held either for productive use in trade or business or for investment (*replacement property*).

A deferred exchange is entitled to the same benefits under Section 1031 as a simultaneous exchange as long as two additional requirements are met: (1) The replacement property must be identified within 45 days after the date of the original transfer of the delinquished property (*identification period*) and (2) the replacement property must be received within 180 days of the transfer of the relinquished property or before the due date (including extensions) of the exchanger's return, whichever occurs sooner (*exchange period*).

NOTE: It is important that the documents be drawn properly so that the transaction does not appear to be merely a sale and purchase. The exchange documents should be drawn by an experienced real estate or tax practitioner and not by the broker. Brokers involved in an exchange should recommend that their clients be represented by experienced real estate or tax counsel.

Identification of Replacement Property

Replacement property received after the end of the identification period must be identified either in a written document signed by the exchanger and hand delivered, mailed, telecopied or otherwise sent before the end of the identification period to the person obligated to transfer the replacement property or any other person involved in the exchange other than the taxpayer or a disqualified person. The replacement property must be unambiguously described by a legal description, street address or assessor's parcel number. Any replacement property received by the exchanger before the end of the identification period will be deemed to have been timely identified.

The maximum number of replacement properties the exchanger may identify (regardless of the number of relinquished properties in the same deferred exchange) is either (1) three properties without regard to the fair market values of the properties (the three-property rule) or (2) any number of replacement properties as long as their aggregate fair market value at the end of the identification period does not exceed 200% of the aggregate fair market value of all the relinquished properties (the 200% rule). If more properties than allowed under these two rules are identified, the exchange will be disallowed unless the exchanger acquires at least 95% of the aggregate fair market value of the identified replacement properties. If the exchanger receives like-kind replacement property simultaneously with the disposition of the relinquished property, that property is counted as replacement property for the purpose of both the three-property rule and the 200% rule.

The exchanger may revoke a designation of a replacement property at any time before the end of the identification period. The revocation must be in a written document signed by the exchanger and sent before the end of the identification period to the person to whom the identification was previously made. If the identification was made in a written agreement, then the revocation must be made in a written amendment to such agreement or in a written document signed by the exchanger and sent to all parties to the agreement before the end of the identification period. If a revocation is timely and properly made, the exchanger may identify new replacement properties, provided that the total number of identified replacement properties at the end of the identification period satisfies either the three-property rule or the 200% rule.

Incidental personal property (furniture or equipment) need not be identified separately nor counted separately in applying the three-property rule or the 200% rule. Personal property is treated as incidental if its value does not exceed 15% of the value of the real property it accompanies. Even if personal property is treated as incidental in a real property exchange, it is still treated as money or other property, and the exchanger's gain is recognized to the extent of its fair market value.

The replacement property received must be substantially the same property as the property that was identified. Although *substantially* is not defined, the regulations provide an example in which the exchanger acquires a parcel with a size and value of 75% of the property identified. Furthermore, when the identified real property consists of real property with improvements to be constructed, that property will generally qualify as being substantially the same property even if improvements are not completed by the time the property is received by the exchanger.

Actual or Constructive Receipt

Gain is recognized to the extent the exchanger is in actual or constructive receipt of money or other nonlike-kind property. An exchanger is in actual receipt of money if he or she actually receives such money or receives the economic benefits thereof. An exchanger is in constructive receipt of money at such time as money is credited to the exchanger's account, set apart for the exchanger or otherwise made available so the exchanger might draw upon it at any time. However, if the exchanger's control over the receipt of monies is subject to substantial limitations or restrictions, then the exchanger will not be in constructive receipt of such monies. But if such restrictions lapse, expire or are waived before the exchanger receives the replacement property, the exchange will be disallowed. Although the term *substantial restrictions and limitations* is not defined, an exchange agreement is considered suitably restrictive if it permits the exchanger to receive money or other property only at the following times: (1) If replacement property is not identified, then after the end of the identification period; (2) If replacement property is identified, then after the exchanger has received all of the replacement property to which he or she is entitled or at the end of the exchange period. In addition, actual constructive receipt of money by an agent or the exchanger is actual or constructive receipt by the exchanger.

Safe Harbors

The regulations allow for the following four *safe harbors* to avoid actual or constructive receipt, which may be provided for in the exchange agreement:

1. Security or guaranty arrangements
2. Qualified escrow accounts and qualified trusts
3. Qualified intermediaries
4. Interest or growth factors

Qualified Intermediaries

The use of qualified intermediaries is probably the most important safe harbor in the regulations. For a person to be a qualified intermediary, the following conditions must be met:

1. He or she may not be a related party to the exchanger.
2. He or she receives a fee for facilitating the deferred exchange.
3. He or she acquires the relinquished property from the exchanger and transfers it to a buyer.
4. He or she acquires the replacement property and transfers it to the exchanger.

Related parties include the exchanger's spouse, ancestors, descendants, siblings, entities in which the exchanger owns at least 10% interest, the exchanger's employees and, under certain circumstances, his or her attorneys and brokers. The exchanger's attorney or broker will not be considered a related party if his or her only relationship with the exchanger is as a provider of services with respect to exchanges of property. The exchanger's regular attorney will be considered a related party. A wide range of people with whom the exchanger has a pre-existing relationship (such as business associates, aunts, uncles and certian in-laws) will qualify as qualified intermediaries. Other qualified intermediaries include financial institutions and professional exchange companies. Exchangers can obtain greater security by requiring security in the form of a standby letter of credit issued by a financial institution or by insisting that the exchange proceeds be impounded in a qualified escrow account.

The regulations permit direct deeding when the qualified intermediary safe harbor structure is used. He exchanger may deed the relinquished property directly to its ultimate buyer, and the owner of the replacement property may deed that property directly to the exchanger. Use of direct deeding saves transfer taxes and avoids exposing the intermediary to risks of ownership.

The regulations also permit assignment to the intermediary of the agreement to sell the relinquished property and the agreement to purchase the replacement property if all parties to the agreement are notified of the assignment. This eliminates the need of novation of these agreements by a superseding exchange agreement and enables the exchanger to retain the intermediary just prior to close of escrow.

Important Factors

Regardless of the timing of the transactor or of the form in which the transaction is set up, it is important to specify the balances of the encumbrances on the respective properties at the time of the transaction and the expected balances at the time of closing so that the mortgage relief may be properly calculated, for the mortgage relief is a trap for the unwary in an otherwise tax-deferred exchange and must be protected against. An otherwise tax-deferred exchange might generate mortgage relief.

Proper planning can eliminate any taxable profit in the exchange. For example, the owner of Property A may pay down the principal of the encumbrance on Property A so there would be no mortgage relief. An alternative might be for the owner of Property B to further encumber his or her property prior to consummation of the exchange to eliminate mortgage relief.

One can see that in order to accomplish a tax-deferred exchange with its attendant benefits, knowledge and timing are prime requisites together with precise analysis of all factors involved in the transaction. All the facts relating to the transaction should be thoroughly analyzed, and the agreement should spell out all the elements of the transaction and especially, as mentioned, the intention to enter into a tax-deferred exchange should be stated.

Impact of Section 1250 on Tax-Deferred Exchanges

Prior to enactment of the TRA '86, accelerated depreciation or cost recovery was allowable on improvements to real property. Such improvements were characterized as Section 1250 property. The excess of the depreciation that would have been allowable under the straight-line method was called excess depreciation and was subject to recapture as ordinary gain in the event the property was sold. Although accelerated depreciation or cost recovery is no longer allowed and capital gain is no longer taxed at a preferential rate, Section 1250 is still in effect and has some tax consequences.

If an exchange otherwise qualifies under Section 1031 but the fair market value of the acquired Section 1250 property is less than the amount of ordinary gain that would have been recognized on account of the excess depreciation, then to the extent that the ordinary gain exceeds the fair market value of the Section 1250 property such gain will be recognized. This can occur where unimproved real property or property with limited improvements is acquired.

If sufficient Section 1250 property is acquired to avoid recognition of the gain, the excess depreciation accumulated on the old property is transferred to the new property and will result in ordinary gain when the new property is sold. This may be important if an installment sale is made of the new property because the ordinary gain must be recognized in the year of sale. Of lesser significance is the fact that deduction of capital loss is limited when it cannot be offset against capital gain, and therefore, whether or not a transaction results in capital gain or ordinary gain may be of some significance in the future.

EXCHANGE ANALYSIS

The Comparative Exchange Analysis, Form 122, is reprinted with permission from Professional Publishing (see page C-47). The form is designed to determine the feasibility of an exchange by computing the client's cash flow and net equity income before and after the exchange. If the comparison is favorable, the broker will have a strong argument in favor of the exchange.

COMPARATIVE EXCHANGE ANALYSIS

PREPARED BY	JOHN REAL ESTATE		DATE:	
PREPARED FOR	MR BROWN			

PROPERTY ADDRESS		100 GREEN ST	22 OCEAN AVE	
TYPE OF PROPERTY		OFFICE WAREHSE	OFFICES	

		For vital pertinent data and tables refer to the REALTY BLUEBOOK I & II published annually by Professional Publishing Corp	GUIDE NUMBERS	CLIENT'S PROPERTY A	CAP RATE	EXCHANGE PROPERTY B	CAP RATE	INCREASE (+) or DECREASE (-) of **B** over **A**	CAP RATE
BALANCING OF EQUITIES	1	Market Values		480,000		800,000			
	2	Less Existing Mortgages		180,000		450,000			
	3	EQUITIES	1 - 2	300,000		350,000			
	4	Personal Property							
	5	Personal Residence							
	6	Notes		20,000					
	7	Cash		30,000					
	8	EQUITY AND BOOT GIVEN	3 + 4 + 5 + 6 + 7	350,000	LINES 8 AND 13 MUST BALANCE				
	9	Personal Property							
	10	Personal Residence							
	11	Notes							
	12	Cash							
	13	EQUITY AND BOOT RECEIVED	3 + 9 + 10 + 11 + 12			350,000			

RECOGNIZED GAIN	14	Transaction Costs		5,000					
	15	Adjusted Basis		300,000					
	16	Realized (Indicated) Gain	1 - 14 - 15	175,000					
	17	Any Net Mortgage Relief	Excess of 2 A over 2 B			0			
	18	Cash or Other Boot Received	9 + 10 + 11 + 12			0			
	19	Total Boot Received	17 + 18			0			
	20	Cash or Other Boot Given	4 + 5 + 6 + 7 + 14			55,000			
	21	Net Boot Received	Excess of 19 over 20			0			
	22	RECOGNIZED (TAXABLE) GAIN	The lower of 16A or 21B			0			

INCOME	23	SCHEDULED ANNUAL INCOME		94,800		190,000			
	24	Less Vacancy and Credit Losses		2,844		7,600			
	25	GROSS OPERATING INCOME	23 - 24	91,956		182,400			
	26	Less Operating Expenses		8,600		17,000			
	27	NET OPERATING INCOME	25 - 26	83,356		165,400			
	28	Less Annual Loan Payments		28,440		66,828			
	29	GROSS SPENDABLE INCOME (Cash Flow)	27 - 28	54,916	18.3	98,572	28.1	+ 43,656	

Transfer Basis	30	Market Value of Property B	1B			800,000			
	31	Less Realized (Indicated) Gain	16A			175,000			
	32	Plus Recognized Gain	22B			0			
	33	BASIS OF PROPERTY B	30 - 31 + 32			625,000			
AFTER – TAX INCOME	34	Allocation to Improvements	INFO			75 %			
	35	Cost Recovery Period				31.5 Years			
	36	Cost Recovery Method				S L			
	37	Cost Recovery Rate p/year				3.1746 %			
	38	Depreciation Allowance	33 × 34 × 37	23,017		14,880			
	39	Interest		25,200		63,000			
	40	Taxable Income from Property	27 - 38 - 39	35,139		87,520			
	41	Other Taxable Income		60,000		60,000			
	42	Total Taxable Income	40 + 41	95,139		147,520			
	43	Total Federal Tax Liability (See Bluebook II)	Tax Rate x 42	23,933		41,219			
	44	Tax Liability Other Income	Tax Rate x 41	12,933		12,933			
	45	Tax Liability due to Property	43 - 44	11,000		28,286			
	46	NET SPENDABLE INCOME	29 - 45	43,916		70,286			
	47	Plus Equity Build-up (See Bluebook II)		3,240		3,828			
	48	NET EQUITY INCOME	46 + 47	47,156	13.5	74,114	21.2	26,958	

OTHER DATA								

FORM 122 (10-88) COPYRIGHT © 1987 BY PROFESSIONAL PUBLISHING CORP 122 PAUL DR SAN RAFAEL CA 94903 (415) 472 1964

PROFESSIONAL PUBLISHING

Exchange Agreements **C-47**

The form is unique in that it has built-in directions for completing all calculations, including balancing the equities, computing recognized gain, transferring the basis, computing cost recovery and, most important, the net equity income. Each pad of forms comes with a built-in example and simple directions. The form teaches anyone to complete a professional exchange analysis in a matter of minutes, a subject that takes many hours to learn in an exchange course.

Directions for Use of Form 122

1. Obtain and fill in the data needed to complete the analysis, where indicated by the arrows at the left margins of columns A and B.
2. The numbers in the column Guide Numbers refer to the line numbers in the far left column.
3. To balance the equities on lines 1 through 13 in columns A and B, compute (and tentatively write in with pencil) the amounts on line 8, column A and line 13, column B. Because these two amounts must balance, erase the smaller of the two and substitute the larger. The difference must now be made up in either: Boot Given (lines 4, 5, 6 or 7 in column A) or in Boot Received (lines 9, 10, 11 or 12 in column B), as the case may be.

    In the following example, 8A amounted to $300,000 and 13B to $350,000. In order to balance 8A and 13B, $350,000 was then substituted for $300,000 in equity plus $30,000 in cash. Therefore, make up the balance of $20,000 in some form of boot; in this case a note for $20,000 was offered.
4. Now complete column A from line 14 to line 48 as directed by the guide numbers. Reading the sections Recognition of Gain and Transfer of Basis under the heading Tax-Deferred Exchanges in the Tax section of the *Realty Bluebook*® is recommended.
5. Upon completion of column A, complete column B, beginning at line 16 down to line 48 as directed by the guide numbers.

6. Finally, show the result of the analysis, by computing the Increase or Decrease in Cash Flow and Net Equity Income after the Exchange in lines 28 and 48 in the last column. An increase in cash flow and/or net equity income should be a strong argument in favor of the proposed exchange.

INSTALLMENT SALES

The taxpayer's use of the installment sale method under Internal Revenue Code Sec. 453 provides a way to spread tax on profit from the sale of an asset over a number of years. This avoids paying tax on the entire gain in the year of sale. The installment sale method is used unless the taxpayer elects not to use it by reporting the entire gain in the year of sale.

Year of sale is usually the year in which title passes. Payments during the year of sale would include the down payment (in whatever form) and the principal portion of installment payments received during the year. In the event that property is sold subject to a mortgage that exceeds the seller's basis, the difference between the principal amount of the mortgage and the adjusted basis of the seller would be treated as a payment made during the year of sale.

This method may be to the advantage of a particular client's overall tax situation. The broker's task is not to advise his or her client in the matter but to alert the client to the fact that the Internal Revenue Code provides for such a method and to refer the client to a tax consultant for advice.

The installment sale method is not available to persons classified as dealers in real property.

Realized Gain

Realized gain is the net selling price (after selling expense) less adjusted basis.

Contract Price

The contract price is the gross selling price (before commission) less mortgages assumed by the purchaser except to the extent that such mortgages exceed the seller's adjusted basis.

Reportable Gain

The reportable gain in each year, including the year of sale, is equal to the amount paid to the principal multiplied by the realized gain and divided by the contract price.

Gain may be capital or ordinary. If the sale resulted in capital gain, then the gain portion of installment payments in subsequent years is also capital gain and vice versa.

If a portion of the gain is ordinary gain due to excess depreciation as defined in Internal Pevenue Code Section 1250, then the entire ordinary gain must be reported in the year of sale, irrespective of the amount received. The amount thus recognized is added to the basis of the property disposed of for the purpose of determining the gross profit ratio and calculating how much of each installment payment is included in income.

The Internal Revenue Code provides that interest will be imputed where no interest is stated or where the interest is too low. If a portion of the installments in future years is held to be interest rather than principal, then such reduction in principal would, of course, also reduce the sales price.

See Imputed Interest in the Tax section.

Computations

Example

Gross selling price	$100,000
Commission	5,000
Adjusted basis	65,000
Loan balance	40,000
Purchaser assumes the existing loan of	40,000
Seller takes back a second mortgage of	34,000
Down payment	26,000

Installment payments in the year
of sale $1,500 of which $1,000 is interest.

Down payment	$26,000
Plus principal payments in year of sale	500
Total paid to principal in year of sale	**$26,500**
Gross selling price	100,000
Less commission	5,000
Net selling price	$95,000
Less adjusted basis	65,000
Realized gain	**$30,000**
Gross selling price	100,000
Less mortgage assumed by purchaser	40,000
Contract price	**$60,000**

Profit Ratio = Realized Gain ÷ Contract Price =
$30,000 ÷ $60,000 = 0.5

Recognized Gain = Profit Ratio ×
Principal Payments Received =
0.5 × $26,500 = $13,250

Mortgages Assumed in Installment Sales

Any amount of mortgage assumed or taken subject to is considered part of the initial payments in installment sale reporting only to the extent that the mortgage exceeds the adjusted basis.

Sellers should be cautioned that in the event the seller encumbers the property to the extent of the adjusted basis immediately before the sale with the intention of obtaining tax-free cash, the IRS may take the position that the refinancing is undertaken in connection with the sale and should therefore be regarded as a single transaction and that consequently the proceeds from the refinancing should be considered as part of the initial payments.

Disposition and Hypothecation of Installment Sale Contracts

With certain limited exceptions, the disposition of the note or contract evidencing the deferred payments in an installment sale results in the recognition of gain or loss. The basis of the note or contract right is the amount of the unrecovered cost of the property sold. The gain or loss recognized will be the difference between the amount received for the obligation and its basis. If the disposition is made by gift, the amount to be recognized will be the difference between the basis of the obligation and its fair market value at the date of the gift.

If an installment obligation is used as collateral for a loan, the full amount of the loan proceeds will be considered to be a payment.

The transfer of an installment obligation on account of the death of a seller would not result in immediate recognition of gain. There are also exceptions relating to various tax-free transfers under the Internal Revenue Code.

Prepayment of Installment Contract by Buyer

Ordinarily, a seller would not be required to accept a prepayment under an installment note or contract that does not allow prepayment by its terms. However, a state statute may permit such prepayment and substantially diminish the tax advantages of the installment sale to the seller. For example, Sec. 2954.9 of the California Civil Code permits a buyer to prepay a real estate loan for residential property of four units or less that is taken back by the seller as part of the purchase price. Under the statute the buyer is not permitted to make such prepayment in the year of sale unless the seller has taken back four or more such loans during that calendar year. The California statute permits a lender to charge a prepayment penalty if specified in the note.

Imputed Interest

When there is a sale of property and a portion of the sale price is deferred, interest will be imputed where no interest is stated or where the interest is less than the minimum allocable.

Subject to the limit set forth below, the interest rate will be equal to the applicable federal rate. When the transaction is a sale and leaseback by the seller, the imputed interest will be 110% of the applicable federal rate.

The applicable federal rate depends upon the term

of the note. There is a rate for notes due in three years or less, one for notes due in more than three years but not more than nine years and one for notes due in more than nine years. The rates are determined by the IRS and published monthly. The lowest rate in effect during the three-month period ending on the first day of the month in which a binding contract is executed will be the applicable federal rate for the transaction.

Ordinarily, both the buyer and seller must report the interest income and deductions on the accrual method. However, when the principal amount does not exceed a specified statutory maximum and when the parties jointly elect, the seller does not use the accrual method of accounting and is not a dealer with respect to the property sold. Then the transaction may be reported by both the buyer and seller on the cash method of accounting.

Section 1274A of the IRC provides that when the deferred payment does not exceed $2.8 million, increased by inflation adjustments after the calendar year 1989, the maximum interest rate will be 9%. Said section provides that the maximum amount permitted under the preceding paragraph for use of the cash method is $2 million, which is also adjusted for inflation after 1989. In 1993, the inflation adjusted amount in order to qualify for the 9% limitation was $3,332,400 and the maximum amount that would quality for the cash method of accounting was $2,380,300.

PERSONAL RESIDENCES

Internal Revenue Code Section 1034

Under IRC Sec. 1034, no gain is recognized if

1. the taxpayer's principal personal residence is exchanged for another principal personal residence, provided the cost of the new residence equals or exceeds the adjusted sale price* of the old residence; or

*Adjusted Sale Prices = Gross Sale Price less Sales Expense less Fixing-Up Expenses. Fixing-Up Expenses equal cost of work performed within 90 days before the sale and paid within 30 days after the sale.

2. the old principal personal residence is sold and another residence is purchased and used as the taxpayer's principal personal residence within 24 months before or after the sale of the old residence, provided the cost of the new residence equals or exceeds the adjusted sale price* of the old residence.

Any costs incurred prior to this period, such as purchase of land upon which the taxpayer constructs a residence, may not be included in computing the cost of the new residence for qualifying purposes.

Gain is recognized (taxable) to the extent that the purchase price of the new residence is less than the adjusted sales price of the old residence.

An exchange of principal personal residences or sale and purchase, without recognition of gain can be repeated but not within 24 months.

NOTE: Generally, a taxpayer is limited to only one rollover in a 24-month period with regard to nonrecognition of gain on the sale of a principal residence. For sales and exchanges made after July 26, 1978, gains on the sales of more than one principal residence within a 24-month period will not be taxed currently if a replacement principal residence is purchased and occupied within that period. This new rule only applies if each sale is employment related and the relocation satisfied the moving expense deductibility requirements. (See section Tax-deductible Moving Expenses.)

Computing Gain on Sale and Basis of a New Residence

If a personal residence is sold and a new one acquired where this section applies, the new basis will be the cost of the new house less the amount of any gain that has been deferred.

In Example A, the cost of the new residence is higher than the adjusted sales price of the old residence; in Example B, the cost of the new residence is lower.

		Example A	Example B
1.	Sales price	$100,000	$100,000
2.	*Less* commission	6,000	6,000
3.	Amount realized	94,000	94,000
4.	*Less* basis of residence sold*	44,000	44,000
5.	**Gain realized on sale**	**50,000**	**50,000**
6.	Amount realized (line 3)	94,000	94,000
7.	*Less* fixing-up expenses	2,000	2,000
8.	Adjusted sales price	$ 92,000	$ 92,000
9.	*Less* cost of new residence	120,000	76,000
10.	**Gain recognized**	**0**	**16,000**
11.	Gain realized on sale (line 5)	50,000	50,000
12.	*Less* gain recognized (line 10)	0	16,000
13.	**Deferred gain**	**50,000**	**34,000**
14.	Cost of new residence	120,000	76,000
15.	*Less* deferred gain (line 13)	50,000	34,000
16.	**Basis new residence**	**70,000**	**42,000**

Basis of old residence = Acquisition Cost plus Cost of Improvements plus Special Assessments less Casualty Losses less Deferred Gain (if any) on the sale or exchange of a previous personal residence.

Basis

Tax basis is the book value of property for income tax purposes. Basis is determined by the method of acquisition, such as purchase, inheritance, gift and so on. If the property is acquired by purchase, its basis is the purchase price plus acquisition expenses.

During ownership of the home, the basis is adjusted upward by adding any *capital expenditures* (the cost of home improvements). In the event a portion of the home is used for rental or business, the basis is adjusted downward by subtracting any *cost recovery (depreciation) deductions* taken. The result is termed *adjusted basis*.

Any profit realized from the sale of real property is taxable and is referred to as *recognized gain*.

The *sale price* less *selling expenses* is the *amount realized*.

The adjusted sales price less adjusted basis is termed *gain realized*.

In the event a new residence is purchased and occupied by the taxpayer as his or her principal residence within 24 months before or after the sale of the old home, gain is recognized (taxable) only to the extent that the cost of the new residence is less than the adjusted sales price of the old residence. The taxable amount is thus termed *recognized gain*.

Realized gain less recognized gain is termed *deferred gain*.

Cost of new residence less deferred gain is the *basis of the new residence*. (See examples on page C-55.)

Residence Interest

Qualified residence interest is deductible as an itemized deduction against ordinary income. Qualified residence interest is defined as interest on debt secured by either the taxpayer's principal residence or a second residence of the taxpayer.

Where the taxpayer is a tenant/stockholder of a housing cooperative, debt secured by stock of the cooperative is treated as debt secured by the residence of the taxpayer. When stock may not be used as security by virtue of restrictions pursuant to local or state law or reasonable restrictions in the cooperative agreement, the stock may be treated as securing such debt if the taxpayer established that the debt was incurred to acquire the stock.

A second residence is a residence owned by the taxpayer that is (1) used by the taxpayer for personal purposes for a number of days exceeding the greater of 14 days or 10% of the number of days during such year as such unit is rented at fair rental or (2) neither used nor rented by the taxpayer during the taxable year.

The amount of interest deductible as residential interest is limited to *acquisition indebtedness* or *home equity indebtedness.* Acquisition indebtedness means indebtedness incurred in acquiring, constructing or substantially improving a qualified residence of the taxpayer secured by such residence. The term also includes any indebtedness secured by such residence resulting from the refinancing of indebtedness meeting the requirements of the definition but only to the extent that the amount of the indebtedness resulting from such refinancing does not exceed the amount of the refinanced indebtedness. There is a $1 million limitation on acquisition indebtedness.

Home equity indebtedness is indebtedness, other than qualified acquisition indebtedness secured by a qualified residence, that does not exceed the fair market value of the qualified residence less the amount of the acquisition indebtedness. There is a limit of $100,000 on home equity indebtedness.

All indebtedness existing on October 13, 1987, is treated as acquisition indebtedness, and the $1 million limitation does not apply. Pre–October 13, 1987, indebtedness also includes indebtedness incurred to refinance such debt. However, the refinancing indebtedness cannot exceed the pre–October 13, 1987, indebtedness existing at the time of the refinancing. The foregoing rule with respect to indebtedness existing on October 13, 1987, means that interest on loans existing on that date will remain fully deductible if they are secured by a qualified residence. However, as the principal amount of the loan is paid down, if the refinancing amount exceeds the amount due at the time of refinancing, the interest will be deductible only to the extent that it qualifies as home equity indebtedness that is limited to $100,000. This rule with respect to refinancing also applies to acquisition indebtedness incurred after October 13, 1987, for which the principal amount is reduced and the principal amount of the refinancing exceeds the amount of the reduced principal.

It is not necessary that the home equity indebtedness be the subject of a separate loan. The principal amount of the indebtedness for which interest is deductible is determined by adding the acquisition indebtedness to the home equity indebtedness.

However, the $1 million limitation on acquisition indebtedness is reduced by the amount of outstanding pre–October 13, 1987, indebtedness.

Deductible Expenses

The following expenses do not adjust the homeowner's basis but may be deducted against ordinary income:

1. Residence interest (both primary and second homes)
2. Discount points to be deductible must:
   - show on settlement statement as loan origination, loan discount, or discount points;
   - be computed as a percentage of the loan amount;
   - conform to an established business practice with respect to home financing in the area in which the residence is located and must not exceed the amount generally charged in that market area; and
   - be paid for financing a principal residence.

   NOTE: In March 1994, the IRS announced that homebuyers are now permitted to deduct points paid on their behalf by sellers for a mortgage to purchase their principal residence. The change is retroactive to homes purchased since 1991. Buyers who purchased since 1991 and did not deduct any seller paid points should contact the IRS about obtaining the deduction.

Points are deductible over the term of the loan if paid in the following situations:

- for refinancings or lines of credit;
- for home improvement loans when the amount borrowed has no connection with an acquisition of a principal residence;
- for loans on second or vacation homes, business or investment properties; and
- in connection with purchases of a principal residence that are allocable to a loan amount exceeding the $1 million limit.

Nondeductible Expenses

Acquisition expenses may not be deducted against ordinary income but are added to the basis. Examples include appraisal fees, credit reports, inspection fees, title fees, attorney fees, property taxes and mortgage insurance premiums.

Fixing-up expenses are the cost of work to assist the sale, performed within 90 days before the sale and paid within 30 days after the sale. Fixing-up expenses are not deductible against ordinary income.

Partial Occupancy by Owner

The sale of a small residential income property, partially occupied by the owner, can result in both capital gain and a nondeductible loss. The sales price and the basis must be apportioned to the owner's unit and the rental portion of the property. Because only the rental portion of the property is depreciable, the basis allocated to the owner's unit is higher. In the following example, an owner occupied one of three flats that he bought for $75,000 and sold at an adjusted sales price of $60,000.

	Total	*Rental*	*Personal*
Adjusted sales price	$60,000	$40,000	$20,000
Cost basis	75,000	50,000	25,000
Less depreciation		12,000	
Adjusted basis		38,000	
Gain (or loss)		2,000	(5,000)*

The $5,000 loss is a nondeductible personal loss and cannot be offset against the $2,000 gain from the rental portion of the building.

Conversion of a Personal Residence to Income-Producing Property

Homeowners cannot deduct maintenance expenses, nor can they take depreciation deductions on personal residences. However, if they convert a home to rental property, maintenance expenses become deductible nonbusiness expenses under IRC Sec. 212; the owners can also take depreciation deductions while the property is held for the production of income or for investment under IRC Sec. 167(a) (2).

However, by converting a home to rental property, homeowners can lose their Sec. 1034 nonrecognition of gain benefits. The property would then only qualify for nonrecognition of gain under Sec. 1031. (See section Tax-Free Exchanges.)

Business Use of a Home

A taxpayer is entitled to deduct certain business expenses attributable to a portion of the home used exclusively and regularly as a principal place of business or as a place of business that is used by patients, clients or customers in meeting or dealing with the taxpayer in the ordinary course of business.

In addition, employees must establish that they are required for their employer's convenience to provide their own space and facilities for the performance of their duties and are not doing so merely because it is appropriate and helpful in their employment. These limitations also apply when an employee leases a portion of his or her home to his or her employer.

Deductible expenses include those made exclusively for the business portion of the home and expenses that must be allocated to the portion of the home used for business, such as utilities, real estate taxes, insurance, mortgage interest, and so on.

In addition, deductions for depreciation may be claimed on the business portion of the home.

Sale of Personal Residences by Persons 55 or Over

Under the Internal Revenue Code Sec. 121 taxpayers 55 or over (at the time they sell their principal residences) may elect to exclude from their taxable income gain from such sale provided that the taxpayer has owned and used the property as his or her principal personal residence for three out of the last five years preceding the sale. The amount of the gain excluded may not exceed $125,000.

Short temporary absences for vacation or other seasonal absences count as periods of use even though the home was rented during such periods.

To be eligible, it is sufficient that either husband or wife meet the above requirements of age, ownership and use as long as they are legally married at the time of sale and the property is held in joint tenancy or as community property.

If single persons own a personal residence as joint tenants or as tenants in common, both meeting age, ownership and use requirements of Sec. 121, each joint tenant or tenant in common is fully exempt on his or her share of the profit up to the maximum of $125,000.

This tax exemption is available to a taxpayer and his or her spouse only once during their lifetimes. However, election of the benefits of Sec. 121, as it existed prior to July 26, 1978, does not preclude a taxpayer from electing the new benefits that became available after that date.

If the taxpayer or his or her spouse already sold a personal residence prior to their marriage and elected to use the tax exemption, then the exemption will not be available again during a subsequent marriage.

If two taxpayers who separately own personal residences and subsequently marry wish to sell both residences after marriage, the exemption can only apply to one residence provided age, ownership and use requirements are met. All requirements must be met by one spouse.

If a taxpayer elects the benefits of Sec. 121 and Sec. 1034 (a situation that might occur if the gain realized on the sale of a personal residence was in excess of $125,000), the basis of the new property would be determined by subtracting the deferred gain from the cost of the new residence. (See following examples.)

Computing Taxable Gain on Sale of a Residence for Persons over 55

1. Sales price	$200,000
2. *Less* selling expenses	12,500
3. Adjusted sales price	$187,500
4. *Less* basis of home	50,000
5. **Gain realized on sale**	**$137,500**
6. *Less* exemption	125,000
7. **Taxable gain on sale**	**$ 12,500**

Computing Taxable Gain and Basis of New Residence for Persons over 55

	Example A	*Example B*	*Example C*
Cost of new residence	$ 90,000	$ 60,000	$ 50,000
8. Adjusted sales price (line 3)	187,500	187,500	187,500
9. *Less* exemption	125,000	125,000	125,000
10. Revised adjusted sales price	62,500	62,500	62,500
11. *Less* cost of new residence	90,000	60,000	50,000
12. **Taxable gain**	**0**	**2,500**	**12,500**
13. Cost of new residence	90,000	60,000	50,000
14. *Less* deferred gain (line 7 minus line 12)	12,500	10,000	0
15. **Basis of new residence**	**77,500**	**50,000**	**50,000**

Tax Savings the Homebuyer Should Know About

The tax deductions of interest and property taxes as well as reduction of the principle loan amount, can considerably reduce the homeowner's actual monthly housing cost, depending upon his or her tax bracket. This is a powerful closing argument with a buyer who finds monthly payments excessive, as the following example illustrates.

Loan amount	$80,000
Term	30 Years
Interest	9%
Monthly payment	$644
Taxes	$200/mo
Insurance	$40/mo
Total monthly payment	$884

First month's interest:	
9% × 80,000 ÷ 12	$600
Property taxes per month	+ 200
Total tax deduction per mo.	$800
Monthly tax savings @ Client's tax bracket of 28%:	
$800 × 28%	− 224
Effective monthly cost	$660
Monthly equity build-up (See Section A, Equity Build-Up Tables)	
$80,000 × 0.683% ÷ 12	− 46
Actual monthly cost	$614

Tax-Deductible Moving Expenses

Certian specified expenses connected with the move to a new principal place of employment are deductible. All employees, old or new, reimbursed or unreimbursed, are treated alike and the self-employed are allowed comparable deductions as well.

Deductible expenses include cost of moving household goods and personal effects and the expense of traveling (including lodging) from the old home to the new home of the taxpayer and members of his or her household. If traveling is done by car, expenses can be deducted either by itemizing or by a standard deduction of $.09 per mile plus tolls and parking.

The foregoing expenses are deductible only if the new principal place of work is at least 50 miles further from the old residence than the old place of work was. This distance is measured by the shortest of the more commonly traveled routes between two points.

The taxpayer must be employed full-time (not necessarily by one employer only) at the new location for a minimum of 39 weeks during the 12 months following the move. This test is waived if employment is terminated due to certain circumstances beyond his or her control. On a joint return, the deduction is allowed if either husband and or wife meet this 39-week test. The self-employed must work at the new location either as a self-employed person or as an employee for at least 78 weeks during the 24 months following the move of which at least 39 weeks must be during the first 12 months.

Reimbursements of any of the above expenses must be included in the taxpayer's gross income.

Energy Tax Credit

A 10% energy credit is allowed to a business for equipment that uses solar power to generate electricity or to heat or cool and for equipment to produce, distribute or use geothermal energy.

Information Reporting on Real Estate Transactions

The TRA '86 requires that real estate transactions be reported to the IRS. The primary responsibility for reporting is on the person or entity responsible for closing the transaction, including any title company or attorney conducting the settlement. If there is no person or entity responsible for closing the transaction, the reporting must be done by the mortgage lender. If there is no mortgage lender, the reporting must be done by the seller's broker. If there is no seller's broker, the reporting must be done by the buyer's broker.

Form 1099 is used to report the necessary information. The provision is effective for real estate transactions that close on or after January 1, 1987.

RISK
MANAGEMENT

To receive advance notice of the
next *Realty Bluebook*® edition
(and information about
what's new), please call
1-800-322-8621
to register your name and address.

CONTENTS

RISK MANAGEMENT

RISK
D

RISK MANAGEMENT

MANAGING RISK

Risk management can be defined as a plan of action to minimize the real estate broker's risk of liability and generally involves four components: (1) education, (2) risk shifting, (3) risk anticipation and (4) risk control.

EDUCATION

Educating the sales staff should be the number one concern of a broker's efforts in reducing legal liability, which has become an increasingly serious risk of doing business. A sales staff able to recognize and deal with the situations that most frequently result in litigation is without a doubt a broker's best insurance to stay out of court. The following chapters are designed to assist in achieving this goal.

RISK SHIFTING

Several approaches are available to shift the risk of liability from the broker.

Errors and Omissions Insurance Coverage

Brokers should plan to devote more time and attention to risk management and their own professional liability insurance needs. To assist in this effort, some tips from insurance experts are offered here:

- E&O policies vary substantially between insurance carriers. It is important to consider the insured activities, exclusions, conditions and definitions.
- Premium savings should be accomplished by taking a higher deductible, not by opting for an inadequate insurance amount. Keep in mind that the primary purpose of E&O insurance is protection against catastrophic, business-threatening lawsuits.
- Read all fine print in the policy.

- Complete the application in every detail, including information on operations, personnel, revenues, descriptive brochures, standard contracts used, resumes and any prior claims.
- Any material misrepresentation made by an applicant for insurance, even though made innocently, whether verbal or written, renders the insurance contract voidable. A misrepresentation is material when the insurance company would not have entered the contract had the complete facts been known at the time the policy was issued. The company has the legal right to rescind or cancel the policy in such an event.
- Liability that may not be covered by E&O insurance includes claims based upon fraud and antitrust violations.

Inspections or Evaluations by Third Party Experts

"I am not qualified to give you an expert opinion on the condition of. . . . A structural engineer could best answer your question." Such conversations should be documented by a follow-up note or letter to the buyer. Real estate professionals should be cautioned that if they hold themselves out to be experts in a certain trade or profession by answering questions, for example, on structural soundness, they may be held to the same performance standards as a structural engineer.

RISK ANTICIPATION

Risk anticipation involves identifying the source of problems and taking steps to ensure that such problems do not arise.

Documenting Information on the Property Provided by the Seller

The law, through court decisions, imposes a duty upon real estate brokers to exercise care in obtaining information about the property. It is a broker's responsibility to check out and document information obtained from the seller. The National Association of

REALTORS® strongly recommends the use of disclosure statements by sellers, and some states have mandated the use of such disclosures.

Written Disclaimers

Another technique to avoid risk is the use of written disclaimers that the broker or salesperson is qualified to advise on matters concerning the marketing of real estate. For questions concerning the legal or tax consequences of the transaction or advice on the condition of the property, the buyer should consult appropriate professionals.

Disclosures in Writing or Confirmed by Letter

Disclosures of agency relationships, possible existence of environmental hazards, due-on-sale clauses, zoning and flood hazards should be confirmed by letter.

Protective Clauses

Listings, Sales Agreements and Buyer-Broker Agreements:

Buyers (Sellers) acknowledge they have not relied upon any representations by Broker with respect to the environmental condition of the property that are not contained in this agreement.

Buyer-Broker Agreements for Purchase of Unimproved Land:

Buyers acknowledge they have not relied upon any representations by Broker to determine the environmental condition of the property or its suitability for the intended project.

Purchase/Sale Agreements:

Conditioned upon a satisfactory environmental audit.

RISK CONTROL

Brokers should establish procedures to identify the first clue of grievances and set up written policies to deal with complaints before they turn into litigation.

- Salespersons and office staff should be required to immediately report the first clues of a buyer's dissatisfaction or "buyer's remorse" to the broker or a designated manager.
- All sales and office staff should be made aware of the importance of answering any complaints with respect and consideration, no matter how ill-founded they may appear.
- Prompt action by the broker is essential, showing understanding, but emphasizing all the positive points of the property. In case of "buyer's remorse," it may be necessary to sell the property all over again. Often an expert opinion may lay a buyer's concerns to rest.
- If the firm is responsible and likely to incur liability, the broker and his or her attorney may consider the possibility of a settlement rather than risk litigation.

MISREPRESENTATION AND NONDISCLOSURE

A broker judged liable for misrepresenting or failing to disclose a material fact could be ordered to pay severe actual damages, punitive damages and even criminal penalties in case of fraud. Other penalties may include disciplinary sanctions for violating the REALTORS® Code of Ethics and suspension or revocation of real estate license.

The 1970s and 1980s witnessed a new concept of consumer protection in the sale of residential real estate and a proliferation of lawsuits against sellers and brokers claiming fraud, misrepresentation and failure to disclose material facts.

In the 1984 landmark case *Easton v. Strassburger,* the California Court of Appeals imposed a new duty on real estate agents: the duty of a seller's agent to disclose to a buyer defects the agent was not aware of but would have been aware of had the agent made a reasonably competent inspection in light of certain red flags. This duty exists even though there is no fiduciary relationship between the agent and the buyer.

Some courts have noted that this duty is limited to a visual inspection and does not necessarily include an obligation to verify facts related by the seller unless there are indications to the contrary.

Misrepresentation imposes liability on several bases of law:

1. Intentional misrepresentation (active fraud): Knowingly making a false statement about a material fact
2. Intentional concealment (constructive fraud or passive fraud): Knowingly failing to disclose a material fact
3. Negligent misrepresentation: Making a false statement about a material fact that the broker did not know but should have known was false
4. Negligent nondisclosure: Failure to disclose a material fact for lack of exercising adequate care in obtaining information about the property

5. Negligent advice: Giving incorrect professional advice when the agent should have known the advice was wrong

INTENTIONAL MISREPRESENTATION (ACTIVE FRAUD)

Active fraud imposes liability for knowingly making a false statement about a material fact or for knowingly attempting to conceal a material defect from a buyer's view or discovery. In *May v. Hopkinson,* 347 S.E.2d 508 (S.C. App. 1986), the real estate agent obtained two estimates for repair work on a window. One estimate did not include repairs to the wall's structural damage. The agent did not disclose this estimate, and despite the fact that there were other indications of termites and additional problems, he informed the purchasers that the house was structurally sound. The South Carolina Court of Appeals held that the agent's actions supported a finding of fraud.

In *Loch Ridge Construction, Inc. v. Barra,* 291 Ala 312, 280 S2d 745 (1973), the buyer claimed the salesperson had fraudulently misrepresented the house to be in perfect condition, constructed in a good and workmanlike manner and in compliance with plans and specifications approved by FHA. The court ruled in favor of the buyer.

In *Pumphrey v. Quillen,* Ohio St 343, 135 NE2d 328 (1956), the court ruled that brokers may be held liable for fradulent misrepresentation if they make a statement they know they cannot justify and the statement is found to be false.

INTENTIONAL CONCEALMENT (CONSTRUCTIVE FRAUD)

Constructive fraud imposes liability for intentionally concealing known material defects to a buyer, particularly if one or more of the following is true:

- The buyer is unable or unlikely to discover such a defect without assistance, sometimes referred to as a latent defect. *Cooper v. Jevne,* 128 Cal. Rpt. 724 (Cal. App. 1976); *Lynn v. Taylor,* 642 P.2d 131 (Kan. App. 1982).
- The defect relates to a health or safety matter. *Cashion v. Ahmadi,* 345 So. 2d 268 (Ala 1977); *Gozon v. Henderson-Dewey & Assoc., Inc.,* 458 A. 2d 605 (Pa. Sup. 1983).
- The real estate agent has led the buyer away from discovering the defect.
- The real estate agent has made a false statement, believing it to be true when made, but later discovering it to be false without correcting it. *Mammas v. Oro Valley Townhouses, Inc.,* 638 P.2d 1367 (Ariz. App. 1981).

In *Lynn v. Taylor,* 7 Kan. App. 369, 642 P2d 131 (1982), the buyer of a termite-damaged residence sued the seller and broker for delivering a clean pest control inspection report while fraudulently concealing a negative report previously obtained by the broker. The appellate court confirmed judgment against the broker and seller and explained a general principle that a party is under legal obligation to disclose information, including existing reports, if it has knowledge the other party would not or could not reasonably be expected to have. Failure to do so can constitute fraud, especially if the other party relies on the first party's advice.

In *Century 21 Page One Realty v. Naghad,* 760 S.W.2d 305 (Tex. App. 1988), the sellers listed their property with a real estate agency. A neighbor promptly called the agency and informed them of a sewage problem and threatened suit if it was not fixed before the property was sold. The real estate agent sold the property without disclosing the problem. Soon after the purchasers moved in, raw sewage leaked into their yard. The Texas Court of Appeal affirmed judgment against the agent and the seller for failing to disclose the problem.

NEGLIGENT MISREPRESENTATION

Negligent misrepresentation imposes liability for false statements that the real estate agent did not know were false but should have known were false.

In *Johnson v. Greer Real Estate Co.*, 720 P.2d 660 (Kan. 1986), the real estate agency filling out the listing agreement transferred information without attempting to verify it from a listing on the same property made several years earlier. The prior listing incorrectly indicated that the house was connected to a sewer system. The property was eventually sold to a couple who specifically informed the agent that they had no interest in any property with a septic tank. The Supreme Court of Kansas affirmed a lower court decision and found that the jury could well have concluded that even if the sellers did not know the property was served by a septic tank system, a real estate agent knowledgeable about the area should have known the true facts and should have disclosed them to the buyers.

The Alaska Supreme Court noted that real estate professionals "hold themselves out to the public as having specialized knowledge of the realty they sell" and "a purchaser who relies on a material misrepresentation, even though innocently made, has a cause of action against the broker originating or communicating the misrepresentation."

NEGLIGENT NONDISCLOSURE

Negligent nondisclosure imposes liability for failure to exercise adequate care to discover material defect and disclose it to the buyer.

In *Easton v. Strassburger,* 152 3rd 90, 199 Cal. Rpt 383 (Cal. App. 1984), the plaintiff purchased a house that was later severely damaged by a massive landslide. Although the property had in the past experienced some earth movement and the listing broker was aware of certain red flags indicating the need for soil testing, no warning was given to the buyer. The California Court of Appeals ruled that in light of certain red flags, the seller's agent was negligent in failing to perform a reasonably competent inspection (or having such an inspection performed by appropriate professionals) and revealing the problems that would have been discovered in the course of such an inspection to the buyer.

NOTE: This decision imposed a duty on the seller's agent to disclose defects to the buyer even though no fiduciary relationship existed between the seller's agent and the buyer.

In *Gouveia v. Citycorp Person to Person Financial Center Inc.* (N.M. App. 1984), the buyer sued the listing broker who had described the property in "all top shape," when in fact it was "replete with major defects," which were not apparent until after the buyer had moved in. The New Mexico Court of Appeals, ruling in favor of the buyer, concluded that a listing broker has a legal obligation to prospective buyers to disclose defects discoverable by reasonable inspection.

In *Provost v. Miller,* 144 Vt. 67, 473 A2d 1162 (1984), the court noted that, as seller's agents, brokers are guilty of negligent misrepresentation only if they pass along information that they know, or have reason to know, may not be true.

In *Hoffman v. Connell,* 108 Wash. 2d 69, 736 P2d 242 (1987), the Supreme Court of Washington ruled in favor of a broker who innocently misrepresented a property's location and boundary lines by telling the buyer what the seller had told him. The court held that the broker would be liable for passing the seller's misinformation only if something had occurred to alert the broker of a problem, in which case the broker would have been negligent in failing to investigate. The court characterized brokers and salespeople as "marketing agents," not "structural engineers or contractors" and explained that brokers have "no duty" to verify a seller's independent representations unless they are aware of facts that "tend to indicate such representations are false." However, it is always prudent to verify information regarding acreage, boundary lines and permitted uses of the property.

In *Amato v. Rathbun Realty, Inc.,* 98 NM 231, 647 P2d 433 (NM Ct. App. 1982), a buyer sued a selling broker for negligent misrepresentation and failure to disclose information. The court ruled for the buyer, noting "a broker is a fiduciary in a position of great trust and confidence and must exercise the utmost good faith." Breaching such a duty can give rise to a cause of action against the broker for both negligence and constructive fraud.

New legislation in this area is constantly being enacted and brokers should become familiar with new developments in their state through local associations and other sources.

NEGLIGENT ADVICE

Negligent advice imposes a liability for giving incorrect professional advice when the agent should have known the advice was wrong. Advice differs from a representation in that advice is a suggestion whereas a representation is a statement of fact. In *Gerard v. Peterson,* 448 N.W. 2d 669 (Iowa 1989), a real estate agent, who had casually advised the buyer that it "probably wasn't necessary" to include a financing contingency in the purchase agreement, was held liable for giving the buyer negligent advice.

FREQUENT CAUSES OF LITIGATION AND HOW TO AVOID THEM

- Failure to disclose to a buyer that an addition or alteration was performed without a building permit and/or not in compliance with code requirements. Courts have held agents liable for failing to verify that a seller obtained a building permit and final inspection, if necessary by inquiring with the local building department.
- Agents should advise sellers to disclose water leaks or drainage problems even though they have been

fixed. Complaints for concealment can be avoided by disclosure of all leaks including when, by whom and how they were repaired.

- Agents should refrain from making representations with respect to boundary lines. Surveying is beyond the expertise of real estate brokers and agents.
- Agents should recommend having a qualified inspector check the septic system including the leach lines. Simply pumping out is not sufficient.
- Failure to disclose pet urine contamination. Buyers should be advised to retain a qualified expert if such contamination is suspected.
- Failure to investigate and disclose red flags pointing to prior land movements or excessive settling, such as sloping floors, distorted garage frames, cracks at window or door corners or cracks in fireplaces.

SUMMARY

- A listing broker who fails to investigate a red flag and to alert the buyer exposes himself or herself to liability.
- A broker who innocently gives a buyer incorrect information furnished by the seller may not be held liable; however, the broker would be obligated to verify the seller's representation if there is any indication the seller's representation may not be true.
- A selling broker representing the buyer may be liable for constructive fraud if he or she fails to disclose material information to the buyer.
- Brokers may be liable for fraud or negligence committed by their salespeople even if they do not participate in, or do not have knowledge of or have forbidden such misconduct.
- A purchaser who relies on a material misrepresentation by a broker or salesperson, even though innocently made, has a cause of action against the broker originating or communicating the misrepresentation.

DISCLOSURE OF ENVIRONMENTAL HAZARDS

The following chapter, Disclosure of Environmental Hazards, is an integral part of the course outline Risk Management III, produced by and reprinted with permission of the Hawaii Association of REALTORS®.

The series of courses, titled Risk Management I, II and III, is based on material provided by NAR during their Risk Reduction Instructors Training Seminar in Chicago. The courses are available for purchase from the Hawaii Association of REALTORS®.

The information contained in this chapter is accurate, reliable and current as of the date of publication. Readers are advised to check the currentness before relying on its information for any type of decision making. The information contained herein is not intended as legal or other technical advice. Readers are advised to consult appropriate experts or licensed professionals on questions concerning its applicability to their particular factual circumstances or situation.

THE REAL ESTATE AGENT'S ROLE

Real estate agents cannot and are not required to understand complicated environmental legislation. This is a field for specialized attorneys and environmental experts. The real estate agent's primary responsibility in this area is (1) to recognize potential environmental hazards in commercial or industrial properties, agricultural or residential properties, and (2) to recommend that the seller retain appropriate experts to evaluate those hazards. Should the agent discover a potential environmental hazard, an attorney ought to be involved in drafting the required disclosure. This may shift any liability from the agent to the respective experts. When representing the buyer, the broker should recommend that any contamination be properly cleaned up. The potential liability resulting from environmental problems is so great that most buyers should not be encouraged to take such risk. A real estate agent representing a buyer who insists on purchasing a property that has potential environmental problems should strongly advise the buyer in writing, with the assistance of an attorney, not to proceed with the purchase.

MAJOR FEDERAL ENVIRONMENTAL LEGISLATION

Hazardous Substances and Environmental Laws

There are a number of federal and state laws that (1) regulate the storage, use, transportation and disposal of hazardous substances and (2) require the removal of hazardous wastes by the owners of real property. One important federal law that affects the real estate industry is the Comprehensive Environmental Response, Compensation and Liability Act of 1980 (CERCLA), which was amended as the Superfund Amendment and Reauthorization Act of 1986.

A major concern of real estate brokers are those laws that make owners of real property responsible for the clean-up of hazardous substances that are found on the property. Under CERCLA, there is no financial limit to an owner's obligation for the clean-up of hazardous wastes found on his or her property. The current owner may be strictly or absolutely liable for the costs of the clean-up whether he or she caused the problem or not. However, CERCLA states that a defense to this liability, known as the *innocent landowner defense,* may be satisfied if an assessment is performed prior to acquisition of the property, which constitutes "all appropriate inquiry into the previous ownership and uses of the property consistent with good commercial or customary practice" as defined in 42 USC Section 9601(35)(B).

In agreements for the sale of real property, buyers will want a comprehensive warranty and indemnity from the seller with respect to the existence of hazardous wastes. Sellers ordinarily will want to limit their representations to facts of which they have actual knowledge and require the buyer to make his or her own investigation. Although an indemnity agreement can be helpful, an indemnification is only good if the indemnifying parties still exist and have the funds to back it up. Some states require sellers of commercial property to notify the buyer of the existence of any hazardous substance known to the seller.

Lenders are concerned with the effect of hazardous wastes upon the value of their security. Because of this, they normally require a comprehensive inspection and report with respect to the environmental integrity of the property. Many lenders require that an environmental inspection be performed by an environmental professional prior to agreeing to lend money on a parcel of real property. This is more often the case with properties zoned commercial or industrial or those that have a history warranting an investigation.

Current commercial leases commonly include a provision prohibiting the use or storage of hazardous substances on the premises or requiring that the lessee comply with all the environmental laws. Some states require a lessee to notify the lessor of the existence of any hazardous substance on the premises.

The Resource Conservation and Recovery Act of 1976 (RCRA)

This law provides a total life cycle control for hazardous waste management including the registration, reporting, permitting, handling, storage, transportation, manifest system and disposal standards.

Small quantity generators that generate less than 100 kilograms (that is about half a 55-gallon drum) per month are not exempt from requirements but have some different responsibilities under RCRA than a large quantity generator.

Under RCRA, a waste is hazardous if it

- is specifically listed as hazardous or
- fails specific characteristic tests that result in it being considered either toxic, corrosive, reactive or ignitable.

A real estate agent should be aware that a transporter of hazardous wastes must be registered. If a potentially hazardous waste is found on a property, it should be left in place until picked up by a certified hauler; a real estate agent is not normally a registered hazardous waster transporter. Additionally, strict documentation requirements apply.

Environmental Responsibilities under CERCLA/Superfund

Environmental liability extends to those who violate environmental quality laws and to those who somehow become responsible for the clean-up of contaminated property. Keep in mind that the issue is not fairness. It is a question of who has "deep pockets" and might be able to afford to pay for the clean-up. The government will seek clean-up costs from innocent purchasers of real estate if the original wrongdoer is insolvent or cannot be found. In other words, this legislation is based on strict liability. It doesn't matter if the contamination was not the owner's fault.

NAR advises that brokers should familiarize themselves with hazards known to be common in their market area and that the broker's investigation should include signs of environmental problems readily apparent to a real estate broker but that the broker should not be expected to discover problems apparent only to the trained eye or judgment of an environmental expert.

When there is a *release* (spill, leak, etc.) of hazardous substances, CERCLA gives the Environmental Protection Agency (EPA) the right to have the substances cleaned up either by

1. cleaning up a release using Superfund resources and suing to recover costs from any responsible party on a strict liability basis or

2. ordering through injunction that responsible parties have to clean up. EPA has the right to fine violators at $25,000 per day.

Note that no minimum amount is required for the definition of a *release*. Even the threat of a release is sufficient to trigger EPA action to require payment for a clean-up.

Liability for Clean-Up

Who can become liable for cleaning up contaminated property? Property owners, lenders who foreclose on contaminated property, parties who have the equivalency of ownership through a sale-leaseback and others can become responsible for clean-up costs. Superfund Section 107(a) imposes liability on persons known as *potentially responsible parties* (PRPs).

1. Those who have operations and processes that release regulated materials or wastes must pay to clean up the contaminated property or property where the wastes were improperly (illegally) disposed. This could include problems from leaking tanks affecting the soil or groundwater. It could range from contamination resulting from illegal dumping of materials to legal disposal of a waste that later caused a problem.
2. The current owner or purchaser may have to pay for clean-up of contamination from previous owners even if the current owner had nothing to do with past contamination.
3. The current owner may have to pay for disposal of illegally disposed wastes without the consent of the owner by an unknown third party.
4. An owner of land may be responsible to pay for the clean-up of wastes that have leached in from an adjoining property.
5. Landlords may be liable for actions of their tenants whenever a tenant improperly disposes of hazardous waste onto a property.
6. Tenants may assume liability for property conditions or may be required to correct a condition

they did not create or contribute to, such as clean-up of a prior tenant's waste or the removal of asbestos necessary for renovation.

Current owners can become responsible for clean-up costs when hazardous substances are discovered unless they can prove they meet the requirements of the *innocent landowner defense* under CERCLA at 42 USC 9601(35)(A). They can also be liable for pre-existing hazardous substances if these are later released into the environment.

Limiting a Landowner's Liability

Defenses include an act of God, an act of war and/or act of an unrelated third party of an innocent owner.

The so-called innocent landowner defense may not stop the purchaser from losing the contaminated asset. It will merely protect other income and assets from being attached for the clean-up costs. The general rule is: To avoid liability for clean-up costs, a purchaser must make all appropriate and customary inquiries into the past ownership and use of the property. If contamination is found later, liability for clean-up costs might not attach although one's equity in the property might be lost. The process of taking all appropriate and reasonable steps to ascertain that there is no contamination is part of what is called *environmental due diligence.*

Example

Part of environmental due diligence is to become aware of red flags that might suggest the possibility of contamination. In *BCW Assoc. Ltd. v. Occidental Chem Corp.,* 3 Toxics Law Reporter 943, No. 88-5847 (E.D. PA September 29, 1988), a purchaser relied solely on an engineer's report of no contamination. Dust had accumulated in the building; the purchaser decided not to have the dust tested even though it was an indication of possible problems. The dust was later found to contain lead, and the purchaser was ordered by the federal court to pay some of the clean-up costs for ignoring an "obvious red flag of contamination."

The Environmental Protection Agency is willing to consider a *de minimis settlement* with innocent landowners that would limit the amount the landowner had to contribute to the cost of hazardous waste clean-up.

1. To meet the requirements of such a settlement the following question must be answered affirmatively: "Did the landowner acquire the property without knowledge or reason to know of the disposal of hazardous substances?"

2. To meet this test, the landowner must show that he or she has conducted "all appropriate inquiry." Factors listed under Section 101(35)(B) for consideration in determining if all appropriate inquiry has been made include
   a. any specialized knowledge of an experienced defendant,
   b. relationship of purchase price to value of the property if uncontaminated,
   c. commonly known or reasonably ascertainable information about the property,
   d. the obviousness of the presence or likely presence of contamination at the property and
   e. the ability to detect such contamination by appropriate inspection.

3. IMPORTANT OBSERVATION: The ability of a purchaser to demonstrate "all appropriate inquiry" and thus be able to receive a de minimis settlement may be based on the issue of whether the real estate agent was diligent in ascertaining and disclosing material facts.

4. The EPA publishes a National Priorities List of sites that require action through the Superfund. There are potentially 30,000 such sites nationally.

SPECIFIC ENVIRONMENTAL HAZARDS

Asbestos

Basically, there is no safe level of asbestos exposure. It is a fibrous material that has been used as construction material because it is a good fire retardant and efficient insulator. When inhaled, asbestos can cause asbestosis, a fibrotic scarring in the lung; lung cancer; and mesothelioma, a cancer of the chest cavity. A 1988 random survey by the EPA found asbestos in about 20% of buildings surveyed. A national hotline on asbestos is (202) 554-1404 (8:30 A.M. to 5 P.M., EST).

Asbestos or asbestos containing material (ACM) can be classified into two general categories: friable and nonfriable.

Friable products are materials that can easily crumble, usually with little mechanical activity. This is considered the most dangerous because when this asbestos becomes airborne, asbestos fibers can be easily inhaled. Activities that can cause friable products to become airborne include routine cleaning, repair and maintenance, renovation, operation of air-conditioning and general deterioration over time.

Nonfriable products typically contain bonding agents like cements, plastics and so on that prevent asbestos from being released into the air. However, problems can occur if the material is physically altered through sanding, drilling and so forth. The owner or operator of a demolition or renovation activity must first thoroughly inspect the pertinent facility area for the presence of asbestos containing material prior to any construction activities. Any contractor working near a potential ACM should be notified of its presence.

The use of asbestos in buildings has been generally prohibited since 1978, with some restrictions as early as 1973. A building constructed prior to 1979, therefore, becomes a red flag property and should be evaluated for asbestos danger. (It should be noted that asbestos still may be present in buildings constructed after 1979, if older building materials were used.)

The EPA has indicated that many homes built during the past 20 years probably do contain asbestos products. (It should be noted that asbestos still may be present in a building constructed after 1979 if older building materials were used.) According to experts, some places where asbestos might be found in the home include

- around pipes and furnaces in older homes as insulating jackets and sheeting;
- in some vinyl flooring material;
- in ceiling tiles and sprayed ceilings;
- in exterior roofing, shingles and siding;
- in some wallboards;
- mixed with other materials and sprayed around pipes, ducts and beams;
- in patching compounds or textured paints; and
- in door gaskets of stoves, furnaces and ovens.

Both the EPA and the Occupational Safety and Health Administration (OSHA) have authority in issues concerning asbestos.

On July 26, 1986, the *permissible exposure limit* (PEL) for an eight-hour period was lowered by OSHA to 0.2 fibers per cubic centimeter.

Removal of asbestos should be performed by experts. Projects involving more than 230 square feet or 160 linear feet of asbestos-carrying materials require notification to the EPA regional office. On July 20, 1990, OSHA proposed new standards that would only exempt repair or removal of asbestos on pipes of less than 21 linear feet and repair and removal of an asbestos panel of less than 9 square feet (see Zachary S. Cowan, "New Asbestos Rules on the Horizon for Building Owners," *Building Operating Management,* January 1991, p. 34).

Experts indicate that "if the material is in good condition and in an area where it is not likely to be disturbed, leave the asbestos-containing material in place." Extreme care should be exercised in handling, cleaning or working with material suspected of containing asbestos. The owner or operator of a demolition or renovation activity must first thoroughly inspect the pertinent facility area for the presence of asbestos-containing material prior to any construction activities. Any contractor working near a potential ACM should be notified of its presence.

Formaldehyde

Formaldehyde is a colorless, gaseous chemical compound that was used for home insulation until the early 1980s. It is also used in some glues, resins, preservatives and bonding agents.

In homes, the most likely source of formaldehyde is adhesives in pressed wood-building materials (used in furniture, kitchen cabinets, etc.) and insulation.

Health risks to humans are undetermined, but it has been found to cause cancer in animals, while humans exposed to sufficient quantities have been affected with skin rash, breathing difficulties and other symptoms.

Formaldehyde emissions decrease over the first two or three years; experts say that older urea-formaldehyde building materials are probably not a significant source of formaldehyde emissions.

Radon

Radon is a naturally occurring, odorless, tasteless radioactive gas. It is the second largest cause of lung cancer after cigarette smoking. Radon is one of the few known Group A carcinogens. It occurs in regions that contain uranium. It also has been discovered in soils with phosphate, granite and certain types of shale. Problems occur when radon passes through cracks and spaces in the foundation and becomes concentrated in tight buildings that do not allow the gas to escape and dissipate to the outside. Radon can also seep into well water, but the likelihood is reduced for homes supplied with municipal water supply. According to the National Council on Radiation Protection and Measurement, radon represents 55% of all radiation sources. A national hotline is 1-800-SOS-RADON.

Radon problems can be corrected by sealing cracks in foundations and by increasing ventilation.

Indoor Air Quality

A broader issue, of which asbestos, formaldehyde and radon are a part, is the problem of indoor air quality in commercial and industrial buildings.

As part of due diligence in the purchase of a commercial building, clients should be advised to consider hiring experts to perform indoor air quality surveys. Buildings that are sealed to promote energy efficiency also can seal in pollution and facilitate radon problems.

One authority, J. M. Kuvalanka, has described something called sick- or tight-building syndrome with symptoms including headaches, fatigue, skin and eye irritations, allergies and upper respiratory problems. An indoor air quality survey can include some or all of the following: tenant and employee questionnaires, ventilation studies, CO_2 profiling, temperature and relative humidity measurements and specific contaminant sampling and analysis.

Lead

The presence of lead in drinking water or paint is dangerous, especially to children who tend to absorb more lead than adults and who are more likely to exhibit hand-to-mouth behavior. Lead excretes from the body slowly and accumulates in bone and tissue. It can cause brain damage, convulsions and paralysis. At press time, the Environmental Protection Agency (EPA) and the Department of Housing and Urban Development (HUD) had proposed new regulations pertaining to lead-based paint, training and certification of contractors, renovation and remodeling guidelines, lead-contamination and laboratory accreditation and testing standards. These proposed rules are expected to be promulgated soon.

Drinking water can become contaminated because it passes through lead pipes. These pipes were in common usage as late as the 1930s. Lead solder was used for copper pipes into the 1980s. Not until 1986 did the Safe Drinking Water Act require the use of lead-free solder, pipes and flux for any facilities connected to a public water system. In 1988, Congress banned the use of lead-based solder in plumbing applications within homes and buildings. Sampling could also be performed on-site, using specific sampling equipment. The reliability of any testing methods should be considered when sampling for lead.

The most likely location of lead-based paint is in bathrooms and kitchens. The use of lead paint was not prohibited until 1980. Lead-based paint is usually found on walls, woodwork and window frames.

There is no practical way to detect the presence of lead without testing. Buyers of older properties should be cautioned to have them tested for lead-based paint. According to experts, likelihood of lead-based paint is related to the age of the house, and it is in

1. approximately two-thirds of the houses built in the U.S. before 1940;
2. approximately one-third of the houses built from 1940 to 1960;
3. an indeterminate (but smaller) portion of houses built since 1960; and
4. industrial facilities in which metalwork, automobile radiator repairs and soldering activities, which are likely candidates for lead contamination, take place.

Checking for lead paint involves removing a sample of paint and having it tested in a qualified laboratory. Sampling also could be performed on site, using specific sampling equipment. The reliability of any testing methods should be considered when sampling for lead.

The Department of Housing and Urban Development (HUD) requires that FHA borrowers buying homes built before 1978 receive and read a Lead-Based Paint Notice before executing the purchase agreement. The notice, promulgated by HUD, is reprinted here.

U. S. Department of Housing and Urban Development

NOTICE TO PURCHASERS OF HOUSING CONSTRUCTED BEFORE 1978

If the home you intend to purchase was built before 1978, it may contain lead-based paint. About three out of every four pre–1978 buildings have lead-based paint.

What Is Lead Poisoning?

Lead poisoning means having high concentrations of lead in the body. Lead can:

- Cause major health problems, especially in children under 7 years old.
- Damage a child's brain, nervous system, kidneys, hearing, or coordination.
- Affect learning.
- Cause behavior problems, blindness, and even death.
- Cause problems in pregnancy and affect a baby's normal development.

Who Gets Lead Poisoning?

Anyone can get it, but children under 7 are at the greatest risk, because their bodies are not fully grown and are easily damaged. The risk is worse if the child:

- Lives in an older home (built/constructed before 1978, and even more so before 1960).
- Does not eat regular meals (an empty stomach accepts lead more easily).
- Does not eat enough foods with iron or calcium.
- Has parents who work in lead-related jobs.
- Has played in the same places as brothers, sisters, and friends who have been lead poisoned, (lead poison cannot be spread from person to person. It comes from contact with lead).

Women of childbearing age are also at risk, because lead poisoning can cause miscarriages, premature births, and the poison can be passed onto their unborn babies.

Where Does It Come From?

The lead hazards that children most often touch are lead dust, leaded soil, loose chips and chewable surfaces painted with lead-based paint. A child may be harmed when it puts into its mouth toys, pacifiers, or hands that have leaded soil or lead dust on them. Lead also comes from:

- Moving parts of windows, and doors that can make lead dust and chips.
- Lead-based paint on windows, doors, wood trim, walls and cabinets in kitchens and bathrooms, on porches, stairs, railings, fire escapes and lamp posts.
- Soil next to exterior of buildings that have been painted with lead-based paint and leaded gasoline dust in soil near busy streets.
- Drinking water, (pipes and solder)
- Parents who may bring lead dust home from work on skin, clothes, and hair.
- Colored newsprint and car batteries.
- Highly glazed pottery and cookware from other countries.
- Removing old paint when refinishing furniture.

In recent years some uses of lead in products that could cause lead poisoning have been reduced or banned. This is true for lead in gasoline, lead in solder used in water pipes, and lead in paint. Still, a great deal of lead remains in and around older homes, and lead-based paint and accompanying lead dust are seen as the major sources.

How Do I Know if My Child Is Affected?

Is your child:
- cranky?
- complaining of stomachaches or headaches?

- vomiting?
- unable to concentrate?
- tired?
- hyperactive?
- unwilling to eat or play?
- playing with children who have these symptoms?

These can be signs of lead poisoning. However, your children might not show these signs and yet be poisoned; only your clinic or doctor can test for sure.

What Can I Do About It?

Your child should first be tested for lead in the blood between six months and one year old. Ask the clinic or your doctor to do it during a regular checkup. Your doctor will tell you how often you should have your child tested after that. A small amount of lead in the blood may not make your child seem very sick, but it can affect how well he or she can learn. If your child does have high amounts of lead in the blood, you should seek treatment and have your home tested for lead-based paint and lead dust.

How Do I Know if My Home Has Lead-Based Paint?

The HUD inspection does not determine whether a home actually has lead-based paint. It only identifies where there is defective paint in a home that might have lead-based paint. Therefore, the only way you can know for sure is to have the home tested by a qualified firm or laboratory. Both the interior and exterior should be tested. You should contact your local health or environmental office for help.

What Do I Do if My Home Does Have Lead?

Do not try to get rid of lead-based paint yourself, you could make things worse for you and your family. If your home contains lead-based paint, contact a company that specializes in lead-based paint abatement. Have professionals do the job correctly and safely. This may cost thousands of dollars, depending on the amount of lead-based paint and lead dust found in your home, but it will also protect you and your children from the effects of lead poisoning. In the meantime, there are things you can do immediately to protect your child:

- Keep your child away from paint chips and dust.
- Wet-mop floors and wipe down surfaces often, especially where the floors and walls meet. Be sure to clean the space where the window sash rests on the sill. Keeping the floor clear of paint chips, dust and dirt is easy and very important. Do not sweep or vacuum lead-based paint chips or lead dust with an ordinary vacuum cleaner. Lead dust is so fine it will pass through a vacuum cleaner bag and spread into the air you breathe.
- Make sure your children wash their hands frequently and always before eating.
- Wash toys, teething rings and pacifiers frequently.

Will HUD Insure a Mortgage Loan on a Home with Lead-Based Paint?

HUD will insure a mortgage on a house even if it has lead-based paint. If you purchase a property with lead-based paint, HUD will not remove it. You will have to pay for the cost of removal yourself.

Acknowledgment

I acknowledge that I have received and read a copy of this Notice before signing the sales contract to purchase my property.
Date: [_____]
Signature(s): [_____]

Underground Storage Tanks (USTs)

Underground storage tanks have been used to store petroleum products, chemicals and liquid wastes since the early 1900s for the convenience of owners and for what was then considered "safety." However, corrosion, stress, faulty construction or installation have caused tanks to leak after 20 years or sooner, depending on the corrosiveness of the soil. Some estimates place the number of USTs in the United States between 3 and 5 million, and the EPA estimates that on a national scale about 40% of USTs are leaking—discharging gasoline, petroleum products and other hazardous liquids into the soil and potential ground-water sources.

In 1984, national requirements governing the underground storage of petroleum and hazardous substances were adopted as part of the Hazardous and Solid Waste Amendments of 1984 to the Resource Conservation and Recovery Act (RCRA).

The presence of a UST should be a red flag triggering advice to the client that further investigation by a qualified expert is needed. Real estate licensees should be familiar with disclosure laws in their state so they can properly advise buyers and sellers.

In states where sellers are not required to make written disclosures, including knowledge of USTs on their property, a buyer would be well advised to ask the seller about the presence of underground storage tanks and to include the seller's statement in the sales agreement. The existence of a UST can often be discovered by fill pipes or vent lines protruding from or flush with the ground, stained soil and odors or fumes, such as fuels or solvents, seemingly coming from nowhere. If the presence of a UST is suspected, a trained consultant should be retained to perform further studies. It should be noted that there may not be any visual signs of a UST such as vent and fill pipes. In some cases, detailed historical investigation may be required to identify a potential UST.

Once it has been established that a UST is in the

ground, further steps need to be taken to determine (1) whether the tank is leaking, (2) the extent of any contamination caused by the leakage and (3) the cost of remediating the contamination.

The first step is a *Phase I Assessment.* This may include a physical examination of the property, review of the property's history, examination of records showing reported incidents and potential problems, and investigation into nearby potential off-site locations of contamination. Sampling is not normally performed during a Phase I Assessment. If it is known that a UST exists, a tank tightness test may be able to determine whether a tank is leaking and to what extent. The result of a Phase I Assessment will help determine if an environmental contamination problem potentially exists. If it appears that a potential problem exists, it usually is verified in a Phase II Assessment.

During a *Phase II Assessment,* sampling is performed to verify the potential problem. If the potential problem is a UST, it is often removed, and samples are taken from under it. If a release has been verified, the pertinent regulatory agencies must be informed. If necessary, the extent of contamination is normally characterized in a *Phase III Assessment.* In this phase, sampling is performed to determine how far the problem has migrated.

Once reported, the pertinent regulatory agency will usually provide guidance on remediation. For a leaking tank, this may include removal of the tank and clean-up of affected soils and/or groundwater. Affected nearby properties must also be cleaned up. Usually, final samples are required to verify that a contaminated site has been properly cleaned up.

It should be noted that different entities may call the assessment phases by different names. For example, a Phase I is sometimes called an ESA (Environmental Site Assessment), and so on. This can result in confusion. It is therefore recommended that any assessment be carefully screened to ensure that the contractors are professional, certified when required and reputable. A mistake by the contractor can ultimately be at the cost of the landowner.

Water Quality and Groundwater Contamination

Surface water and groundwater contamination can result from many sources, including leaking tanks, surface spills, hazardous wastes and materials, mining waste and runoff, agricultural chemicals, septic and sewer systems and boat traffic. The EPA Safe Drinking Water Hotline may be contacted at 1-800-426-4791 for additional information.

Polychlorinated Biphenyls (PCBs)

PCBs are used in electrical equipment because they provide a good insulating medium. The EPA has determined that "PCBs may cause adverse reproductive effects, developmental toxicity, and tumor development in humans" (Freeman, 1989, pp. 4–13). PCBs have been found to remain in the environment for a long time and have been shown to be passed on with the food chain and offspring of contaminated species.

PCBs are used in electrical transformers, capacitors, fluorescent light ballasts, heat transfer and hydraulic systems, and other electrical equipment.

A real estate agent should be aware of the types of equipment that may contain PCBs. PCBs may remain in place as long as the equipment they are contained in does not appear to be leaking. For example, older light ballasts may contain PCBs. These do not represent a contamination problem unless they are leaking or are disposed of improperly. If a piece of equipment containing PCBs is observed to be leaking, the local regulatory agency may be contacted for direction. It should also be noted that specific recordkeeping requirements apply to threshold quantities of PCBs.

HANDLING ENVIRONMENTAL PROBLEMS

General Precautionary Measures To Avoid Liability for Environmental Problems

Real estate agents may advise their clients to obtain environmental audits before purchasing property in order to

1. discover the extent of any environmental contamination and
2. be able to utilize the innocent landowner defense under CERCLA if contamination is subsequently discovered.

Avoid Advising Parties on Environmental Issues. Sellers and real estate agents should avoid making any representations or offering any advice, not only about the environmental condition of the property but also about the status of the law or the meaning of any environmental provision contained in a contract.

Listing Agreements/Engagement Letters. These documents should include language stating that no warranties, representations or characterizations as to the environmental condition of the property are made that are not expressed in writing.

Environmental Questionnaires. Language requiring sellers to disclose any information known to them about the environmental condition of the property is sometimes added to the disclosure checklists presently used by many real estate agents. These questionnaires can be the basis for communicating information regarding environmental problems to prospective buyers. However, completion of a questionnaire should not be solely relied upon to determine whether a site is clean as the seller may not know enough to answer all the questions.

Environmental Site Assessments. Only an environmental assessment performed by a competent environmental professional in accordance with good commercial or customary practice should be relied upon. In some instances, even with the use of a competent environmental professional, a problem may not be uncovered. No environmental assessment can wholly eliminate uncertainty regarding the potential for recognized environmental conditions in connection with a property. An environmental assessment is intended to reduce, but not to eliminate, uncertainty regarding the existence of recognized environmental conditions, recognizing reasonable limits of time and cost.

Buy and Sell Agreements. Provisions may be included in the buy and sell agreement allocating the risk of environmental problems among the parties to the agreement. Contingencies also may be included in the buy and sell agreement making the sale conditional upon a satisfactory environmental audit.

Vacant Land. Real estate agents who represent buyers seeking vacant land for a particular project should be careful not to make representations about the suitability of the land for the project. A buyer representation agreement should contain explicit language stating:

> *Buyer does not rely on any representation by the agent to determine the environmental condition of the property, or its suitability for the intended project."*

Visual Inspections. If a real estate agent spots certain red flags indicating possible environmental problems, the agent should recommend that the buyer obtain an environmental audit.

DRUG PROPERTY FORFEITURES

The real estate agent's role in this area is similar to the role in environmental hazards except that no amount of disclosure will compensate for a seizure of the property. A buyer should obviously be discouraged from purchasing a property that could conceivably be subject to seizure. A seller cannot sell a property that could conceivably be subject to seizure. In short, the property should not be listed or sold until the condition subjecting the property to drug seizure has been corrected and eliminated.

If illegal drug activity is taking place on real property, that property could be seized even though the actual owner of the property was not in any way involved with such activity. The right of the federal drug enforcement authorities to seize this property is contained in the Federal Drug Enforcement Act of 1988 (Title 21 USC Section 853). Property subject to criminal forfeiture includes real property and tangible and intangible personal property.

To avoid seizure, a property owner would use the *innocent owner* defense and must demonstrate that either

1. he or she had no knowledge of the use of the property for illegal drug activity or
2. he or she had knowledge and made reasonable efforts to keep the property from being used for such illegal activity.

The burden of proof is on the property owner or lessor.

AGENCY

Agency is a relationship in which one person (the agent) is authorized to represent the interests of another (the principal or client) in business dealings with third parties.

AGENCY PROBLEMS IN REAL ESTATE

Many buyers, sellers and even professionals still wrongly believe that selling agents represent the buyer when in fact they may be subagents of the seller.

CONSEQUENCES OF BREACH OF AGENCY DUTIES

- Loss of commission
- Rescission of transaction
- Loss or suspension of license
- Actual damages
- Punitive damages over and above actual damages in severe cases
- Criminal penalties in severe cases of fraud

RISK REDUCTION RECOMMENDATIONS

- Education and training in agency relationships
- Use of disclosure forms
- A written company policy addressing agency relationships (as recommended by NAR, April 28, 1992)

SUBAGENCY VERSUS BUYER AGENCY

With the exception of some states, traditional MLS policy has been a blanket unilateral offer of subagency, making any MLS member automatically a subagent of the seller unless subagency was specifically rejected.

On April 28, 1992, NAR changed its MLS policy to read:

"NAR's multiple listing policy shall be modified to delete the mandatory offer of subagency and make offers of subagency optional. Participants submitting listings to the MLS must, however, offer cooperation to other MLS participants in the form of subagency or cooperation with buyer agents or both. All offers of subagency or cooperation made through an MLS must include an offer of compensation."

While subagency in MLS has a definite marketing advantage to sellers, it also creates liability because a seller is bound by the acts, representations and misrepresentations of a subagent. Thus, the new MLS policy of optional subagency offers a choice to reject subagency to both sellers and MLS members; sellers may reject subagency because they may not want the added liability that goes hand in hand with subagency; agents may reject it because they prefer to represent buyers rather than be subagents of sellers.

SUBAGENCY

A subagent, under a listing agreement with a seller, acts as the agent for the seller only. A seller's agent, or a subagent of that agent, has the affirmative obligations listed below.

Duties of a Seller's Agent to the Seller

Fiduciary Duties. Fiduciary duties include loyalty, utmost care, integrity and honesty in dealings with the seller.

Duty of Obedience. The seller's agent must obey all lawful instructions from the seller within the scope of his or her authority.

Duty of Confidentiality. The seller's agent must keep secrets that may weaken the seller's position.

Duty of Disclosure. The seller's agent is obliged to disclose to the seller

- at time of listing, the fact that subagency is optional and that the seller is responsible for the subagents' acts and representations,
- the identity of all potential buyers,
- information about the willingness of a buyer to complete the sale or offer a higher price,
- the buyer's intention to subdivide or resell property at a profit and
- any business or family relationship between agent and buyer.

Duty of Accounting. The seller's agent must

- account for all monies entrusted to the agent and
- keep accurate and complete records of all transactions.

Duties of a Seller's Agent to the Buyer

- Diligent exercise of reasonable skill and care in the performance of the agent's duties
- A duty of honest and fair dealing and good faith
- A statutory duty to present all offers
- A duty to disclose all facts known to the agent materially affecting the value or desirability of the property that are not known to, or within the diligent attention and observation of, the parties (including disclosure of material facts the broker knew or should have known)
- A duty to verify critical information received from the seller

SUGGESTION: To avoid falling into the trap of accidental undisclosed dual agency, it is good for agents to caution buyers to avoid any discussion of what they might be willing to pay or anything they would not tell the seller directly.

BUYER AGENCY

A selling agent can, with a buyer's consent, agree to act as agent for the buyer only. As such, the agent is not the agent or subagent for the seller. A buyer's agent has the affirmative obligations listed below.

Duties of the Buyer's Agent to the Buyer

Fiduciary Duties. Fiduciary duties include loyalty, utmost care, integrity and honesty in dealings with the buyer.

Duty of Obedience. The buyer's agent must obey all lawful instructions from the buyer within the scope of his or her authority.

Duty of Confidentiality. The buyer's agent must keep secrets that may weaken the buyer's position.

Duty of Disclosure. The buyer's agent is obliged to disclose to the buyer

- the willingness of a seller to accept a lower price,
- any facts relating to the urgency of a seller's need to dispose of the property,
- the length of time a property has been on the market and any other offers or counteroffers that have been made on the property,
- all facts known to the agent materially affecting the value or desirability of the property that are not known to, or within the diligent attention and observation of, the buyer and
- any business or family relationship between agent and seller.

Duty of Accounting. The buyer's agent must account for all monies entrusted to the agent.

Duties of the Buyer's Agent to the Seller

- Diligent exercise of reasonable skill and care in the performance of the agent's duties
- A duty of honest and fair dealing and good faith

THE CHOICE

After explaining subagency and buyer agency, an agent may offer the buyer a choice: "I can represent the seller, or I can represent you as the buyer. Which do you prefer?"

Whichever the choice, there are certain buyers who, for several reasons, cannot be treated as customers. For example, a close relative or long-term client becomes interested in a house listed by Agent Smith's broker. As an agent or subagent of the seller, Smith is duty bound not to disclose to her relative any confidential information that might harm the seller's bargaining position, nor is Smith supposed to give advice on matters of price, and so on. Should this relative or long-term client be treated as a customer or as a client?

Buyers Who Should or Must Be Clients

- Buyers who require anonymity, such as famous or wealthy people or corporations moving into the area
- Relatives
- Close friends
- Close business associates or partners
- Buyers who want to be represented
- Former clients and former customers
- First-time buyers who need help
- Out-of-town buyers who need help with property values and location

BUYER REPRESENTATION AGREEMENT

A buyer representation agreement provides for the exclusive right to represent the buyer for a certain period of time, to assist the buyer in locating real property of a specific nature and to negotiate terms for its acquisition acceptable to the buyer. The form also includes clauses such as possible dual agency, possible conflicts with other buyer clients, compensation options, optional retainer fee and binding arbitration.

Disclosures to Listing Broker, Seller and Closing (Escrow) Agent

In a transaction in which the broker represents a buyer, the listing broker should be informed of the buyer-broker arrangement at first contact, again at the time the appointment is made and once more when the offer is presented. The closing agent should also understand the representation arrangements.

Compensation

Payment of commission does not necessarily establish agency. It makes no difference who pays the commission—the seller, the buyer or both. Commissions are disbursed at closing as part of the transaction as any other closing cost. The closing document should clearly show two commissions—one marked "on behalf of the sellers" to the listing office, the other marked "on behalf of the buyers" to the selling office.

Advantages of Buyer Brokerage

- Minimum legal risk
- No liability for subagents
- Closer control over buyers
- No marketing expenses

DUAL AGENCY

Dual agency situations can arise with in-house sales if a buyer-client, represented by one of the broker's agents, becomes interested in one of the broker's listings. Exchanges, syndications and purchases by real estate agents for their own account are other potential dual agency situations. A real estate broker can legally be the agent of both the seller and the buyer in a transaction, provided full disclosure is made and both parties give their informed consent. Because seller and buyer in a transaction have conflicts of interest, the dual agent can only act as an intermediary between the parties. A *dual agency disclosure addendum* form is designed to present the predicament to seller and buyer and to provide full disclosure of the limitation in services the agent is able to provide in such a dual agency situation. Provided both parties give their informed consent to such dual agency, the broker is under obligation not to disclose any information of a confidential nature that could harm one party's bargaining position or benefit the other's. For example, the broker could not disclose to the seller information about what price or terms the buyer might be willing to pay other than what is offered in writing or disclose to the buyer information about what price or terms the seller might accept other than what is contained in the listing agreement.

Duties of a Dual Agent to Both Seller and Buyer

Fiduciary Duties. Fiduciary duties include utmost care, integrity, honesty and loyalty in dealings with the seller and the buyer.

Duty of Disclosure and Honest and Fair Dealings

- A dual agent has a duty to disclose all material facts required by law and information the agent believes might affect the principals' decisions with respect to the transaction.
- A dual agent has a duty to disclose any business or family relationship between the agent and either the seller or the buyer.
- A dual agent may not disclose to the seller information about what price or terms the buyer may offer other than those offered in writing by buyer.
- A dual agent may not disclose to the buyer information about what price or terms the seller may accept other than the listed price or terms.

- A dual agent may not disclose any information of a confidential nature that could harm one party's bargaining position or benefit the other's.

Unintended or Accidental Undisclosed Dual Agency. Undisclosed dual agency is unlawful, whether intended, unintended or accidental. The broker who fails to disclose dual agency is likely to (1) violate both state licensing law and general agency law, (2) jeopardize any right to a commission and (3) justify having either the seller or the buyer rescind the underlying transaction. The broker is then potentially liable for monetary damages. This right of rescission exists even if there is no injury, the transaction is fair and the agent acts in good faith. Even though the dual agent obtains the required consents, the agent must still be extremely careful not to favor one side over the other.

Risk of Dual Agency. Because the dual agent owes the same fiduciary duties to both principals, the dual agent walks a legal razor's edge trying to avoid situations in which the agent might unintentionally compromise one principal in favor of the other.

Dual agency has been described as a time bomb. As long as the buyer and the seller are happy with the transaction, the question of dual agency probably will never arise, but if either party becomes unhappy for whatever reason, even months after closing, undisclosed dual agency may provide the mechanism to undo the transaction. It is no legal defense that the dual agency was unintended or was performed with all good intentions to help both the buyer and the seller. Buyers and sellers generally neither care nor know about the subject of dual agency until one of them wants to back out of the deal and consults an attorney. Dual agency cases have a high rate of success for plaintiffs and a high value for settlement purposes.

DISCLOSURE OF AGENCY RELATIONSHIP

Written Disclosure with Informed Consent

Written disclosure of agency relationship with informed consent is an essential risk reduction tool. Most states have disclosure regulations (most of them oral).

Article 21 of the NAR Code of Ethics requires disclosure of agency relationship to buyers and sellers.

Timing of Disclosure

Disclosure to sellers should be made at time of listing; disclosure to buyers at first meaningful contact.

COMPANY AGENCY POLICIES

Seller Agency Exclusively

All sellers are clients; all buyers are customers.

Advantages. The public, as well as the real estate agencies, is familiar with this traditional method of conducting real estate transactions.

Drawbacks

- The agency may lose agents who want to represent buyers.
- The agency may lose buyers who want to be represented.
- There is a high risk potential of unintended undisclosed dual agency.
- Maximum liability exists for breach of subagents' fiduciary duty.

Buyer Agency Exclusively

All buyers are clients. Buyers do not list property.

Advantages

- There is a minimum risk policy legally.
- There is no liability for subagents.
- There is no closer control over buyers.
- There are no marketing expenses.

Drawbacks

- A buyer agency discourages agents who want to list.
- Sellers do not contact buyer agencies, and thus, business is lost.

Single Agency Whether Listing or Selling

The agent represents either buyer or seller but never both in same transaction.

Advantages. There is no risk of undisclosed dual agency.

Drawbacks. A single agency whether listing or selling is difficult to manage and only works in very small firms.

Dual Agency for In-House Sales

One agent works with a seller-client while another agent works with a buyer-client. A listing agent selling his or her own listing to a buyer-client should be avoided.

Advantages. The flexibility allows for buyer brokerage and subagency.

Drawbacks. A dual agency for in-house sales requires extensive training, constant monitoring and consent of both parties. The liability of creating a dual agency exists.

For an in-depth coverage of agency relationships and office policies, refer to the following books:

Agency Disclosure: The Complete Office Policy Guide, John W. Reilly and Michael Somers

Agency Relationships in Real Estate, John W. Reilly

Consensual Dual Agency, John Reilly, Gail Lyons and Don Harlan

FEDERAL FAIR HOUSING LAWS

Title VIII of the Civil Rights Act of 1968, amended in 1988, is administered by the Department of Housing and Urban Development (HUD). The act is herein referred to as Title VIII.

The Secretary of HUD is authorized to review state and local statutes and certify those that are substantially equivalent to Title VIII. "Substantially equivalent" may include those statutes that provide broader protection than title VIII.

Title VIII is a comprehensive fair housing law that prohibits discrimination on the basis of the following criteria:

1. Race
2. Color
3. Religion
4. Sex
5. National origin
6. Handicap* or
7. Familial status*

The 1988 amendment to Title VIII includes handicapped persons and families with children as so-called protected classes.

CONDUCT PROHIBITED BY THE FAIR HOUSING LAWS

Refusal To Sell or Rent

The following acts are illegal:

- Any refusal based on race, color, sex, religion, national origin, handicap or familial status to sell, rent or otherwise make unavailable a dwelling after receipt of a bona fide offer
- Discrimination in terms, conditions, privileges or services in the sale or rental of a dwelling based on prohibited criteria
- Representation that a dwelling is not available when in fact it is, based on prohibited criteria

- Denial of access to or participation in a multiple listing service based on prohibited criteria
- Discrimination in granting requested financial assistance based on prohibited criteria

Racial Steering

Racial steering, or influencing a person's housing choice based on prohibited criteria, is, for example, directing minority prospects to integrated or all minority neighborhoods and white prospects to all white neighborhoods. Evidence of steering is often gathered through the use of testers.

Advertising that Expresses a Preference

Publishing any material or advertisement that indicates a preference, limitation or discrimination based on prohibited criteria is illegal. HUD has promulgated advertising guidelines designed to clarify permissible and nonpermissible real estate advertising. It is also inappropriate to make explicit reference to the proximity of the dwelling to a commonly known racial or ethnic landmark, such as a synagogue, ethnic center or predominantly black institution.

Blockbusting

Blockbusting or panic selling refers to the suggestion when soliciting a listing that crime is increasing or that persons of a minority are moving into the neighborhood.

Handicapped Discrimination

The law defines handicap as a "physical or mental impairment which substantially limits one or more of a person's major life activities."

NOTE: A physical or mental impairment includes any physiological disorder or condition, cosmetic disfigurement or anatomical loss, mental and/or psychological disorders, specifically including alcoholics and persons with HIV virus, AIDS and other diseases that cannot be transmitted by casual contact. However, the handicap classification specifically excludes "those who are illegally using or are addicted to a controlled substance and those whose tenancy would constitute a direct threat to the health or safety of other individuals," or those "whose tenancy would result in substantial physical damage to the property of others."

NOTE: Major life activities are considered caring for oneself, performing manual tasks, walking, seeing, hearing, speaking, breathing and learning.

HUD regulations state that real estate brokers or agents may not inquire whether a person has a handicap or the extent of any handicap in evaluating a person's qualifications to buy or rent a dwelling. A broker or agent may, however, ask questions about a prospect's rent history as long as the same questions are asked of every prospect. For example, a broker may inquire whether a prospect will be able to meet the monthly payments or whether the prospect is a current abuser of or addict of a controlled substance.

Title VIII prohibits property owners from refusing to allow a tenant to make reasonable structural modifications to a unit, at the tenant's expense, to allow the handicapped tenant full enjoyment of the premises. The property owner may, however, condition any structural modifications to the interior of a unit on the tenant's agreement to restore the unit to its original condition upon termination of occupancy.

Title VIII requires property owners to make reasonable accommodations in any rules or regulations governing the housing development that are necessary to permit the tenant to fully enjoy the premises (e.g., allowing a seeing eye dog notwithstanding a no pet rule, assignment of a parking space to a handicapped tenant near a building entrance, a waiver of a rule banning vans in a building's parking lot when a van is necessary to a handicapped person's transportation).

Title VIII further provides that all new *covered*

multifamily dwellings meet certain basic accessibility and adaptability requirements. A covered multifamily dwelling includes all units in a building of four or more dwelling units if the building has an elevator, and ground floor dwelling units in buildings of four or more dwelling units without an elevator.

Covered multifamily dwellings must meet the following design and construction requirements:

- Public and common use areas readily accessible to handicapped
- Doors wide enough to allow passage by a wheelchair
- An accessible route into and through the unit
- Reinforcements in bathroom walls to allow later installation of grab bars around toilet, tub, shower, stall and shower seat, where provided
- Kitchens and bathrooms allowing an individual in a wheelchair to maneuver about the space
- Light switches, electrical outlets, thermostats and other environmental controls in accessible locations

Families with Children

Familial status means a parent or guardian in the legal custody of children under the age of eighteen, and pregnant women.

Title VIII forbids property owners or agents from refusing to sell or rent a dwelling to an otherwise qualified prospect simply because the prospect has children under the age of eighteen in his or her household. While Title VIII prohibits discrimination based upon familial status, the statute does not pre-empt reasonable state or local regulations limiting the number of persons who may occupy a particular dwelling.

According to HUD regulations, property owners may not establish dual purpose facilities where certain sections of a housing complex are reserved for adults only and other sections for families with children.

Housing for Older Persons

Title VIII specifically authorizes the exclusion of children from housing for older persons, notwithstanding the prohibition of discrimination against families with children. This exemption includes the following:

1. Housing provided pursuant to a state or federal program designed to accommodate the needs of senior citizens
2. Housing occupied solely by persons 62 years or older
3. Housing where 80% of the units are (at all times) occupied by at least one person 55 years or older per unit, and where
   a. the development is intended for, and marketed as, housing for older persons and
   b. the development provides significant facilities and services specifically designed to meet physical or social needs of older persons (e.g., social and recreational programs, continuing education, information and counseling, accessible physical environment, emergency and preventive health care programs, congregate dining facilities, transportation to facilitate access to social services).

CONSEQUENCES OF FAIR HOUSING LAWS VIOLATIONS

The potential penalties for violation of fair housing laws are so severe that responsible real estate brokers simply cannot assume the risk. Furthermore, fair housing cases are almost always excluded from errors and omissions policies.

An *aggrieved person* who believes himself or herself to be a victim of a discriminatory housing practice may bring an action directly in federal court or may file a complaint with HUD. If HUD finds reasonable cause, the case may be tried before a *HUD administrative law judge (ALJ)* or before a *federal district judge*.

If state or local law is deemed by HUD to be substantially equivalent to Title VIII, HUD will refer all complaints from that jurisdiction to the state or local agency for processing.

Both ALJs and federal courts may award *actual damages,* attorneys fees and issue injunctions to prevent any further discriminatory practices. An ALJ may also assess *civil penalties* limited to $10,000 with no prior offense, $25,000 with one prior offense within five years and $50,000 with two prior offenses within seven years. A federal court judge may also impose an unlimited amount in punitive damages plus attorneys fees and costs.

Also, the United States attorney general may bring an action where a pattern of practice of discrimination has occurred, as opposed to a single isolated act, and secure *injunctive relief and damages,* together with civil penalties of $50,000 for the first offense and $100,000 for any subsequent offense.

To highlight the importance of complying with federal fair housing laws, in July 1992 a jury ordered a Washington, D.C., area property management company to pay $2.41 million in damages to a woman who said the company refused to rent an apartment to her because she has children. In 1990, after being told for the second time that the building in which she and her children had hoped to rent was an "all adult" building, plaintiff Carrie H. Timus sued the management company, claiming it violated federal fair housing laws that prohibit discrimination on the basis of familial status.

NAR General Counsel Laurence K. Janik noted that the damages award underscores the seriousness with which juries are viewing cases that involve discrimination against families with children. "The extraordinary amount of the damages award sends a message that society is not going to tolerate discrimination against families with children," said Janik.

RISK REDUCTION RECOMMENDATIONS

The Real Estate Firm's Public Commitment

A personal commitment includes, among other things, subscribing to the HUD/NAR Voluntary Affirmative Marketing Agreement (VAMA) and the affirmative advertising, recruitment, training and documentation obligations that are set forth in VAMA.

Education and Training

Risk will be reduced by

- providing education and training to all sales associates, directly or through the board, and making available the NAR "Fair Housing Handbook."
- educating individual clients, who may put the greatest source of pressure on a broker to discriminate or steer. Sellers must understand that the broker will not accept a listing on any conditions that are in violation with the fair housing laws. NAR developed an informative brochure titled "What Everyone Should Know About Equal Opportunity in Housing" that can be given to clients and customers.

Documentation

When an agent is confronted with a complaint of discriminatory housing practice, especially when the complaint is grounded upon the use of a tester, it is imperative to have records showing the prospect's name, address, telephone number, race, stated requirements for housing, price range, as well as dates and addresses of properties offered and/or shown.

The agent may have only a hazy memory of the prospect as one of hundreds encountered in the last month or year. Without a written record to refresh his or her recollection, the agent has no basis to establish whether the prospect was in fact afforded equal professional service. A paper trail is the strongest defense!

Testing of Lenders

In May 1993, the office of the Comptroller of the Currency announced it would be using testers to identify discrimination in the loan application process. The pilot program, which will target about 900 national banks, will use minority and nonminority testers to find out how potential borrowers are treated before they file a loan application.

As part of its Fair Housing Initiatives Program, HUD has committed to fund a $1 million contract with the National Fair Housing Alliance in Washington, D.C.

THE AMERICANS WITH DISABILITIES ACT (ADA)

The Americans with Disabilities Act (ADA), signed by President George Bush in 1990, is intended to protect individuals with disabilities from various forms of discrimination in employment, public services, transportation, public accommodations and telecommunications services. The requirements of the law pertaining to employment discrimination and removal of barriers in public accommodations are of particular importance to real estate brokers.

TITLE I—EMPLOYMENT

Title I of the ADA became effective July 26, 1992, for employers with more than 25 employees, and on July 26, 1994, for employers with 15 or more employees. It is enforced by the Equal Employment Opportunity Commission.

Title I prohibits employers from discriminating against "qualified individuals with disabilities."

A qualified individual with a disability is one who meets the skill, experience, education and other job-related requirements of a position held or desired and who, with or without "reasonable accommodation," can perform the "essential functions of a job."

Disability means a physical or mental impairment that "substantially limits" one or more of a person's major life activities. This also includes a record of such impairment or being regarded as having such impairment.

Reasonable accommodation is a logical adjustment made to a job or the work environment that enables a qualified person with a disability to perform the functions of that employment position. It is considered to be discrimination under the ADA to refuse to make a reasonable accommodation to the known physical or mental limitations of a qualified applicant or employee with the disability unless the accommodation would pose an undue hardship on the business.

Examples of Reasonable Accommodations

- Reserved parking spaces that must be accessible and clearly labeled
- Level or ramped entrance
- Access to conference rooms, restrooms and cafeterias
- Widening doorways for wheelchair access
- Job restructuring
- Providing readers to blind employees
- Providing interpreters for conferences and training courses for hearing-impaired persons
- Schedule modifications
- Retraining
- Reassignment to vacant positions
- Adjusting or modifying examinations, training materials or policies
- Buying special equipment and devices

Essential functions of a job are fundamental job duties and not just the marginal functions of a particular position.

Major life activities are functions such as caring for oneself, performing manual tasks, walking, seeing, hearing, speaking, learning and working.

"Substantially limits" means unable to perform a major life activity that the average person in the general population can perform or being significantly restricted as to the condition, manner or duration under which an individual can perform a particular major life activity.

The Federal Government has developed a number of guidelines for undue hardships under a previous law known as the Rehabilitation Act of 1973. In judging what an undue hardship is, the government looks at business activity; financial cost and expenses; overall size of the firm including number of employees and budget; the structure of the workforce and the nature and cost of the accommodations needed.

Also protected is anyone associated with an individual who has a disability. A person currently on illegal drugs or engaged in alcohol abuse is not considered by the ADA provisions to be impaired, but a person who has been rehabilitated and is not using drugs or a person currently in a drug rehabilitation program may be protected under ADA.

An employer is not required to hire a person who poses a direct threat to health or safety. This threat, however, must create "a significant risk of substantial harm" and not just slightly increase the risk. The burden of proof is on the employer.

Pointers for Avoiding Claims of Discrimination Under the ADA

- Employers should not ask job applicants about their medical condition. However, employers may require them to undergo a medical exam as a condition of a job offer.
- Employers should not ask applicants how many days they missed from work last year due to illness. However, it is all right to ask how many days they were absent from work.
- Employers should not ask applicants whether they would need reasonable accommodation or what type of accommodation they would need to perform the job. However, employers may ask applicants whether they can perform the specific job-related functions with or without reasonable accommodation.
- Alcoholism is considered a disability, so employers should not ask applicants how much alcohol they drink or if they have ever been treated for alcoholism. However, it is correct to ask applicants if they drink alcohol.
- Psychiatric disorders are also considered disabilities. Asking applicants if they have ever sought treatment for inability to handle stress is not allowable. Instead, employers may ask them how well they handle stress or if they work better or worse under pressure.

Even if applicants volunteer information about their disability, employers should not follow up with questions about the disability.

For more information on complying with the ADA, contact the local office of the Equal Employment Opportunity Commission (EEOC).

TITLE III—PUBLIC ACCOMMODATIONS AND COMMERCIAL FACILITIES

Title III of the ADA, effective January 26, 1992, prohibits discrimination against persons with a disability in places of public accommodation and commercial facilities.

The law requires removal of architectural and communications barriers in existing privately owned places of public accommodations.

A privately owned public accommodation includes virtually all commercial facilities including office buildings, convention centers, hotels, restaurants, theaters, museums, retail establishments, day care centers and medical buildings. ADA applies to private entities that own, lease or operate such public accommodations.

The requirement to remove architectural and communications barriers assumes that these changes are readily achievable. The obligation to remove barriers does not require extensive restructuring or burdensome expense. However, there is no specific monetary formula to determine that an action is readily achievable. Factors to be considered in determining whether removal of a barrier is readily achievable include the nature and cost of the work needed, the overall financial resources of the facility itself and the overall financial resources of the parent corporation.

An employer who takes the position that an accommodation needed by a disabled person is not readily achievable has the burden of proof.

In examining the "readily achievable" test, the government has suggested priorities to remove barriers where all accessibility goals might not be readily achievable, in this order:

1. Providing access to site from public sidewalks, parking or public transportation
2. Providing access to all areas where goods and services are made available to the public
3. Providing access to restroom facilities
4. Providing access to all remaining areas

Tax Credits

Real estate brokers and clients should consult an accountant about possible tax relief to offset any financial burden resulting from ADA requirements. Tax credits for up to 50% of eligible expenditures greater than $250 but less than $10,250 are available to businesses with annual gross receipts not exceeding $1 million or fewer than 30 full-time workers. Eligible expenditures include costs for removing barriers and providing auxiliary aids. A tax deduction of up to $15,000 per year for qualified removal of architectural and transportation barriers may be taken by any business regardless of its size.

New Buildings

A new building intended for first occupancy after January 26, 1993, must for all practical purposes be barrier free or readily accessible to people with disabilities.

The readily accessible standard does not require elevators to be installed in facilities less than three stories high and less than 3,000 square feet in area unless these facilities are shopping centers or offices of a health care provider.

REDUCING RISK OF ADA LIABILITY

Noncompliance with the ADA exposes violators to stiff penalties and significant liability.

Steps Brokers Can Take To Avoid Legal Problems with the ADA

- Brokers may advise building owners, tenants and property managers to review their leases to determine who is responsible for compliance mandated by legislation or regulation.
- If a lease is due to expire, ADA compliance might be discussed during renewal negotiations.
- Brokers should have their offices inspected by an architect familiar with ADA regulations.
- Brokers might alert their commercial clients to the existence of the ADA and suggest they have their buildings inspected by a knowledgeable architect.
- Brokers and their commercial clients should document their awareness of the legislation and any steps they have taken or costs they have incurred to comply, including all discussions, correspondence, reports, costs of inspections, building modifications and purchases of auxiliary aids.

ADA REQUIREMENTS FACT SHEET

(U.S. Department of Justice)

Employment

- Employers may not discriminate against an individual with a disability in hiring or promotion if the person is otherwise qualified for the job.
- Employers can ask about one's ability to perform a job but cannot inquire if someone has a disability or subject a person to tests that tend to screen out people with disabilities.
- Employers will need to provide reasonable accommodation to individuals with disabilities. This includes steps such as job restructuring and modification of equipment.
- Employers do not need to provide accommodations that impose an undue hardship on business operations.

- Who needs to comply: All employers with 15 or more employees must comply effective July 26, 1994.

Public Accommodations

- Private entities such as restaurants, hotels and retail stores may not discriminate against individuals with disabilities effective January 26, 1992.
- Auxiliary aids and services must be provided to individuals with vision or hearing impairments or individuals with other disabilities unless an undue burden would result.
- Physical barriers in existing facilities must be removed if removal is readily achievable. If not, alternative methods of providing the services must be offered if they are readily achievable.
- All new construction and alterations of facilities must be accessible.

Transportation

- New public transit buses ordered after August 26, 1990, must be accessible to individuals with disabilities.
- Unless an undue burden would result, transit authorities must provide comparable paratransit or other special transportation services to individuals with disabilities who cannot use fixed route bus services.
- Existing train systems must have one accessible car per train by July 26, 1995.
- New rail cars ordered after August 26, 1990, must be accessible.
- New bus and train stations must be accessible.
- Key stations in rapid, light and commuter trail systems must be made accessible by July 26, 1993, with extensions up to 20 years for commuter rail (30 years for rapid and light rail).
- Who needs to comply: Effective July 26, 1994, all employers with 15 or more employees must comply.

State and Local Government

- State and local governments may not discriminate against qualified individuals with disabilities.
- All government facilities, services and communications must be accessible consistent with the requirements of Section 504 of the Rehabilitation Act of 1973.

Telecommunications

- Companies offering telephone service to the general public must offer telephone relay services to individuals who use telecommunications devices for the deaf (TDDs) or similar devices.

Examples

The following fact situations were prepared by the Hawaii Real Estate Research & Education Center, University of Hawaii.

Fact Situation A. Ms. X is in a wheelchair. She holds a real estate sales license and has applied to work in the residential sales division of Broker B's office, a firm with 45 salespersons. Because of the wheelchair, Broker B does not think that Ms. X will be effective in showing houses to prospective buyers and advises her that she is not qualified to apply for a job with his firm. Broker B is also concerned that Ms. X's wheelchair is too big to fit through the door of the conference room in which the firm's sales meetings are held.

Fact Situation B. Mr. Y is a prospective buyer of a small, four-story medical office building. Mr. Y is very, very rich. The building does not have an elevator and the stairs are narrow. The current owner has had a negative cash flow problem for the past three years and is seeking to sell the property. Mr. Y tells Broker B that he plans to keep the property. Mr. Y tells Broker B that he plans to keep the building in its existing condition for a few years until he can tear it down and develop a high rise hotel in its place.

In both fact situations, Broker B has problems created by the passage of ADA. In the Fact Situation

A, Broker B is guilty of employment discrimination in violation of Title I. Ms. X has the right to file a charge of discrimination with the U.S. Equal Employment Commission.

In Fact Situation B, Mr. Y will need to spend capital to remove barriers that discriminate against the disabled. This may be an expense he may not have expected. Having failed to disclose the provisions of ADA as they apply to this situation, Broker B may be sued by Mr. Y.

DISCLAIMER

The material presented in this section is for general education purposes and is not intended to provide specific legal advice. Because the ADA requirements are very technical, licensees are advised to consult their attorney for guidance.

Other Sources of Information

For information concerning Title I, Employment Discrimination:

Equal Employment Opportunity Commission
Telephone: 800-669-EEOC

For information concerning Title III, Public Accommodations and Commercial Facilities:

U.S. Department of Justice
Telephone: 202-514-0301

The Americans with Disabilities Act
Title III Technical Assistance Manual
U.S. Department of Justice
Civil Rights Division

Accessibility Guidelines for Buildings and Facilities
U.S. Architectural & Transportation Barriers Compliance Board
Telephone: 202-653-7834
Fax: 202-653-7863

ANTITRUST LAWS

Antitrust laws protect competition and prevent monopolies. Violation of federal and/or state antitrust laws result in severe sanctions the law can inflict upon a business, its partners and corporate officers. Therefore, real estate brokers and sales associates must have a basic understanding of antitrust laws and how they are applied to the real estate industry. Antitrust violations are generally not covered by errors and omissions policies.

THE SHERMAN ACT

Section 1 of the Sherman Act (1890) provides: "Every contract combination in the form of trust or otherwise, or conspiracy, in restraint of trade or commerce among several states, or with foreign nations, is declared to be illegal."

Conspiracy means that two or more separate business entities participate in a *common scheme or plan* and that the effect of the scheme is *restraint of trade.*

Conspiracies To Fix Real Estate Commission Rates or Commission Splits

In *United States v. National Association of Real Estate Boards (NAREB),* the Supreme Court in 1950 held that the concept of *trade* as used in the Sherman Act included real estate brokerage and that mandatory fee schedules that were promulgated and enforced by a real estate board through disciplinary proceedings violated Section 1 of the Sherman Act.

While commission rates are the most common object of price fixing allegations against real estate brokers, a conspiracy among brokers to fix the duration of listing agreements, the form of compensation or the type of listings that will be accepted would also be in violation of the Sherman Act.

Restraint of Trade

The 1980 decision in *McLain v. New Orleans Real Estate Board,* the court held that a conspiracy to fix real estate commissions can have the necessary effect upon interstate commerce because the transaction that results from the successful marketing effort often involves the use of out-of-state mortgage lenders or insurers. As such, an artificially inflated real estate brokerage commission raises the total cost of closing a real estate transaction that in turn affects interstate commerce in mortgage lending and insurance. This decision established without a doubt that the federal antitrust laws apply to the real estate brokerage business despite the local character of the real estate being sold or leased.

The language in the Sherman Act that *every* contract or combination in restraint of trade is declared to be illegal brought about a dispute that was decided in *Standard Oil v. United States.* Reasoning that every business contract is a restraint upon the commercial freedom of the parties, the Supreme Court interpreted the words *in restraint of trade* to mean only those contracts, combinations or conspiracies that unreasonably restrain trade. This judicial editing of the Sherman Act is known as the *Rule of Reason.*

Applying the Rule of Reason to various types of trade restraints, the Supreme Court eventually identified that their anticompetitive effects can be presumed. This conclusive presumption of an anticompetitive effect is known as the *per se rule.* If a particular restraint is found to be within the per se category, the antitrust laws do not allow any evidence, justification or excuse to be presented in defense of a per se offense. Thus, the issue in a per se case is not to determine if there is a conspiracy but whether the defendant is found to have participated in the conspiracy.

There are two categories of restraints subject to the per se rule that are of most concern to real estate brokers: (1) conspiracies to fix commission rates or commission splits and (2) group boycotts.

In *United States v. Foley,* a conspiracy to fix real estate commissions was found when a member of the Montgomery County (Maryland) Board of REALTORS® announced at a board function that he was raising his gross commission rate and that "he did not care what others did." The announcement was construed as an invitation to conspire, and the subsequent action by the other competitors was construed as an acceptance of this invitation. This case demonstrates that an inference of conspiracy based upon the actions of alleged conspirators is permissible as evidence without proving that alleged conspirators actually consulted with each other concerning a fee structure.

Group Boycotts

Group boycotts having the primary objective of harming or destroying a competitor or a supplier of goods and services occur in the real estate business when two or more brokers agree to refuse to cooperate or to cooperate on less favorable terms with a third broker, often a discount broker, in order to force a change in the competitor's behavior or to drive the competitor out of business. Such boycotts are per se (as a matter of law) illegal under the antitrust laws.

Real estate brokers or salespeople who act as if there were a conspiracy to boycott a competitor are just as vulnerable to an antitrust lawsuit as those who actually participate in the conspiracy.

Tying Agreements

The Supreme Court has defined a tying agreement as "an agreement to sell one product, only on the condition that the buyer also purchases a different (or tied) product . . ."

Courts have concluded that when the effect of a tying arrangement is to extend the seller's market power in the tying product into the market for the tied product, the tying arrangement is per se illegal under the antitrust laws.

As a result of *Northern Pacific Railway Co. v. United States,* real estate brokers should treat with caution any contract for the sale of land that conditions the sale on the buyer's agreement that he or she will engage the services of the seller or the seller's subsidiary.

Examples of possible antitrust violations are

- a list back clause in an agreement for the sale of subdivision lots whereby the developer sells a subdivision lot to a builder conditioned upon the builder's agreement to list back the improved property with the developer's brokerage firm for subsequent sale to homebuyers.
- a property management agreement that binds the owner to list the property with the broker-manager.

ANTITRUST ENFORCEMENT

The Department of Justice

The U.S. attorney general, through the Antitrust Division of the Department of Justice, may bring criminal and civil actions to enforce the Sherman Act.

The Antitrust Division has brought criminal antitrust indictments against real estate brokers, all of which have alleged that the defendants engaged in a conspiracy to fix real estate commissions.

A corporation found guilty of violating the Sherman Act may be fined up to $1 million. An individual may be fined up to $100,000 and imprisoned up to three years, or both.

Private Enforcement

Section 4 of the Clayton Act authorizes private persons to recover damages for injuries to their business or property by reason of anything forbidden by the antitrust laws.

Under the act, injured persons may recover three times actual damages plus reasonable attorney's fees.

REDUCING RISK OF ANTITRUST LIABILITY

Office Policies

Education. Education is imperative because brokers are held accountable and liable for the actions and statements of their sales associates. Each new salesperson should attend an orientation program. For this purpose NAR has prepared a videotape, *A Look at the Law: Antitrust,* as well as a booklet entitled "Antitrust and Real Estate Compliance Program for REALTORS® and REALTOR-ASSOCIATES®."

Training. When discussing fees with actual or prospective clients, sales associates should use language conveying the impression that the firm sets commission rates unilaterally and independently.

Sales associates should provide positive reasons for the firm's fee structure when sellers ask to lower the commission rate. Any suggestion that commissions are established by agreement among brokers or that an individual competitor is the object of a boycott must definitely be avoided.

Brokers or salespeople who find themselves in the midst of a prohibited discussion of commission rates with competitors must immediately take affirmative steps to disavow any connection with it. Being silent may imply that the silent broker participated in the price-fixing conspiracy.

To avoid antitrust liability, real estate brokers and salespeople should be particularly careful to avoid any communications or discussions with their competitors that relate in any way to the commission rates charged to sellers or the compensation levels paid to other firms for cooperative brokerage services.

Sales associates should report any suggestions by salespeople from other firms that could imply an invitation to fix commissions or boycott a competitor.

Standard Forms. Printed forms should *not* contain *preprinted* commission rates, predetermined listing periods, automatic renewal clauses or predetermined protection periods. There should be blanks to be filled out in each transaction.

Antitrust Investigations or Complaints. In the event of an antitrust investigation or complaint, the matter should be referred immediately to the firm's attorney. The local board or Association of REALTORS®, state association and the general counsel's office of NAR may also provide legal assistance.

What To Do

- The key to avoiding inferences of antitrust conspiracy is to establish independently fees and other listing policies including commission rates (flat fee or percentage of sales price), commission splits, length of listing, length of protected period after expiration and type of listing without consulting any competing brokerage firms.
- Documenting that commission rates and commission splits are set and/or adjusted as a result of independent business judgment is recommended. Such documentation may take the form of a confidential memo restricted solely to sales associates of the firm and to the office file.
- In the event a broker finds it necessary to deviate from his or her cooperative compensation split to one particular cooperating broker, it is essential to document that the deviation is based upon an independent evaluation of the circumstances. Such documentation would be necessary to rebut a possible inference of conspiracy in the event one or more other firms also lowered their cooperative compensation to the same firm.

What Not To Do

Real estate brokers must never
- mention or intimate intentions concerning commissions, fees or other business plans to competitors.

- refer to pricing policies of competitors when responding to questions about fees.
- include representatives of a third office when discussing a commission split with a cooperating broker.
- tell prospective clients they should not work with another firm because other brokers will not do business with that firm.
- suggest that other brokers have agreed not to cooperate for less than a particular commission split.

Dangerous Words and Phrases

(From the booklet entitled "Antitrust and Real Estate, Compliance Program for REALTORS® and REALTORS-ASSOCIATES®," by permission of the National Association of REALTORS®. All rights reserved.)

The following are examples of words or phrases occasionally used by salespeople that would permit a judge or jury to infer that real estate brokers are engaged in an illegal conspiracy:

- "I'd like to lower the commission rate, but the board has a rule . . ."
- "This is the rate that everyone charges."
- "The MLS will not accept less than a 120-day listing."
- "Before you list with XYZ Realty, you should know that nobody works on their listings."
- "If John Doe was really professional (or ethical), he would have joined the board."
- "The board requires all REALTORS® to make their salespeople join."
- "The best way to deal with John Doe is to boycott him."
- "If you valued your services as a professional, you wouldn't cut your commission."
- "No board member will accept a listing for less than ninety days."
- "Let him stay in his own market. This is our territory."

- "If he was really a professional, he wouldn't use part-timers."
- "This is the rate every firm charges."
- "I'd like to lower the commission, but no one else in the MLS will show your house unless the commission is X%."
- "Before you decide to list with XYZ Realty, you should know that because they are a 'discount' broker, members of the board won't show their listings."
- "I'd like to (reduce the commission ... shorten the listing term ... accept an exclusive agency listing), but if I do the MLS won't accept the listing."
- "This is what all brokers do."
- "No one else will cooperate unless you accept the listing on these terms."

UNAUTHORIZED PRACTICE OF LAW

Practice of Law

Quoting John Reilly's *The Language of Real Estate*, practice of law is defined as: "Rendering services that are peculiar to the law profession, such as preparing legal documents, giving legal advice and counsel, or construing contracts by which legal rights are secured. A real estate broker's license can be suspended or revoked for the unauthorized practice of law, regardless of whether or not fees are charged. The broker also has an ethical duty to recommend that legal counsel be obtained when the interest of either buyer or seller requires it.

"There is universal uncertainty as to whether the broker's use of certain forms constitutes the practice of law. While it is permissible for the broker to help complete certain standard forms, such as a sales contract, the broker has a duty to do so with accuracy and with certainty. Such completion of forms is permissible only where it is incidental to the broker's earning a commission and not where he or she makes a separate charge for filling in the form. In most states the broker may not prepare documents such as contracts for deed, deeds, mortgages, deeds of trust, options, and certain leases.

"Only attorneys and the parties to a transaction are authorized to prepare legal instruments. However, many state Associations of REALTORS® and Bar Associations have broker-lawyer accords that recognize that the real estate broker must have authority to secure some kind of agreement between buyer and seller, evidence of the transaction, and provisions for payment of the broker's compensation. This usually gives a broker the authority to fill in the blanks of pre-printed documents only, and not to draft legal documents or close transactions (as some states recognize these acts as the practice of law)."

Thus, in many states real estate licensees may fill in the blanks in printed, standardized forms approved by a lawyer and in connection with transactions handled by the broker in the usual course of business. However, the broker may not charge for filling in the blanks or give advice or counsel as to the legal effect and validity of such documents.

The standard of care demanded of an attorney will be the standard applied to a real estate licensee who practices law.

In an effort to help resolve the unauthorized practice of law problem, the National Association of REALTORS® adopted Article 17 of the Code of Ethics: "The REALTOR® shall not engage in activities that constitute the unauthorized practice of law and shall recommend that legal counsel be obtained when the interest of any party to the transaction requires it." This article has been introduced in court [*Crutchley v. First Trust & Savings Bank,* 450 N.W. 2d 877 (Iowa 1990)] as the standard of a case against which a salesperson's conduct should be measured. Proof of a violation of this standard is evidence upon which the judge and jury may find a salesperson negligent.

Legal Advice or Judgment

Exercising legal judgment as to which competing real estate form to use or giving advice about legal effects of executing a joint tenancy deed constitutes a practice of law [*State Bar of New Mexico v. Guardian Abstract and Title Company, Inc.,* 575 P.2d 943 (NM 1978)].

A real estate broker who counseled a seller on the tax consequences of various forms of property transfer engaged in unauthorized practice of law [*Wolfenberger v. Madison,* 357 N.E.2d 656 (IL 1976)].

BIBLIOGRAPHY

Agency Relationships in Real Estate by John W. Reilly

Agency Disclosure: The Complete Office Policy Guide by John W. Reilly and Michael Somers

Antitrust and Real Estate Compliance Program for REALTORS® *and* REALTOR-ASSOCIATES® by NAR

Blueprint for Office Risk Reduction Practices by NAR

Buyer Agency by Gail G. Lyons and Donald L. Harlan

Buyer Brokering by James B. Warkentin

Buyer's Broker Registry, P.O. Box 23275, Ventura, CA 93002; 800-729-5147

Consensual Dual Agency by John Reilly, Gail G. Lyons and Donald L. Harlan

Fair Housing Act Amendments, cassette course, by NAR

Fair Housing in the '90s, course, by the National Association of REALTORS®

Leading Guide to Buyer Brokering by Barry M. Miller

Reference Handbook: Antitrust and Real Estate by NAR

Risk Management I, course outline, by the Hawaii Association of REALTORS®

Risk Management II, course outline, by the Hawaii Association of REALTORS®

Risk Management III, course outline, by the Hawaii Association of REALTORS®

The How & Why of Buyer Agency by Pat M. Goodover II

The Language of Real Estate by John W. Reilly

SALES
TECHNIQUES

To receive advance notice of the
next *Realty Bluebook*® edition
(and information about
what's new), please call
1-800-322-8621
to register your name and address.

CONTENTS

SALES TECHNIQUES

SALES TECHNIQUES

This section of the *Realty Bluebook*® offers comprehensive outlines on listing and selling techniques for both study and quick reference.

Each chapter is an independent unit. Consequently, there is some repetition of data from chapter to chapter relevant to the subject presented.

Throughout this section several Professional Publishing products are recommended for efficient use in the respective activities. A list of these products and order information may be found at the end of the Sales Techniques section.

PREREQUISITES FOR SUCCESS

Appearance

- You never get a second chance to make a good first impression!
- Impeccable personal grooming is important.
- Dress in keeping with your clients' lifestyles.
- Keep late model automobile in immaculate condition.

Personal Attributes

- Cultivate a positive attitude about yourself.
- Be enthusiastic about your ability to market real estate.
- Be enthusiastic about your company.
- Be enthusiastic about real estate in general.
- Your enthusiasm affects your clients and creates business. (How can a client possibly be excited about a property if you, the expert, are just lukewarm about it?)
- Be relaxed.
- Wear a million-dollar smile.
- Address people by their names—pronounced correctly!
- Maintain good eye contact.
- Be a good listener.

- Find out what the other person wants and help him or her find the best way to get it.
- Find common interests.
- Be tactful and courteous in every way.
- Always be prompt; if delayed, call to apologize.
- Show understanding of clients' problems.
- Be genuinely interested in people.
- Make an effort to recognize and allow for human behavior patterns. (People who are basically extroverts, introverts, factual, friendly, hostile, suspicious, etc.)
- The name of the game is helping people own their dream house.

Effective Words and Phrases

- The word *you* and the person's name are magic sounds—use them often.
- Pronounce names correctly; ask if in doubt.
- Use *please* and *thank you*.

LISTING TECHNIQUES

Listing Goals

Striving toward a goal makes your listing efforts more exciting and more effective.

1. Begin by setting a goal of the annual income you plan to earn from your listing efforts, taking into account how much of your total real estate effort you plan to devote to listing.

2. Calculate the number of properties you need to list per year in order to achieve your goal by using the formula in the example shown below, substituting your own numbers for income goal and commission splits.

A. Listing income goal: $ 50,000
B. Average sale price: 140,000
C. Average seller's commission: 6% of B _____
D. Listing broker's commission*: 50% of C _____
E. Average agent's share: 60% of D _____
F. Average agent's commission:
$B \times C \times D \times E$
$\$140,000 \times 0.06 \times 0.5 \times 0.6$ 2,520
G. Average percentage of listings sold: 60%
Number of Listings needed per year:
$A \div F \div G$
$\$50,000 \div \$2,520 \div 0.6$ **33**

Therefore, you need to list 33 properties per year in order to attain your goal of $50,000 in listing commissions.

Based on co-op sales.

TIME MANAGEMENT IN LISTING

Treat your time as you treat your money. Because time is the most valuable commodity a real estate professional has to offer, its effective control is essential to success.

Serious Sellers versus Maybe Sellers

Identify fake sellers quickly or you'll waste precious time.

- Real sellers have specific reasons for selling (transfer, retirement, marriage, birth, divorce, death, financial, tax).
- Real sellers have a time frame for selling (transfer, closing date of new home).
- Real sellers will accept the concept of fair market value (as opposed to fake sellers who sell only if they get their price).
- Real sellers will cooperate in providing needed documentation and disclosures (as opposed to fake sellers who would balk at such inconvenience).

Maintain a Priority List

- List your activities in priority groups (A, B and C).
- Your most important priority is to concentrate on the specific number of listings you must obtain to achieve your goal.
- Schedule 75% of your time for talking to clients and no more than 25% for paperwork.
- Delegate unproductive detail work to hired help (escrow work, mailing farm letters, etc.).
- Use a computer and laser printer for direct mail letters.
- Use your priority list each evening to plan the next day.
- Consult the list often, especially between appointments or during lulls in your business day.
- Always carry productive reading material in case you are kept waiting.

Suggested Daily Schedule of a Dedicated Lister

- Early A.M.—Check morning newspapers for leads (by owner ads, marriages, divorces, births, transfers, promotions, garage sales, furniture for sale, rezoning). Write thank-you notes, address sales aids. Service escrows.

- Mid A.M.—Preview new listings. Service own listings (for more efficiency use *Listing and Transaction Folder* by Professional Publishing).
- Late A.M.—Prospect.
- Early P.M.—Prospect.
- Mid P.M.—Prepare and mail newsletters.
- Evenings—Check evening papers for leads. Plan the next day. Attend civic and club functions.

FARMING

Two Types of Farms

1. Territorial or geographical farm. The objective of territorial farming is to build a clientele through a concentrated effort in a limited geographic territory in which the agent develops an expertise.
2. Social or sphere of influence farm. In social farming, the agent concentrates listing efforts within social groups or organizations in which he or she is extremely active.

Considerations in Selecting a Territorial Farm

- Turnover in the territory.
- Average selling price in the territory.
- Whether you can relate easily to the people in the farm or share similar interests.
- Competition from other agents. If you see a number of different real estate signs in the territory, you may assume that no agent has as yet been able to establish a beachhead. However, if the signs of one broker are dominating the territory, you are probably up against considerable competition.
- In a new subdivision, you will find less competition than in a more established neighborhood, but you may have to wait a few years for the first listings.

Establishing the Size of a Farm

Limit the farm to a number of properties that make in-person contacts feasible every four to six months and telephone contacts every three months. Between 150 to 400 homes should be an acceptable range depending on these factors:

1. The number of listings you expect your farm to yield. The example under the heading Listing Goals shows 33 listings per year to achieve a $50,000 annual listing income from all sources. Estimate how many of these listings you expect to come from farming and how many from other sources.
2. The turnover rate of the farm. Compute the turnover rate by dividing the number of homes sold during the previous year in the MLS district in which the farm is located by the total number of homes in that district.
3. Your estimated share of homes listed in the farm. Your share of the homes listed will depend upon your efforts, such as the amount of time devoted to farming, diligence, attitude and use of hired help or computer for direct mail. The results are necessarily lower in a newly initiated farm but should increase after the first year.

Based on these three factors, you can calculate the size of your farm using the formula in the example below:

Number of listings the farm
   is expected to yield: 10   [A]

Number of sales in MLS
   district in previous year: 150

Number of homes in MLS district: 1,400

Annual turnover:
   $150 \div 1,400 = 0.107$ [B]

Estimated share of homes
   listed in farm: 45% = .45   [C]

Size of farm needed:
   [A] ÷ [B] ÷ [C]
   $10 \div 0.107 \div 0.45 =$ **208 Homes**

Therefore, you need a farm of 208 homes in order to attain your goal of ten listings per year.

Farm Mailing List

Sources of Mailing Lists

- Reverse telephone directory
- County Assessor's officer has records with information on:
  - Homeowners' names
  - Assessed value
  - Date of property transfer
  - Owner occupied or rented
  - Title companies
  - Multiple listing services
  - Commercial services—Real Estate Data, Inc. (REDI) operates nationwide

Farm Records

Duplicate records, cross indexed by name and address, are strongly recommended for success in farming.

SUGGESTION: Prepare small self-adhesive mailing labels in duplicate. Apply one label to top corner of the record filed by address, the other to the record filed by client name.

There are many types of record systems. The following method is offered as a guideline.

1. Client record by address. This record may be kept in small 3-by-5-inch cards containing simply the client's name and address (mailing label applied at top corner).
2. Client record by name. Use 8½-by-11-inch sheets for alphabetical filing in a 3-ring binder. By selecting fields from the following outlined data, you can design your own form and have it printed or duplicated.

Personal Information

- Name and address (mailing label applied at top corner)
- Small colored stickers marked AO (Absentee Owner) and R (Renter)
- Phone number
- Names of all occupants

- Occupation, employer
- Best day and time to contact
- Anniversary
- Birthdays
- Hobbies

Property Information

- Type or model house
- Assessed value

Contacts Made

- Date
- Telephone/mail/in-person
- Remarks: (lots of space)

Transaction Information

- Date of purchase
- Purchase price (or assessed value)
- Date listed
- Listed price
- Listing office/agent
- Date of sale
- Sale price
- Selling office/agent
- Date off market

3. Direct mail farming record. Design a tabular form on an 8½-by-11-inch paper with columns labeled *Mailing Number, Mailing Date, How Many Letters Rec'd* and *How Many Responses*. Assign a number to each mailing, and attach a copy of the newsletter with the number of the mailing written at the top.

Updating all records regularly is essential for success! It is advisable to make the first mailing with "Address Correction Requested." Contact your local post office for further information.

4. Farm map. Set up a farm map showing with colored stickpins your listings and sales, as well as those of the competition.

Be a Specialist in Your Farm

- Become thoroughly familiar with the type of homes in the farm, floor plans, construction, sale prices, public transportation, shopping facilities, schools (college, private, parochial), churches, recreational facilities; any proposed changes in zoning, proposed construction (commercial, churches, sports arenas, industrial, etc.).
- Attend neighborhood functions, get involved in PTA, etc.
- Drive through the territory at least once a week—look for new signs, construction, changes, new landscaping.
- Keep up with current events in the farm (local newspapers).

Rejection-Free Method of Farming

Because most of us fear being rejected, develop an approach that makes rejection extremely unlikely.

- Offer service, make positive statements, do not ask favors.
- Never ask for a listing when knocking on someone's door. Introduce yourself as a specialist, and offer your services whenever needed. Ask if anyone in the neighborhood has plans to move.
- Write letters of introduction and follow-up with telephone calls before making personal contacts.

1. Letter of Introduction

- Introduce yourself as the specialist in the territory.
- You plan to provide a service to homeowners by keeping them informed on matters concerning real estate, especially in the neighborhood.
- Provide service by offering to:
  - Answer questions concerning real estate.
  - Provide information on properties listed by any broker.
  - Prepare a free market analysis.

- Remember to mention if you can be reached evenings at home.
- Provide a brief background of your company including its track record.
- Provide a brief background of yourself.
- Ask for referral of friends who may plan to move.
- Mention that you hope to introduce yourself in person in the very near future.

2. Telephone Follow-Up—Three to Four Days after the Mailing Arrives

"Mr./Mrs. Owner, I'm with ABC Realty. My name is Jim Ross. I mailed you a card [letter] telling you about [subject matter]. Is this a convenient time to talk for a minute or two? Real estate in Westlake is my specialty. I'd be happy to be of service if you have any questions concerning any Westlake home that has a For Sale sign. . . ."

With any favorable response, offer to look at the house and give a complimentary market analysis.

3. Mail Handwritten Note

"I enjoyed our telephone conversation yesterday. Thank you for taking time from your daily schedule."

Include business card and confirm appointment, if any.

4. Personal Contact At Least Twice a Year

- Knock on door.
- Stand away from door.
- Look relaxed.
- Wait until acknowledged.
- Introduce yourself.
- "You probably received my postcard—I specialize in homes in this area."
- Be complimentary.
- Do not solicit listing!
- Do ask about anyone considering moving in the neighborhood.
- "Do you happen to know of anyone interested in buying or selling?"

- Examples of handouts to offer:
  - New listing cards (Choose your neighbor cards)
  - Open house invitations
  - Newsletter (see Topics for Newsletters)
  - Real estate–related handout
  - Consumer discount program with local businesses
  - Baseball, football or basketball schedules
  - After leaving, make notes of conversation, names, and so on to add to records later.
  - Immediately upon listing a home, inform surrounding neighbors.

5. Mail Handwritten Note

"I enjoyed meeting you and (other persons) on Wednesday. (Compliment owner on any particularly attractive feature of the house or garden, etc.) Any interested buyers or sellers you may wish to refer will be assured of prompt professional attention. Sincerely,".

Individual Farming Newsletters

A number of publishers produce monthly real estate newsletters that can be personalized with your name and photo. Because of quantity production, they are reasonable and quite convenient. However, there is no substitute for the individual style and personal touch of your own newsletter. You may find the following guidelines helpful should you decide to produce your own. Today's desktop publishing (using personal computers and laser printers) makes production of quality newsletters a breeze, individually addressed with matching envelopes to boot. An individual newsletter mailed every other month should be more effective than a commercially produced one mailed monthly.

Topics for Newsletters

- Current neighborhood real estate news (recent sales, new homes for sale—not only your own listings)—Ask if owner knows of any potential purchasers for these new listings.

- Annual summary sheet or card of neighborhood activities
  - Homes listed by your company
  - Homes sold by your company
  - Homes listed and sold by your company
- Real estate market and tax information
  - Interest rates
  - Price trends (sellers' or buyers' market)
  - New types of financing
  - Real estate statistics
  - Purchasing a home as income property
  - Recent tax news affecting property owners
- A glimpse into the life of a real estate agent
  - Professional services free for the asking
  - Advantages of working with your own agent
  - How the real estate profession is organized
  - Types of listings, advantages and disadvantages
- Answers to common questions about real estate
  - Types of home improvements that add value to a home in terms of sale price
  - What to look for in floor plans
  - News about energy conservation
  - Security in the home
  - Safety in the home
- Thumbnail sketches of articles or ideas of interest to homeowners—new products, fix-it ideas, storage ideas, gardening, home improvement, maintenance, repairs, consumer information, recipes. Your imagination is the only limit. Always identify your source ("I just read in *XYZ Magazine, Readers Digest, New York Times* or saw on TV or heard from Joe the Chef or Mary the Gardener, etc.").
- Monthly bulletin offering free ads
- Neighborhood directory of hobbies, services, interests
- Discount coupons from new (or established) neighborhood businesses
- Remember to ask for referrals of friends or relatives who may be moving.

- Always offer to
  - prepare complimentary market analysis,
  - provide information on properties listed by any broker and
  - answer questions concerning real estate.
- Give home phone number in case you cannot be reached in the office.
- Enclose self-addressed, stamped return postcard.

Style and Technique for Writing a Newsletter

- Write in a personal, conversational style as one individual to another. Create a friendly tone.
- Put yourself in the readers' shoes and try to read your story from their point of view.
- Avoid real estate lingo.
- Use short, easy-to-read sentences (maximum 15 words per sentence) and short paragraphs.
- Write interesting stories.
- Present your case in an understandable manner.
- Use specifics, not generalities, ("Interest rates have dropped from 10% to 9% during the last three months" instead of "Interest rates have been going down").
- Emphasize the benefits to the client of the topic under discussion instead of listing its features, qualities or statistics. (Example: "Over 100 L&H sales associates are in contact with many prospective buyers; what this means to you is immediate exposure to an active portion of the market!" instead of saying: "L&H Realty Company has over 100 sales associates.")
- Make sure what you write is believable.
- Use a bold headline as an attention getter:
  - Year's Real Estate Activity in Westlake
  - Is It Worth Improving Your Home?
  - You Asked Me about Real Estate . . .
  - Free Homebuyers' Guide
- Use informal language (try simple words instead of intellectual ones). Your letter will run smoother and have a more emotional effect on a reader. Examples:

Try *Simple Words*	*Instead of* *Intellectual Words*
speed up	accelerate
there's more	additionally
let	allow
expect	anticipate
anxious	apprehensive
find out	ascertain
good looking	attractive
helpful	beneficial
begin	commence
finished	completed
agreement	covenant
hope	desire
too much	excessive
show	exhibit
because	for
hopeless	futile
gardening	horticulture
funny	humorous
tell	inform
I'm sorry	I regret
has	is provided with
teamwork	joint effort
find out	learn
own	possess
stop	prevent
buy	purchase
get	receive
asked for	requested
take care of	service
enough	sufficient
better than	superior to
late	tardy
end	terminate
news	tidings
pure	unadulterated
use	utilize
rich	wealthy

- Salutation—be specific: "Dear Westlake Neighbor" or "Dear Westlake Homeowner" (instead of just "Dear Neighbor").
- Start your letter with an attention getter.
  - "As I drove through Westlake this morning...."
  - "If you are like most of your neighbors...."
  - "Have you noticed...?"
  - "Remember the days when...."
  - "The other day I read an interesting article in...."
- Use transition phrases to lead into the next paragraph:
  - "That's why...."
  - "In short...." (Refer to topic of
  - "You too...."   the newsletter)
  - "Here's how ..."
- End your letter with an appropriate closing—"Sincerely yours" or "Sincerely" with your first and last name.
- Always add a postscript, an effective call for action!
  - P.S. If you miss me at the office, don't hesitate to call me at home: 123-4567.
  - P.S. There is no obligation for a market analysis.
  - P.S. Return the enclosed card now while you're thinking about it.
  - P.S. When you have a minute, don't forget to read....
  - For ethical reasons (which will also impress an owner), add: P.S. Please disregard this letter if your home is listed with another broker.
- Always enclose a stamped, self-addressed return postcard with printed check blocks for easy replies.

Telephone Consumer Protection Act of 1991 (TCPA)

REALTORS® who use the telephone to contact potential clients and customers must comply with a new regulation effective December 20, 1992, on telephone solicitations.

ιe new regulation, issued October 16, 1992, by the
αl Communications Commission, implements
ιons of the TCPA and applies to all telemarketers.
The use of automated telephone dialing systems and
prerecorded voice messages is severely restricted by the
regulation, which places only minor limitations on per-
son-to-person telephone solicitations.

A rundown of the regulation's restriction and the
steps real estate brokers and sales associates must
take to comply with them are listed below.

Person-to-Person Calls

- No calls may be made to residences before 8 A.M.
  or after 9 P.M.
- A solicitor must identify himself or herself and
  the company and provide the company's telephone
  number. If an established business relationship
  exists with a consumer, a solicitor is exempt from
  this requirement. An established business relationship exists when there has been prior, voluntary two-way communication between a business
  entity and a consumer whether or not the contact
  results in an actual business transaction involving
  the services offered by the solicitor.
- A real estate firm whose sales associates conduct
  live cold calling must honor consumers' request
  not to be called again by maintaining in writing a
  do-not-call list of residences. A company must also
  have a written policy for maintaining its list.
- A firm must advise employees and independent
  contractors engaged in any aspect of telephone
  solicitation about its do-not-call list and must
  train employees and independent contractors on
  how to maintain the list as required by the firm's
  written policy.
- A consumer's request not to be called applies to
  the business entity making the call and not affiliated business entities unless the consumer reasonably would expect the affiliated businesses to be
  included, given the identification of the caller and
  the product of service being advertised.

Autodialers and Faxes

- No calls may be made to any residential telephone line using an automatic telephone dialing system or artificial or prerecorded voice to deliver a message unless there is prior consent from the called party, an established business relationship exists, the call is an emergency or the call is made by a tax-exempt nonprofit organization.
- Audodialers may not be used in such a way that two or more telephone lines of a multiple-line business are engaged simultaneously.
- All automatic systems shall identify the name and address or telephone number of the person or firm making the call.
- No individual or firm may use a telephone fax machine, computer or other device to send unsolicited advertisements to a telephone fax machine.

Penalties

- Consumers, state authorities and the FCC may sue telemarketers up to $500 in damages for violating the regulation. Telemarketers who have established a record of compliance with the regulation may present examples of this compliance—such as a do-not-call list and a written policy for maintaining the list—as a defense to alleged violations.

Telephone Techniques for Farming

- Call at appropriate times.
- Make the maximum number of calls in the shortest possible time.
- The purpose of the call is to get an appointment.
- Set the appointment for a time when both owners are at home.
- Keep calls short and simple.
- Keep asking questions beginning with how, what, when, where, why, who or which; such questions prompt specific answers whereas questions beginning with are, is, have or do merely require a yes or no answer.

ow when to stop talking.

sten carefully—do not occupy yourself with anything but paying attention to what the other person has to say.

- Never interrupt or finish someone's sentence.
- Never argue.
- Speak into the mouthpiece so your words are clearly heard.
- Smile while talking on the phone.
- Use everything you know about people and their home.
- Never patronize or talk down to people (never use expressions like "my friend" or "your understand" or "you see").
- Do not put a client on hold if at all possible.
- Never hang up first; wait for your client to hang up.
- If you call at an inconvenient time, apologize and reschedule.
- Wrap up a conversation as soon as you have an appointment.
- If the prospect is not interested, end the conversation in a pleasant way, such as "it was nice talking with you."

Effective Words and Phrases To Use

- The word *you* and a person's name are sweet music in the listener's ear; use them often.
- Pronounce names correctly—ask if in doubt.
- Use *please* and *thank you*.
- Thank the prospect for his or her time.
- Thank the prospect for waiting.

Openers

Begin with a friendly, casual greeting.

- "Mrs. Whitmore, good evening. I'm with Sunshine Realty here in Westlake. My name is Terry Ross. Do you have a minute to talk?"
- "Hello, is Mr. Goodman at home? Mr. Goodman, my name is Patricia Riley, do you have a moment to talk on the phone?"

- "Mr. Bentley, I'm Tammy Bowman with Sta. Realty. Did you receive my letter?"

Telephone Topics

Make an outline of topics that will stir the prospect's interest.

- Talk about peoples' hobbies, children, schools, college and their homes. Get to know people.
- Offer free home evaluations.
- Offer financing and refinancing information.
- Discuss income property.
- Discuss the possibility for renters to own a home.
- Remember to ask for referrals of friends or relatives who may be moving.
- Offer to answer questions concerning real estate.

FOR SALE BY OWNER (FSBO)

Sources for Leads

- Search the classifieds daily for FSBO ads, and update as you obtain information (reason for selling, deadline, property data, asking price, contacts, appointments, etc.).
- Look for FSBO signs.

First Contact with Seller

Put the seller at ease during the first conversation whether it is on the phone or in person. Speak calmly, listen attentively and show understanding for the seller's problems in order to establish a relaxed climate. It takes an average of four to five weeks for a FSBO to be ready to list, so take it easy.

Qualifying the Seller

Find out if the listing is worth pursuing by discovering

- the reason for selling (unless the FSBO—the seller—has a strong motivation to sell, you will probably waste your time);
- if they have found (purchased) another home;

...ere they are moving;

...here is any deadline for moving;

...here are any meaningful commitments to other brokers, agents or buyers (a friend or relative in the business? Find out a name to check if it is an excuse.); and

- if the property is in excessively poor condition.

Asking Permission To See the House and Meet the FSBO

Once the seller is qualified, your objective is to gain permission to see the seller in his or her home.

Techniques and Dialogue

- Show understanding of the seller's problems.
- Emphasize your expertise.
- FSBO: "Why do you want to see the house?"
  Agent: "For the benefit of several of my buyers."
  FSBO: "We're not interested."
  Agent: "If I had a good offer on your house today, would you turn it down?"
  FSBO: "Do you have an interested buyer? I never heard of your firm."
  Agent: "I'm sure I'll be able to show evidence that we have an excellent reputation."

The First Meeting inside the Home

Your first impression, which includes personality, appearance, manners, dress, automobile, counts. Be positive and confident in your ability to successfully market properties. Show understanding of the seller's problems and offer assistance even though they are not prepared to list with you. It may take several weeks before a FSBO is ready.

Leading questions to ask in a subtle manner:

- Have you sold a home before?
- How long did it take?
- How much time do you have to make a sale?
- If you have not sold by then, have you considered retaining a professional real estate person?

- What qualities would you expect in a real estate person to entrust him or her with the marketing of your property?
- Do you want me to do a market analysis for you—without obligation? (If the answer is yes set up a listing appointment. CAUTION: Do not make this offer unless or until you feel the seller is ready to list.)

Be sure to ask the sellers for a commitment to meet with you before deciding to list the property for sale. Follow up with a handwritten note thanking them for their commitment. Make weekly follow-up telephone calls asking about their progress and offer continued assistance.

To List or Not To List

"Mr. and Mrs. Seller, selling a house and carrying the transaction through to a successful completion is no easy task. You can, of course, retain a professional to do the job or you can try to save the commission by making the sale yourself. Remember, though, the typical direct-from-owner buyer expects you to knock off the commission for his own benefit and is likely to have experience in such negotiations. Before you decide to go the for-sale-by-owner route, ask yourself the following questions (listed below and on page E-22). Unless you can answer yes to most of them, it will be to your advantage to list your home with the best real estate professional you can find."

YES   NO

☐   ☐   Do you have ample time to sell your house?

☐   ☐   Is your house easy to find?

☐   ☐   Do you have the know-how to price your house at the highest figure that will attract buyers?

☐   ☐   Are you capable of running an effective advertising campaign? Do you have time to answer phone calls at all hours and to keep your house in top condition ready for prospects at any time?

☐ Do you know how to show your house to best advantage?

☐ ☐ Can you answer objections and criticism without showing irritation?

☐ ☐ Are you familiar with today's disclosure laws?

☐ ☐ Do you know how to protect yourself against the legal liabilities sellers are subject to as a result of numerous recent court decisions?

☐ ☐ Can you tell the difference between a prospective buyer answering your ad by phone and a criminal disguised as a buyer, using ads to get into homes?

☐ ☐ Are you able to call back prospects without placing yourself in a poor bargaining position to negotiate an offer?

☐ ☐ Can you show prospects comparable properties, so they can see why your home is worth the money you ask?

☐ ☐ Do you have the ability to bargain successfully for price, terms, moving date and so on?

☐ ☐ Are you familiar with today's financing techniques and sources?

☐ ☐ Do you have an outlet for second mortgages?

☐ ☐ Do you have the professional skill necessary to draw legally binding contracts?

☐ ☐ Can you handle all the details and paperwork required to close the transaction?

EXPIRED LISTINGS

Seller Qualification by Telephone

- Is your home off the market?
- Would you sell it if you had a buyer?
- Why do you think it has not sold?
- How was it exposed to the market?

- How many showings did you have?
- Did you have any offers?
- At what price and terms?
- What will you do when it is sold?
- May I come by between three and four o'clock this afternoon to see your home?

The Appointment

- Find some feature in the house to admire.
- Show understanding for their situation.
- Do you think your house was realistically priced?
- Do you think your terms were attractive to a typical buyer?
- Do you feel your house was in a condition to attract buyers?
- What qualities would you expect in a real estate person to entrust him or her with marketing your property?

PERSONAL REFERRALS

National statistics show that personal referrals account for almost half the listings generated. A successful referral system, built over the years, will replace the hard work necessary in the early years of one's career.

Up-to-Date Records

Constant updating of your records is essential in building an effective personal referral system. It requires an efficient record system, one that can be maintained with a minimum expenditure of time.

Personal and Telephone Contacts

It is vital to make regular contacts by telephone (at least every 60 days) and in person (three to four times per year) with everyone in your personal referral system.

Always remember to send a thank-you note for the referral. Keep the referring source informed of the transaction status at regular intervals.

- .iversary cards
- Dirthday cards to all family members on a regular basis
- Personal brochures
- Choose-your-neighbor cards
- New-neighbor cards
- Open house invitations
- Monthly informative newsletters (local developments, taxes, storage ideas, home maintenance suggestions, etc.)
- Consumer discount programs with local businesses
- Short investment seminars (two or three hours)
- Promotional products calendars, key tags, etc.

PREPARATION FOR LISTING INTERVIEW

Armed with facts and knowledge, an agent reflects professionalism and credibility, causing most sellers to give serious consideration to what they have to say. The result is usually a more salable listing.

Research

- Consult the Checklist section of **_Realty Bluebook_**® for the appropriate listing data checklist (single family, condominiums, multifamily, etc.), concerning ownership, location, site, improvements, interior, financing, market analysis and price.
- Find out the date and cost of acquisition (transfer stamps are on recorded deed at county recorder's office).
- Check recorded deed for all persons having an interest in the title.
- Become thoroughly familiar with
  - the type of homes in the neighborhood, floor plans, construction and recent sale prices; and
  - public transportation, shopping facilities, schools (elementary, junior high, high school,

college, private), churches, recreational fac_{ti}ties as well as any proposed changes in zoning, proposed construction (commercial, churches, sports arenas, industrial etc.).

Comparative Market Analysis

Determine a realistic price range and terms; establish a price limit beyond which the listing becomes unattractive. The market analysis should show

- properties for sale,
- properties sold past 12 months and
- expired listings.

Listing Kit

- Completed residential market analysis
- Current **Realty Bluebook**® and financial tables
- *Red Flags Property Inspection Guide*
- The following forms:
  - Listing contract
  - Estimated seller's proceeds
  - Red Flags Inspection Checklist*
  - Seller's property disclosure statement
  - Agency disclosure statement
  - FIRPTA Nonforeign seller affidavit
  - Home warranty forms
- Listing presentation manual
- Visual aids
- Legal pad
- Lock box and lock box agreement
- Tape measure
- Camera with film
- Calculator
- Ball point pen
- Business cards

Red Flags Property Inspection Checklist, Form 109-RF, is reprinted in the "Checklist section" with permission from Professional Publishing, San Rafael, Calif.

Personal Attitude and Technique

- Be prompt and call to apologize if delayed.
- Be relaxed.
- Wear a million-dollar smile.
- Address people by their names, pronounced correctly!
- Maintain good eye contact.
- Be a good listener.
- Find common interests.
- Be tactful and courteous in every way.
- Be positive about the home, your company, yourself.
- Show confidence in your ability to market real estate.
- Show understanding of client's problems.
- Be genuinely interested in people.
- Make an effort to recognize and make allowance for human behavior patterns (people who are basically extrovert, introvert, factual, friendly, hostile, suspicious, etc.).

Tips

- Try to be in a quiet room with plenty of light (kitchen or dining room) undisturbed by children, TV or radio.
- Never seat yourself between husband and wife.

Seller's Motivation

Find out the seller's needs (if not yet discussed previously).

- Why are they selling?
- Where are they moving?
- Have they purchased another home?
- Do they need their equity to close the new house?
- When do they plan to move?
- Any deadline for selling their house?

Seller's Prior Experience in Selling Real Estate

- Sold by owner?
- Through a broker?
- Was experience good or bad?

Inspecting the Home

- Most salable features—Have seller point them out and make notes.
- Problem areas—Discuss with seller, reinspect later for red flags.
- Fixtures that are not to be included in the sale—A fixture is anything permanently affixed to real estate and that, therefore, goes with the house. Fixtures usually include trees, shrubs and plants, built-in appliances, drapery hardware, wall-to-wall carpets, light fixtures, chandeliers, TV antennae. If any of such fixtures are not to go with the house, they should be replaced with something comparable now or, at least, specifically excluded from the sale.
- Improvements that help the sale—Certain improvements add value to a home in terms of sale price; others do not.
  - Expensive improvements, such as a spa or swimming pool, should be avoided because their cost usually does not increase the sale price enough to warrant the effort.
  - To bring top dollars, a home should be in top physical condition. Listed below are some cost-effective improvements.
    - Clean if and where needed; wash off fingerprints on doors.
    - Painting, if needed, increases salability.
    - Remove/replace stained or torn wallpaper.
    - Remove stains from kitchen and bathroom counters.
    - Replace worn kitchen and bathroom floor coverings.
    - Shampoo carpets.

- Replace missing or broken door and cupboard hardware.
- Use soap to lubricate sticking windows and drawers.
- Oil creaking door hinges.
- Repair broken windows, shower doors, shutters and storm windows.
- Repair clogged plumbing lines, leaky faucets and leaks underneath sinks.
- Fix creaky floors.
- Make sure all mechanical systems and appliances are in good working order; make repairs where needed.
- Repair roof, if needed.
- Repair worn and leaky rain gutters and downspouts.
- Fix and paint fence, if needed.
- Remove oils and stains from garage floor and driveway.

Remodeling Job	Average Job Cost	Average Resale Value	Cost Recouped
Minor Kitchen Remodel	$ 6,234	$ 6,551	104%
Bath Addition	10,552	10,020	95
Major Kitchen Remodel	19,261	18,021	94
Bath Remodel	7,207	6,109	85
Family Room Addition	28,455	24,069	85
Master Bedroom Suite	22,060	18,320	83
Attic Bedroom	21,904	17,715	81
Deck Addition	5,731	4,456	78
Replace Windows	7,315	5,289	72
Replace Siding	9,052	6,403	71
Sun Space Addition	24,929	17,416	70

Source: *Realtor News,* week of May 24, 1993

Reasons for Listing with You and Your Firm

- Be positive, demonstrate your confidence in your ability to fill the seller's most important needs:
  - To net them the most money

- In the shortest possible time
- With the least amount of inconvenience to the owner
- Company's sources of buyers:
  - Current list of prospective buyers
  - Multiple listing
  - Classified and display advertising
  - Personal referrals
  - Corporate relocation referrals
  - National referral organizations
  - Open houses
  - For Sale signs
- Visual Aids
  - Track record (listings sold by you and your firm showing listed price, sold price, time on the market)
  - Company background
  - Company sales activities
  - Clipping of ads
  - Packet of required listing and selling forms

The Right Asking Price

Present Comparative Market Analysis:

The following excerpt, "The Right Asking Price" is reproduced from *Home Sellers Guide* by Professional Publishing.

"Establishing the right price range is a critical consideration in marketing real property. Over-pricing, as well as underpricing, can be detrimental to the sale.

"Many sellers tend to price their house far above market value for a number of reasons: sentimental attachment, expensive improvements made over the years (not necessarily always appreciated by prospective buyers), false rumors of high priced sales in the neighborhood, and often unrealistic opinions of well meaning friends.

"An overpriced house discourages serious buyers and real estate people. It usually remains on the market too long causing people to wonder if something is wrong with the house.

"On the other hand, unfamiliarity with the market may cause sellers to underprice their home, only to find it snapped up by a speculator for quick resale at a profit."

Agency Relationships

An increasing number of states are requiring real estate agents to disclose their intended agency relationship with sellers and buyers.

Need for Property Inspections and Disclosures

Real estate brokers and agents have always been responsible for faithfully representing the condition of a property without concealing any known defects. In the 1980s, the courts and legislatures of various states, notably California, required brokers and agents to inspect a property for any visible defects, also called red flags, that may affect its value or desirability and to disclose them to prospective buyers.

Closing

Obtaining the sellers' signatures should be no more than the logical result of a well-prepared, smooth listing interview with all the sellers' questions and objections convincingly answered. When that point has arrived, it is up to the agent to take the initiative by filling in the listing contract and asking the necessary questions in the process. All that remains is simply to hand the contract to the sellers for their signatures—with a pen!

MARKETING AND SERVICING THE LISTING

Marketing a real property efficiently involves exposure of the property's benefits to the ultimate extent via a maximum number of channels in order to reach the greatest possible number of potential buyers.

Channels

- Current list of prospective buyers in contact with your firm
- Multiple listing
- Classified and display advertising
- Personal referrals
- Corporate relocation referrals
- National referral organizations
- Open houses
- For Sale signs

Advertising

Advertising, a major part of marketing, falls beyond the scope of this section.

Product Knowledge

Intimate knowledge of the home is not only a prerequisite of successful marketing but also a sign of professionalism. The Listing Data checklists (see Checklist section) provide the data you need to market almost any type of real estate.

Servicing the Listing

An essential part of servicing the listing entails

- constant communication with the seller;
- adjusting the listing price, if needed;
- making sure landscaping, exterior and interior of the home are in top condition;
- preparing the best possible financing packages for the typical buyer;
- exposing the property to the market through all available channels;
- enthusiastically discussing the listing at every opportunity; and
- for the vacant house, insurance requirements, lights, water, maintenance, and so on.

SELLING TECHNIQUES

Agency Relationships

Definitions

Agency A relationship in which one person (the agent) is authorized to act on behalf of the best interests of another (the principal or client) in business dealings with third persons.

Fiduciary A person in a position of trust and confidence.

Agent's fiduciary duties to a principal Obligations a fiduciary owes to a principal under the law of agency include loyalty; obedience to (lawful) instructions; and honesty, full disclosure, utmost care and diligence in working for the principal's best interests within the scope of business for which he or she has been retained. An agent must avoid any conflicts of interest that might compromise his or her undivided loyalty. An agent is duty bound to disclose to his or her principal all relevant information concerning the agency relationship and to protect the principal's confidences (such as a seller's confidentially expressed willingness to sell below the listed price or a buyer-client's confidentially expressed willingness to pay a price higher than is offered.)

Real Estate Agency Alternatives

Subagency versus Buyer Agency. This is, of course, a policy choice for the broker to make.

Until April 1992, traditional MLS policy in most states was a blanket unilateral offer of subagency, making any MLS member automatically a subagent of the seller, unless subagency was specifically rejected.

On April 28, 1992, NAR changed its MLS policy to delete the mandatory offer of subagency and make offers of subagency optional. Participants submitting listings to the MLS must, however, offer cooperation to other MLS participants in the form of subagency or cooperation with buyer-agents or both. All offers of subagency or cooperation made through an MLS must include an offer of compensation.

While subagency in the MLS has a definite marketing advantage to sellers, it also creates liability because a seller is bound by the acts, representations and misrepresentations of a subagent. Thus, the new MLS policy of optional subagency offers a choice to reject subagency to both sellers and MLS members—to sellers because they may not want the added liability that goes hand in hand with subagency, to agents who may prefer to represent buyers rather than be subagents of sellers.

Subagency. A seller's agent (and subagent) under a listing agreement with the seller acts as the agent for the seller only. A seller's agent has the following obligations to the seller:

- A fiduciary duty of loyalty, utmost care, integrity and honesty in dealings with the seller
- A duty to obey all lawful instructions from the seller within scope of authority
- A duty not to disclose confidential information that may weaken the seller's bargaining position
- A duty to disclose
  - the identity of all potential buyers.
  - information about what price or terms the buyer may be willing to offer other than those contained in the written offer.
  - the buyer's intention to subdivide or resell property at a profit.
  - any business or family relationship between agent and buyer.

A seller's agent has the following obligations to a buyer:

- Diligent exercise of reasonable skill and care in the performance of the agent's duties
- A duty of honest and fair dealing and good faith
- A statutory duty to present all offers
- A duty to disclose all facts known to the agent materially affecting the value or desirability of the

property that are not known to, or within the diligent attention and observation of, the parties (including disclosure of material facts the broker knew or should have known)

- A duty to verify critical information received from the seller

SUGGESTION: To avoid falling into the trap of accidental undisclosed dual agency, it would be well for agents to caution buyers to avoid any discussion of what they might be willing to pay or anything they would not tell the seller directly.

Buyer Agency. A selling agent can enter into an agreement with a buyer to represent the buyer only. As such, the agent is not the agent or subagent of the seller.

A buyer's agent has the following obligations to the buyer:

- A fiduciary duty of loyalty, utmost care, integrity and honesty in dealings with the buyer
- A duty to obey all lawful instructions from the buyer within scope of authority
- A duty not to disclose confidential information that may weaken the buyer's bargaining position
- A duty to disclose
  - information about what price or terms a seller might be willing to accept other than the listed price or terms.
  - any facts relating to the urgency of seller's need to dispose of the property.
  - the length of time the property has been on the market and any other offers or counteroffers that have been made on the property.
  - all facts known to the agent materially affecting the value or desirability of the property that are not known to, or within the diligent attention and observation of, the buyer.
  - any business or family relationship between agent and seller.

Buyer-Broker Contract. Unless the buyer employs his or her own agent to protect and represent him or her, the buyer is without adequate representation. The buyer retains the agent for the purpose of locating property acceptable to the buyer and conducting negotiations on the buyer's behalf. The agent must advise the seller and the seller's agent that he or she is the agent of the buyer and not the agent of the seller.

The greatest benefit to a buyer in employing his or her own agent is that the buyer's best interests are represented in negotiations with sellers. Another important benefit is that the agent's search for the right property for the buyer is no longer limited to listed properties. Because his or her fee is protected, a buyer's agent can negotiate on properties that are for sale by owner or seek out properties that are not on the market or are in foreclosure or probate.

Buyer's Choice. After explaining subagency and buyer agency, an agent should offer the buyers a choice: "I can represent the sellers, or I can represent you as the buyers. Which do you prefer?"

Dual Agency. Dual agency situations can arise with in-house sales if a buyer-client, represented by one of the broker's agents, becomes interested in one of the broker's listings. A real estate broker can legally be the agent of both the seller and the buyer in a transaction, provided full disclosure is made and both parties give their informed consent. Because the seller and buyer in a transaction have conflicts of interest, the dual agent can only act as an intermediary between them. Provided both parties give their informed consent to such limited agency, the broker is obligated not to disclose any information of a confidential nature that could harm one party's bargaining position or benefit the other's.

SELLING GOALS

Striving toward a goal makes your selling efforts more exciting and more effective. The following format enables you to estimate what you need to do in order to achieve your goal.

Based on last year's commissions [A], number of transactions [B], estimated number of appointments

[C], and contracts [E], you can establish the earnings value per transaction [H], per appointment [I] and per contract [J].

Now establish a commission goal [K], and calculate the number of transactions, appointments and contacts needed to achieve your commission goal.

The example below assumes 5 working days per week and 50 working weeks per year.

Commissions earned last year: $48,000   [A]
Number of transactions* last year: 24   [B]
Est. appointments†/week last year: 8   [C]
Est. appointments†/year last year:
  [C × 50 wks] = 400   [D]
Est. contacts‡/day last year: 10   [E]
Est. contacts‡/week last year:
  [E × 5 days] = 50   [F]
Est. contacts‡/year last year:
  [F × 50 wks] = 2500   [G]
Earnings value/trans.: [A ÷ B] = $2,000   [H]
Earnings value/appt.: [A ÷ D] = $120   [I]
Earnings value/contact.: [A ÷ G] = $19.20   [J]
Commission goal: $60,000   [K]
Transactions/yr needed to achieve goal:
  [K ÷ H] = 30   [L]
Appointments/yr needed to achieve goal:
  [K ÷ I] = 500   [M]
Appointments/wk needed to achieve goal:
  [M ÷ 50 wks] = 10   [N]
Contacts/yr needed to achieve goal:
  [K ÷ J] = 3,125   [O]
Contacts/wk needed to achieve goal:
  [O ÷ 50 wks] = 62.5   [P]
Contacts/day needed to achieve goal:
  [P ÷ 5 days] = 12.5   [Q]

*Transactions (for the purpose of this calculation) means your sale of another listing, or your listing sold by another. Your sale of your own listing would count as two transactions.

†Appointment means an appointment to show property or to discuss a listing.

‡Contact means talking to anyone about real estate, either in person or by phone.

Summary:

You need 12.5 contacts on average per day (5 working days per week) to obtain 10 appointments each week (working 50 weeks per year) to make 30 transactions to earn $60,000 per year.

SOURCES OF BUYERS

- Past clients
- Relatives
- Acquaintances
- Referrals
- Service people (professionals, trades people, etc.)
- Farming owners
- Farming tenants
- Relocation services
- Neighbors of listings
- Ad and sign calls
- Walk-ins
- Open houses
- Investors
- Enrollees at your investment seminars
- Groups such as homeowners' association, PTA , Little League, service clubs, etc.

TIME MANAGEMENT IN SELLING

Because time is the most valuable commodity a real estate professional has to offer, its effective control is essential to success.

Distinguish Real Buyers from Shoppers

Identify shoppers quickly or you will waste precious time. A serious buyer

- is motivated, ready, willing and able to enter and fulfill a contract;
- will be prompt and forthright in providing needed information (for loan qualification, family needs, etc.);

- has specific reasons for buying;
- has a time frame for buying a home; and
- will accept the concept of fair market value.

Qualify Your Prospects
- Determine what price range the prospect can afford.
- Discover the prospect's real needs and tastes. People often end up buying homes quite different from what they originally specified.

Show Fewer Properties to More Buyers
Preview the market before making a sales presentation. It is less time consuming, more professional and more effective than wasting your buyers' time by dragging them needlessly from house to house.

Maintain a Priority List
- List your activities in priority groups (A, B and C).
- Use the list each evening to plan the next day.
- Consult it often, especially between appointments or during lulls in your business day.

Plan Your Day
- Schedule your appointments, important phone calls, and so forth the previous evening.
- Use your priority list to fill in.
- Schedule 65% of your time working directly with motivated buyers and sellers, 10% prospecting for potential buyers and sellers, 15% preparation time and 10% for professional development.

Use Every Minute of Your Day
- Start your day early.
- Read the classifieds.
- In case of floor time, read and clip the company ads and search for comparable listings.

- Listen to educational cassettes while driving to and from work.
- Carry education or professional reading material in case you are kept waiting.

The Makings of a Superstar Sales Agent

- Superstars determine a buyer's motivation at first contact; they don't waste precious time working with poorly motivated buyers without deadlines.
- Superstars qualify a buyer's ability to afford what they want as soon as possible; they don't waste time working with buyers who won't accept the concept of fair market value.
- Superstars have done their homework; they know their market.

QUALIFYING THE BUYER

Prequalifying Questions

A prospect's time frame and reason for buying are the most important clues for telling a real buyer from a shopper.

- How soon do they need occupancy?
- Do they own or rent?
- How many in their family live with them?
- Do they have to sell their present home before they purchase?
- Do they have their home listed with another real estate broker?
- What price range do they have in mind?
- How much have they set aside for an initial investment?
- How much have they budgeted for monthly loan payments?
- How long have they been looking?
- Are they looking for a house as an investment?

Before taking a prospect on a home showing tour, it is highly recommended to have a further qualifying session to establish a realistic price range. Explain to the prospects the need for obtaining answers to a number of questions prior to looking at homes in the interest of saving them valuable time and zeroing in on the right home. The more you know about the buyer's needs, family, likes and dislikes, living style, background and financial situation, the better equipped you will be to help them. It is, therefore, important to establish a pleasant, frank relationship. Meeting buyers in their home can provide valuable clues about their living style.

At this stage, it is not practical nor possible to gather all the information a lender needs to underwrite a loan. However, what you can determine is the buyer's stable income, recurring monthly obligations and funds available for down payment. You should be familiar with the debt-to-income ratios for the type of financing prevalent in your area (FHA, VA, Fannie Mae, Freddie Mac).

For detailed information, please refer to Loan Underwriting and Qualifying Ratios under Conventional, FHA and VA in the "Financing" section.

KNOWING THE MARKET

Knowing your market is not only your obligation to your clients, it is essential to a successful selling career.

- Be informed about every aspect of your listings and the needs of your sellers.
- Have a working knowledge of every property listed by your company.
- On a regular basis, drive by and inspect as many other brokers' listings within your farm and/or within the realm of your specialty as practicable.
- Inspect new listings of interest to any of your prospective buyers.

FLOOR CALL TECHNIQUES

Advertising is by far the biggest item on most brokers' budgets, so each ad call represents more dollars than most agents realize.

Advance Preparation

Prepare an ad sheet, and be sure you have familiarized yourself with these properties as well. Inspect them prior to your floor time.

Objective

- The primary purpose is to get an appointment.
- You must show excitement about a property to make your client want to see it.
- Follow your answers with your own qualifying questions—then be a good listener.

General Telephone Tips

- The purpose of the call is to get an appointment!
- Keep calls short and simple.
- Keep asking qualifying questions beginning with how, what, when, where, why, who or which; such questions prompt specific answers whereas questions beginning with are, is, have or do merely require a yes or no answer.
- Listen carefully—do not occupy yourself with anything but paying attention to what the other person has to say.
- Never interrupt or finish someone's sentence.
- Know when to stop talking.
- Never argue.
- Speak into the mouthpiece so your words are clearly heard.
- Smile while talking on the telephone.
- Remember to use *please* and *thank you*.
- Frequently use the words *you* and the person's name.
- Pronounce names correctly—always ask if in doubt.
- Do not put a client on hold if you can possibly help it.
- Never hang up first. Wait for your client to hang up the phone.
- If you call at an inconvenient time, apologize and reschedule.

- Wrap up a conversation as soon as you have an appointment.
- End a call politely if the prospect is not interested.

Effective Words and Phrases To Use

- *You* and a person's name pronounced correctly (ask if in doubt) are sweet music in the listener's ear; use them often.
- Use *please* and *thank you*.
- Thank the prospect for his or her time.
- Thank the prospect for waiting.

Openers

Begin with a friendly, casual greeting.

- "Mrs. Whitmore, good evening. I'm with Sunshine Realty here in Westlake. My name is Terry Ross. Do you have a minute to talk?"
- "Hello, is Mr. Goodman at home? Mr. Goodman, my name is Patricia Riley, do you have a moment on the phone?"
- "Mr. Bentley, I'm Tammy Bowman with Star Realty. Did you receive my letter?"

How to Talk on the Phone with a Prospect

- "Good morning, Star Realty. How can I help you?"
- "Yes, that's one of the best listings we've had in the area, let me pull the detail folder for you. By the way, I'm Julie Goodman, who am I speaking with?"
- "By the way my name is. . . , and your name please?"
- "Incidentally, if you have any other ads circled in your paper, I could save time by checking them out. I can report back to you within the hour. We cooperate with all brokers and there would be no cost or obligation. If you would just read the ads to me please."
- "May I show you the home now or would this afternoon be better?"

- "Let me give you my home phone number, in case you need to call after office hours . . . What's your number?"

Make an Outline of Topics that Will Stir the Prospect's Interest

- Talk about prospects' hobbies, children, schools, college and their homes. Get to know people.
- Offer free home evaluations.
- Offer financing and refinancing information.
- Discuss income property.
- Discuss the possibility for renters to own a home.
- Remember to ask for referrals of friends or relatives who may be moving.
- Offer to answer questions concerning real estate.

What if the Caller Wants the Address?

A problem most agents have to deal with is the buyer who keeps asking for the address of the property. Because giving out the address means essentially losing the prospect, the trick is to obtain an appointment without giving out an address.

Demonstrated below is a telephone dialogue between a most persistent buyer wanting to know the address of the property advertised and a real estate agent equally determined to obtain an appointment without giving the address. Notice how the agent follows each answer with a significant question (underlined).

Agent: **Good morning, Blue Sky Realtors, how may I help you?**

Buyer: I'm calling on your ad in . . . .

Agent: **Oh, I'm glad you called. This is one of the more interesting homes we have had in this area.**

Buyer: What's the address?

Agent: **If you'll pardon me for just a moment, I'll get the folder that has all the information.**

By the way, my name is Fred Drake. May I ask your name?

Buyer: Mr. Friendly.

Agent: **Mr. Friendly,** when we listed this home we searched the market to find other properties for sale similar to this one. I think you will be interested in seeing one or two of these. But before I take up your time in giving you the details of these homes, let me just ask you a few questions that will help me to understand your needs. (Fill in the answers on your sheet).

Buyer: What is the price?

Agent: **$..., what price range did you have in mind?**

Buyer: What down payment?

Agent: **What did you have available as an initial investment? Do you have to sell your present home before you purchase?**

Buyer: How many bedrooms?

Agent: **This home has four bedrooms. May I ask how many you have in your family living with you?**

Buyer: Where is the property located?

Agent: **(Give general area; near college, park, major intersection, etc.—do not give the address.) Is this an area you would consider?**

Buyer: Yes.

Agent: **May I show you the home now or would this afternoon be better?**

Buyer: What is the exact address?

Agent: **I would be glad to give you the address; however, one of the conditions of our contract with the sellers is that we accompany each client to their home. I would be glad to show it to you now, or this afternoon between two** and three. <u>Which time would be more convenient for you?</u>

Buyer: I just want to drive by the property.

Agent: **It's always a good idea to see the exterior of a home first as well as the neighborhood. <u>When do you plan to drive by?</u>**

Buyer: Oh, say 5 P.M.

Agent: **Fine, in order to save you time, I'll be available at 5 P.M. to answer any questions you may have about this home. <u>Shall I pick you up or would you prefer to stop by the office?</u>**

Buyer: I would prefer to drive by the home myself first.

Agent: **Mr. Friendly, maybe this home is not for you . . . but then again, maybe it is. . . . The only way I can assist you is to show you a home and let you tell me your likes and dislikes. <u>After all, it is difficult to determine your true needs over the telephone, isn't it?</u>**

Buyer: I don't have time to look with you.

Agent: **I understand your frustration. Buying a home is an important decision, one that takes a great deal of time. When you are busy time is hard to find. Printed detailed information on several homes as well as professional guidance can save you time and money. <u>Where would you like me to mail this information?</u>**

Buyer: The last broker showed me a bunch of real dogs. Are you going to waste my time?

Agent: **Mr. Friendly, to assure you that your time will not be wasted, I'll prepare detailed information on several excellent homes that fit your requirements. I'll drop these off for your consideration before you visit the properties. <u>What is your address and phone number?</u>**

Buyer: I prefer not to give you my phone number. I don't want to be hounded.

Agent: **I know how you feel. No one likes to be pressured. However, I feel that over eager selling is an unnecessary act. The important skill I can offer you is to find the home you want and show you how you can own it. <u>Suppose such a home becomes available tomorrow, how can I reach you?</u>**

Buyer: I only want information. I have my own broker.

Agent: **May I suggest it sounds as if you need a broker, one that will do the work for you. <u>Are there any other ads you would like information on? I'd be happy to obtain the information for you and call you back if you would let me know how I can get in touch with you.</u>**

SHOWING THE HOME

Preparation

You have determined the buyers' price range and have discovered their true needs and tastes. In the interest of professionalism, it is your job to search the market before making a sales presentation. As a result, you will show fewer homes to more satisfied buyers. Try not to present more than three homes at any one session.

Bear in mind that most homebuyers base their decision primarily on emotion. They often purchase homes entirely different from their original specifications, so do not hesitate introducing them to a home you feel would suit their fancy even though it is not what they said they were looking for.

Ask the buyer to take notes. Let them know that you will be discussing with them what they liked most, what they liked least, what they would change ... and that before looking at another home they will be eliminating one property. That means they are constantly selecting a property, and when they have found the right one, you'll be able to say, "I think we've found your home ... Let's see how it looks on paper."

Planning

- Plan appointments to allow enough time between properties.
- Obtain keys of lock-box combinations, where needed.
- Arrange for the home to look inviting—lights on, draperies open, soft music, a roaring fire in the fireplace in the winter, windows open or air-conditioning on in the summer.
- Decide on the sequence in which to show the homes you have selected.
  - Showing your best choice last generally works better with buyers who are inexperienced and need to be educated or buyers who have not looked before and need to compare homes in the area before making a decision.
  - Showing the best choice first, and additional homes only if necessary, is the correct method for buyers who are familiar with the market and know what they want.
- Select the route and approach to the property that shows off the home to its best advantage.

On the Way to the Home

- Meet the buyers (preferably both of them if there are two) at your office or pick them up at their home. Do not meet them at the property.
- At this time, confirm your agency relationship with the buyers (if required by state law).
- Do not tell your buyers how many homes you have selected to show them (you may not want to show more once you have found the right one).
- Set them at ease by making them feel you will stay at their side in their search for the right home.

Let them know your feelings are not hurt by negative comments.
- Keep asking qualifying questions.
- On the way to the home tell them about people living in the neighborhood, community, schools, shopping centers and transportation. Remember to disclose obvious negatives.
- Parking across the street often provides the best position from which to favorably display the setting and exterior of the home.

Let the Buyers Discover the Home

- If the sellers are home, introduce the buyers.
- Precede the buyers to the area of the home you want them to see first. It is usually a good idea to save the most attractive part of the home until last.
- Let them discover the home at their own pace.
- Keep quiet, except to point out features that are not obvious.
- Observe and listen carefully for any positive or negative reactions and comments.
- Make mental notes for later use in closing.
- If they show signs of real interest, encourage them to go through the home again, and leave them alone.
- If they show signs that this is not the house they want, cut the inspection short. Do it in a manner that will not hurt the sellers feelings.
- If they don't know, try to make them decide. "How soon will you know? . . . How will you know?"

Tips

- If the home is occupied, knock on bedroom doors before entering.
- Do not stand in the way of a scenic view.
- Do not argue if the buyers voice objections.
- If you answer objections, do it in the form of a question.

OBTAINING THE OFFER

At this point, you have identified the prospects as real buyers with a strong motivation to purchase; you have successfully established a relationship of trust, qualified the buyers and found them a home they like. The culmination of these actions should simply be the writing and signing of an offer to purchase.

For most of us, the purchase of a home is a big decision and it usually takes some type of initiative by the agent to get the process started, such as:

- "I can tell you love the house. You do, don't you? Shall I write it up?"
- "Why don't we make them an offer?"
- "I have the impression this is the home you want. Right?"
- "You like the house, don't you? Let's see what it looks like on paper."

Whether you are sitting at a kitchen table or at a computer in your office, simply ask the questions you need answered to fill in the blanks of the deposit receipt and start writing. Once completed, review the offer with the buyers and hand it to them, with a pen, for the signature. It's as simple as that.

What if They Cannot Decide?

There may be valid reasons why the house is not right for your buyers. If that is the case, find out the reasons and search for another home. In most cases, however, the indecision is caused by a fear of making a decision. This is a normal reaction and may be easily resolved by using one of these proven methods:

- Repeat previously acknowledged benefits.
  - "How important is the quality of the schools to you?"
  - "Would you agree this is the only home you've seen that has the spaciousness and privacy your family needs?"
  - "Didn't you mention that the proximity to shopping and transportation would mean the need for only one car?"

- "I'm afraid you're not the only people attracted by the comfortable family room with its cozy fireplace and the pleasant patio to spend a cool evening. It wouldn't be the first time more than one buyer makes an offer on a house, which would put you at a serious negotiating disadvantage."
- Use the Ben Franklin approach.
  Assist the client in making a decision by weighing the advantages against the disadvantages, a method used by Ben Franklin and referred to as the Ben Franklin method. Divide a sheet of paper in two by drawing a vertical line in the center with a horizontal line at the top. Write the heading REASONS FOR on the left and REASONS AGAINST on the right. Then help the client list all the reasons for buying the home on the left side of the sheet and the reasons against buying on the right. If the reasons against buying outweigh those in favor, you will probably need to find another house. If the opposite occurs, you might say, "It sure seems the reasons in favor of buying outweigh those against. Shall we go ahead?"

PREPARING THE OFFER AND COUNTEROFFER

Please refer to Legal Aspects of Contract Preparation and Purchase Agreements in the Contract Clauses section.

Need for Property Inspections and Disclosures

Real estate brokers and agents have always been responsible for faithfully representing the condition of a property without concealing any known defects. In the 1980s, the courts and legislatures of various states, notably California, required brokers and agents to inspect a property for any visible defects—also called red flags—that may affect its value or desirability and of making appropriate disclosures to prospective buyers.

NEGOTIATING THE TRANSACTION

If you are the selling agent, you should call the listing agent as soon as you have a signed deposit receipt and request an appointment with the seller to present the offer. As a general rule, letting the seller know the price and terms of an offer on the telephone is not recommended. Therefore, the listing agent would be wise to have a secretary or an associate call the seller for the appointment because that person can honestly say he or she has no knowledge of the terms of the offer.

Preparation for Presentation of the Offer

The listing agent should ask himself or herself these questions:

- Is it a fair offer?
- What does my comparative market analysis say?
- Have market conditions changed?
- Have I prepared a seller's proceeds sheet?
- Am I thoroughly familiar with the details of the offer—price, terms, dates of closing and occupancy, etc.?
- What are the benefits of the offer?
- Is the possibility of a slightly higher price worth the burden of keeping the home on the market?
- Can I honestly recommend this offer to the seller?
- What is my agency relationship with the seller? Whom do I represent?

Tips

- Select a quiet room with plenty of light such as kitchen or dining room, where you will undisturbed by children, TV or radio.
- Never seat yourself between husband and wife.

Presenting the Offer

- Tell the sellers about the buyers; portray them as real people with real needs, not as someone waiting to take advantage of them.
- Tell the seller how you obtained the offer, that the buyers were interested in several homes but finally favored this one.
- Point out the benefits of the offer.
- Ask if the possibility of a slightly higher price is worth the burden of keeping the home on the market.
- The benefits of a second mortgage, if offered, include:
  - High interest
  - Security commensurate with a buyer's cash investment
  - A buyer's credit check by the lender
  - Its use as collateral
  - Its potential sale to an investor for cash at a discount (refer to yield Tables with Examples in the *Realty Bluebook® Financial Tables*).
- If sellers stall, are undecided, need more information, object or give reason why they can't accept, ask:

  "I can respect (appreciate). . . ."

  "Does that mean. . . ?"

  "Other than. . . , is there anything else preventing you from. . . ?"

  "If I could. . . , would you. . . ?"
- If seller wants to think it over:
  - Ask what part of the proposal they are uncomfortable with.
  - Point out the buyers may also be thinking it over and have the right to withdraw the offer.
- Get seller to accept, reject or counter.
- If the offer contains provisions not in the best interest of the sellers, it is your obligation to recommend a counteroffer with the necessary corrections.

- It is not only your obligation to represent the best interest of the sellers, it is also good business sense. After all, you want their referral business.
- If the offer is unacceptable in its present form, try to obtain a counteroffer on the best possible terms.

Multiple Offers

Occasionally, more than one offer is received simultaneously on the same property. In such an event, each offer should be presented separately by only the listing agent and the respective selling agent. If one of the offers is procured by the listing agent, the broker or manager of the listing office should take his or her place.

Also refer to Multiple Counteroffers in Section B, Contract Clauses.

TRANSACTION FOLLOW-THROUGH

Reiterating a statement from earlier in this section: Personal referrals account for almost half the listings generated, according to national statistics. Without conscientiously taking care of your clients' interests until the transaction is successfully completed, all the good efforts put forth so far may be wasted.

Much detail work needs to be done to ascertain that all conditions of the contract are carried out in a proper and timely fashion. Many brokers find it profitable to have trained staff assist the agent with most of this detail work. This method enables the agent to remain in touch with the client until the transaction is satisfactorily completed while at the same time allowing him or her to do more productive activities.

CHECKLISTS

To receive advance notice of the
next *Realty Bluebook*® edition
(and information about
what's new), please call
1-800-322-8621
to register your name and address.

CONTENTS

CHECKLISTS

CHECKLISTS

RESPA INFO TO LENDER WITH COMMITMENT REQUEST

- ☐ Copy sales contract
- ☐ Name of escrow holder with buyers' and sellers' fees
- ☐ Name of title company with buyers' and sellers' fees
- ☐ Commission split information
- ☐ Name, address and phone number of buyer
- ☐ Request lender to delete from seller's copy of advance disclosure statement confidential information of concern only to the buyer and vice versa
- ☐ Request lender to allow agent to look over advance disclosure statement before mailing to principals
- ☐ Request copy of statement to be mailed to broker
- ☐ Title report, if available
- ☐ Pest control report, if available

CHECKLIST OF BUYER'S CLOSING COSTS

Nonrecurring Costs

- [ ] Title insurance (where payable by buyer)
- [ ] Escrow fee (where applicable)
- [ ] Legal fee (where applicable)
- [ ] Survey fee (where applicable)
- [ ] Loan fee
- [ ] Appraisal fee
- [ ] Tax service
- [ ] Credit report
- [ ] Notary fee
- [ ] Recording fee
- [ ] Pest control inspection
- [ ] Document preparation fee
- [ ] Review fee
- [ ] Application fee
- [ ] Underwriting fee
- [ ] Courier fee
- [ ] Verification fee
- [ ] Warehousing fee

Recurring Costs

- [ ] Hazard insurance
- [ ] Trust fund or impound account
- [ ] Prorated taxes (if paid beyond recordation)
- [ ] Prorated interest (if charged in arrears, to end of month; if charged in advance, to date of first payment)

Credits, If Any

- [ ] Prorated taxes (if not paid to recordation)
- [ ] Prorated rents, if any
- [ ] Security deposits on hand, if any

CHECKLIST OF SELLER'S CLOSING COSTS AND CREDITS

Costs

- ☐ Selling commission
- ☐ Title insurance (where payable by seller)
- ☐ Escrow fee (where applicable)
- ☐ Survey fee (where applicable)
- ☐ Legal fee (where applicable)
- ☐ Prepayment penalty, if any
- ☐ State or local revenue stamps or transfer tax, if any
- ☐ Pest control inspection fee, in case of VA loan
- ☐ Pest control work, if any
- ☐ Recording fee
- ☐ FHA or VA points, if any
- ☐ Forwarding fee
- ☐ Reconveyance fees (on any deeds of trust to be reconveyed)
- ☐ Notary fee
- ☐ Prorated taxes (if not paid to date of recordation)
- ☐ Personal property tax
- ☐ Interest, if paid in arrears (from date of last payment to date of recordation)
- ☐ Prorated rents, if any
- ☐ Security deposits on hand, if any

Credits

- ☐ Interest, if paid in advance (from recordation to date of next loan payment)
- ☐ Refund existing trust fund (impound account), if any
- ☐ Prorated taxes (if paid beyond recordation)

ESCROW CHECKLIST FOR SELLING BROKER

- ☐ Obtain increase of deposit
- ☐ Open an escrow
- ☐ Order credit report on buyer (if required)
- ☐ Order pest control inspection
- ☐ Order other inspections (roof, etc., if required)
- ☐ Check on any contingencies to be eliminated
- ☐ Check occupancy permit
- ☐ Order loan commitment
- ☐ Assist buyer with loan application and submit to lender
- ☐ Arrange for hazard insurance
- ☐ Have closing instructions prepared and signed by buyer

ESCROW CHECKLIST FOR LISTING BROKER

- ☐ Notice of sale to multiple listing office
- ☐ Check on increase of deposit
- ☐ Examine preliminary title report and assist in eliminating clouds on the title, if any
- ☐ Check on any contingencies to be eliminated
- ☐ Request title or escrow company to order payoff demand or statement of condition and assumption papers from lender(s)
- ☐ Check with selling office on buyer's loan
- ☐ If income property, obtain: rent schedule, rent due dates, security deposits, copies of leases, names and phone numbers of tenants
- ☐ Have seller's instructions prepared and signed
- ☐ If seller carries a second loan, have seller record a request for copy of notice of default and subscribe to a tax agency
- ☐ Obtain seller's future address and phone number

DATA CHECKLIST FOR SINGLE-FAMILY DWELLINGS

1	Date information was obtained
2	Property location
3	Type of home
100	**OWNERSHIP**
101	Owner's name, address (if other than above), residence phone, business phone
102	Occupation
103	Title vested in (list all persons having an interest in the title)
104	To inspect property
105	Acquisition date/cost of acquisition
106	Previously listed/how long/at what price
107	Reason for selling/degree of urgency
108	Date occupancy can be given
200	**LOCATION**
201	Nearest cross street
202	District/subdistrict/tract
203	Public transportation
204	Shopping facilities
205	Schools (elementary, junior high, high school, college, private)
206	Churches
207	Recreational facilities
208	View
300	**Site**
301	Lot size
302	Corner
303	Zoning
304	Legal description
305	Utilities and street improvements in
306	Yard (front, rear)/fenced/condition
307	Patio/lanai
308	Lawn sprinklers
309	Pool
310	Condition of grounds
400	**IMPROVEMENTS**
401	Estimated age
402	Style
403	Attached or detached

404	Type and quality of construction
405	Builder
406	Exterior finish/condition
407	Stories/levels
408	Type of roof/condition
409	Basement
410	Garage/number of cars
411	Storage space
412	Wiring (110 or 220 volt)/condition
413	Plumbing (copper or galvanized)/condition
414	Sewer
415	Type of heating
416	Air-conditioning
417	Insulation
418	Weather stripping
419	Type of flooring
420	Window screens
421	Storm windows
422	Intercom system
500	**INTERIOR**
501	Floor plan
502	Square footage of living space
503	Number of bedrooms/sizes
504	Number of bathrooms/tubs/stall showers/ over tub showers
505	Living room/size/fireplace
506	Dining room/size/separate or combination
507	Breakfast room
508	Family room/social room
509	Kitchen/gas or electric/built-in range or oven/disposal/dishwasher/other
510	Laundry room
511	Carpeting
512	Draperies
513	Other personal property included/inventory
514	Unusual extras
515	Interior condition
600	**EXISTING FINANCING** (List first and junior liens)
601	Loan balance/as of what date

602	Monthly payments (taxes and insurance included)
603	Interest rate
604	Lender/address/phone number
605	Loan number
605-A	Loan owned by FNMA
605-B	Blended interest rate
606	Prepayment penalty
607	Transferable/assumption fee/can loan be taken subject to
608	Due date/balloon payment
609	Original amount/term/year of inception
610	If there is a second loan, can it be bought at a discount/what discount
611	Improvement bond/prepayment penalty
700	**POTENTIAL FINANCING**
701	Loan commitment/amount/term/interest/ payments/loan fee/lender
702	Will seller pay FHA or VA points?
703	Will seller help finance? If so, amount/ interest/monthly pay-off rate/due date
704	Is seller interested in installment sale
800	**COMPETITIVE MARKET ANALYSIS**
801	For sale now
802	Sold past year
803	Expired past year
900	**PRICE**
901	Listed price
902	Predicted probable sale price (Use comparative market approach)
903	Possible rental value
904	Taxes 19__/19__
905	Assessed value

Address	Style	Bedrooms	Baths	Family room	Electric kitchen	View	Pool	Other	Number of days on market	List price	Sale price	Terms

CONDOMINIUM BUYER'S CHECKLIST

1. Hazard and liability insurance included in association fee? What limits of liability?
2. Amount of association fee. Is fee guaranteed fixed for a certain period?
3. In case of a resale unit, check with the association regarding possible problems with the unit, such as unapproved changes or alterations, delinquent fees, etc.
4. Common areas owned or leased?
5. Is maintenance budget realistic?
6. Obtain comprehensive listing of which items are standard and which are optional.
7. If purchase includes extras, obtain written work orders with price quotations signed by a responsible person.
8. Check completion date of unit and common areas. Are penalties provided for delay in completion?
9. Security: intercom, closed-circuit TV?
10. Parking space designated, ample, how close to unit? Guest parking?
11. Storage space ample?
12. Soundproofing adequate?
13. Warranties covering structural defects, equipment, systems and appliances in effect until what date?
14. In case of a conversion, obtain copy of engineer's report on condition of building and its equipment (roof, foundations, heating and cooling systems, elevators, plumbing and electrical systems).
15. Restrictions, if any, on owner's right to resell? Does the association have the right of first refusal?
16. Check restrictions imposed by the declaration of condominium (children, pets, storage of recreational vehicles or boats in common areas or driveways, advertising signs, architectural alterations, etc.).

Condominium Documents

☐ C&R's or declaration of condominium (also referred to as master regulations or master deed). The declaration authorizes the board of directors of the owners' association, through the bylaws, to manage the affairs of the development with regard to the common areas and facilities.

The declaration establishes the ratio of each unit to the total of all units affecting the assessments for common expenses, votes in the association and real estate taxes apportioned to each unit. The declaration further deals with the description of the units and the common areas, common expenses, the owners' and the association's obligations, use restrictions, options in case of partial or total destruction, rules for amending the declaration, remedies for violation of the declaration and termination of the condominium by the members.

☐ Bylaws of the association of owners set forth certain rules and regulations for the internal government of the condominium development.

☐ Financial statement of the association

☐ Operating budget and schedule of monthly assessments

☐ Regulatory agreement, used only in FHA-financed condominium projects.

☐ Engineer's report on condition of building and equipment in case of a condominium conversion.

In addition, state law may require other documents, such as:

☐ Articles of incorporation of the owners' association

☐ Final subdivision report

DATA CHECKLIST FOR MANUFACTURED (MOBILE) HOMES

1	Date information obtained
2	Property location
3	Type/brand name
100	**OWNERSHIP**
101	Registered owner(s)
102	Legal owner's name, address and phone number
103	Title vested in (list all persons having an interest in title)
104	Title information/serial number, year, model, license number
105	How to inspect property
106	Acquisition date and cost
107	If previously listed, for how long and at what price
108	Reason for selling/degree of urgency
109	Date occupancy can be given
200	**LOCATION**
201	Name of park
202	Address
203	Space
204	Public transportation
205	Shopping facilities
206	Schools (elementary, junior high, high, college, private)
207	Churches
208	Recreation facilities, clubhouse, pool, playground
300	**SITE**
301	Park/poor, standard, excellent
302	Children
303	Pets
304	Number of spaces/% occupancy
305	Space rental cost
306	Manager's name and phone number
307	Laundry/showers
400	**IMPROVEMENTS**
401	Estimated age

402	Brand name, manufacturer, year, width, length
403	Construction quality/economy, average, good, custom
404	Skirting
405	Patio size
406	Carport size
407	Window awnings/number
408	Front porch/size/awnings
409	Rear porch/size/awnings
410	Hitch/detachable/missing
500	**INTERIOR**
501	Square footage
502	Bedrooms
503	Bathrooms/shower/tub
504	Living room
505	Dining/breakfast area
506	Kitchen/gas or electric
507	Appliances and equipment/refrigerator, range, oven, dishwasher, disposal, other
508	Air conditioner/serial number and tonnage
509	Furniture
600	**EXISTING FINANCING**
	(List all loans)
601	Loan balance/date
602	Monthly payments
603	Interest rate
604	Lender/address/phone number
605	Loan numbers
606	Prepayment penalty
607	Transferable/assumption fee/Can loan be taken subject to?
608	Balloon payment/due date
609	Original amount/term/year of inception
610	If there is a second, can it be bought at a discount?
700	**POTENTIAL FINANCING**
701	Loan commitment/amount/term/interest/ payments/loan fee lender
702	Will seller pay points?

703 Will seller help finance, and if so, under
what terms and conditions?

800 COMPETITIVE MARKET ANALYSIS

Address - Park	Brand name - Year	Width - Length	Bedrooms	Baths	Appliances	Other	How long on market	List price	Sale price	Terms

801 For sale now
802 Sold past year
803 Expired past year
900 PRICE
901 Listed
902 Probable sale price
903 Possible rental value
904 Taxes

DATA CHECKLIST FOR APARTMENT HOUSES

1	Date information was obtained
2	Property location
3	Number of units
100	**OWNERSHIP**
101	Owner's name, address, residence phone, business phone
102	Owner's occupation
103	Property operated by owner or manager/manager's duties
104	Title vested in (list all persons having an interest in the title)
105	Adjusted basis/depreciation reduction/depreciation method/useful life
106	Owner's tax bracket/legal status
107	Owner's attorney/tax counsel/accountant
108	Resident manager's name, apartment number, phone number
109	To inspect property
110	Acquisition date/cost of acquisition
111	Previously listed/how long/at what price
112	Reason for disposition/degree of urgency
113	Investment objective

    a. Tax shelter
    b. Estate building
    c. Equity return (how much)
    d. Spendable (how much)
    e. Other

200	**LOCATION**
201	Proximity to central business district
202	Public transportation
203	Access to arterial roads, freeways, etc.
204	Shopping facilities
205	Churches
206	Schools
207	Recreational facilities
208	Other
300	**SITE**
301	Lot size
302	Zoning

303	Legal description
304	Off-street parking
305	Pool
306	Patios
307	Lawn sprinklers
308	Condition of grounds
400	**IMPROVEMENTS**
401	Builder
402	Age of building
403	Architectural design
404	Number of stories
405	Type of construction
406	Type of roof/condition
407	Exterior finish/condition
408	Basement/foundations
409	Storage facilities for tenants
410	Laundry facilities (owned or leased)
411	Garbage chutes
412	Elevator
413	Separate meters
414	Wiring/condition
415	Plumbing (copper or galvanized)/condition
416	Type of heating/age/condition
417	Air-conditioning/age/condition
418	Adequate sprinklers and fireproofing system
419	Recent pest control clearance
420	Interior halls/type of floor covering/ condition
500	**APARTMENTS**
501	View
502	Floors
503	Carpeting
504	Draperies
505	Stoves/built-in
506	Refrigerators
507	Dishwashers
508	Garbage disposals
509	Bathrooms/tubs/showers over tub/stall showers
510	Amount of storage space and closets
511	Intercom system

512	TV antenna/outlets
513	Fireplaces
514	Decks, balconies, patios
515	General condition of apartments
516	Furniture/condition
517	Inventory of personal property
518	General size of rooms (large/average/small)
519	General quality of interior (deluxe/average/economy)
520	Typical occupants/families/couples/single people/age groups/occupation (economic level)
521	Other
600	**RENTALS**

Apartment No.	No. of bedrooms	No. of baths	Furnished	Leased	Rent per month	Square footage	Rent per square foot	Tenant turnover last 12 months	Vacancy period per turnover	Rent loss due to vacancies	Potential rent

601	Totals of above schedule
602	Income from garages and/or laundry
603	Scheduled annual gross income (based on unfurnished units; adjust if furnished)
604	Total rent loss due to vacancies last 12 months in dollars
605	Vacancy factor in percent of scheduled annual gross income
606	Last two or three years' audited rental income
607	Normal source for new tenants
608	Check prepaid rents, security deposits, rent arrears, side agreements, concessions
609	Are rents comparable, higher or lower than average rents of similar units in neighborhood

700 EXPENSES

701 Taxes 19__/19__ (assessed value land and building)
702 Operating license fee
703 Hazard insurance/premium/coverage
704 Liability insurance/premium/coverage
705 Workmen's compensation insurance
706 Social Security
707 Electricity
708 Gas
709 Water
710 Garbage collection
711 Sewer service charge
712 Elevator inspection service
713 Pool maintenance service
714 Janitor and/or gardener
715 Resident manager's salary or rent allowance. List duties
716 Legal and accounting fees
717 Administrative management
718 Reserve for maintenance, repairs and supplies/Does property show signs of substandard maintenance?/What needs to be done soon?
719 Reserve for replacement of personal property/What needs replacement soon?
720 Are expenses in keeping with similar expense items in neighborhood
721 Other

800 EXISTING FINANCING
(List all loans on real and personal property)
801 Loan balance/as of what date
802 Monthly payments, including taxes and insurance
803 Interest rate
804 Annual debt service/interest payments/equity build-up
805 Lender/address/phone number
806 Loan number
807 Prepayment penalty
808 Loan locked in/until when?

809	Transferable/assumption fee/Can loan be taken subject to?
810	Due date/balloon payment
811	Original amount/term/year of inception
812	If there is a second loan, can it be bought at a discount?/If so, what discount?

900   POTENTIAL FINANCING

901	Loan commitment/amount/interest/term/payments/loan fee/lender
902	Will seller help finance?/amount/interest/payoff rate/due date
903	Is seller interested in installment sale?

1000   YIELD COMPUTATION ON FIRST YEAR'S INCOME

1001		Scheduled annual income
1002	Less	Vacancy reserve
1003	Equals	Gross operating income
1004	Less	Operating cost
1005	Equals	Net operating income
1006	Less	Annual debt service (payments on principal and interest
1007	Equals	Cash flow (gross spendable income)
1008	Plus	Equity build-up (annual principal payments)
1009	Equals	Equity return

(See the section on Tax Effects for computations of after-tax equity return and after-tax cash flow)

1100   NEIGHBORHOOD AND MARKET ANALYSIS

1101	Economic level of people in area (typical occupation)*
1102	Average income per family/per capita*
1103	Typical family size in area*
1104	Ratio of homeowners to tenants in area*
1105	Population growth in area*
1106	Number of competitive apartment houses in area
1107	Level of rent in comparable competitive buildings

1108   Gross multipliers of comparable properties recently sold

For sources of information, contact public utility companies, lending institutions, local building department, chamber of commerce, telephone company, local newspapers and U.S. Department of Commerce (Census Bureau)

1200   PRICE

1201   Listed price

1202   Predicted probable sale price/apply average gross multiplier to scheduled annual gross income of subject property/Make adjustments for higher than average rents due to exceptionally efficient management and for lower than average rents due to poor management.

1300   IMPORTANT EXHIBITS

1301   Preliminary title report (Watch for and examine covenants, conditions and restrictions on record.)

1302   Survey report

1303   Plot plan

1304   Photographs of property

1305   Area map with property plotted

1306   Recent inspection reports (pest control, roof, heating system, elevators, etc.)

1307   Certified operating statements for last few years

1308   Copies of leases and rental agreements

1309   Copies of management contracts

1310   Inventory of personal property

1311   Statistical reports on economic and population growth of area

DATA CHECKLIST FOR OFFICE BUILDINGS

1   Date information was obtained
2   Property location
3   Number of stories

100   **OWNERSHIP**
101   Owner's name, address, residence phone, business phone
102   Owner's occupation/is owner occupant of property
103   Building operated by owner or manager
104   Title vested in (list all persons having an interest in the title)/ground lease
105   Adjusted basis/depreciation deduction/ depreciation method/useful life
106   Owner's tax bracket/legal status
107   Is owner classified as dealer
108   Owner's attorney/tax counsel/accountant
109   Manager's name, address, phone number
110   To inspect property
111   Acquisition date/cost of acquisition
112   Previously listed/how long/at what price
113   Reason for disposition/degree of urgency
114   Investment objective
     a. Tax shelter
     b. Estate building
     c. Equity return (how much)
     d. Spendable (how much)
     e. Other
115   Sale and leaseback/tax-deferred exchange/ installment sale

200   **LOCATION**
201   Quality of location: 100% location (main business section in town); 90% location, etc.
202   Proximity to: transportation/freeways/ financial institutions/service facilities/ restaurants/stores/etc.
203   Parking facilities nearby
204   Any foreseeable trends toward shift in business section

300   **SITE**

301	Lot size
302	Corner
303	Zoning
304	Legal description
305	Off-street parking
306	Landscaping
400	**IMPROVEMENTS**
401	Number of stories
402	Basement/foundations
403	Type of entrance and lobby
404	Parking garage in building
405	Square feet of rentable office space
406	Number of offices
407	Age of building
408	Architectural design
409	Condition/functional obsolescence
410	Recent pest control clearance
411	Type of construction
412	Type of roof/condition
413	Exterior finish/condition
414	Type of floors/load factors/floor coverings/condition
415	Type of ceilings/concealed lighting
416	Ceiling height
417	Interior halls/floor coverings/condition
418	Design/potential for altering size and layouts of offices
419	Storage facilities for tenants
420	Elevators/automatic/service elevators
421	Wiring/voltages/condition
422	Plumbing (copper, galvanized)/condition
423	Size of windows
424	View
425	Lighting/intensity level
426	Type of heating/age/condition
427	Air-conditioning/age/condition
428	Ventilation
429	Adequate sprinklers and fireproofing system/fire alarm system
430	Adequate locks and burglar alarm system
431	Toilet facilities

432   Special equipment
433   Special facilities
500   TENANCIES

Floor	Tenant	Type business	Financial rating	Lease term	Lease expiration	Square feet	Rent per month	Rent per sq. foot	Vacant

501   Income from parking garage
502   Scheduled annual gross income
503   Last few years audited gross income
504   Are rents comparable, higher or lower than
      average rents in similar buildings with equal
      location

600   EXPENSES
601   Taxes 19__/19__ (assessed value of land and
      building)
602   Hazard insurance
603   Liability insurance
604   Workmen's compensation insurance
605   Social Security
606   Electricity
607   Gas
608   Water
609   Garbage collection
610   Elevator inspection service
611   Janitor/window cleaning
612   Manager/list duties
613   Legal and accounting fees
614   Adminstrative management/leasing fees/
      signs of substandard maintenance/what
      needs to be done soon
615   Replacement reserve for personal property
616   Are expenses in keeping with similar expense
      items in comparable buildings with equal
      location

617	Other
700	**EXISTING FINANCING**
	(List first and junior liens)
701	Loan balance/as of what date
702	Monthly payments
703	Interest rate
704	Annual debt service/interest payments/equity build-up
705	Lender/address/phone number
706	Loan number
707	Prepayment penalty
708	Loan locked in/until when
709	Transferable/assumption fee/can loan be taken subject to
710	Due date/balloon payment
711	Original amount/term/year of inception
712	If there is a second loan, can it be bought at a discount/if so, what discount
800	**POTENTIAL FINANCING**
801	Loan commitment/amount/interest/term/payments/loan fee/lender
802	Will seller help finance/amount/interest/payoff rate/due date
803	Is seller interested in installment sale
900	**PRICE**
901	Listed price
902	Predicted probable sale price/use capitalization approach (usually for lack of sufficient comparable buildings)/make adjustments for above-average income due to over-efficient management or below-average expenses due to poor management
1000	**IMPORTANT EXHIBITS**
	See items 1301 through 1311

DATA CHECKLIST FOR COMMERCIAL PROPERTIES

1	Date information was obtained
2	Property location
3	Type of property
100	**OWNERSHIP**
101	Owner's name, address, residence phone, business phone
102	Owner's occupation/is owner occupant of property
103	Title vested in (list all persons having an interest in title)/ground lease
104	Adjusted basis/depreciation deduction/depreciation method/useful life
105	Owner's tax bracket/legal status
106	Is owner classified as dealer
107	Owner's attorney/tax counsel/accountant
108	To inspect property
109	Acquisition date/cost of acquisition
110	Previously listed/how long/at what price
111	Reason for disposition/degree of urgency
112	Investment objective

    a. Tax shelter
    b. Estate building
    c. Equity return (how much)
    d. Spendable (how much)
    e. Other property to occupy
    f. Other

113	Sale and leaseback/tax-deferred exchange/installment sale
200	**LOCATION**
201	Median strip/left-turn lane
202	Advertising value of property
203	Public transportation
204	Proximity to main arteries and freeways
205	Traffic patterns/projected streets/street widening
206	If shopping center/neighborhood center/community center/regional center
300	**SITE**
301	Lot size/square footage or acreage

302	Zoning
303	Legal description
304	Deed restrictions
305	Parking lot/number of cars/paving/condition
306	Access for loading
307	Landscaping
308	Room for expansion
400	**IMPROVEMENTS**
401	Square footage/front footage/depth/layout
402	Number of stories or levels
403	Basement/foundations
404	Use restrictions, if any
405	Expansion possibilities
406	Age of building
407	Architectural design
408	Condition/functional obsolescence
409	Recent pest control clearance
410	Type of construction
411	Exterior finish/condition
412	Type of roof/condition
413	Type of floors/condition/load factor of each floor
414	Ceiling height
415	Wiring/voltage
416	Lighting/intensity level
417	Heating/age/condition
418	Air-conditioning/age/condition
419	Number and location of toilets
420	Adequate sprinklers and fireproofing system
421	Adequate locks/burglar alarm
422	Any special equipment
423	Loading dock height
500	**INCOME**
501	Lessee's name/original or sublessee
502	Type of business/how long in business
503	Capital
504	Dun & Bradstreet rating
505	Bank reference
506	Other financial and/or credit information
507	Monthly rent/monthly rent per square foot/ per front foot

508	Percentage lease/method of computing coverage
509	Overage last few years
510	Number of years remaining on lease/option to renew, at what rent
511	Tax clause in lease
512	Owner responsible for exterior maintenance
513	Other terms of lease (including option to buy, option to renew, right of first refusal)
514	Annual gross income
600	**EXPENSES**
601	Taxes 19__/19__ (assessed value land and improvements)
602	Hazard and liability insurance (classification)/coverage/premium
603	Services
604	Utilities
605	Salaries
606	Reserve for maintenance and repairs/signs of substandard maintenance/what needs to be done soon
607	Promotion
608	Legal and accounting fees
700	**EXISTING FINANCING** (List first and junior liens)
701	Loan balance/as of what date
702	Monthly payments
703	Interest rate
704	Annual debt service/interest payments/equity build-up
705	Lender/address/phone number
706	Loan number
707	Prepayment penalty
708	Loan locked in/until when
709	Transferable/assumption fee/can loan be taken subject to
710	Due date/balloon payment
711	Original amount/term/year of inception
712	If there is a second loan, can it be bought at a discount/if so, what discount
800	**POTENTIAL FINANCING**

801	Loan commitment/amount/interest/term/loan fee/lender
802	Will seller help finance/amount/interest/pay-off rate/due date
803	Is Seller interested in installment sale
900	**AREA SURVEY**
901	Traffic count in front and at nearest intersection (per day, week, month, year)
902	Distance to nearest competitive business
903	Estimated number of families within service radius of business*
904	Average family size*
905	Average income per family*
906	Trend of population growth*
907	Is area, district or street deteriorating*

*For sources of information contact public utility companies, chamber of commerce, lending institutions, local building department, telephone company, local newspapers and U.S. Department of Commerce (Census Bureau)

1000	**IMPORTANT EXHIBITS**
1001	Preliminary title report (watch for and examine covenants, conditions and restrictions on record)
1002	Survey report
1003	Plot plan
1004	Photographs of property
1005	Area map with property plotted
1006	Recent inspection reports (pest control, roof, heating system, elevators, etc.)
1007	Certified operating statements last few years
1008	Copies of leases and rental agreements
1009	Copies of management contracts
1010	Inventory of personal property
1011	Statistical reports on economic and population growth of area

DATA CHECKLIST FOR INDUSTRIAL PROPERTIES

1   Date information was obtained
2   Property location
3   Type of property/present use/highest and best use

100   **OWNERSHIP**

101   Owner's name, address, residence phone, business phone
102   Owner's occupation
103   Is owner occupant or absentee owner
104   Title vested in (list all persons having an interest in the title)/ground lease
105   Adjusted basis/depreciation deduction/ depreciation method/useful life
106   Owner's tax bracket/legal status
107   Is owner classified as dealer
108   Owner's attorney/tax counsel/accountant
109   To inspect property
110   Acquisition date/cost of acquisition
111   Previously listed/how long/at what price
112   Reason for disposition/degree of urgency
113   Investment objective
       a. Tax shelter
       b. Estate building
       c. Equity return (how much)
       d. Spendable (how much)
       e. Other property to occupy
       f. Other
114   Sale and leaseback/tax-deferred exchange/ installment sale

200   **LOCATION**

201   Proximity to nearest city or metropolitan area
202   Proximity to major highways, freeways, etc./ highway weight, height and length limitations of vehicles
203   Advertising value of property
204   Railroad sidings/spots/team-track service
205   Trucking services/availability/rates/schedules
206   Access to waterways

207	Proximity to airport
208	Proximity of raw material sources/delivery/storage
209	Nature of industry in area
210	Proximity of research facilities or a major university
211	Proximity of major Defense Department contractors or other prime contractors
212	Proximity of major markets
213	Radius of overnight shipping
214	Public transportation
215	Proximity of motels, hotels, restaurants
300	**COMMUNITY**
301	Community acceptance of industry/attitude of local officials
302	State and local tax structure and assessment policies
303	Local government's financial status/budget/per capita debt/sources of revenue
304	School districts/water, sewage and drainage districts/park and library districts
305	Police Department/personnel/crime rate
306	Fire Department/number of stations/personnel/rating
307	Medical and hospital facilities
308	Insurance classification
309	Adequate supply of housing, schools, recreation, churches, universities, libraries*
310	Road maintenance
400	**POPULATION**
401	Present population of area*
402	Average income per family and family size*
403	Present sources of income in percentages
	a. Industry
	b. Farming
	c. Government
	d. Military
	e. Other
404	Population growth trend*
405	Projected growth,* due to new industries

(list), new military contracts or bases, new
tracts, freeways, rapid transit, other

*For sources of information, contact public utility companies,
chamber of commerce, lending institutions, local building
department, local planning commissions, U.S. Army Corps of
Engineers, U.S. Department of Commerce (Census Bureau),
telephone company and local newspapers.*

500 CLIMATE AND NATURAL HAZARDS
501 Temperatures/average/minimum/maximum
502 Average length of frost period
503 Rainfall in inches/rainy season
504 Humidity/average/minimum/maximum
505 Fog conditions
506 Fire hazards
507 Storm hazards
508 Inundation hazards
509 Earthquake faults

600 LABOR MARKET
601 Total estimated employment*
602 Breakdown:* agriculture/construction man-
ufacturing/transportation/trade/finance/
insurance/real estate/service/government/
military
603 Availability of skilled and unskilled labor*
604 Union or nonunion/history of strikes*
605 Wage rates/hours overtime/fringe benefits*

*For sources of information, contact the Census Bureau, U.S.
Department of Commerce.*

700 SITE
701 Lot dimensions and square footage, shape,
plot
702 Size of off-street loading, parking and expansion areas
703 Zoning/heavy or light industry/foreseeable
shift in zoning
704 Building code requirements
705 Legal description
706 Easements
707 Deed restrictions and covenants: use/con-
struction/zoning/setbacks/signs/parking/

	storage/waste disposal/maintenance of building grounds/loading
708	Topography/grading needed/cost of grading
709	Elevation relative to highest known high water level
710	Soil/load-bearing characteristics/subsoil/depth to bedrock/depth to groundwater
711	Drainage/natural run-off capacity for industrial waste/need for artificial drainage/need for flood protection
712	Type of paving/condition
713	Landscaping
800	**IMPROVEMENTS**
801	Building dimensions and square footage/layout/stories
802	Office dimensions and square footage/number of private offices/condition
803	Expansion possibilities/master plan for development
804	Adaptability for various uses
805	Age of building
806	Architectural design
807	General condition of building/functional obsolescence
808	Type of construction (tilt-up, concrete, concrete blocks, corrugated metal, other)
809	Building code classification of structure
810	Type of roof/condition
811	Type of floors/condition/load factor
812	Ceiling height
813	Clear span or posts/column space
814	Floor/truss clearance
815	Number of skylights/sizes
816	Exhaust vents
817	Wiring/voltage/amps/H.P.
818	Lighting/intensity level
819	Number of drains
820	Number and location of toilets
821	Adequate sprinkler and fireproofing system
822	Adequate locks/burglar alarm
823	Number of truck doors/size

824	Number of rail doors/interval
825	Dock height/excavated loading dock/covered
900	**UTILITIES AND FUEL**
901	Power/availability/capacity/connections/rates
902	Gas/availability/capacity/storage factors/connections/rates
903	Water/source/capacity/pressure/rates/chemical analysis
904	Telephone
905	Cost of coal and oil
1000	**EQUIPMENT**
1001	Number of freight elevators/size/capacity/passenger elevator
1002	In-plant rail
1003	Cranes/type/capacity in tons/clearance
1004	Type of heating
1005	Air-conditioning
1006	Boiler(s)/type/rating in BTU
1007	Air and steam lines
1008	Transformers/capacity/location/bus ducts
1009	Auxiliary power generator
1010	Condition of equipment/obsolescence
1100	**INCOME**
1101	Lessee's name/original or sublessee
1102	Type of business/how long in business
1103	Capital
1104	Dun & Bradstreet rating
1105	Bank reference
1106	Other financial and/or credit information
1107	Monthly rent
1108	Number of years remaining on lease/option to renew, at what rent
1109	Tax clause in lease
1110	Owner responsible for exterior maintenance
1111	Other terms of lease (including option to buy, option to renew, right of first refusal)
1112	Annual gross income
1200	**EXPENSES**
1201	Taxes 19__/19__ (assessed value land and improvements)

1202	Hazard and liability insurance (classification)/coverage/premium
1203	Reserve for maintenance and repairs/signs of substandard maintenance/what needs to be done soon
1204	Legal and accounting fees
1205	Other
1300	**EXISTING FINANCING**
	(List all loans on real property and equipment)
1301	Loan balance/as of what date
1302	Monthly payments
1303	Interest rate
1304	Annual debt service/interest payments/equity build-up
1305	Lender/address/phone
1306	Loan number
1307	Prepayment penalty
1308	Loan locked in/until when
1309	Loan transferable/assumption fee
1310	Due date/balloon payment
1311	Original loan amount/term/year of inception
1312	If there is a second loan, can it be brought at a discount/what discount
1400	**POTENTIAL FINANCING**
1401	Loan commitment/amount/interest/term/payments/loan fee/lender
1402	Will seller help finance/amount/interest/payoff rate/due date
1403	Is seller interested in installment sale
1500	**PRICE**
1501	Listed price, price per acre
1502	Price range per acre of comparable sites recently sold
1503	Predicted probable sale price
1600	**IMPORTANT EXHIBITS**
1601	Preliminary title report (watch for and examine covenants, conditions and restrictions on record)
1602	Survey report
1603	Plot plan

1604	Photographs of property
1605	Area map with property plotted
1606	Recent inspection reports (pest control, roof, heating system, elevators, etc.)
1607	Certified operating statements last few years
1608	Copies of leases and rental agreements
1609	Copies of management contracts
1610	Inventory of personal property
1611	Statistical reports on economic and population growth of area

DATA CHECKLIST FOR MOTELS

1	Date information was obtained
2	Name of motel
3	Property location
4	Number of units
5	Type/resort motel/roadside motel/perimeter motel/in-city motel
100	**OWNERSHIP**
101	Owner's name/address/residence phone/ business phone
102	Owner's occupation
103	Motel operated by owner or manager
104	Franchise chain/motel chain
105	Independent operator/affiliation with recommending organization
106	Title vested in (list all persons having an interest in the title)
107	Adjusted basis/depreciation deduction/ depreciation method/useful life
108	Owner's tax bracket/legal status
109	Is owner classified as dealer
110	Owner's attorney/tax counsel/accountant
111	Manager's name/phone
112	To inspect property
113	Acquisition date
114	Acquisition cost/land/construction/furniture and fixtures/total
115	Previously listed/how long/at what price
116	Reason for disposition/degree of urgency
117	Investment objective

    a. Tax shelter
    b. Estate building
    c. Equity return (how much)
    d. Spendable (how much)
    e. Other motel to operate
    f. Other

118	Sale and leaseback/tax-deferred exchange/ installment sale/sale of an operating lease
200	**GROUND LEASE**
201	Ground rent
202	Expiration date of lease

203	Option/what rent/length of option
204	Subordination clause in lease
205	Who pays land taxes/amount
206	Summary of lease terms
207	Can land be purchased/when/at what price
300	**LOCATION**
301	Traffic counts per day, week, month, year, season
302	Traffic patterns/present road conditions/ projected road improvements/contemplated rerouting of traffic
303	Adequacy of signs/on site/highway signs/how many/owned or rented
310	**Resort Motels:**
311	Scenic and/or recreational values
312	Self-contained resort
313	Closest tourist attractions
314	Visibility to entering traffic
320	**Roadside Motels:**
321	On main interstate route
322	Is route part of national master road plan
323	Accessibility to freeway on and off ramps
324	Strategic location between major cities
325	Proximity to resort area, industrial, manufacturing and financial centers, and military installations
330	**Perimeter Motels:**
331	Proximity to airport/central business district
332	On downtown feeder road
333	Access to freeways
340	**In-city Motels:**
341	Proximity to central business district
342	Proximity to tourist attractions
343	Proximity to convention centers
344	Access to freeways
345	Fire and police protection
346	Adjoining properties
347	Can adjoining property be bought
348	Nearest competition
400	**SITE**
401	Acreage/dimensions/shape/plot

537	Picture windows overlooking grounds and pool area
538	Decks, patios, cabanas
540	**Public facilities:**
541	Lobby/size/how furnished
542	Office/size/equipment
543	Pool/size/children's pool/pool equipment
544	Children's play area
545	Patios/cabanas
546	Ice and beverage machine
547	Restaurant/seating capacity/leased/who owns equipment
548	Cocktail lounge/leased/who owns equipment
549	Meeting facilities
550	Banquet facilities
551	Gift shop/barber shop/beauty salon/ newsstand/leased
552	Manager's living quarters/size/furnishings included
600	**FURNISHINGS AND FIXTURES**
601	Quality and style of furnishings/condition
602	TVs/how many/age/make/condition
603	Radios
604	Room telephones
605	Other equipment
606	Linens owned or rented/5-day minimum linen inventory
607	Detailed inventory
700	**SERVICES**
701	Valet and laundry service
702	Babysitter
703	Bellhop service
704	Free continental breakfast
705	Room service
706	Pool lifeguard
707	Number of maids used/salaries/how long employed
708	Clerical employees/salaries
709	Maintenance employees/salaries
800	**INCOME STATEMENT (3 years)**
801	Number of rooms

802	Asking price
803	Gross multiplier
804	Total room gross income
805	Gross income per room
806	Cost per room
807	Other income
808	Income bar and food
809	Rate schedules
810	Occupancy percentages
811	Is income in keeping with room gross income per unit and occupancy percentages of comparable motels in area
900	**EXPENSES**
901	Taxes 19__/19__ (assessed value land and improvements)
902	Hazard and liability insurance/premium/coverage
903	Workmen's compensation insurance
904	Social Security
905	Payrolls
906	Utilities
907	Water
908	Garbage collection
909	Supplies
910	Linen service or laundry
911	Elevator inspection service
912	Pool maintenance service
913	Payrolls/clerical/maids/service/maintenance
914	Legal and accounting fees
915	Advertising/sign on property/roadside signs/AAA
916	Maintenance and repairs/signs of substandard maintenance/what needs to be done soon
917	Reserve for replacement of personal property
918	Are expenses in keeping with similar expense items of comparable motels in area
1001	**EXISTING FINANCING** (List all loans on real and personal property)
1001	Loan balance/as of what date

1002	Monthly payments/taxes and insurance included
1003	Interest rate
1004	Annual debt service/interest payments/equity build-up
1005	Lender/address/phone number
1006	Loan number
1007	Prepayment penalty
1008	Loan locked in/until when
1009	Transferable/assumption fee/can loan be taken subject to
1010	Due date/balloon payment
1011	Original amount/term/year of inception
1012	If there is a second loan, can it be bought at a discount/if so, what discount
1100	**POTENTIAL FINANCING**
1101	Loan commitment/amount/interest term/payments/loan fee/lender
1102	Will seller help finance/amount/interest/payoff rate/due date
1103	Is seller interested in installment sale
1200	**PRICE**
1201	Listed price (times-earnings ratio applied to net income before debt service and depreciation)
1202	Overall rates and occupancy percentages of comparable motels in area
1203	Predicted probable sale price/apply to subject property average times-earnings ratios of comparable motels recently sold/make adjustments for above-average income due to over-efficient management or below-average expenses due to poor management and vice versa.
1400	**IMPORTANT EXHIBITS**
1401	Preliminary title report (watch for and examine covenants, conditions and restrictions on record)
1402	Survey report
1403	Plot plan
1404	Photographs of property

1405	Area map with property plotted
1406	Recent inspection reports (pest control, roof, heating system, elevators, etc.)
1407	Certified operating statements last few years
1408	Copies of leases and rental agreements
1409	Copies of management contracts
1410	Inventory of personal property
1411	Statistical reports on economic and population growth of area

DATA CHECKLIST FOR FARM PROPERTIES

1   Date information was obtained
2   Property location
3   Type of farm/grain/livestock/special purpose
4   Highest and best use

100   OWNERSHIP

101   Owner's name/address/residence phone/ business phone
102   Owner's occupation/absentee owner
103   Farm operated by owner or manager
104   Title vested in (list all persons having an interest in the title)
105   Tax basis/owner's tax bracket/legal status
106   Owner's attorney/tax counsel/accountant
107   Manager's name/address/phone number
108   Acquisition date/cost of acquisition
109   Previously listed/how long/at what price
110   Reason for disposition/degree of urgency
111   Investment objective
     a. Expansion of operation
     b. Tax shelter
     c. Estate building
     d. Equity return (how much)
     e. Spendable (how much)
     f. Other
112   Sale and leaseback/tax-deferred exchange/ installment sale

200   LOCATION

201   Proximity to metropolitan area or nearest town
202   Proximity to recreational area/lakes/ reservoirs
203   Potential alternative use of land/subdivision/ industrial/recreational
204   Proximity to local grain, livestock and other markets
205   Proximity to canneries, dairies, grain or cereal plants
206   Proximity to farm equipment service
207   Access to arterial roads, freeways, etc.

208	Access to waterways
209	Access to railroads
210	Proximity of schools, school bus, churches, shopping center, recreational facilities
211	Availability of farm labor/wages
300	**CLIMATE AND HAZARDS**
301	Length of growing season
302	Temperatures/average/minimum/maximum
303	Average length of frost period/begin and end
304	Rainfall in inches/rainy season
305	Humidity/average/high/low
306	Fog conditions
307	Fire hazards
308	Storm hazards
309	Inundation hazards
310	Diseases
311	Weeds
400	**LAND**
401	Legal description/easements/deed restrictions
402	Neighbors
403	Total acreage/boundary lines
404	Tillable land/orchards/pasture/timberland/ waste land
405	Fences/type/condition
406	Soil/type and quality of topsoil and subsoil/ crops most adaptable to soil/productivity/soil test
407	Topography/level/degree of slope/rolling/can tractor be used
408	Drainage/natural, surface or tile drainage/ adequacy for peak rainfalls/assessment drainage district
409	Adequacy of water supply/chemical composition/safe for human consumption
410	Source of water supply/well/riparian rights to river or creek
411	Irrigation/method/irrigation district/cost
412	Utilities/electricity/gas/telephone
413	Livestock/dairy/cattle breeding/hog/poultry/ other

414	Special purpose/orchard/vegetable/berry/timber/other
415	Crop history/rotation of crops/type of crops
416	Government alloted acreage to crops, if any
417	Annual yield per acre of common crops/average annual yield per acre in area
418	Fertilizer/type/average annual amount used/average annual cost
500	**IMPROVEMENTS**
501	Buildings/use/construction/size roof/foundation/age/condition/value
502	Dwelling/type/age/construction/exterior/roof/basement/foundation/stories/flooring/wiring/plumbing/heat/air-conditioning/insulation/weather stripping/window screens/storm windows/number of rooms/kitchen (built-ins)/baths/extras/condition
503	Roads/paving/blacktop/gravel/other
600	**PERSONAL PROPERTY INCLUDED**
601	Machinery/other equipment
602	Growing crops
603	Livestock/ancestery
700	**TENANCY**
701	Lessee's name/address/phone number/experience/capital/credit rating
702	Lease/length/terms
703	Monthly rent
800	**INCOME AND EXPENSES**
801	Annual gross income past few years
802	Taxes 19__/19__ (assessed value land and improvements)
803	Insurance coverage and premium/hazard/liability,/crop/workmen's compensation/Social Security
804	Utilities
805	Maintenance of buildings and personal property/signs of substandard maintenance/what needs to be done soon
806	Soil and water conservation
807	Fertilizer
808	Development/clearing land

| 809 | Wages |
| 810 | Are income and expenses in keeping with comparable items in the area/if so, does it reflect over-efficient or poor management |

900   **FINANCING**

901	Private mortgage
902	Land contract of sale (installment contract)
903	Federal Land Bank Loan
904	Bank/insurance company loan
905	Farmer's Home Administration loan (FHA)
906	Terms: Cash down payment required/ payments/interest/term/subordination/due-on-sale/prepayment penalty/lock-in/due date

1000   **PRICE**

| 1001 | Listed price/price per acre |
| 1002 | Prices per acre of comparable farm land recently sold in the area (excluding buildings and personal property) |

1100   **IMPORTANT EXHIBITS**

1101	Preliminary title report
1102	Survey report
1103	Plot plan
1104	Photographs of property
1105	Area map with property plotted
1106	Recent inspection reports (pest control, roof, heating system, elevators, etc.)
1107	Certified operating statements last few years
1108	Copies of leases and rental agreements
1109	Copies of management contracts
1110	Inventory of personal property

DATA CHECKLIST FOR UNDEVELOPED LAND

1	Date information was obtained
2	Property location
3	Present land use
100	**OWNERSHIP**
101	Owner's name/address/residence phone/business phone
102	Owner's occupation
103	Title vested in (list all persons having an interest in the title)
104	Tax basis/owner's tax bracket/legal status
105	Is owner classified as dealer
106	Acquisition date/cost of acquisition
107	Previously listed/how long/at what price
108	Tax-deferred exchange/installment sale
109	Reason for disposition/investment objective
110	Will owner sell in parcels or only as a whole
111	Will owner sell only, lease or build to lease
112	Investment objective

    a. Tax shelter
    b. Estate building
    c. Equity
    d. Spendable (How much)
    e. Other

200	**SIZE AND DESCRIPTION**
201	Size of pracel/dimensions/boundaries/plot or survey map
202	Legal description
203	Deed restrictions/covenants/easements

Surveyors terminology/abbreviations

IPF	Iron pin found by surveyor
IPP	Iron pin placed by surveyor
LLL	Land lot line
BL	Building line
DE	Draining easement
MH	Man hole
R/W	Right of way

300 CHARACTERISTICS AND UTILITIES

301 Highest and best use (recommendations from qualified engineer or land planner)
   a. Farm, ranch or timberland
   b. Recreation or resort property
   c. Industrial property
   d. Commercial property
   e. Residential property

302 Topography of terrain (contour map)

303 Elevation relative to highest known high water level

304 Drainage/natural run-off capacity/need for artificial drainage/need for flood protection

305 Sanitary sewerage system/adequacy/proximity

306 Subsoil (soil engineer's report)/depths to bedrock and groundwater

307 Estimate of clearing, grading and cut and fill operations, if any

308 Cost estimates of off-site and on-site improvements to obtain finished lots or plots

309 Pure drinking water/adequacy of supply

310 Source of water supply/well/riparian rights to river or creek

311 Spot location of the following items on a general location map:
   a. Existing easements/size and purpose
   b. Sanitary sewer outfall lines
   c. Storm sewer outfall lines
   d. Drainage directions
   e. Existing water service lines/sizes
   f. Existing gas service lines
   g. Existing electrical lines

312 Letters from public utilities or governmental agencies regarding present or projected services to the property

400 LOCATION

401 Proximity to what metropolitan area, city or district

402	Proximity to central business district and regional shopping center*
403	Proximity to neighborhood shopping centers*
404	Proximity to and quality of schools (grade, junior high, high, college, private)*
405	Proximity to churches/recreational centers/parks/theatres/hospital/medical center*
406	Industrial or cemetery property nearby
407	Public transportation
408	Access to main traffic arteries and freeways
409	Contemplated new roads, freeways, transportation facilities
410	Traffic count/in front and at nearest intersection (if commercial lot)
411	Median strip/left turn lane (if commercial lot)
412	Located in city or county/fire and police protection
413	Type and quality of adjoining properties
414	Other site and neighborhood characteristics

Generally acceptable maximum distances from homes:
Regional shopping center 4 miles
Neighborhood shopping center ¾ mile
Recreation facilities 4 miles
Public school 1 mile
High school 12 miles
Church 4 miles
Work 45 minutes

500   SOCIAL REGULATIONS

501	Zoning/existing and proposed
502	Dedication of land to public use
503	Requirements as to location and width of streets
504	Requirements as to curbs, gutters, sidewalks
505	Requirements as to lot size
506	Use restrictions
507	Building restrictions
508	Bond required for improvements

600   TAXATION

601	Tax rate
602	Assessment policies and trends
603	Assessed value

604	Taxes 19__/19__
605	Special assessments
700	**POPULATION**
701	Present population in above area*
702	Average income per family and family size*
703	Present sources of income in percentages*:

    a. Industry
    b. Farming
    c. Government
    d. Military
    e. Other

704   Projected growth due to the following factors*:
    a. New industries (list)
    b. New military contracts
    c. New military bases
    d. Freeways
    e. Rapid transit
    f. Other

705	Ratio of homeowners to tenants in area*
800	**CLIMATE AND NATURAL HAZARDS**
801	Temperatures/average/minimum/maximum
802	Average length of frost period
803	Rainfall in inches/rainy season
804	Humidity/average/minimum/maximum
805	Fog conditions
806	Fire hazards
807	Storm hazards
808	Inundation hazards
809	Earthquake faults
900	**LOCAL BUILDING TRENDS**
901	Number of new subdivisions in area/location
902	Number of new homes under construction in area*/finished home costs
903	Number of new apartment houses under construction in area*
904	Number of existing shopping centers in area

For sources of above data, contact chamber of commerce, local building department, public utilities (for number of recent and planned installations), title insurance companies, lending institutions, local planning commission, U.S. Department of Commerce and U.S. Army Corps of Engineers.

1000 PRICE
1001 Listed price/price per acre
1002 Price range per acre of comparable land recently sold
1003 Predicted probable sale price
1100 IMPORTANT EXHIBITS
1101 Preliminary report
1102 Survey report
1103 Plot plan
1104 Photographs of property
1105 Area map with property plotted
1106 Recent inspection reports (pest control, roof, heating system, elevators, etc.)
1107 Certified operating statements last few years
1108 Copies of leases and rental agreements
1109 Copies of management contracts
1110 Inventory of personal property
1111 Statistical reports of economic and population growth in the area

CHECKLIST FOR PURCHASE OF DEVELOPMENT LOTS

(Courtesy of Colonial Mortgage Company, Fort Wayne, Indiana)

1. Are there large, successful builders nearby (especially on the same road closer to town) who will provide very tough competition?
2. Have any builders failed recently in the immediate neighborhood?
3. Have out-of-town builders considered moving here (taken options, etc.) and then changed their minds?
4. Are efficient subcontractors and labor available?
5. Is the market so competitive that you could not afford to do as much advertising or as expensive a job of merchandising as other nearby builders?
6. Has a qualified engineer walked over the property and, if necessary, made soil tests and other studies to assure you this is buildable land?
7. Has this parcel been peddled to other builders and rejected?
8. Do you understand the zoning and can you live with it?
9. Are there easements over the property?
10. Can you solve any drainage problems?
11. Are there mosquitoes, fog, smog, noise, or smells?
12. Is that part of town a one-industry area that could be hurt badly by layoffs?
13. Is the area heavily dependent on Army, Navy, or Air Force units that might be withdrawn?
14. Is the area overbuilt with apartments that offer serious competition to new houses?
15. Is it likely that real estate taxes soon will be increased substantially?
16. Are new highways with uncertain locations planned, which might tie up the whole area for a year or more?
17. Is nearby land zoned for outdoor movies, commercial buildings, or any other purpose which homeowners would consider a liability?
18. Has the property a poor approach?

19. Are there nearby shack towns or other undesirable elements?
20. Are you surrounded by subdivisions where houses sell for several thousand dollars less than yours?
21. Are you so far out of town that you need to sell for $2,000 less than builders closer in?
22. Can you offer as much house for the money as nearby competitive builders?
23. Has a big local builder, or an out-of-town builder, an option on land nearby that could spoil your sales once he opens up?
24. Would an experienced local broker refuse to try to sell houses here?
25. What is the tax rate now? Two years ago?
26. How many foreclosures are there in the area?

DATA CHECKLIST FOR MOBILE HOME PARK SITES

1	Date information was obtained
2	Property location
3	Present land use
100	**OWNERSHIP**
101	Owner's name/address/residence phone/business phone
102	Owner's occupation
103	Title vested in (list all persons having an interest in the title)
104	Acquisition date/cost of acquisition
105	Previously listed/how long/at what price
106	Tax-deferred exchange/installment sale
107	Reason for disposition/investment objective
108	Will owner sell in parcels or only as a whole
200	**SIZE AND DESCRIPTION**
201	Size of parcel/dimensions/boundaries/plot or survey map
202	Legal description
203	Deed restrictions/covenants/easements
300	**CHARACTERISTICS AND UTILITIES**
301	Topography: level, rolling, hilly, rough, low, rocky
302	Existing structures on property
303	Elevation relative to highest known high water level
304	Drainage/natural run-off capacity/need for artificial drainage/need for flood protection
305	Sewer at property line/proximity
306	Subsoil (soil engineer's report)/depths to bedrock and groundwater
307	Estimate of clearing, grading and cut and fill operations, if any
308	Cost estimate of off-site and on-site improvements to obtain finished lots or plots
309	Water at property line/pure drinking water/proximity
310	Source of water supply/well/riparian rights to river or creek

311	Gas at property line/proximity
312	Power at property line/proximity
313	Spot location of the following items on a general location map:

    a. Existing easements/size and purpose
    b. Sanitary sewer outfall lines
    c. Storm sewer outfall lines
    d. Drainage directions
    e. Existing water service lines/sizes
    f. Existing gas service lines
    g. Existing electrical lines

| 314 | Letters from public utilities or governmental agencies regarding present or projected services to the property |

400 LOCATION

401	Proximity to what metropolitan area, city or district
402	Proximity to central business district and regional shopping centers*
403	Proximity to neighborhood shopping centers*
404	Proximity to and quality of schools (grade, junior high, high, college, private)*
405	Proximity to churches/recreation centers/ parks/theatres/hospital/medical center*
406	Industrial or cemetery property nearby
407	Public transportation
408	Access to main traffic arteries and freeways
409	Contemplated new roads, freeways, transportation facilities
410	Located in city or county/fire and police protection

For sources of above data, contact chamber of commerce, local building department, public utility companies (for number of recent and planned installations), title insurance companies, lending institutions, local planning commission, U.S. Department of Commerce and U.S. Army Corp of Engineers.

500 ZONING

| 501 | Present zoning |
| 502 | Proposed zoning |

503	Purchase subject to zoning
504	Planning department opinion of chances to obtain zoning for mobile home site
600	**TAXATION**
601	Tax rate
602	Assessment policies and trends
603	Assessed value
604	Taxes 19__/19__
605	Special assessments
700	**POPULATION**
701	Present population in above area*
702	Average income per family and family size*
703	Present sources of income in percentages*
	a. Industry
	b. Farming
	c. Government
	d. Military
	e. Other
704	Projected growth due to the following factors*
	a. New industries (list)
	b. New military contracts
	c. New military bases
	d. Freeways
	e. Rapid transit
	f. Other
705	Ratio of homeowners to tenants in area*
800	**CLIMATE AND NATURAL HAZARDS**
801	Temperatures/average/minimum/maximum
802	Average length of frost period
803	Rainfall in inches/rainy season
804	Humidity/average/minimum/maximum
805	Fog conditions
806	Fire hazards
807	Storm hazards
808	Inundation hazards
809	Earthquake faults
900	**LOCAL BUILDING TRENDS**
901	Number of mobile home parks in area/proximity/quality/other characteristics
902	Number of new subdivisions in area/location

903	Number of new homes under construction in area*/finished home costs
904	Number of new apartment houses under construction in area*
905	Number of existing shopping centers in area
1000	**PRICE**
1001	Listed price/price per acre
1002	Price range per acre of comparable land recently sold
1003	Predicted probable sale price
1100	**TERMS**
1101	Loan balance, if any/interest rate/payments/due date/prepayment penalty
1102	Lender/loan number
1103	Loan assumable
1104	Can loan be subordinated
1105	Will seller help finance/amount/interest/pay-back rate/due date/subordinate
1106	Amount of cash required
1200	**IMPORTANT EXHIBITS**
1201	City or county map with location of property
1202	Assessor's or parcel map with dimensions
1203	Topographical map
1204	Aerial photo
1205	Survey report
1206	Statistical reports on economic and population growth of area

For sources of above data, contact chamber of commerce, local building department, public utility companies (for number of recent and planned installations), title insurance companies, lending institutions, local planning commission, U.S. Department of Commerce and U.S. Army Corp of Engineers.

SELLER'S PROPERTY DISCLOSURE STATEMENT

1. Title and Access

a. Is the property currently leased? If so, when does the lease expire? Does the lessee have an option to extend the lease?

b. Does anyone have a first right of refusal to buy, option or lease the property? If so, who?

c. Do you know of any existing, pending or potential legal actions concerning the property or the homeowners' association?

d. Has there been a notice of default filed against your property? If yes, please explain.

e. Are there any bonds, assessments or judgments that are either liens upon the property or that limit its use?

f. Do you own real property adjacent to, across the street from or in the same subdivision as the subject property? If yes, please describe.

g. Do you know of any encroachments, easements, licenses, boundary disputes or third party claims affecting the property (rights of other people to interfere with the use of the property in any way)? If so, explain.

h. Are you aware of any pending real estate development in your area (such as condominiums, planned unit developments, subdivisions or property for commercial, educational or religious use)?

i. Do you experience any excessive noises, for example, airplanes, trains, trucks, freeway, etc.?

j. Are you aware of any other conditions that could affect the value or desirability of the property?

2. Land

a. Does the property have any filled ground? If so, is the house built on filled or unstable ground?

b. Do you know of any past or present settling or soil movement problems on the property or on adjacent properties? If so, have they resulted in any structural damage? What was the extent of damage?

c. Do you know of any past or present drainage or flooding problem on your property or adjacent properties? If so, explain on separate sheet. Is there water standing on the property after rainfall? Any active springs?

d. Is the property in a designated flood zone?

e. Is the property in a Special Studies Zone as provided by the Alquist-Priolo Geological Hazard Zones Act?

f. Are you aware of any past or present problems with driveways, walkways, patios or retaining walls on your property or adjacent properties due to drainage, flooding or soil movement (such as large cracks, potholes, raised sections)? If so, please describe.

3. Structural Disclosures

a. Do you know of any structural additions or alterations or the installation, alteration, repair or replacement of significant components of the structures upon the property completed during the term of your ownership or that of a prior owner with or without an appropriate permit or other authority for construction from a public agency having jurisdiction?
☐ Explanation attached

b. Approximate age of structure: Do you know of any condition in the original or existing design or workmanship of the structure that would be considered substandard? If so, please explain.

c. Are you aware of excessive settling, slanted floors, large cracks in walls, foundations, garage floors, driveways, chimneys or fireplaces? If so, explain.

d. Are you aware of any structural wood members, including mudsills, being below soil level?

e. Is crawlspace, if any, below soil level?

f. Do you know of any inspection reports, surveys, studies, notices and so on concerning the property? If so, please list each one even if you have already made them available.

g. Date of last structural pest control inspection? By whom?

h. Do you prefer a presale structural pest control inspection?

    i. Date of last city/county mandatory inspection report?

    j. Have you any notice(s) of violations relating to the property from any city, county or state agencies? If so, please explain.

    k. Do you know of any violations of government regulations, ordinances or zoning laws regarding this property? If so, explain.

4. Roof, Gutters, Downspouts

    a. Type of roof: □ Tar and gravel, □ Asphalt shingle, □ Wood shingle, □ Tile, □ Other. Age of roof?

    b. Has roof been resurfaced? If so, what year? Is there a guarantee on the roof? For how long? By whom?

    c. Has roof ever leaked since you owned the property? If so, what was done to correct the leak?

    d. Are gutters and downspouts free of holes and excessive rust?

    e. Do downspouts empty into drainage system or onto splash blocks? Is water directed away from structure?

5. Plumbing System

    a. Source of water supply: □ Public, □ Private well. If well water, when was water sample last checked for safety? Result of test?

    b. Well water pump? Date installed? Condition? Sufficient water during late summer?

    c. Are water supply pipes copper or galvanized?

    d. Are you aware of below normal water pressure in your water supply lines (normal is 50 to 70 lbs.)?

    e. Are you aware of excessive rust stains in tubs, lavatories and sinks?

    f. Are you aware of water standing around any of the lawn sprinkler heads?

    g. Are there any plumbing leaks around and under sinks, toilets, showers, bathtubs and lavatories? If so, where?

h. Pool? Age? Pool heater: ☐ Gas, ☐ Electric, ☐ Solar. Pool sweep? Date of last inspection? By whom? Regular maintenance?
i. Hot tub/spa? Date of last inspection? By whom?
j. ☐ City sewer, ☐ Septic tank: ☐ Fiberglass, ☐ Concrete, ☐ Redwood. Capacity? Is septic tank in good working order?

6. Electrical System

a. 220 Volt?
b. Are there any damaged or malfunctioning receptacles?
c. Are you aware of any damaged or malfunctioning switches?
d. Are there any extension cords stapled to baseboards or underneath carpets or rugs?
e. Does outside TV antenna have a ground connection?
f. Are you aware of any defects, malfunctioning or illegal installation of electrical equipment in or outside the house?

7. Heating, Air-Conditioning, Other Equipment

a. Is the house insulated?
b. Type of heating system?
c. Is furnace room or furnace closet adequately vented?
d. Are fuel-consuming heating devices adequately vented to the outside directly or through a chimney?
e. Date of last inspection of heating equipment? By whom?
f. Solar heating? In working order?
g. Air-conditioning? Date of last inspection? By whom?
h. Does fireplace have a damper?
i. Provision for outside venting of clothes dryer?
j. Approximate age of water heater? Capacity? Is your water heater equipped with temperature

pressure relief valve, which is a required safety device?

k. Electric garage door opener? Condition? Number of controls?

l. Burglar alarm? make? In working order? Owned? Leased? Rented?

m. Smoke detectors? How many? ☐ 110V, ☐ Battery. In working order?

n. Lawn sprinklers? Automatic clock? In working order?

o. Water softener? In working order?

p. Sump pump? In working order?

q. Are you aware of any of the above equipment that is in need of repair or replacement or is illegally installed?

8. Built-In Appliances

a. Are you aware of any built-in appliances that are in need of repair or replacement? If so, which?

9. Personal Property Included in the Purchase Price

a. List items of personal property that are included in the purchase price.

b. Are there any liens against any of these items? If so, please explain.

10. Home Protection Program

a. Do you want to provide a home protection program at your expense?

11. Condominiums

a. Please check availability of copies of the following documents: ☐ CC&Rs, ☐ Condominium declaration, ☐Association bylaws, ☐ Articles of incorporation, ☐ Subdivision report, ☐ Current financial statement, ☐ Regulations currently in force.

b. Does the condominium declaration contain any resale restrictions?

c. Does the homeowners' association have the first right of refusal?

d. Please check occupancy restrictions imposed by the association, including but not limited to: ☐ Children, ☐ Pets, ☐ Storage of recreational vehicles or boats on driveways or in common areas, ☐ Advertising or For Sale signs, ☐ Architectural or decorative alterations subject to association approval, ☐ Other.

e. In case of a conversion, do you have an engineer's report on the condition of the building and its equipment?

f. Monthly/annual association dues? How much? What is included in the association dues?

g. Has your association notified you of any future dues increases or special assessments? If so, please give details.

h. Are all dues, assessments and taxes current?

i. I shall provide a statement from the condominium homeowners' association documenting the amount of any delinquent assessments, including penalties, attorney's fees and any other charges provided for in the management documents to be delivered to Buyer.

j. Security: ☐ Intercom, ☐ Closed circuit TV, ☐ Guards, ☐ Electric gate, ☐ Other.

k. Parking? Does each unit have its own designated parking spaces? How close to unit? Is space ample? Guest parking?

l. Is soundproofing adequate? Are there noisy trash chutes?

m. Property management company.

12. Newly Constructed Residences

a. Is deposit held in trust fund?

b. Bond guaranteeing completion of unit and common area and facilities?

c. Is builder a member of Home Builders Association? Is Home Owners' Warranty (HOW) available?

d. Will carpets, draperies and appliances be identical to those shown in model unit?

e. Please list expiration dates of warranties covering appliances and equipment. Final inspection date? Occupancy permit date? Contractor? License?

13. Ownership

a. Are you a builder or developer?

b. Are you a licensed real estate agent?

c. Have all persons on the title signed the listing agreement?

d. Please list all persons on the title who are not U.S. citizens.

e. Are you aware of anything else you should disclose to a prospective buyer? If so, please explain. (Use addendums if necessary.)

The foregoing answers and explanations are true and complete to the best of my/our knowledge and I/we have retained a copy hereof. I/we herewith authorize the Agent in this transaction to disclose the information set forth above to other real estate brokers, real estate agents and prospective buyers of the property.

Dated: _____ Seller: _____ Seller: _____

I/we acknowledge receipt of this Seller's Property Disclosure Statement, including additional explanations, if any, attached hereto.
Dated: _____ Buyer: _____ Buyer: _____

I am satisfied with the above Seller's property disclosure statement.
Dated: [_____] Buyer: [_____] Buyer: [_____]

I am not satisfied with the above Seller's property disclosure statement and herewith rescind my offer to purchase above property.
Dated: [] Buyer: [_____] Buyer: [_____]

I reserve the right to have the property inspected by the following professional(s) and to submit a copy of the inspection report(s) to Seller's Agent on or before _____.

Dated: [_____] Buyer: [_____] Buyer: [_____]

INSTRUCTIONS

The law in some jurisdictions requires that the broker make a physical inspection of the property and that notice of any defects observed during such an inspection be disclosed to buyers.

The purpose of the Seller's Property Disclosure Statement (Forms 110.11, 110.12 and 110.13) is to give a buyer such notice.

RED FLAGS INSPECTION CHECKLIST

	CIRCLE APPROPRIATE SYMBOL OR MARK ⊠		
_____ Property	⌐	⌐	🌐
_____ Agent			
_____ Date			
Red Flags Property Inspection Guide page numbers provided for reference.	Red Flag	Possible Red Flag	Nothing Observed or Not Applicable

1. INSPECTING FOR RED FLAGS OUTSIDE THE HOME

	Red Flag	Possible Red Flag	Nothing Observed or Not Applicable
Cracks in sidewalks, driveways, or decks? (2/4)	⌐	⌐	☐
Cracks in foundation? (2/5)	⌐	⌐	☐
Cracks in fireplace? (2/26)	⌐	⌐	☐
Visually distorted structure? (2/7)	⌐	⌐	☐
Visual evidence of drainage problems? (2/8)	⌐	⌐	☐
Building ventilation screens damaged? (2/10)	⌐	⌐	☐
Visual evidence of hillside instability, landsliding? (2/11)	⌐	⌐	☐
Visual evidence of erosion? (2/12)	⌐	⌐	☐
Visual evidence of roof deterioration? (2/15)	⌐	⌐	☐
Hazardous vegetation observed? (2/16)	⌐	⌐	☐
Hazardous deck or stair railings? (2/18)	⌐	⌐	☐
Hazardous stairs? (2/19)	⌐	⌐	☐
Hazardous walkways or steps? (2/20)	⌐	⌐	☐
Visual evidence of failing retaining walls? (2/39)	⌐	⌐	☐
Swimming pool out-of-level? (2/40)	⌐	⌐	☐
Cracks in swimming pool? (2/40)	⌐	⌐	☐
Hazardous play structure or treehouse? (2/41)	⌐	⌐	☐

2. INSPECTING FOR RED FLAGS INSIDE THE HOME

	Red Flag	Possible Red Flag	Nothing Observed or Not Applicable
Cracks in basement walls? (2/21)	⌐	⌐	☐
Water stains, or white powdery deposits on basement walls? (2/21)	⌐	⌐	☐
Sump pump(s)? (2/21)	⌐	⌐	☐
Water stains on ceiling or around windows? (2/14)	⌐	⌐	☐
Wall or ceiling cracks? (2/22)	⌐	⌐	☐
Hidden wall cracks? (2/23)	⌐	⌐	☐
Any noticeable sloping floors? (2/24)	⌐	⌐	☐
Cracks in tile floors? (2/24)	⌐	⌐	☐
Sticking doors or windows? (2/25)	⌐	⌐	☐
Uneven spaces between doors and frames? (2/26)	⌐	⌐	☐
Cracks in fireplace? (2/26)	⌐	⌐	☐
Hazardous fireplace hearth? (2/27)	⌐	⌐	☐
Visual evidence of sagging beams? (2/28)	⌐	⌐	☐
Burned or damaged electrical outlets? (2/29)	⌐	⌐	☐
Any extension cords under carpet or stapled to wall? (2/29)	⌐	⌐	☐
Any exposed wiring? (2/30)	⌐	⌐	☐
Electrical panel accessible and intact? (2/30)	⌐	⌐	☐
Gas shut-off valve accessible? (2/32)	⌐	⌐	☐
Hazardous water heater? (ie. no pressure valve, etc.) (2/33)	⌐	⌐	☐
Visual evidence of illegal additions? (2/34)	⌐	⌐	☐
Hazardous steps? (2/35)	⌐	⌐	☐

3. DURING YOUR INSPECTION DID YOU OBSERVE?

	CIRCLE YES OR NO	
Safety glass emblem on sliding doors (2/36)	Yes	No
Ground fault interrupters (2/31)	Yes	No
Safety wire on garage door springs (2/37)	Yes	No
Smoke alarm(s) (2/37)	Yes	No
	Yes	No

This form is designed to be used in conjunction with the **Red Flags Property Inspection Guide.** In California the completed checklist may be made an attachment to the Real Estate Transfer Disclosure Statement (Statutory Form) part 3 or 4 as applicable. (PPC 109.3 & 109.4 CAL)

FORM 108 RF (10-87) COPYRIGHT © 1987 BY PROFESSIONAL PUBLISHING CORP. 122 PAUL DR. SAN RAFAEL, CA 94903 (415) 472-1964 ▇ PROFESSIONAL PUBLISHING

INDEX

M

N

O

P

S

T

U

V

NOTES

NOTES

NOTES

NOTES

NOTES

NOTES

NOTES

NOTES

NOTES

NOTES